# Harnessing Generative Artificial Intelligence for Science Education

Michail Kalogiannakis
https://orcid.org/0000-0002-9124-2245
*University of Thessaly, Greece*

Dimitrios Sotiropoulos
https://orcid.org/0000-0001-7367-5760
*University of Thessaly, Greece*

IGI Global
Scientific Publishing
Publishing Tomorrow's Research Today

| | |
|---|---|
| Vice President of Editorial | Melissa Wagner |
| Director of Acquisitions | Mikaela Felty |
| Director of Book Development | Jocelynn Hessler |
| Production Manager | Mike Brehm |
| Cover Design | Jose Rosado |

Published in the United States of America by
IGI Global Scientific Publishing
701 East Chocolate Avenue
Hershey, PA, 17033, USA
Tel: 717-533-8845 | Fax: 717-533-7115
Website: https://www.igi-global.com E-mail: cust@igi-global.com



Library of Congress Cataloging-in-Publication Data

Names: Kalogiannakis, Michail, 1969- editor | Sotiropoulos, Dimitrios 1974- editor
Title: Harnessing generative artificial intelligence for science education / edited by Michail Kalogiannakis, Dimitrios Sotiropoulos.
Description: Hershey, PA : IGI Global Scientific Publishing, [2026] | Includes bibliographical references and index. | Summary: "This book aims to discuss the latest advances in the use of Generative Artificial Intelligence (GenAI) in science education and its new methods, tools, and approaches in integrating GenAI into practice and learning environments"-- Provided by publisher.
Identifiers: LCCN 2025034543 (print) | LCCN 2025034544 (ebook) | ISBN 9798337329130 hardcover | ISBN 9798337329147 paperback | ISBN 9798337329154 ebook
Subjects: LCSH: Science--Computer-assisted instruction | Science--Study and teaching | Artificial intelligence--Educational applications | Generative artificial intelligence
Classification: LCC Q182.7 .H37 2026 (print) | LCC Q182.7 (ebook)
LC record available at https://lccn.loc.gov/2025034543
LC ebook record available at https://lccn.loc.gov/2025034544

British Cataloguing in Publication Data
A Cataloguing in Publication record for this book is available from the British Library.

# Table of Contents

# Detailed Table of Contents

This chapter outlines a design framework for employing generative AI chatbots (GenAI) as Socratic dialogue partners to enhance students' engagement with fundamental scientific concepts through historically informed discourse. The proposed framework consists of four components: Initiation, Dialogue, Reflection, and Evaluation and Transfer. Feedback loops connect these parts to ensure that teachers' goals, AI prompts, classroom activities, and formative assessments are all aligned. This study concentrates on ancient Greek natural philosophy, particularly Presocratic and Aristotelian concepts regarding matter, change, and causality. The chapter argues that Socratic dialogues with GenAI, placed in historical contexts, can facilitate better understanding of core scientific concepts, foster critical and reflective thinking, as well as help students to locate modern scientific knowledge within a broader historical and cultural context. It also addresses the moral, legal, and management issues that arise when utilising GenAI to facilitate Socratic dialogue responsibly.



Effective feedback is crucial for deep learning, yet providing timely, personalized guidance remains a challenge in education, especially in science. This paper introduces the "Feedback Loop Architect," a human-centered GenAI platform designed to create personalized feedback ecologies. The platform addresses the need for iterative feedback by simulating and supporting student-platform interactions. A key contribution is our novel methodology for creating a realistic synthetic dataset capturing the dynamics of feedback dialogues. This dataset, informed by established practices like "Sticky Note Feedback," serves as a testbed for the platform. We demonstrate how the platform simulates learning progressions, visualizes feedback impact, and provides personalized guidance. Results from a simulation of 450 interactions across 50 students show significant improvements in scores (mean increase: 2.69 points) and answer elaboration. This work provides a framework for researchers developing educational AI, offers insights for managers, and explores ethical considerations in such systems.

The transformation of science curricula in the digital age requires the integration of advanced technologies such as Generative Artificial Intelligence (GenAI). This chapter discusses the urgency of using GenAI in science education at the secondary level to enhance personalization, scientific simulation, and interdisciplinary collaboration. Despite its significant potential, the implementation of GenAI is still hindered by teachers' digital literacy, infrastructure, and ethical considerations. Global studies highlight best practices that can be adapted through teacher training, smart curriculum design, and the development of AI literacy laboratories as critical and ethical learning spaces.



This chapter explores the integration of GenAI into STEM education with a primary focus on Science education. It examines how GenAI can revolutionize teaching and learning by providing adaptive learning environments, personalized assessments, and real-time feedback that cater to the diverse needs of students also ensuring the ethical challenges associated with the implementation of GenAI, including concerns around bias, transparency, data privacy, and academic integrity. The chapter emphasizes the importance of balancing technological innovation with ethical practices to ensure equitable access and responsible use of GenAI tools. Looking ahead, the chapter outlines key future directions, including the refinement of adaptive learning tools and the need for AI literacy programs for educators. The chapter concludes by highlighting the potential of GenAI to transform science education while ensuring that it is used in ways that promote fairness, inclusivity, and accountability.

# Preface

Generative Artificial Intelligence (GenAI) has rapidly moved from a technological novelty to a consequential socio-technical infrastructure that reshapes how knowledge is produced, represented, negotiated, and assessed across educational settings. In science education specifically, GenAI raises foundational questions about what it means to learn with and through models, to reason with evidence, to communicate scientific explanations, and to participate in inquiry in environments where language, images, simulations, and feedback can be generated at scale. Yet, the educational value of GenAI cannot be reduced to speed, automation, or convenience. Its pedagogical significance depends on intentional design, transparent epistemic goals, and a careful balancing of human judgement with computational affordances.

This volume addresses a primary academic need: bridging the gap between broad discussions of GenAI and GenAI in relevant and meaningful school settings, thereby enhancing teachers' research and practice. In this respect, each chapter in this edited volume adopts a distinct approach. Rather than approaching GenAI as merely another "thing" to add to an already-established curriculum, the authors take a much more holistic approach, looking at how GenAI could provide an opportunity to rethink the various components of science education (e.g., how to form and construct representations, how dialogue should work, how to create an ecology of feedback, how to connect curriculum goals with assessment, how to prepare teachers in their professional development, etc.). Although the chapters in this volume come from diverse teacher education and school contexts and represent multiple disciplines, they all share a common theme: that effective GenAI integration occurs when GenAI's technological capabilities align with the pedagogical purposes, ethical considerations, and developmental stages of learners.

A distinctive contribution of this volume is its emphasis on theory, evidence, and practice as complementary commitments. "Theory" foregrounds the conceptual lenses that clarify what counts as scientific understanding, how learners build explanations, and how tools mediate reasoning and participation. "Evidence" highlights methodological rigour and the types of data and analytical approaches required to evaluate GenAI-enhanced learning designs and outcomes. "Practice" addresses implementation in real educational ecosystems, where curricular demands, assessment cultures, teacher expertise, institutional policy, and inclusivity considerations determine whether innovation translates into educational improvement. Together, these commitments support a coherent agenda for GenAI-enhanced science education that is empirically attentive, pedagogically disciplined, and responsive to the broader implications of automation, authorship, equity, and accountability.

The volume is intended for researchers and graduate students in science education and educational technology, for curriculum and instructional designers, and for teachers and teacher educators seeking actionable frameworks that can guide classroom integration. While GenAI capabilities continue to evolve, the chapters in this collection emphasize enduring educational questions: how learners make sense of concepts, how representations mediate understanding, how feedback shapes learning trajectories, and how professional learning enables ethical adoption. In this sense, the volume aims to remain relevant even as specific platforms change, because it concentrates on principles, design logics, and pedagogical commitments rather than transient features.

## HOW TO USE THIS VOLUME

There are a few distinct but related audiences for this volume, each with diverse interests and needs.

Researcher and Graduate Students: Methodologies and Design Principles for GenAI Research in Science Education are outlined within Chapters 1-4 of the Volume. Chapter 1 presents foundational perspectives on design and methodology, while Chapters 2-4 create the innovative frameworks for student authorship, dialogic learning, and feedback architectures.

Practicing Educators: The implementation strategies documented in Chapters 2, 3, and 5 provide information and resources to practice classroom integration. The Build, Refine and Learn (BRaL) Framework outlined in Chapter 2, the Dialogic Approaches outlined in Chapter 3, and the Curriculum Integration Strategies discussed in Chapter 5 all offer practitioners practical, actionable guidance.

Curriculum Designers and Administrators: Chapters 5-7 document systemic integration, resource development and curriculum transformation. These chapters provide practical roadmaps and blueprints that support the system-level adoption of pedagogical integrity and ethical standards.

For Teacher Educators and Professional Development Specialists: Chapter 8 offers comprehensive professional development frameworks essential for preparing educators to work effectively and ethically with GenAI tools.

Cross-cutting Themes: All readers will benefit from the volume's consistent attention to ethical considerations, equity, and the balance between technological capability and human judgment that runs through every chapter.

## ORGANIZATION OF THE BOOK

Chapter 1 written by Agyabeng N. Yeboah and Leila Goosen examines methods and methodologies for harnessing learner-generated content and creating usable interfaces to support the effective application of technology in basic education. The

chapter details methods and design for conducting research that connects learner-generated data with usability and teacher-intended instruction, and presents a conceptual framework through which researchers can explore ways to improve GenAI-supported learning environments. The design aspect of the chapter focuses on how learners experience content within a learning system through an interface, and how they add their own content to the system.

Chapter 2 is titled: Student-Created Generative Artificial Intelligence (GenAI) Physics Simulations: A Build, Refine and Learn (BRaL) Framework for Conceptual Understanding and was authored by Dimitrios Sotiropoulos. The chapter presents a conceptual framework for developing deep conceptual understanding through students' authorship. The author does not view simulation use as using existing tools, but rather views building simulations as a means of constructing knowledge through a series of iterative steps in designing, testing, improving, and explaining scientific models. The BRaL framework connects GenAI-enabled construction of knowledge through simulation with conceptual development in physics and describes GenAI tools as supportive scaffolds for students developing modeling practices and developing epistemic agency in physics learning.

Chapter 3, "GenAI and Ancient Greek Natural Philosophy: Exploring the Foundations of Science Concepts through Interactive Dialogues" (Dimitrios Sotiropoulos, Christos Xenakis, Apostolos Xenakis, & Michail Kalogiannakis), takes this theme of dialogue beyond the interactions provided by GenAI to the way in which we might connect GenAI to the history of the development of scientific concepts. The chapter examines the way in which the use of conversational methods of engagement with the ideas that formed the foundation for Natural Philosophy provides opportunities for developing a better understanding of science concepts. It is not the intent to replace traditional methods of instruction, but rather to provide an enriched instructional experience that will allow for the development of a deeper understanding of science concepts through guided inquiry and argumentative reasoning and comparative contrast. The chapter also offers insight into how GenAI conversational methods of dialogue may serve as an interpretive link between the methods of reasoning used by the ancient Greeks and current approaches to establishing educational objectives for Science Learning.

Chapter 4, "The 'Feedback Loop Architect': A Human-Centred GenAI Platform for Refining Personalized Feedback Ecologies in Science Education" (Hossein Jamali), addresses one of the most consequential areas of GenAI application: feedback. Rather than treating feedback as a single message delivered after performance, the chapter conceptualizes feedback as an ecology distributed across time, tasks, tools, and human roles. The proposed platform foregrounds human-centred design principles, aiming to support personalization while preserving transparency, teacher oversight, and pedagogical alignment. The chapter contributes a design language for building feedback systems that enhance learning without collapsing evaluation into automation.

Chapter 5, "Bridging the Gap: 'Integrating GenAI into Secondary Science Curricula'" (Nofamataro Zebua & Yan Piter Basman Ziraluo), examines the use of GenAI as an addition to the secondary science curriculum. The authors examine how to align GenAI with the curriculum's desired outcomes, the limitations of teaching and learning in secondary science, and the practices associated with specific scientific disciplines. The chapter identifies the importance of coherent curriculum thinking that connects the objectives of the curriculum, the activities within the classroom, the assessment techniques used, and the guidelines for responsible use of GenAI, thereby allowing schools to take advantage of the possibilities offered by GenAI to create innovative changes to their current.

Chapter 6, "Transforming Science Education through Generative AI: Adaptive Learning, Ethical Practices, and Inclusive Curriculum Design" (Dipta Gomes, Saikat Baul, Jubayer Ahamed, Dip Nandi), broadens the dialogue surrounding systemic transformation of how we educate students in science at the university level via GenAI. The chapter organizes its contribution to the conversation into four interrelated areas: (a) GenAI-enabled adaptive learning and personalized learning; (b) AI-supported formative assessments and feedback practices; (c) Strengthening students' scientific reasoning and ability to make sense of data using representations and visualizations; and (d) Ethical Practices, Governance, Academic Integrity, and Inclusive Curriculum Development. In conclusion, this chapter presents integrated recommendations for pedagogical design and institutional implementation, stating that there must be a balance between innovating while maintaining transparency, equity, and responsible practices in the use of technology in higher education.

Chapter 7, "Authoring Academic Resources for Science Education with a Generative AI Tool" (María Lucía Barrón-Estrada, Ramón Zatarain Cabada, Víctor Manuel Bátiz-Beltrán, Aldo Uriarte-Portillo), discusses how Generative AI can be used as an Authoring Engine for Academic Science Educational Resources and discusses a Cloud-Based Solution using Large Language Models (LLMs) and XR / WebXR which supports developing, adapting, and repurposing of Create Interactive Learning Resources for Both Teachers and Students. The platform's Authoring Workflow(s) and its primary

functions (e.g., create Courses, Create Presentations, Create Learning Experiences including Immersive Learning Experiences, etc.) are described as well as providing key Implementation Considerations for Creating Digital Solutions that are being used in Real-World Classroom Environments (including Usability and Feasibility). In addition, this chapter discusses some of the Unique Validation Requirements (including Validation for Disciplinary Accuracy & Validation for Representational Clarity) of Generated Learning Materials, especially in areas where Clarity and Accuracy are the Cornerstones of Student Learning in the Sciences.

Chapter 8, "Empowering Science Educators in the Age of Generative AI: Frameworks for Effective Professional Development" (Debbie Diana Devonish), identifies the teacher as the critical lever for the responsible use of GenAI resources. In this chapter, frameworks for professional development have been synthesised to assist teachers in evaluating GenAI output, designing effective learning tasks, maintaining academic integrity and supporting equitable learning outcomes. The chapter argues that the use of GenAI has significant social and ethical implications that must be addressed through extensive professional development, a culture of collaboration, and practical models that link research to classroom practice.

Collectively, these eight chapters present a coherent pathway for GenAI-enhanced science education: from design methodology and learner-facing interfaces, to student authorship of models and simulations, to dialogic learning with scientific ideas across time, to feedback architectures and curriculum integration, and finally to resource authoring and teacher professional learning. The volume does not offer a single "best practice" template; instead, it provides conceptual tools, frameworks, and exemplars that support informed decision-making in diverse educational contexts.

As this volume goes to press, the GenAI landscape continues to change quickly. New models, new policies, and new institutional responses will undoubtedly shape what is possible—and what is permissible—in classrooms. Nevertheless, the central message of this collection remains stable: educational value emerges when GenAI is embedded within pedagogically meaningful designs, ethically defensible practices, and inclusive learning environments. We hope this volume contributes to a more disciplined, evidence-attentive, and human-centred conversation about how GenAI can support science learning—and about the boundaries that must be maintained to protect learners, teachers, and the integrity of education.

This work emerges at a critical juncture in educational history, as generative artificial intelligence transforms not only how we teach and learn science, but also how we conceptualize knowledge construction, assessment, and educational equity. We are grateful to all who are working to ensure that these transformations serve the best interests of learners and society.

Volos, Greece, January 2026
Michail Kalogiannakis & Dimitrios Sotiropoulos (Editors)
University of Thessaly, Department of Special Education

## REFERENCES – FURTHER READING

Kalogiannakis, M., Papakonstantinou, N., & Sotiropoulos, D. (2025). From Support Tool to Learning Partner: A Systematic Review of GenAI Integration in University Science Labs. *Creative Education, 16*, 1364–1401. DOI: 10.4236/ce.2025.169083

Spasopoulos, T., Sotiropoulos, D., & Kalogiannakis, M. (2025). Generative AI in Pre-Service Science Teacher Education: A Systematic Review. *Advances in Mobile Learning Educational Research*, *5*(2), 1501–1523. DOI: 10.25082/AMLER.2025.02.007

Sotiropoulos, D., Raikou, N., & Kalogiannakis, M. (2025). Views of future Special Education teachers on teaching Natural Sciences during Practicum. Review of Science, Mathematics and ICT Education, 19(2), 137-159. https://doi.org/DOI: 10.26220/rev.5423

Sotiropoulos, D., & Kalogiannakis, M. (2025). Using GenAI Tools to Enhance Teaching and Learning in Science. In Proceedings of the 14th Hybrid Edition of the International Conference New Perspectives in Science Education, 293-301, Italy-Florence: Filodiritto-Pixel, 19-21 March 2025, https://doi.org/DOI: 10.26352/L319_2420-9732

Sotiropoulos, D. J., & Meletiou-Mavrotheris, M. (2025). Postgraduate student teachers' perspectives concerning AI and its integration into STEAM teaching and learning. In Papadakis, S. (Ed.), *AI roles and responsibilities in education* (pp. 3–21). Springer., DOI: 10.1007/978-3-031-96855-6_1

Uğraş, H., Uğraş, M., Papadakis, S., & Kalogiannakis, M. (2025). Innovative early childhood STEM education with ChatGPT: Teacher perspectives. Technology. *Knowledge and Learning*, *30*(2), 809–831. DOI: 10.1007/s10758-024-09804-8

Uğraş, M., Çakır, Z., Zacharis, G., & Kalogiannakis, M. (2025). ChatGPT in Early Childhood Science Education: Can It Offer Innovative Effective Solutions to Overcome Challenges? *Computers*, *14*(9), 368. DOI: 10.3390/computers14090368

Xenakis, A., Dimos, I., Feidakis, M., Sotiropoulos, D., Kalovrektis, K., & Nikolaou, G. (2025). An LLM-based smart repository platform to support educators with computational thinking, AI, and STEM activities. In *Empowering STEM educators with digital tools* (pp. 107–136). IGI Global Scientific Publishing., DOI: 10.4018/979-8-3693-9806-7.ch005

# Acknowledgment

The editors express their profound gratitude to the authors whose original research and creative ideas have influenced this book. We are grateful to researchers from multiple countries across four continents who worked diligently to contribute diverse perspectives on the timely topic of using Generative Artificial Intelligence (GenAI) in Science Education.

We appreciate the peer reviewers' valuable input during the editorial process, which helped ensure that all contributions met high scholarly standards.

This publication occurs at a critical time in educational history. We extend our gratitude to all teachers/researchers and practitioners who are leading the way in demonstrating the Ethical and Effective Use of GenAI in science classrooms worldwide.

Volos, Greece,

January 2026

Michail Kalogiannakis & Dimitrios Sotiropoulos

# Chapter 1
# Harnessing Learner Content and User Interface Design for Basic Education:
## Research Methodology and Design

**Agyabeng N. Yeboah**
*University of South Africa, South Africa*

**Leila Goosen**
https://orcid.org/0000-0003-4948-2699
*University of South Africa, South Africa*

## ABSTRACT

*The purpose of this chapter is to describe the research methodology and design to be implemented in a study towards harnessing learner content and user interface design for basic education. Against the background of harnessing generative Artificial Intelligence (AI) for science education, the main focus of the chapter will include an emphasis on the challenges and opportunities related to ethical Generative Artificial Intelligence (GenAI) use in Science, Technology, Engineering and Mathematics (STEM) education.*

## INTRODUCTION

This section will describe the general perspective of the chapter and end by specifically stating the *objective*.

DOI: 10.4018/979-8-3373-2913-0.ch001

## Harnessing Generative Artificial Intelligence for Science Education

Generative Artificial Intelligence (GenAI) had quickly become one of the most revolutionary *emerging trends* across most sectors, including education, healthcare, and creative fields. As part of this book, the purpose of the chapter is to investigate the theoretical foundations, empirical studies, and *practical* uses of generative artificial intelligence (GAI) in science education, with the chapter covering a variety of *issues*, such as instructional design, adaptive learning interfaces, and ethics in school and tertiary education.

## Harnessing Learner Content and User Interface Design for Basic Education: Research Methodology and Design

As part of a book with a theme similar to the current volume, on *Integration Strategies of Generative AI in Higher Education*, the most recent chapter by Yeboah and Goosen (2025) presented integration strategies of learner content and user interface design in higher education for teaching and learning online in times of crises, while a previous chapter by Yeboah and Goosen (2024) explained the impact of learner content and user interface design on e-learning quality as part of a book presenting *Cases on Economics Education and Tools for Educators.*

The research approach for the study discussed in this chapter is detailed. This chapter will explain the research strategy and paradigm. It will also describe the population of the study, as well as the sampling strategies and data collection procedures used for the study. It further proposes the instruments that will be used for data collection and covers the steps to be taken to guarantee the development, validity and reliability of the study. The chapter will also touch on the pilot study to be undertaken and the data gathering techniques, the implementation of the actual intervention, as well as what make up the ethical **issues**, which need to be addressed throughout the research study.

## Recommended Topics

From the *recommended topics* suggested for the book, this chapter will discuss e.g.,

- Ethical GenAI Use in Science, Technology, Engineering and Mathematics (STEM) Education: *Challenges* and Opportunities
- Gambling on the *future* of creativity in science education with the integration of GenAI
- GenAI-Integrated Curriculum Models for *Future*-Ready Scientists

- *Teacher Training* and GenAI: Preparing *Future* Educators for Digital Transformation

## Target Audience

Like the *target audience* for this book, that of the chapter includes academics, science educators, educational technologists, policymakers, and researchers, who require evidence-based information and **practical** guidance on integrating generative AI into their curricula and teaching practice.

## Objective

As part of this book, the chapter will address the latest advances in the use of generative artificial intelligence in science education and new methods, tools, and approaches in integrating GenAI into practice and learning environments. The chapter will specifically examine how GenAI applications and tools can enable inquiry learning, promote scientific *problem-solving* and enhance learner-centered experiences in virtual and physical laboratories.

# BACKGROUND

This section will provide broad definitions and discussions of the topic on *Harnessing Learner Content and User Interface Design for Basic Education* regarding *Research Methodology and Design* and incorporate the views of others (in the form of a literature review) into the discussion to support, refute, or demonstrate the authors' position on the topic.

"As personal computing devices transition from traditional computers to contemporary mobile platforms, a global revolution in technology-based learning is underway. In" this context, the book edited by Papadakis and Kalogiannakis (2024) provided *new approaches* to *mobile learning for early childhood education.*

Also in early childhood education, within the context of physical and natural *science* courses, Kalogiannakis and Kanaki (2022, p. 197) reported on a pilot study in Greece, as part of a *research anthology on computational thinking, programming, and robotics in the classroom.* In the contemporary digital era, introducing computational thinking concepts is considered an imperative need at all stages of schooling, since" these "are inextricably linked to skills".

In the same book discussed in the previous paragraph, a chapter on learning computational thinking development in young children with Bee-Bot educational robotics was presented by Papadakis and Kalogiannakis (2022, p. 926). "It is widely known that when used intentionally and appropriately, technology and interactive media are effective tools to support learning and development."

A chapter in a book on *integrating micro-credentials with AI in open education* indicated that micro-credentials "are transforming digital education by offering flexible, targeted, and *accessible* ways for learners to acquire and demonstrate skills." Micro-credentials can therefore be used to establish new realities in digital education (Stamatakis, Logothetis, Petridis, Kalogiannakis, & Vidakis, 2025, p. 19).

As part of a book on *the digital folklore of cyberculture and digital humanities*, Barianos, Logothetis, Kalogiannakis and Vidakis (2022, p. 186) presented the *case* of ThimelEdu with regard to teaching ancient Greek theatre through in-game exploration. "Serious games are increasingly integrated into official learning settings due to their effectiveness as teaching tools, especially in *cultural* heritance."

In the same book discussed in the previous paragraph, a chapter on gamification techniques capitalizing on state-of-the-art technologies by Logothetis, et al. (2022, p. 206) pointed out that teachers are rapidly incorporating "gamification techniques and game-based learning (GBL) into the learning material", aided by technological "advancements on the world wide web".

Ansu-Kyeremeh and Goosen (2022) were exploring the socioeconomic facets of online learning technologies with regard to inclusive education in Ghana relating to the effects of technological advancement in academia.

The aim of the study reported on by Opara and Ogbanu (2023, p. 462) in a *journal* article on *advances in education and philosophy* was to investigate the "effect of item order on" the reliability of a "mathematics test among senior secondary school students in Rivers State", Nigeria. Students "were allowed 35minutes of testing time on an 80-item test."

An *international business* and *management studies journal* article by Sürücü and Maslakci (2020, p. 2694) discussed validity and reliability in quantitative research: The validity and reliability "of the scales used in research are essential factors that enable the research to yield beneficial results."

Ethics, integrity, and the scientific method were the main foci of a chapter by Lewis (2020, p. 459) as part of the *handbook of research ethics and scientific integrity*. "Experimental design is one aspect of a scientific method. A well-designed, properly conducted experiment aims to control variables in order to isolate and manipulate causal effects and thereby maximize internal validity, support causal inferences, and guarantee reliable results."

## Universal Design Principles

*Universal Design* for Learning (UDL) was the main focus of a content analysis of peer reviewed journals from 2012 to 2015 by Al-Azawei, Serenelli and Lundqvist (2016) in a *journal* article on *the scholarship of teaching and learning*.

A *computer science review* journal article on "adaptive or intelligent user interfaces (AUI or IUI)" were presented by Miraz, Ali and Excell (2021, p. 1), with the "three core domains being focused upon" including "Artificial Intelligence (AI), User Modelling (UM) and" *universal* usability through plasticity of user interface *design*.

## Blended Learning

An *international journal* article on *advanced science and technology* by Adri, Wahyuni, Zakir and Jama (2020) described using the Analysis, Design, Development, Implementation, and Evaluation (ADDIE) instructional model to design *blended* project-based *learning* based on a production approach.

The focus of the PhD dissertation of Alenezi (2023) was on *blended learning motivation support at the Saudi Electronic University* by *utilizing self-determination theory*.

Singh, Steele and Singh (2021) were combining the best of online and face-to-face learning in a hybrid and *blended learning* approach for COVID-19, post vaccine, & post-pandemic world in their *journal* article on *educational technology systems*.

# MAIN FOCUS OF THE CHAPTER

## Issues, Controversies, Problems

This section will present the authors' perspectives on the *issues, controversies, problems*, etc., as these relate to theme of the book on *Harnessing Generative Artificial Intelligence for Science Education* and arguments supporting the authors' position on *Harnessing Learner Content and User Interface Design for Basic Education* regarding *Research Methodology and Design*. It will also compare and contrast with what had been, or is currently being, done as it relates to the specific topic of the chapter and the main theme of the book.

The systematic strategy or plan of action that describes the precise technique adopted to bring about the desired results in a study is referred to as research methodology (Creswell & Creswell, 2018). It explains how the researcher handles the research *problems* and develop *solutions* to these. In essence, research methodology is a collection of techniques adopted to gather, arrange and evaluate the needed data so that the researcher can make logical judgements and make sense of the findings (Walliman, 2021). The purpose and type of data to be collected in the study determine the approach to be used and has a significant influence on the entire research process (Kivunja & Kuyini, 2017).

A *social sciences* journal article by Sebele-Mpofu (2020) provided a literature review on the complexities and underlying assumptions related to saturation *controversy* in qualitative research.

## Reliability of the Questionnaire

The Cronbach Alpha coefficient will be employed by this research for the assessment of the reliability of the questionnaire, where the internal consistency of the questionnaire items will be measured. In this regard the deployment of the pilot study will be used to address the *issue* of reliability. The deployment of the questionnaire will be done after the learner had been given the opportunity to be engaged with the e-learning model at the pilot study stage. The selection of the Cronbach Alpha will be used to since it is able to cater for the use of multiple response for each item in the questionnaire (Bujang, Omar, Foo, & Hon, 2024). The Cronbach Alpha values are used to measure the extent to which the test items are interrelated (Hoekstra, Vugteveen, Warrens, & Kruyen, 2019).

## Research Ethics

Ethical **issues** are very important aspects in all research and this study will pay attention to it. Leidner and Tona (2021) opined that interpersonal ethics require concern for the dignity, privacy and well-being of those who are studied in the process of data collection, analyses and reporting. These include the right to privacy, voluntary participation, no harm to participants, confidentiality and the right to withdraw from the intervention. To gather data from the eligible participants, the researcher will submit a copy of the instrument to the Cape Coast municipal Directorate of Education to be reviewed. All ethical requirements, such as academic honesty, plagiarism, acknowledgement of copyright materials used and institutional ethical clearance will be address. Again, permission will be asked from the eligible schools and an introductory letter and ethical clearance given by the Cape Coast Municipal Directorate of Education.

The respondents' consent will be sought and they will be duly informed about the voluntary nature of their participation. The respondents will be assured of their anonymity and it will be clearly stated on the questionnaire. No respondent will be allowed to disclose his/her name or even the name of the school, which they teach as teachers or learn as students. Hence, the views of the respondents will be handled with the utmost care and confidentiality.

### Limitations and Delimitations of the Study

This study will investigate the relationship between learner content and user interface design and how it impacts on the quality of an e-learning environment. This study will be delimited to only the grade six students in the Cape Coast Municipality. The study will be delimited to two schools, which will be randomly chosen from ten schools in the Cape Coast Municipal Directorate of Education. The instruments for the study will include a questionnaire and an academic performance test in computing for grade six, which will be constructed by the researcher and will be proofread by the teachers who are not in the selected schools.

There will be fifteen questions for use as a pre-test and post-test. The study will use grade six learners who possess a considerable number of computing skills to manipulate the intervention given. They also exhibit traits or characteristics of junior high learners. Finally, only teachers in the selected schools will be used to administer the interventions.

The research will focus primarily on two basic schools in Cape Coast municipality in the Central Region of Ghana. This might affect the **issue** of generalization. The study could be “more reliable if it was conducted in” all basic schools in Ghana.

The main instrument for data collection will be a questionnaire. A questionnaire could have a “low response rate and the possibility of” learners’ responses being biased cannot be ruled out. These weaknesses associated with questionnaires can “negatively influence the validity of the conclusions” that will be drawn from the study.

## Ethical Generative Artificial Intelligence Use in Science, Technology, Engineering and Mathematics Education: Challenges and Opportunities

As part of a *Handbook of Research on Using Educational Robotics to Facilitate Student Learning*, the chapter by Chatzopoulos, et al. (2021, p. 441) presented “the design and development of” DuBot, “an open-source, low-cost robot for K12 students, suitable for use in educational robotics and *science, technology, engineering” and mathematics.*

In the same book as discussed in the previous paragraph, the aim of the study reported on in the chapter by Vlasopoulou, Kalogiannakis and Sifaki (2021, p. 235) was to investigate the attitudes and behavioral “intentions of primary school teachers regarding the” impending “integration of *STEM* education in primary school grades”.

Featuring insights from administrators' perspectives, the study reported on by Taşdan, Kartal, Gözüm and Kalogiannakis (2025, p. 275), as part of a book on *Empowering STEM Educators with Digital Tools*, aimed to explore school administrators' perspectives on the digital transformation of school management processes. It" also examined "the tools used in digital transformation".

In their chapter in the same book referred to in the previous paragraph, Xenakis, et al. (2025, p. 107) aimed "to describe the design technology and educational necessity of" a Large Language Model (LLM) "smart repository platform, which supports educators with all necessary materials", as well as computational thinking, *AI*, and *STEM* activities.

In a similar context as the study, which is the main focus of this chapter, the *education* journal article by Kwaah (2024) was exploring *challenges and opportunities* with regard to social media use among basic school teachers in Ghana.

A paper published in the *proceedings of the Institute of Science and Technology Education (ISTE) conference on Mathematics, Science and Technology Education* by Ngugi and Goosen (2017) explored the effects of *Course Design* Characteristics (CDCs), *Self-Regulated Learning* (SRG) and knowledge sharing in facilitating the development of innovative among technology students at universities, while their *smart innovation, systems and technologies behavior* journal article (Ngugi & Goosen, 2019) was modelling motivation, *metacognitive strategies* and affective aspects of learning towards smart innovation for information systems and technology students.

## Research Approach

A research paradigm shapes a researcher's perspective on both the methodology and philosophy of research (Khatri, 2020). A research paradigm serves as a conceptual framework that outlines appropriate theories and methods for addressing a specific research *problem* (O'Donoghue, 2018). It shapes a researcher's approach to a *problem* by reflecting their underlying beliefs, values, and perspectives on the world (Kamal, 2019). This framework aids the researcher in defining reality, truth, and knowledge (Rahi, 2017). An *international journal* article on *economics* and *management sciences* by the latter author provided a systematic review of research paradigms, sampling *issues* and instruments development in the context of research design and methods. The choice of a research paradigm has significant methodological implications, influencing the formulation of research questions, the selection of study participants, the development of data collection tools, and the strategies for data processing and analysis (Kivunja & Kuyini, 2017).

Davies and Fisher (2018) similarly noted that a research paradigm significantly shapes the research questions and the methods used for data collection. Bogna, Raineri and Dell (2020) identified the primary research paradigms as positivism (realism), interpretivism (constructivism), pragmatism (pluralism), critical theory and realism. Positivism asserts that knowledge is relative and that a singular objective reality exists. It suggests that research should move from general theories to specific data, implying that an established theory can generate data. Research under the positivist paradigm typically employs quantitative methods.

Contrasts this with interpretivism, which regards knowledge as a subjective reality that can be interpreted. According to Van der Walt (2020), interpretivist epistemology, knowledge is not only existent but can also be constructed and applied. This perspective suggests that theory is derived from data, meaning that research progresses from specific instances to general theories. Interpretivist epistemology research in nature usually employs the qualitative method. Whereas, pragmatism combines elements of from the area of positivism and constructivism (interpretivism), this then recognizes the fact that knowledge that can be viewed objectively can also be subjectively interpreted. This then makes research from the pragmatic paradigm point of view often employs mixed methods. A quick reflection of these facts makes it easy for the research under consideration to be grounded in pragmatic philosophy and accordingly will adopt the mixed methods in this research inquiry.

Critical theory comes from the background of challenging and criticizing convention and this deals with probing societal structures that concerns with *issues* such as inequality, oppression, and domination (Bogna, et al., 2020). The choice of this paradigm normally focuses on how to improve and empower the disadvantage groups in the society and advocate for the need for social change. The critical theory then adopts both the qualitative and quantitative methods in their approach but then pay attention to social *issues* and how to promote social justice. The realism paradigm also turn attention to the reality that exists independently with regard to human thoughts and beliefs, but of which the construct of understanding of it is inevitably shaped or obscured by characteristics as human and the kind of meaning we make of such things from the environment. Realist will usually opt for the use of a scientific method to investigate *issues*, however there is the acceptance that what we choose to observe and what fact we look out for might be from a theoretical perspective. They typically use a combination of qualitative and quantitative methods to understand and represent reality.

The choice of a paradigm for this study will be the pragmatic research paradigm and this is carefully done as its corresponds well to the dynamic complexities of online learning technologies in modern contexts this study wants to unravel. Elder-Vass (2022) noted that pragmatism determines the validity of an idea or theory based on its *practical* effectiveness, with the understanding that truth evolves through successful real-world application. The pragmatic approach deal with the promotion of the selection of the best methods that works best for a study and that is whether it means the use of quantitative, qualitative or both. When different research techniques are mixed based on what will best satisfy a question, then it makes room for gathering a much richer information and thereby giving a better information about the phenomenon under study (Allemang, Sitter, & Dimitropoulos, 2022). Thus, a multidimensional and multimethodological strategy is essential for a comprehensive exploration of reality.

Rather than focusing on the contentious aspects of truth and reality, pragmatism emphasizes the effectiveness of *solutions* in addressing the research questions posed (Elder-Vass, 2022; Ormerod, 2021). Pragmatism accepts both singular and multiple realities that are amenable to scientific inquiry and prioritizes the resolution of *practical*, real-world *issues*. This approach liberates researchers from the limiting dichotomy between constructivism and post-positivism, offering flexibility in choosing research methods (Racine, Kusch, Cascio, & Bogossian, 2021). Consequently, the current study will benefit from not being confined to a specific research methodology.

Pragmatism focuses on the use of whatever methods we adopted that works best to effectively address research *problems*. Pragmatism projects the truth as anything that works in real-life settings as oppose to what is just considered as an idea. In contrast to interpretivism it projects what is our personal meanings, whiles pragmatism consider the way an action produces results. It explains when we learn by doing and get to see the result from what actually happens as articulated by Dewey (1938; Bhat & Neelam, 2023). The work of Dewey (1938) underscores pragmatism as a philosophy geared towards *problem-solving*, viewing knowledge as arising from action and experience, which he describes as warranted assertions (Verawati & Sarjan, 2023). The journal article by the latter authors provided a perspective on the philosophy of critical thinking in *problem*-based *science* learning.

The pragmatic paradigm will be used for this study in order to ensure a thorough understanding and analysis of how user interface design and learner content affect the quality of e-learning design and go a long way to improve the performance of student upon interacting with the model. The pragmatic paradigm will be selected because it lays a high value on *practical* outcomes and directs the choice of research techniques which will be in line with how well they solve the research *problems* identified. A thorough inquiry that takes into account different kinds of view point and data type either a qualitative or quantitative data can be collected and analyze with the pragmatic paradigm (Hampson & McKinley, 2023). In their *research in education* journal article, the latter authors were criticizing pragmatism as a paradigm for mixed research against the background of *problems* posing as *solutions*.

This study will have the freedom to choose the best research strategies, procedures and methods that is appropriate and fits the aims and objectives by the choice of a pragmatic paradigm. Therefore, the pragmatic paradigm is deemed highly suitable for this investigation, as it allows for an adaptive methodological approach to effectively explore the impact of e-learning models on student satisfaction.

## Population and Sampling

In research population refers to every person or elements that are related to the referred topic being studied. As Stratton (2021) posited, a population can simply be said to be a group that when selected meets certain criteria for being relevant to be included in the study. The selection of the right population is very crucial since it helps to define the study's findings and make them relevant and can be applied more broadly. In a similar vein, Casteel and Bridier (2021) describe the population as a group of individuals who share certain attributes and characteristics, underscoring the significance of precisely defining the population to ensure the relevance and accuracy of the study outcomes.

The study under consideration will focus on a specific set of population, which will be students from public and private basic schools in the Cape Coast Municipality, which can be found in the Central Region of Ghana. There are 99 public and private schools in the Cape Coast Metropolis. Of these, there are 61 public basic school and 38 private basic schools. Most of these school were not able to organize online learning technologies and classes for their students during the Covid-19 pandemic era and some that made the attempt were reaching the students through the parents the WhatsApp platform (Kwaah, 2024).

From these schools, focus will be given to schools with computer laboratory which is the main tools needed for the experiment to take place. The schools with more functioning computers will be factored in the population needed for the research. To ensure fair representation, both public and private schools will be selected. 10 basic schools will be selected from the 99 basic schools in the Cape Coast Metropolis, which will be made up five public schools and five private schools. These schools should have the highest number of computers in within the Metropolis to allow the inclusion of more participants and must also be widely apart so that it does not lead to contamination.

### Sampling Techniques

The method of sampling, which involves the selection of a representative subset from the larger population for inclusion in the study, is critical for maintaining the methodological integrity of the research. According to Ahmed and Ishtiaq (2021), when sampling strategy is carefully selected, it sets the ground for guaranteeing the validity, accuracy and more importantly the reliability and validity of the data gathered. For study findings and its reliability and to the extent to which it represents the target population, Mweshi and Sakyi (2020) reiterated how important it is to choose a good sampling technique.

The sample for this study will consist of grade 6 students from initially identified ten schools identified. The study will use grade six learners who possess a considerable number of computing skills to manipulate the intervention given. They also exhibit traits or characteristics of junior high learners. Only teachers in the selected schools will be used to administer the interventions. This will ensure consistency of the implementation process. To this end, this will also ensure that the interventions are delivered in a consistent manner and go on to reduce variability that might results from different teaching styles or school environment. The teachers in these schools are familiar with the needs of their students given that they have been in the school setting for some time. Participants from the public and private schools will be will be randomly assigned experimental or control groups. The schools will be put into two groups; private and public. To this end, the researcher will employ a simple random sampling approach to choose two schools from the initially identified two group of five. This method ensures an equitable and unbiased selection process, thereby facilitating a comprehensive and accurate representation of the population in the research sample. This meticulous approach to sampling is to enhance the study's credibility and contribute to a deeper understanding of the e-learning model's impact within the context of basic education in the Cape Coast Metropolis.

## Instrumentation and Data Collection Techniques

The influence of an e-learning model especially at the basic school level in Cape Coast Metropolis in the Central Region of Ghana is the main focus of this study's instrumentation and data collection methodologies, which will employ a methodical approach for the collection of data, to measure and also to analyze evaluate data relevant to the study's goals.

### Instrumentation

The instruments for data collection will be an e-learning model, a custom questionnaire, a semi-structured interview and classroom observation. To assess students' performance before and after the use of the e-learning model intervention, a pre-test and post-test assessments will be administered to students to measure the learning gains attributable to the e-learning model. The items in the assessments will come from topics thar aligned with the curriculum and will carefully be constructed to test students' knowledge and skills in computing topics taught through the e-learning platform.

Custom-made questionnaires will be constructed to collect data on students' engagement, satisfaction of the e-learning model, custom-designed questionnaires will be developed. These custom-made instruments will have both closed-ended questions which will be used for quantitative analysis and open-ended questions to capture qualitative insights into students' experiences and perceptions which will be analyze qualitatively in thematically.

Computing teachers, as well as selected students will take part in semi-structured interviews with the aim of gathering detailed information on the e-learning model implementation process, challenges faced and the perceived efficacy of the chosen e-learning model. This interview will then provide qualitative information about how e-learning functions in schools and how it improves teaching and learning methods in the schools.

Direct observations of e-learning sessions will be carried out to assess the interaction between students and the e-learning platform, the use of digital tools and resources, and the overall classroom dynamics in an online learning technologies environment. Observation checklists will be developed to systematically record the use of e-learning features, student engagement levels, and instructional delivery methods.

## The E-learning Model

The e-learning model will be developed using the Articulate Storyline 3 open software with the guided topic. The design will incorporate learner engagement strategies, user interface design principles and interactive content development. To make sure this is achieved below will be the step-by-step guide to creating the e-learning model.

Step 1: The purpose of the design will be well defined and that will be to create and interactive e-learning module that improves learner engagement and provide satisfaction and improve on learning outcomes. The objectives of learner engagement will be clearly stated. This should be how the model can actively engage with content through interactive elements. It should also include how learners can achieve the intended learning outcomes through a well design structured content. And finally, how the students will find the interface intuitive and visually attracting.

The reader should note that due to length limits for this chapter, only the first step is described.

## Data Collection Techniques

### *Pilot Study*

According to Teresi, Yu, Stewart, and Hays (2022), a pilot study is conducted on a small scale before the actual study is organized with the aim to evaluate the data collection instruments to ascertain that they meet the needs of the study under consideration and whether they should be maintained or changed accordingly.

This study will employ the pilot study to ascertain whether the students can navigate the buttons such as the forward, backward to *access* the multimedia elements without difficulty. To this end it will help to check the responsiveness of the model across different devices such as computers and smartphones. This will also ensure that branching scenarios, test and instant feedback features of the model perform the intended task and that the formative and summative assessments are correctly graded.

The pilot study will help to check for the clarity of test items and how they align with the content and the objective. It will be used to test if the closed-ended scale and open-ended prompts returns a relevant behavior and that they elicit meaningful insights on challenges and perceived efficacy.

The pilot test will again help to measure how long the students will need to complete a module and how long they will take to complete an assessment. The pilot study will also be used to identify barriers for students with home computers or basic computer skills. The pilot study will be used to measure the sample of two schools in Cape Coast Metropolis to see whether is a good representation and whether the duration for the experiment will be adequate.

### *Semi-Structured Interviews*

Semi-structured interviews, from the view point of Creswell and Guetterman (2024), represent a two directional conversation where the role of the interviewer is to direct questions to the participant with the sole purpose of collecting data. Semi-structured interviews are seen in most research due it its flexibility and as it provides room for follow-up questions to asked for an incomplete or a response that is considered unclear (Creswell, 2012; Buys, Casteleijn, Heyns, & Untiedt, 2022). In this regard a total is twelve (12) learners and two (2) teachers will be selected from the experimental and control groups. Six (6) learners will be purposively selected from each group. This will be made up of two (2) learners who performed poorly, two (2) learners who performed averagely and two (2) learners who performed well in the post-test from each group. The semi-structured format will allow the researcher to come up with follow-up question for unclear answers.

All the respondents will be asked the same set of questions. All the interview will be conducted within the same interview schedule. The interview sections will be voice-recorded as it will be analyzed further. The interview will focus on gathering qualitative perspectives into the interplay between user interface design, learner content, demographic factors and end with academic outcomes in e-learning. Under each theme the learner will answer two questions while teachers will answer one question. There will be a total of fifteen questions for the semi-structured interview.

### *Classroom Observation*

Classroom observation is a practice of gathering information on a phenomenon or activity as it happens in a natural environment which is generally done as unnoticeably as possible (Creswell, 2012). According to Caldarella, et al. (2020), teacher-student interaction, how student behave and how teacher also behave in their natural environment can best be learnt through are observation. The current study will try and avoid bias and uphold objectivity as much as possible. Direct observations of e-learning sessions will be carried out to assess the interaction between students and the e-learning platform, the use of digital tools and resources, and the overall classroom dynamics in an e-leaning model environment. Observation checklists will be developed to systematically record the use of e-learning features, student engagement levels, and instructional delivery methods.

## Reliability and Validity

A quasi-experimental design is known for its inability to control extraneous variables. To maximize internal validity, researchers must control extraneous variables so as to rule out these variables as explanations for any effects observed (Lewis, 2020). Extraneous variables are the variables that the researcher does not deploy but may affect the outcomes of the experiment. It can produce uncontrolled effect that can affect the viability of the dependent variable which will consequently affect the independent variable.

The steps that follow will be taken to control the extraneous variables in this study:

1. The venues for the experimental and control group activities will be kept widely apart. The computer laboratories of control groups will be far from the experimental group. This is to prevent contamination, which could come up as a result of interaction between the control and the experimental groups.
2. The same questions will be used for all groups for pre-test and post-test. This will make the groups as homogenous as possible; however, only the treatment package will differ so that any change could be ascribed to the sole cause of the treatment package.
3. All the questions will be trial tested in different places not part of control and experimental groups. The questions will be proofread by ICT teachers, who are

not part of the experiment to confirm that they are items from the curriculum for the term.

4. To reduce experimental mortality, learners will be given exercise books, pens and pencils, and *access to computers (at the computer laboratory) to encourage them to be regular and punctual.*
5. The time for activity will be incorporated into the normal school's timetable so that learners will not have to be in school before normal school reporting time or stay in school long after normal hours.
6. Learners are sometimes used to their regular teachers hence the researcher will not be engaged in the training of the learners. The ICT teachers in the school will administer the model prepared by the researcher.
7. The appropriate statistical tools will be used to analyze the data collected.

### Reliability of the Test

Reliability and consistency are synonymous in value; therefore, reliability of a test refers to the level of consistency in a test construct (Sürücü & Maslakci, 2020). To check for the reliability of the test items in this research, a pilot study will be employed at sampled schools outside the Cape Coast metropolis. The pre-test items will be tested in the sampled schools and the result will be computed using the Spearman-Brown reliability coefficient. The choice of the Spearman-Brown formula to measure the reliability of the test items was ideal for the research since it helps to reduce errors in the constructions that leads to poor test items. According to Opara and Ogbanu (2023), this formula helps to evaluate the consistency in a test items ability to measure only a single idea or concept, for *example* measuring the consistency in performance in computing as a subject. The Spearman-Brown formula will then be very ideal for this research as the student will engage in learning using the e-learning model in a particular subject (Computing) after the pre-test and this will mean that the pre-test and post-test scores when compared are likely not to be similar.

## SOLUTIONS AND RECOMMENDATIONS

This section will discuss *solutions and recommendations* in dealing with the *issues, controversies, or problems* presented in the preceding section.

## Solutions

### Research Design

Research design acts as a structured framework used to address a research problem (Adeoye-Olatunde & Olenik, 2021). It outlines the procedures for conducting research, including crucial details such as whom to collect data from, when to collect it, and the conditions under which it should be gathered (Creswell & Poth, 2007). Essentially, research design is the methodology or approach used to tackle a problem and find *solutions* or a developed framework aimed at answering research questions (Goldschmidt & Matthews, 2022). Every research design selected for a particular study is shaped by underlying presumptions (Sebele-Mpofu, 2020). A good understanding of these presumptions aids in defending the chosen research methodology (Siddiqua, 2023). For this study, a mixed method approach will be considered and this will be combined with a quasi-experimental approach along with a non-equivalent control group as well as a qualitative methodology that makes use of an action interpretive research design.

Learner content and user interface design can be looked at from different perspective but this study will use the mixed method research design where it will utilize a quasi-experimental design with a non-equivalent, pre-test, and post-test control group. The selected design will give room for an in-depth investigation into the research questions that guides the study and it will combine both the quantitative and qualitative methods to solve the problem. For this research the mixed method approach will be selected to provide a good understanding of the impact of learner content and user interface design on e-learning quality. Comparisons between the experimental and the control groups will employ the mean scores before and after the intervention and this becomes possible using this design. It will facilitate measurement of the effects of the independent variables (learner content and user interface design) on the dependent variable (e-learning quality)

Numerous studies, including e.g., Awuah and Ogbonnaya (2020), Bedada (2021), Chidziva (2021), Ofori-Kusi (2017), Yimer and Feza (2019), as well as the *journal* article on *technology and science education* by Mendezabal and Tindowen (2018) employed a quasi-experimental design with a non-equivalent control group, which proves useful in situations where true experimental designs are impractical. Since this approach does not need participants to be randomly assigned for the experiment to be done for both the control and the experimental groups, intact learner groups from school participating can be used as study participants. As the experiments will take place in a natural setting, researchers can directly evaluate participants, measure the impact of the intervention prescribed and reduce the impact of unrelated variables by using quasi-experimental designs. In this design, the researcher lacks control over the assignment of subjects to conditions. Specifically, in the non-equivalent control group design, both control and experimental groups are compared and assigned based on convenience rather than randomization (Singh, 2021).

The quasi-independent variables in this study are learner content and user interface design, and these are what will be manipulated to assess their influence on the independent variable which is the e-learning quality. This design can be symbolically represented as follows:

Experimental Group (N1): O1 → X1 → O2

Control Group (N2): O1 → O2, where:

- O1 represent the pre-test
- O2 represent the post-test,
- X1 represent the intervention (e-learning model with optimized learner content and user interface design).

The experimental group will be given the intervention (X1), whiles the control group will continue with the traditional classroom face to face teaching and learning method. The pre-test and post test scores mean will be compared to measure the effect of the independent variables on e-learning quality. The statistical analysis, that is analysis of covariance (ANCOVA), will be used to determine the significance of the results.

To complement the quasi-experimental design and facilitate data triangulation, the current study will incorporate a qualitative interpretive design of participatory action research (PAR). The design is chosen to explore the understanding the social and contextual factors influencing participants' experience with the e-learning model (William, 2024). It allows for an analytical perspective where external variables influence an individual's interpretation of the world, as illustrated by Kodisang (2022) in *a framework towards improved instruction of probability to grade seven students* based on *a case study of South African schools in Mpumalanga province*. Interpretivism aims to enhance knowledge by exploring and valuing people's unique perspectives (Creswell & Poth, 2007). With its foundation in PAR, the interpretive design in this study will prioritize experiential knowledge to tackle issues stemming from unequal social structures and develop actionable *solutions* (Lenette, 2022).

The study will adopt the interpretive research design and will make use of questionnaire, classroom observations and semi-structured interviews which will serve as the primary data collection tools and can be used to collect both qualitative and quantitative data. Structured questionnaire will be given to the participants in the experimental group to gather standardized data in both quantitative and qualitative format about their experience with the e-learning model. The questionnaire will measure specific aspects of the e-learning model which will include the interface design, the learner content, their learning experience and their overall satisfaction with the e-learning model. The classroom observations will be involving a recording of the classroom natural activities on a day-to-day basis (Cents-Boonstra, Lichtwarck-Aschoff, Denessen, Aelterman, & Haerens, 2021) taking key notes of how participants engage with the proposed e-learning model. The classroom observation is selected so that first-hand evidence of how participant engage with the e-learning model and how the model works in a real learning environment and the kind of effect it has on students' interaction.

To complement the questionnaire and the classroom observation, semi-structured interviews will also be conducted. The participants for the semi-structured interview will be purposively selected and this will be made up of six students and the computing teacher who will be in charge of the day-to-day instructions in the experimental group. The participants will be two students each from the categories of those who performed very well, averagely well and poorly in the post-test. These interviews will target several key dimensions including the perception on how the interface design and learner content impact their learning with the model, their learning experience and their overall satisfaction with the e-learning model. This qualitative approach will make possible for data about user experiences, the perceived benefits and the *challenges* in the implementation to be unearth. These data will be put into themes for thematic discussion (Lochmiller, 2021) to bring out the reoccurring patterns, the important findings as well as the meaningful insights which are important to the research objectives. This careful process will be coded, where major themes which will be interpreted to address how it answers the core research questions which borders on the e-learning model's potential to improve the quality of learning.

The use of the questionnaire, observation and semi-structured interview responses will give a strong, multi-perspective explanation of the e-learning model's *practical application*. This will produce great insights into the e-learning model's theoretical strength as well as its real-world application which can influence the model's success to be adopted in educational settings. These findings will contribute greatly to improving academic understanding and *practical* improvements in e-learning design and delivery.

The mixed methods approach selected for this research is justified in several ways (Dawadi, Shrestha, & Giri, 2021). A *journal* article on *practical studies in education* by the latter authors offered a discussion on the types of, as well as *challenges* and *criticisms*.

These methods build on the strengths of both quantitative and qualitative data, and provide a wider understanding of the research *problem*. The combination of quantitative and qualitative data produces a powerful mix where the quantitative data offer statistical insights whereas the qualitative data provide contextual depth. From this combined strength the issue of a limitation by a single method by ensuring that the research questions are fully answered. In their *journal* article on *mixed methods research*, Yousefi Nooraie, Sale, Marin, and Ross (2020) provided an *example* of the fusion between quantitative and qualitative methods and suggested that the integration of quantitative and qualitative methods is not exclusive but complementary. This approach ensures that the study captures both the measurable outcomes of the e-learning model and the nuanced experiences of its users.

## Recommendations

### Data Interpretation

By integrating the outcomes from regression analysis and ANCOVA, the study will offer a robust evaluation of the e-learning model's effectiveness. This will involve interpreting how specific design elements and content quality directly contribute to learning enhancements. The analysis will reveal the differential impact of the e-learning model on student learning, providing evidence-based insights into which aspects of interface design and content are most beneficial. Based on the statistical analysis, the study will propose actionable strategies for optimizing e-learning environments. This may include *recommendations* for interface adjustments, content enrichment, and pedagogical approaches to enhance learning efficacy.

The findings will highlight areas for further investigation, suggesting how subsequent research can build upon the observed effects of interface design and learner content on e-learning success. The study will reflect on the limitations inherent to its methodological approach, such as potential biases or the representativeness of the sample. This reflection will contextualize the findings within the broader landscape of educational research, ensuring a balanced interpretation of the data.

### Validity of the Semi-Structured Interviews

The check for the validity of the semi-structured interview, the data gathered from the interview will be compared to the data gathered from the distributed questionnaire. The chosen approach which is referred as convergent validity is explained as the comparison of data that are scaled from the same variable that are gathered using the different instrument (Cheung, Cooper-Thomas, Lau, & Wang, 2024). An *Asia Pacific journal* article on *management* by the latter authors presented a review and best-practice *recommendations* related to reporting on reliability, as well as convergent and discriminant *validity* with Structural Equation Modeling (SEM).

The study under consideration will use data from both the questionnaire and the semi-structured interviews as a measure of learners' perceptions of the e-learning model they were introduced to. This will be used to measure precisely their satisfaction with the interface design as well as the content quality. After this the results from the two instruments used will then be compared so as to establish their validity. To share more light on how this will be carried out, this *example* will make it clearer, that is if the data collected with the questionnaire shows that the learners were very satisfied with the interface design of the e-learning model, the interview responses too will be checked to see if it conforms with the finding of the questionnaire. But if there are discrepancies between what was collected by the questionnaire and that of the interview, then there will be a need to identify potential biases or the limitation of the selected instruments used. This data source triangulation will enhance the validity of the findings, thereby providing a more holistic understanding of the research problem.

## FUTURE RESEARCH DIRECTIONS

This section will discuss *future* and *emerging trends*, as well as provide insight about the *future* of the theme of the book on *Harnessing Generative Artificial Intelligence for Science Education* from the perspective of the chapter focus on *Harnessing Learner Content and User Interface Design for Basic Education* regarding *Research Methodology and Design*. The viability of a paradigm, model, implementation *issues* of proposed programs, etc., may be included in this section. If appropriate, the section will suggest *future research opportunities* within the domain of the topic.

### Gambling on the Future of Creativity in Science Education with the Integration of Generative Artificial Intelligence

Unveiling *the future of creativity* and innovation management in the era of *generative artificial intelligence*, Crupi, Costa, Thomas and Khatri (2024) invited submissions that delved into the extensive effects of Gen-AI on *creativity* and innovation, as shifts in GenAI "reshapes the limits of *creativity* and innovation".

### Generative Artificial Intelligence-Integrated Curriculum Models for Future-Ready Scientists

The journal article by Jaouadi and Maaradji (2024, p. 72) presented a hybrid model powered by Information and Communication Technology (ICT) "and using *generative AI* represents an innovative and promising approach to *future* education." With the capabilities of AI, the latter model had "the potential to deliver more personalized, engaging, and *accessible* educational experiences for learners worldwide."

## Teacher Training and Generative Artificial Intelligence: Preparing Future Educators for Digital Transformation

An *international journal* article on *education and humanities* by Zhang and Villanueva (2023) discussed *generative artificial intelligence* preparedness and technological competence towards a digital education *teacher training* program.

## Data Analysis

Quantitative data from questionnaires, and performance assessments will be analyzed using statistical software to identify patterns, *emerging trends*, and correlations. Qualitative data from interviews and observations will be analyzed thematically to extract meaningful insights into the experiences and perceptions of participants regarding the e-learning model. By employing a combination of quantitative and qualitative instruments and data collection techniques, the study aims to comprehensively evaluate the effectiveness of the e-learning model in enhancing educational outcomes within basic schools in the Cape Coast metropolis.

### Data Analysis and Interpretation

The study will employ SPSS for the comprehensive analysis of questionnaire data, focusing on extracting meaningful patterns and relationships. To explicitly ascertain the influence of interface design and learner content on student learning within the e-learning model, regression analysis will be conducted. This statistical technique will pinpoint the direct effects and predictive value of these variables on educational outcomes.

Following the methodology of Creswell (2012), ANCOVA will be applied to compare the post-test scores of the experimental and control groups. This comparison, crucially, will adjust for pre-test scores, ensuring any observed differences in post-test outcomes are attributable to the e-learning intervention rather than baseline discrepancies. Prior to conducting ANCOVA, an independent samples t-test will be employed to assess the equality of pre-test scores between groups. This preliminary step ensures that any subsequent differences found through ANCOVA are a result of the e-learning model's impact.

The study will collect primary data directly from students participating in the e-learning model. This approach ensures the reliability and relevance of the data, as it reflects firsthand experiences and outcomes. Data collection will focus on capturing students' performance through pre-test and post-test scores. This metric serves as a concrete measure of learning progression and the effectiveness of the e-learning model.

## CONCLUSION

This last section will provide discussion of the overall coverage of the chapter and concluding remarks.

This chapter outlines the research methodology for the implementation of an e-learning model that evaluates the impact of e-learning in ICT education which used a quasi-experimental pretest-posttest non-equivalent design. Two groups of students were used for this study: one group focused on an e-learning model and formed the experimental group and other receiving traditional instruction. The study will employ a deductive approach, which will be used to determine the influence of user interface design and learner content have on e-learning quality and it culminative effect on student performance. The research will manipulate variables related to the impact of user interface design and learner content affect student interaction as well as student satisfaction, the performance differences between genders, and outcomes for students how have **access** to ICT tools and possess some basic IT skills. This approach allows for a structured exploration of the specific impacts of e-learning on educational outcomes in ICT subjects.

To ensure the study's reliability and validity, measures will be taken to control extraneous variables, such as using consistent pre-test and post-test questions and ensuring that learning environments for control and experimental groups are separated to avoid contamination. Ethical considerations for this study will focus on obtaining consent from participants, roadmap to ensure confidentiality and projecting voluntary participation. The study's limitation will be in terms of scope which is the selection of two schools within the Cape Coast municipality, which may affect generalizability. Another limitation will be the collection of data which will be done questionnaires and academic performance tests, semi-structured interviews and classroom observation which all have the potential for biases in responses and this may impose some limitation on the study *conclusion.*

## REFERENCES


Adeoye-Olatunde, O. A., & Olenik, N. L. (2021). Research and scholarly methods: Semi-structured interviews. *Journal of the American College of Clinical Pharmacy: JAACP*, *4*(10), 1358–1367. DOI: 10.1002/jac5.1441

Adri, M., Wahyuni, T. S., Zakir, S., & Jama, J. (2020). Using ADDIE instructional model to design blended project-based learning based on production approach. *International Journal of Advanced Science and Technology*, *29*(6), 1899–1909.

Ahmed, I., & Ishtiaq, S. (2021). Reliability and validity: Importance in medical research. *Methods (San Diego, Calif.)*, *12*(1), 2401–2406. DOI: 10.47391/JPMA.06-861 PMID: 34974579

Al-Azawei, A., Serenelli, F., & Lundqvist, K. (2016). Universal Design for Learning (UDL): A content analysis of peer reviewed journals from 2012 to 2015. *The Journal of Scholarship of Teaching and Learning*, *16*(3), 39–56. DOI: 10.14434/josotl.v16i3.19295

Alenezi, M. (2023). *Blended Learning Motivation Support at the Saudi Electronic University: Utilizing Self-Determination Theory.* (PhD dissertation). Northern Illinois University.

Allemang, B., Sitter, K., & Dimitropoulos, G. (2022). Pragmatism as a paradigm for patient-oriented research. *Health Expectations*, *25*(1), 38–47. DOI: 10.1111/hex.13384 PMID: 34748689

Ansu-Kyeremeh, E. K., & Goosen, L. (2022). Exploring the Socioeconomic Facet of Online Inclusive Education in Ghana: The Effects of Technological Advancement in Academia. In Garcia, M. (Ed.), *Socioeconomic Inclusion During an Era of Online Education* (pp. 47–66). IGI Global., DOI: 10.4018/978-1-6684-4364-4.ch003

Awuah, F. K., & Ogbonnaya, U. I. (2020). Grade 12 Students' Proficiency in Solving Probability Problems Involving Contingency Tables and Tree Diagrams. *International Journal of Instruction*, *13*(2), 819–834. DOI: 10.29333/iji.2020.13255a

Barianos, A. K., Logothetis, I., Kalogiannakis, M., & Vidakis, N. (2022). Teaching Ancient Greek Theatre Through In-Game Exploration: The Case of ThimelEdu. In *The Digital Folklore of Cyberculture and Digital Humanities* (pp. 186-205). IGI Global.

Bedada, T. B. (2021). *The use and effect of Geogebra software in Calculus at Wachemo University, Ethiopia: An investigation.* (Doctoral dissertation). University of South Africa (UNISA).

Bhat, B. A., & Neelam, N. (2023). An overview of the life and philosophy of John Dewy. *International Journal of Advanced Multidisciplinary Scientific Research, 6*(12). https://ijamsr.com/issues/6_Volume%206_Issue%2012/20240120_082027_6951.pdf

Bogna, F., Raineri, A., & Dell, G. (2020). Critical realism and constructivism: Merging research paradigms for a deeper qualitative study. *Qualitative Research in Organizations and Management, 15*(4), 461–484. DOI: 10.1108/QROM-06-2019-1778

Bujang, M. A., Omar, E. D., Foo, D. H., & Hon, Y. K. (2024). Sample size determination for conducting a pilot study to assess reliability of a questionnaire. *Restorative Dentistry & Endodontics, 49*(1), e3. Advance online publication. DOI: 10.5395/rde.2024.49.e3 PMID: 38449496

Buys, T., Casteleijn, D., Heyns, T., & Untiedt, H. (2022). A reflexive lens on preparing and conducting semi-structured interviews with academic colleagues. *Qualitative Health Research, 32*(13), 2030–2039. DOI: 10.1177/10497323221130832 PMID: 36194785

Caldarella, P., Larsen, R. A., Williams, L., Downs, K. R., Wills, H. P., & Wehby, J. H. (2020). Effects of teachers' praise-to-reprimand ratios on elementary students' on-task behaviour. *Educational Psychology, 40*(10), 1306–1322. DOI: 10.1080/01443410.2020.1711872

Casteel, A., & Bridier, N. L. (2021). Describing populations and samples in doctoral student research. *International Journal of Doctoral Studies, 16*(1), 339–362. DOI: 10.28945/4766

Cents-Boonstra, M., Lichtwarck-Aschoff, A., Denessen, E., Aelterman, N., & Haerens, L. (2021). Fostering student engagement with motivating teaching: An observation study of teacher and student behaviours. *Research Papers in Education, 36*(6), 754–779. DOI: 10.1080/02671522.2020.1767184

Chatzopoulos, A., Kalogiannakis, M., Papadakis, S., Papoutsidakis, M., Elza, D., & Psycharis, S. (2021). DuBot: An open-source, low-cost robot for STEM and educational robotics. In *Handbook of Research on Using Educational Robotics to Facilitate Student Learning* (pp. 441-465). IGI Global Scientific Publishing.

Cheung, G. W., Cooper-Thomas, H. D., Lau, R. S., & Wang, L. C. (2024). Reporting reliability, convergent and discriminant validity with structural equation modeling: A review and best-practice recommendations. *Asia Pacific Journal of Management, 41*(2), 745–783. DOI: 10.1007/s10490-023-09871-y

Chidziva, J. (2021). *Using ubuntu values to enhance disruptive pedagogies for effective and meaningful teaching of grade 12 Euclidean geometry.* (PhD thesis). UNISA.

Creswell, J. (2012). *Educational research: planning, conducting and evaluating quantitative and qualitative research* (4th ed.). Pearson Education, Inc.

Creswell, J. W., & Creswell, J. D. (2018). *Research design: qualitative, quantitative, and mixed methods approaches* (5th ed.). SAGE.

Creswell, J. W., & Guetterman, T. C. (2024). *Educational research: Planning, conducting, and evaluating quantitative and qualitative research.* Pearson.

Creswell, J. W., & Poth, C. N. (2007). *Qualitative inquiry and research design: choosing among five approaches.* SAGE.

Crupi, A., Costa, A., Thomas, A., & Khatri, P. (2024). *Unveiling the Future of Creativity and Innovation Management in the era of Generative Artificial Intelligence.* Retrieved from https://rnd2024.org/wp-content/uploads/2024/01/RND2024-Track-P3.pdf

Davies, C., & Fisher, M. (2018). Understanding research paradigms. *JARNA*, *21*(3), 21–25.

Dawadi, S., Shrestha, S., & Giri, R. A. (2021). Mixed-methods research: A discussion on its types, challenges, and criticisms. *Journal of Practical Studies in Education*, *2*(2), 25–36. DOI: 10.46809/jpse.v2i2.20

Dewey, J. (1938). *Experience and education.* Macmillan.

Elder-Vass, D. (2022). Pragmatism, critical realism and the study of value. *Journal of Critical Realism*, *21*(3), 261–287. DOI: 10.1080/14767430.2022.2049088

Goldschmidt, G., & Matthews, B. (2022). Formulating design research questions: A framework. *Design Studies*, *78*, 101062. Advance online publication. DOI: 10.1016/j.destud.2021.101062

Hampson, T., & McKinley, J. (2023). Problems posing as solutions: Criticising pragmatism as a paradigm for mixed research. *Research in Education*, *116*(1), 124–138. DOI: 10.1177/00345237231160085

Hoekstra, R., Vugteveen, J., Warrens, M. J., & Kruyen, P. M. (2019). An empirical analysis of alleged misunderstandings of coefficient alpha. *International Journal of Social Research Methodology*, *22*(4), 351–364. DOI: 10.1080/13645579.2018.1547523

Jaouadi, A., & Maaradji, A. (2024). ICT & Generative Artificial Intelligence Powered Hybrid Model for Future Education. *Cadmus*, *5*(3), 61–75.

Kalogiannakis, M., & Kanaki, K. (2022). Introducing computational thinking unplugged in early childhood education within the context of physical and natural science courses: A pilot study in Greece. In *Research Anthology on Computational Thinking, Programming, and Robotics in the Classroom* (pp. 197-222). IGI Global. DOI: 10.4018/978-1-6684-2411-7.ch010

Kamal, S. S. (2019). Research paradigm and the philosophical foundations of a qualitative study. *PEOPLE: International Journal of Social Sciences*, *4*(3), 1386–1394. DOI: 10.20319/pijss.2019.43.13861394

Khatri, K. K. (2020). Research paradigm: A philosophy of educational research. *International Journal of English Literature and Social Sciences*, *5*(5), 1435–1440. DOI: 10.22161/ijels.55.15

Kivunja, C., & Kuyini, A. B. (2017). Understanding and applying research paradigms in educational contexts. *International Journal of Higher Education*, *6*(5), 26–41. DOI: 10.5430/ijhe.v6n5p26

Kodisang, S. M. (2022). *A framework towards improved instruction of probability to grade seven students: A case of South African schools in Mpumalanga province.* (PhD thesis). UNISA.

Kwaah, C. Y. (2024). Social media use among basic school teachers in Ghana: Exploring opportunities and challenges. *Cogent Education*, *11*(1), 2310978. Advance online publication. DOI: 10.1080/2331186X.2024.2310978

Leidner, D. E., & Tona, O. (2021). The CARE Theory of Dignity Amid Personal Data Digitalization. *Management Information Systems Quarterly*, *45*(1), 343–370. Advance online publication. DOI: 10.25300/MISQ/2021/15941

Lenette, C. (2022). What is participatory action research? Contemporary methodological considerations. In *Participatory action research: Ethics and decolonization* (pp. 1–18). Oxford University Press., DOI: 10.1093/oso/9780197512456.003.0001

Lewis, J. (2020). Experimental design: ethics, integrity, and the scientific method. In *Handbook of research ethics and scientific integrity* (pp. 459–474). Springer International Publishing. DOI: 10.1007/978-3-030-16759-2_19

Lochmiller, C. R. (2021). Conducting thematic analysis with qualitative data. *The Qualitative Report*, *26*(6), 2029–2044. DOI: 10.46743/2160-3715/2021.5008

Logothetis, I. B., Christinaki, E., Charalampakos, O., Katsaris, I., & Vidakis, N. (2022). Gamification techniques capitalizing on state-of-the-art technologies. In *The digital folklore of cyberculture and digital humanities* (pp. 206–229). IGI Global. DOI: 10.4018/978-1-6684-4461-0.ch012

Mendezabal, M. J., & Tindowen, D. J. (2018). Improving students' attitude, conceptual understanding and procedural skills in differential calculus through Microsoft mathematics. *Journal of Technology and Science Education, 8*(4), 385–397. DOI: 10.3926/jotse.356

Miraz, M. H., Ali, M., & Excell, P. S. (2021). Adaptive user interfaces and universal usability through plasticity of user interface design. *Computer Science Review, 40*, 100363. Advance online publication. DOI: 10.1016/j.cosrev.2021.100363

Mweshi, G. K., & Sakyi, K. (2020). Application of sampling methods for the research design. *Archives of Business Research, 8*(11), 180–193. DOI: 10.14738/abr.811.9042

Ngugi, J., & Goosen, L. (2017). The Effects of Course Design Characteristics, Self-Regulated Learning and Knowledge Sharing in Facilitating the Development of Innovative Behaviour among Technology Students at Universities. *Proceedings of the Institute of Science and Technology Education (ISTE) Conference on Mathematics, Science and Technology Education* (pp. 80-86). Mopani Camp, Kruger National Park: UNISA Press.

Ngugi, J., & Goosen, L. (2019, October 25). Towards Smart Innovation for Information Systems and Technology Students: Modelling Motivation, Metacognition and Affective Aspects of Learning. (Á. Rocha, & M. Serrhini, Eds.) *Smart Innovation, Systems and Technologies, 111*, 90-99. DOI: 10.1007/978-3-030-03577-8_11

O'Donoghue, T. (2018). *Planning your qualitative research thesis and project: An introduction to interpretivist research in education and the social sciences.* Routledge. DOI: 10.4324/9781351165563

Ofori-Kusi, D. (2017). *An investigation into the use of problem-solving heuristics to improve the teaching and learning of mathematics.* (PhD thesis). UNISA.

Opara, I. M., & Ogbanu, G. I. (2023). Effect of Item Order on the Reliability of Mathematics Test among Secondary School Students in Rivers State. *Journal of Advances in Education and Philosophy, 7*(11), 460–466. DOI: 10.36348/jaep.2023.v07i11.003

Ormerod, R. J. (2021). Pragmatism in professional practice. *Systems Research and Behavioral Science, 38*(6), 797–816. DOI: 10.1002/sres.2739

Papadakis, S., & Kalogiannakis, M. (2022). Learning computational thinking development in young children with Bee-Bot educational robotics. In *Research anthology on computational thinking, programming, and robotics in the classroom* (pp. 926–947). IGI Global. DOI: 10.4018/978-1-6684-2411-7.ch040

Papadakis, S., & Kalogiannakis, M. (Eds.). (2024). *New Approaches in Mobile Learning for Early Childhood Education*. IGI Global., Retrieved from https://www.igi-global.com/book/new-approaches-mobile-learning-early/332803 DOI: 10.4018/979-8-3693-2377-9

Racine, E., Kusch, S., Cascio, M. A., & Bogossian, A. (2021). Making autonomy an instrument: A pragmatist account of contextualized autonomy. *Humanities & Social Sciences Communications*, *8*(139), 139. Advance online publication. DOI: 10.1057/s41599-021-00811-z

Rahi, S. (2017). Research design and methods: A systematic review of research paradigms, sampling issues and instruments development. *International Journal of Economics & Management Sciences*, *6*(2), 1–5. DOI: 10.4172/2162-6359.1000403

Sebele-Mpofu, F. Y. (2020). Saturation controversy in qualitative research: Complexities and underlying assumptions. A literature review. *Cogent Social Sciences*, *6*(1), 1838706. Advance online publication. DOI: 10.1080/23311886.2020.1838706

Siddiqua, A. (2023). Critique of Research Methodologies and Methods in Educational Leadership. *World Journal of Education*, *13*(4), 16–24. DOI: 10.5430/wje.v13n4p16

Singh, A. (2021). Quasi experimental design in scientific psychology. SSRN *Electronic Journal*. DOI: 10.2139/ssrn.3793568

Singh, J., Steele, K., & Singh, L. (2021). Combining the Best of Online and Face-to-Face Learning: Hybrid and Blended Learning Approach for COVID-19, Post Vaccine, & Post-Pandemic World. *Journal of Educational Technology Systems*, *50*(2), 140–171. DOI: 10.1177/00472395211047865

Stamatakis, A., Logothetis, I., Petridis, K., Kalogiannakis, M., & Vidakis, N. (2025). Micro-Credentials Establish New Realities in Digital Education. In *Education, Integrating Micro-Credentials With AI in Open* (pp. 19-38). IGI Global Scientific Publishing.

Stratton, S. J. (2021). Population research: Convenience sampling strategies. *Prehospital and Disaster Medicine*, *36*(4), 373–374. DOI: 10.1017/S1049023X21000649 PMID: 34284835

Sürücü, L., & Maslakci, A. (2020). Validity and reliability in quantitative research. *Business & management studies: an international journal, 8*(3), 2694-2726.

Taşdan, M., Kartal, M., Gözüm, A. İ., & Kalogiannakis, M. (2025). Digital Transformation in School Management: Insights From Administrators' Perspectives. In *Empowering STEM Educators With Digital Tools* (pp. 275-320). IGI Global Scientific Publishing.

Teresi, J. A., Yu, X., Stewart, A. L., & Hays, R. D. (2022). Guidelines for designing and evaluating feasibility pilot studies. *Medical Care, 60*(1), 95–103. DOI: 10.1097/MLR.0000000000001664 PMID: 34812790

Van der Walt, J. L. (2020). Interpretivism-constructivism as a research method in the humanities and social sciences–more to it than meets the eye. *International journal of philosophy and theology, 8*(1), 59-68. doi:DOI: 10.15640/ijpt.v8n1a5

Verawati, N. N., & Sarjan, M. (2023). The philosophy of critical thinking in problem-based science learning. *Prisma Sains: Jurnal Pengkajian Ilmu dan Pembelajaran Matematika dan IPA IKIP Mataram, 11*(4), 992-1001. DOI: 10.33394/j-ps.v11i4.9101

Vlasopoulou, M., Kalogiannakis, M., & Sifaki, E. (2021). Investigating teachers' attitudes and behavioral intentions for the impending integration of STEM education in primary schools. In *Handbook of research on using educational robotics to facilitate student learning* (pp. 235–256). IGI Global Scientific Publishing. DOI: 10.4018/978-1-7998-6717-3.ch009

Walliman, N. (2021). *Research methods: The basics.* Routledge., DOI: 10.4324/9781003141693

William, F. K. (2024). Interpretivism or constructivism: Navigating research paradigms in social science research. *International Journal of Research Publications, 143*(1), 134–138. DOI: 10.47119/IJRP1001431220246122

Xenakis, A., Dimos, I., Feidakis, M., Sotiropoulos, D., Kalovrektis, K., & Nikolaou, G. (2025). An LLM-Based Smart Repository Platform to Support Educators With Computational Thinking, AI, and STEM Activities. In *Empowering STEM Educators With Digital Tools* (pp. 107–136). IGI Global Scientific Publishing.

Yeboah, A. N., & Goosen, L. (2024). The Impact of Learner Content and User Interface Design on E-Learning Quality: Teaching in Times of Crises. In Scott, B., & Fox, M. (Eds.), *Cases on Economics Education and Tools for Educators* (pp. 136–159). IGI Global., DOI: 10.4018/978-1-6684-7583-6.ch006

Yeboah, A. N., & Goosen, L. (2025). Integration Strategies of Learner Content and User Interface Design in Higher Education: Teaching and Learning Online in Times of Crises. In Arinushkina, A. (Ed.), *Integration Strategies of Generative AI in Higher Education* (pp. 51–70). IGI Global., DOI: 10.4018/979-8-3693-5518-3.ch003

Yimer, S. T., & Feza, N. N. (2019). Learners' conceptual knowledge development and attitudinal change towards calculus using jigsaw co-operative learning strategy integrated with GeoGebra. *International Electronic Journal of Mathematics Education, 15*(1). Advance online publication. DOI: 10.29333/iejme/5936

Yousefi Nooraie, R., Sale, J. E., Marin, A., & Ross, L. E. (2020). Social network analysis: An example of fusion between quantitative and qualitative methods. *Journal of Mixed Methods Research*, *14*(1), 110–124. DOI: 10.1177/1558689818804060

Zhang, C., & Villanueva, L. E.Lizelle E. Villanueva. (2023). Generative artificial intelligence preparedness and technological competence: Towards a digital education Teacher Training Program. *International Journal of Education and Humanities*, *11*(2), 164–170. DOI: 10.54097/ijeh.v11i2.13753

Chapter 2

# Student-Created Generative Artificial Intelligence (GenAI) Physics Simulations: A Build, Refine and Learn (BRaL) Framework for Conceptual Understanding

**Dimitrios Sotiropoulos**
https://orcid.org/0000-0001-7367-5760
*University of Thessaly, Greece*

## ABSTRACT

*This chapter presents a pedagogical framework that aims to enhance physics teaching method from high school level to early college by enabling students to create interactive simulations with the help of generative AI tools which are large language models-powered. The BRaL framework recognizes learners as model builders who can develop and refine simulations without programming skills. This framework ensures students learn physics instead of merely remembering it. They create their own models, then take a break to reflect on what they're thinking, and test their arguments against theory and data. The framework has three stages and it includes educators and AI guidance to students on how to design diagrams, conduct virtual experimentation, and identify errors with clear assumptions. Hooke's law simulation as a case study presented in the chapter and depicts how students transition from simple idealized problems to harder, more complex ones.*

DOI: 10.4018/979-8-3373-2913-0.ch002

## INTRODUCTION

New developments in Generative Artificial Intelligence (GenAI) are changing the way students learn science. Generative AI tools, such as large language models (e.g., ChatGPT), may be of immense value for physics learning, as they simulate the process of a human tutor explaining challenging concepts, answering questions and providing feedback, and directing inquiry through conversation in natural language (Ding & Li, 2023; Leon, 2024). In this study, we examine the innovative Build, Refine and Learn method in which students can develop substantive understanding of core physics concepts by building their own physics simulations with GenAI, followed by furthering their understanding by means of continuous feedback and experimentation.

This process aligns well with constructivist approaches- students learn deeply when they actively build and refine their own thinking by creating a mental model (El Fathi et al., 2025; Xavier & Oliveira, 2024). Recent research highlights how bringing students into the process—actually having them create and review models—boosts their understanding and sharpens their problem-solving skills (Magana et al., 2024). GenAI as a creative partner enables students to do genuine modeling and simulation without the need for programming; thus, they can focus their cognitive resources on physics reasoning rather than coding syntax (Robledo-Rella & Toh, 2024; Hamerski, 2024; Aligato & Saligumba, 2025).

The Build, Refine and Learn method in science education is a solution for the two major problems that have been identified. Firstly, it allows students to generate simulations (not only users) which is a technique based on Papert's constructionism (learning-by-making) and contemporary model-based learning theory. Secondly, it reduces the technical challenge: GenAI "coders" facilitate simulation authoring which implies that students can execute their ideas in code through natural language prompts (El Fathi et al., 2025; Mukherjee & Le, 2025; Xavier & Oliveira, 2024).

GenAI lets students turn their mental models into working simulations fast, without forcing them to learn programming first. They can focus on thinking like physicists: figuring out how to represent a system, choosing the right variables and laws, testing their models. No more getting stuck on code. The real work becomes about understanding physics, not wrestling with syntax errors.

Thischapter presents the pedagogical framework for learning by creating and refining models, understanding the importance of mental models and simulations in grasping physics concepts, and explaining how GenAI-supported student-created simulations facilitate learning. We establish the educational worth of carefully planned virtual experimentation using standard representational conventions and provide examples of how repeated build-and-refine cycles (led by teachers or AI coaches) result in a more profound conceptual understanding and the development of skills that can be transferred to other .

## THEORETICAL FOUNDATIONS: LEARNING BY MODEL CONSTRUCTION AND ITERATIVE REFINEMENT

Model-based learning (MBL) offers a conceptual framework to grasp how students develop, verify, and amend mental models that help them understand physical phenomena. MBL at its core is about turning students into modelers who are not just passively receiving information but actively creating, representing, and revising their explanatory structures. In fact, this reflects the epistemology of science itself: researchers build models, check the predictions, and update the models in a cyclical manner using the new data and conceptual feedback (Seel, 2014). Such cyclic processes are also aligned with the principles of teaching–learning sequences, which emphasize structured progression from students' initial conceptions to scientifically accepted models through guided inquiry and reflection (Méheut & Psillos, 2004).

Physics education through the repeated cycle of revision has been especially effective in achieving profound conceptual knowledge. Students in model-based curricula are often reported to outperform those in traditional classes (Liang et al., 2011) on assignments that evaluate understanding of concepts such as the Force Concept Inventory. These methods encourage learners to articulate their assumptions, predict, observe, and change their models—a process that is very close to scientific reasoning (Zwickl et al., 2014).

At the same time, model-based experiments in laboratories and simulations help the development of metacognitive skills as they prompt learners to assess the degree to which their representations address the problem and to identify the parts that are not explained by their models (Odden et al., 2023). This is consistent with the constructivist viewpoint, which holds that the source of conceptual change is the learner's work in resolving the conflict between what the model predicts and what is observed (Mufit et al., 2018). The cognitive conflict feature thus helps in acquiring more profound knowledge and reorganization of models.

Various empirical studies have supported the claim that adopting model-based or problem-based methods along with digital tools can improve understanding and motivation in physics. The example of problem-based learning with PhET simulations wherein students showed higher post-test performance and greater consistency in conceptual understanding (Rianti et al., 2024) can be cited in this regard.

Moreover, research in cognitive neuroscience has shown observable neural changes related to learning through modeling. Brewe et al. (2018) demonstrated that students enrolled in Modeling Instruction (MI) courses exhibited increased activation in brain regions associated with working memory, problem-solving, and conceptual integration, thus providing neurobiological evidence of the learning gains achieved through iterative modeling (Brewe et al., 2018).

Furthermore, problem-structured physics curricula supporting model reconstruction, discussion, and prediction rather than memorizing algorithms have been shown to achieve conceptual retention and transfer of problem-solving skills (Becerra-Labra et al., 2012). Ongoing interactions of model building and model refinement promote deeper conceptual understanding and through scientific reasoning develop reflection and adaptation – the key skills of a contemporary physics learner. The result of modeling supplemented by experimentation and simulation using generative AI has shifted the learning of science from procedural to representational.

When students develop and improve their simulations, they are not only testing their hypotheses, but also representing the physical laws in symbolic, graphical, and narrative forms. The emphasis of this transition from "doing experiments" to "representing phenomena" is that scientific understanding is mainly a portrayal of the different media used—how equations, diagrams, and models signify within a community of practice. Thus, the following section investigates the representational conventions that determine successful modeling and learning and how students can become proficient in switching between symbolic, visual, and computational representations in order to have a more profound conceptual understanding of physics.

## MENTAL MODELS AS THE STARTING POINT OF LEARNING

To grasp physics, students need to develop, evaluate and improve models in their mind which explain the cause and the structure of the relationships of physical entities and processes. The models in their minds become the basis of the user's logic, forecast, and explanation. In physics education, mental models are the students' attempts to produce logical explanations of phenomena which may or may not be similar to scientific models (Greca & Moreira, 2000).

Results from a wide array of comparative studies provide evidence of a strong positive correlation between representational competence and deep and stable conceptual knowledge of students (Edelsbrunner & Malone, 2023; Edelsbrunner & Hofer, 2024). Likewise, a meta-analysis conducted in 2025 found that physics learners increasingly depend on multiple external representations (graphs, diagrams, and symbolic expressions) to develop and verify mental models, thus representational flexibility is a plausible predictor of conceptual learning (Ate, Parno, & Munfaridah, 2025).

Understanding or conceptual change in physics is mostly the outcome of the confrontation between students' intuitive mental models and scientifically validated frameworks. This happens when learners identify the gaps between their explanatory structures and expert models and then get guidance to resolve the differences, thus, triggering a profound conceptual restructuring (Gadgil, Nokes-Malach, & Chi, 2012). Wittmann (2006) goes beyond this frame and suggests "resource graphs" as a means to depict the fluctuating nature of conceptual resources, thereby explaining how conceptual change is not only incremental but also can happen through restructuring (Wittmann, 2006). Present-day classrooms' digital simulations and generative AI systems are becoming a new and effective way to help students externalize their mental models for feedback and refinement. Research reveals that if students express or depict their models with the help of simulations or AI-mediated representations, teachers will be in a better position to spot the wrong concepts and then lead to their rectification (Pedrera, 2025). Finally, as physics learners progress, their mental models evolve to integrate successive scientific theories—a process described as "model evolution" rather than replacement.

One such example is transitions from classical to modern physics, which involve reframing rather than discarding prior conceptual structures, thus showing how learners repurpose existing mental models within new representational frameworks (Zuccarini & Malgieri, 2024). Recent studies in physics education point out that such representational transitions are not only cognitive but also epistemological in nature, as they require learners to internalize new conventions of reasoning, symbolic mediation, and visualization practices that are in line with changes in scientific paradigms (Davishahl & Zhang, 2024; Ate, Parno, & Munfaridah, 2025).

Experiential and simulation-based methods of learning that help students to be proficient in representations and at the same time develop their spatial reasoning have been able to expedite these epistemic shifts as students, both physically and conceptually, reconstruct their knowledge in different fields of physics (Davishahl & Haskell, 2024).

## MODELING, EXPERIMENTATION, AND SIMULATION IN BUILDING PHYSICS UNDERSTANDING

For a long time, modeling has been at the heart of physics education, helping students to go from the theoretical and the abstract to the experimental and the actual. The best way for students to learn is by repeatedly building, checking, and updating models that explain things they can see happen—a cycle that is very much the Build, Refine, and Learn framework. GenAI has the potential to change this cycle, which can now also be understood as the automatic or guided creation of dynamic simulations, visualizations, or even interactive experimental environments. One of the recent examples of physics education change through GenAI is a case where this technology acts as a model-building assistant, thus changing the traditionally student-driven creative process of simulation design. Ben-Zion et al. (2024) illustrated that through generative instruments, students are capable of developing AI-powered simulations of physical systems—thus they virtually create the laboratories that enable them to understand a concept by means of visual experimentation (Ben-Zion et al., 2024).

The study from the field of engineering-physics by Cervantes Juárez and Sánchez Guzmán (2024) indicates that significant learning improvements were observed (Normalized Conceptual Gain = 0.75) when the students were following an AI-led learning cycle that combined spreadsheet-based modeling, generative-AI tutoring, and feedback on students' self-designed experiments. The "Learning Science and Engineering with Electronic Spreadsheets Cycle" (LSEESC) really helps students understand hard ideas. It makes those abstract ideas come to life by linking them to real-world experiments (Cervantes Juárez & Sánchez Guzmán, 2024; Pinho-Lopes & Powrie, 2025).

The capabilities of GenAI extend even further. They can produce animations, design experiments, or even generate activities from scratch on request, based on what students ask and what kinds of problems they are doing. Just yesterday, physics teachers used this capability to demonstrate how physics theories work in practice. This opened the door to a whole new realm of teaching both fun and engaging, a new mode of engaging students. This approach really assisted students in developing their math skills and the capacity to synthesize ideas across subject areas, like kinematics, electricity, etc. (Cervantes Juárez & Sánchez Guzmán, 2024). This is not just with the experiments. AI simulated experiences lead to more student engagement, and, more importantly, to meta-cognitive thinking. That is critical for real learning.

In a study with 91 undergraduate physics students, Robledo-Rella and Toh (2024) used ChatGPT integrated with WolframAlpha to co-solve mechanics problems. The conceptual test scores for the experimental group remained statistically the same as those of the control group. This means that students have reported, through the questionnaire, a significantly higher engagement, motivation, and confidence in their ability to debug and explain AI errors, which serves as an indication of their reflective understanding of the modeling processes (Robledo-Rella & Toh, 2024).

The artistic aspect of modeling is also going to be reframed. Her and Hamerski (2024) explored student perceptions of creativity in a computational-physics course, using GenAI, and saw that the students considered the tool to be a co-actor in idea generation and model-making, thus expanding their agency. Simultaneously, students were also prompted to engage in critical reflection on accuracy and authorship (Her & Hamerski, 2024). More broadly, Nurjanah et al. (2024) undertook a bibliometric review of the literature from 2000-2023 on the use of AI in physics education, including precision of studies applying AI for modeling, simulation, and adaptive feedback. They found that from 2020 onward, there was a significant increase in studies applying AI, identifying twelve thematic clusters, such as 3D virtual laboratories, AI-based modeling systems, and learning analytics for experimental design, indicating simulation-based inquiry with AI has become a definitive trend for physics education research (Nurjanah et al., 2024).

Collectively, prementioned studies reveal that AI-enabled modeling and simulation can help students to switch seamlessly between conceptual reasoning, experimental exploration, and creative synthesis. Such a technological integration is in line with the Refine stage of the framework as it offers instant feedback loops, adaptive scaffolding, and multimodal visualization - thus assisting students in not only verifying their physical hypotheses but also in changing their conception of the way scientific models represent.

## REPRESENTATIONAL CONVENTIONS

Students' scientific understanding is influenced not only by their knowledge but also by their ability to articulate that knowledge in the conventional languages of science. When students can read and create diagrams, equations, visual models, and scientific explanations that follow the rules of their field, they show a deeper understanding of the concepts because these representations make scientific meanings clear and public (Edelsbrunner et al., 2023; Tang, 2023). In physics, these representational conventions act as the grammar of meaning-making: they structure how learners express and coordinate ideas across multiple modes of representation. Decades of research show that mastering these conventions is central to conceptual change and to the development of expert-like reasoning (Ainsworth, 2006; Kozma & Russell, 2005; Airey & Linder, 2009).

Recent evidence confirms that multimodal representation strategies substantially enhance inquiry and explanation in science learning. In a controlled classroom study, Ortiz and Aliazas (2021) found that pupils who engaged in multimodal representational tasks (verbal + diagrammatic + experimental) progressed from basic pattern recognition to proficient scientific reasoning, showing significant gains in inquiry skills (Ortiz & Aliazas, 2021)

In physics education, studies show that representational (multi-representation) competence is positively related to conceptual understanding and problem-solving, especially in physics/engineering cohorts (Edelsbrunner et al., 2024). Experimental and design-based studies likewise indicate that tasks integrating two or more representations within the same learning sequence promote representational fluency better than treating each form in isolation (Lichtenberger et al., 2024; Distrik et al., 2021).

Linet al. (2025) discovered that students' use of GenAI for constructing digital multimodal compositions which involved the integration of text, imagery, and conceptual visualizations led students to a higher level of engagement in representational reasoning as they used AI feedback to both formalize and deepen their understanding (Lin et al., 2025). In a similar vein, Wasielewski (2024) argued that multimodal generative systems such as DALL-E blur the boundaries between an image, an illusion, and a conceptual model thereby students getting involved in questioning the role of visualizations in influencing perception and scientific truth (Wasielewski, 2024).

Research underscores the significance of technological literacy necessary for teachers to work with multimodal representations. Masrifah et al. (2022) identified that physics teachers using e-books with simulations and animations demonstrated higher ICT literacy and pedagogical awareness than their peers who used text-only materials. This is coherent with the Technological Pedagogical and Content Knowledge (TPACK) framework, which connects teachers' work with the use of ICT in their subject-specific pedagogy. More recent literature suggests that pairing TPACK with AI literacy prepares educators to architect adaptive, interactive and data-informed learning environments that support science education in a contemporary context (Peikos, Giannakos, & Papamitsiou, 2025). In the same direction, Blonder, Feldman-Maggor, and Rap (2024) used generative AI with pre-service science teachers to surface their PCK and to strengthen their preparation, showing that AI can function not only as content but as a diagnostic and developmental tool for teacher knowledge.

Meta-analytic evidence indicates that by 2024-2025, educational research will frame representation increasingly as multimodal co-construction in collaboration with AI. A recent bibliometric study by Întorsureanu et al. (2025) found that themes such as 'multimodal GenAI', 'AI-as-peer', and 'AI-mediated representation' are among the fastest growing topics in educational research. This illustrates a shift towards shared authorship of representations as a learner and algorithm (Întorsureanu et al. 2025).

These findings collectively suggest that the rules of representation are no longer confined to disciplinary norms but are evolving into socio-technological literacies. Today's students are not only required to know the syntax of equations and diagrams, but also the semiotics of AI-generated representations, i.e., how to interpret, judge, and ethically apply them. Therefore, the evolution of representational fluency in physics merges human symbolic reasoning with generative co-creation, introducing a new paradigm of *"thinking in physics"*.

## STUDENT-AUTHORED SIMULATIONS WITH GENAI: FOCUSING ON PHYSICS, NOT CODING

GenAI one of the most transformative contributions to physics education is its concept to remove from simulation the barrier of challenging programming. In the past, students who want to model a system physically interactive through programming would have to learn a programming language such as Java, Python, or JavaScript. Now GenAI tools take the learners description of the system and produce the working code—essentially GenAI tools acting as on-demand expert programmers. This transformation brings computational physics within everyone's reach: Ben-Zion et al. (2024) noticed that with large-language-model prompting "educators and students are enabled to design custom simulations without programming expertise," thus advanced conversational linguistics became the medium through which both high school and undergraduate students could create and further refine simulations (Ben-Zion et al., 2024).

Interdisciplinary research studies in the last years resonate with this democratizing pattern, which in turn empowers GenAI tools leveraging in a matriculating of engineering & computing fields/subjects, as efforts aimed at lowering the technical entry barriers and facilitating the cognitive focus on design and reasoning rather than syntax (Johri et al., 2023).

The learning advantage is huge: students would be able to decide on physics—the assumptions, variables, and interpretations—over code debugging. In the Build–Refine–Learn construct, this is in accordance with the rule that cognitive work should be handed over to model-making and investigation, not to the low-level tasks. In their study, Her and Hamerski (2024) found evidence indicating that students perceiving the use of GenAI for research or modification of simulations as creative and exploratory, thereby they deepen their physical reasoning engagement rather than programming syntax (Her & Hamerski, 2024).

Studentsiterate their interaction—prompt, result, critique, refine—thus cognitively anchoring to physics. Every new version comes from a scientific query: "Is this motion governed by Hooke's law?" or "What causes energy to drift over time?" This reflection loop resembles the process of real scientific investigation. Recent studies on AI-generated or AI-supported visualizations in science education show that when students design or adapt AI-based animations/simulations, they spend more time inspecting parameters and checking physical plausibility, which in turn supports causal/explanatory reasoning (Pellas, 2025; Zhou, Xu, & Zhao, 2024). Similar effects were also observed in a wide range of GenAI-education studies that reveal that students' epistemic engagement gets deepened when AI is used for routine tasks and students are free to focus on conceptual inquiry (Întorsureanu et al.,2025).

The task of debugging an AI-generated simulation, in fact, can reveal a deep understanding of the students' mental models. When the omission of an assumption—like resuming air resistance—is the cause of the most obviously unrealistic results, the learners are forced to not only identify the mistake but to also explain it. According to the report by Ben-Zion et al., this "mirrors scientific inquiry," since the process of validation of an AI-generated simulation requires checking its results with empirical or theoretical ones.

Students are being taught to describe a physical system in natural language, and concentrate on the set of governing equation's and constraints rather than the particular syntax to represent them in an FEA code. This approach provides conceptual sense-making as learners engage in explaining the principles and relationships that constitute a system before they formalize them mathematically or computationally. Recent research suggests that this activity, known as representational translation moving back and forth among verbal, mathematical, and symbolic forms of expressions helps students build coherent physical models and to reason across modalities (Marshman et al., 2024).

For example, having explicit phases of reflection and articulation embedded within modeling activities has been identified as a way to promote the development of students' representational and meta-representational competence by necessitating that learners make their reasoning explicit and align symbolical/mathematical representations with the computational simulation models (Magana et al., 2024; Edelsbrunner et al., 2024).

The options go beyond mere mechanics. Using a descriptive prompt, GenAI can help students build complex models, like wave interference, orbital motion or thermodynamic cycles. As attention shifts to the lucidity of physical modeling rather than programming itself, students arrive at a new form of scientific authorship: they propose and refine models that are correct in physics but incorrect in syntax.

In short, GenAI-supported simulation authoring lets students become scientific modellers instead of just learning how to code. It could help people be more creative, think more clearly, and make better decisions by using simulation design as a way to learn physics through active representation and iterative refinement.

## KNOWLEDGE TRANSFER, GUIDED INQUIRY, AND THE ROLE OF ITERATIVE REFINEMENT

One of the primary purposes of education is knowledge transfer: learners should be able to take what they have learned and use it in novel situations and adjacent domains. Studies on model-based and simulation-rich physics instruction show that transfer is more likely when students construct the model themselves and regulate their own learning processes, rather than only receiving worked-out examples (Brewe et al., 2018; Magana et al., 2024).

In AI-supported physics courses, when students are guided to build or co-build artefacts, they have to externalize their often-incomplete conceptions into an explicit representational structure, which is exactly the kind of productive struggle that precedes transfer (Cervantes Juárez & Sánchez Guzmán, 2024; Robledo-Rella & Toh, 2024). GenAI-assisted, student-created simulations are a particularly suitable setting for this: tools that auto-generate or rapidly prototype simulations let students translate their conceptual understanding into an executable model (Ben-Zion et al., 2024; Álvarez-Siordia et al., 2025). When the simulation output, or AI-generated feedback, does not match the expected behaviour, students must revise the model, which triggers reflection on principles and promotes abstraction that can be applied beyond the immediate task (El Fathi et al., 2025; Nareklishvili & Polson, 2025). In this way, GenAI does not replace the transfer process but stages it more frequently and more visibly inside the learning environment, provided that it is embedded in a pedagogical design that keeps students cognitively engaged (Zawacki-Richter et al., 2024; Kaldaras et al., 2024; Pellas, 2025).

Older studies already showed the effectiveness of simulation-based learning for deep understanding and transfer. Banda and Nzabahimana (2021) discovered that students who used PhET simulations improved their mental representations of physical systems in a more coherent way, which allowed them to solve unfamiliar problems and apply the same principles in different contexts. By visualizing processes that are not visible and changing variables, learners established strong conceptual connections that later helped them to recall and generalize.

Present developments lead to new possibilities of GenAI-supported modeling learning environments that combine simulation, reasoning, and guided reflection. Nareklishvili and Polson (2025) provided evidence that generative AI architectures can follow the scientific process by continuously generating, testing, and refining physical laws—thus producing a teaching model similar to students' learning cycles.

Albano and Longo (2025) show something important: when design students use AI to iteratively refine their work, they don't just pick up step-by-step skills—they actually transfer both conceptual and procedural knowledge to new projects. GenAI doesn't just speed up tinkering; it helps students build flexible, higher-level thinking. Instead of memorizing steps, they learn to reason, adapt, and solve new problems.

## THE BUILD, REFINE AND LEARN (BRAL) FRAMEWORK: A STRUCTURED PEDAGOGICAL APPROACH

The Build, Refine and Learn (BRaL) framework has developed this concept into a more formal process for conducting physics education with GenAI support. It is important to point out that BRaL does not offer typical simulation-based lessons, where students explore a tool that someone else built. The best way to distill this is through a driving analogy: students are in the driver's seat with BRaL; the students are creating, testing out, and tinkering with models while the AI is assisting them -- as opposed to traditional lessons where students were passengers. BRaL synthesizes many approaches to teaching and learning including: constructivism (where students construct knowledge); constructionism (where students learn by making something real); inquiry-based learning (where the students' questions guide the process); model-based learning (where understanding comes from building and revising models); and metacognition (thinking about thinking). BRaL weaves all of these strands together with AI to create a learning space for students where the technical impediments to learning physics mostly disappear, allowing students to focus their reasoning about physics.

### Stage 1: Build—Constructing Initial Models

The following process enables students to translate their understanding of a phenomenon into words, and, by using generative AI tools such as ChatGPT or Claude, into working simulations (no coding).

For example; a student might type: "Build a simulation that shows a pendulum with adjustable length and amplitude of initial angle with the energy transformation more visible."

The AI tool does the coding; the student is focused on the science. The learning experience demonstrates Papert's position of constructionism - that learning happens through constructing public artifacts (1980). In externalizing their mental models into a simulation, students confront their assumptions and gaps in understanding of the phenomenon.

The AI is acting as an "on demand expert coder" (Ben-Zion et al., 2024), which saves all of the implementation details in code, which enables students' cognitive load to remain focused on conceptualizing the physics.

In particular pedagogical utilization, the Build stage focuses on several principles: conceptual clarity to be able to make claims about the physical relationships (striving to be explicit), model assumptions based on which factors will or will not be included, decisions on representation (color, arrows, graphs, etc.), and predictive reasoning (students offer predictions before running the simulation regarding the behaviours they expect).

Research supports this approach - constructing/building their model first draws on what students already know about the phenomenon and the student experiences surprise when the simulation cannot match their expectations. It's the surprise that typically leads to real learning (El Fathi et al., 2025).

## Stage 2: Refine—Iterative Testing and Improvement

The Refine stage represents the test-revise cycle from the scientific method. Students run their Now comes the scientific method in action. Students run their simulations, view what happens, then check to see whether what happened matches what the tested something related to their theory or the data they had. When what happened does not match, they engage in a conversation using the AI or a teacher, identify what is incorrect, and then make an applicable revision.

This stage of the argument aligns with empirical research showing that iterative revision when engaged in modeling, encourages deeper understanding than simply creating a model one time (Magana et al., 2024).

Students engage in behaviors that consist of:

- Validation: Checking if the simulation behavior matches the laws of physics
- Debugging: Identifying points in which outputs did not match expectations (i.e., energy drift, truncated unphysical trajectory)
- Parameter exploration: Systematically varying one of the inputs in the simulation to clarify relationships, corresponding to level of the difficulty proposed
- Model extension: The student adding additional complexity to their design (i.e., adding air resistance or damping)

Refinement is not only fixing bugs, but also refinement of the ideas that are underlying. For example, if a spring simulation runs forever, the student will actually have to engage with energy lost and not only the coding. Importantly, the AI provides immediate feedback to the students, so they can run through multiple iterative processes quickly; this is challenging without an interactive simulation (Cervantes Juárez & Sánchez Guzmán, 2024).

The Refine stage incorporates metacognitive scaffolding through prompts like: "Why does your simulation disagree with theory?" or "What physical assumption might be missing?" This guided inquiry prevents unproductive trial-and-error while maintaining student agency (Steinert et al., 2024).

## Stage 3: Learn—Consolidating Understanding Through Reflection

After students have refined the simulation and achieved an outcome that is in line with the theory, they step back to reflect on what they changed, and why their changes then worked. They relate their simulation to the equations and concepts they learned about. They begin to recognize patterns and principles that allow them to extend their understanding to other situations beyond the situation they modeled.

These self-reflective activities include, for example:

- Describing changes: Articulating how or why each revision improved the model
- Relating to theory: Linking the behaviors of the simulation to governing equations
- Generalizing patterns: Recognizing principles that apply to contexts beyond the situation modeled
- Transfer tasks: Noticing trends and applying their understanding to similar phenomena

Research on GenAI-supported self-reflection is promising, and it indicates that Ai-supported academic tutors can develop self-explanation effectively, transcending their reasoning and letting the students assess their own understanding (Yuan & Hu, 2024; Chen et al., 2023). The Learn phase also introduces analogy—they need to compare changes to see that radioactive decay, for example, has similar exponential modeling to capacitor discharge and thermal cooling—which begins to establish structural knowledge, rather than just contextually-specific knowledge that is not applicable to other topics.

## The Cyclical Nature of BRaL

BRaL is not a linear sequence but rather a spiral one (see Figure 1). Each learning phase and cycle will produce new questions that will prompt the next phase or cycle. If a student has a model for ideal projectile motion, they may generate questions based on real-world features or factors that would modify their model, and thus begin a Build phase to include factors such as air resistance. This is analogous to authentic scientific practice where each solved problem reveals a new question that needs to be addressed.

The BRaL cycle, represents a source of multiple paths of transfer. Every iterative refinement pushes a student's generalization. In the case of a model that does not hold under novel conditions, a student will be forced to modify their assumptions and to extend the conceptual scope of generalization. As an example, consider a projectile motion simulation that may work well without air resistance for short distances, but begins to fail for longer trajectories when air resistance plays a role—prompting the student to change the model and incorporate drag in the simulation. Through iterative refinement the students move from procedural knowledge to principled generalization, which is a hallmark of transferable expertise.

Reflection is also another element that helps transfer to a higher level. After changing a model, the students are urged to question their reasoning: What and why did it change? What physical principle can be used to explain this behavior? The process of reflective abstraction helps to recognize generalizable laws and separate them from the details that are specific to the context. Contemporary studies also support this position: Yuan and Hu (2024) revealed that GenAI-based reflective tutoring systems metacognitive engagement by providing a tailor-made feedback that facilitates self-explanation and hence, transfer. Likewise, Chen, Zhu, and Castillo (2023) discovered that the use of GenAI in classroom knowledge-building activities enhances learners' epistemic agency and structured inquiry since learners can refine and verbalize their thinking through AI-mediated dialogue.

Reflection and iteration don't go far without the right scaffolding in place. When students dive into inquiry without guidance, they can misread simulation results or just fiddle around without real understanding. Park and Zhang (2023) point out that instructors play a crucial role here. Their "reflective noticing" helps students stay on track during modeling, so they dig deeper without drifting away from core concepts.

*Figure 1. The BRaL stages*

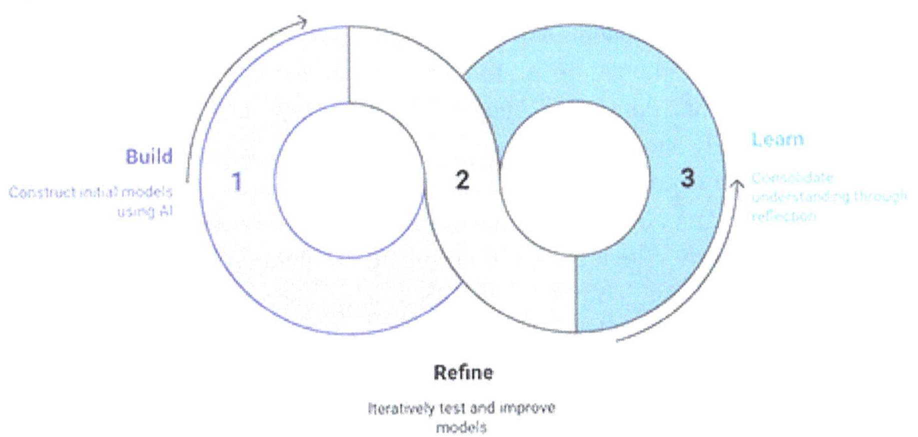

One example of this is the research of Steinert et al. (2024), which found that GPT-4 may be utilized as an effective inquiry tutor that gives relevant helpful information, and by its nature, it leads students to explain their thought process thus increasing user interaction and experimental physics tasks accuracy.

GenAI technology could provide scaffolding. That is, the same generative models that might be used to generate the codes for the simulation, may also serve as cognitive coaches that encourage students to hypothesize, diagnose, and reason to explain the observed behavior of the model. This is a particularly intriguing consideration, because it is leveraging GenAI to not simply serve as a device for students to construct and manipulate in the physical context—but using GenAI as a tutor such that the issue of dependence on "AI as oracle" (i.e. students simply engaging in "just fix it for me" interactions) is being very effectively addressed, but students' practice and learning experience having been redirected toward needing to arrive at a diagnosis, formulate hypotheses, and reflect, conceptually, which are cognitive foundations of their transferrable expertise. In addition to this, Wetzel and Kani (2025) suggest restructuring practices—GenAi assisted scaffolding also encourages students to become more adept in their critical and ethical reasoning—with the caveat that although we cultivate students evaluative judgement skills in the context of physics, students critical and ethical reasoning and literacy and evaluative judgement skills are not confined to the domain of physics.

Furthermore, GenAI radically shortens the iteration cycle time to a level which was previously impossible for traditional settings. One can think of a scenario where within a single class period, students get to build and refine several related simulations—say radioactive decay, capacitor discharge, and thermal cooling—while all of these are governed by the same exponential decay law. This kind of fast comparative modeling allows students to become familiar with the structural similarities among different areas and, moreover, to be able to extract the same mathematical principles from various domains. Chung et al. (2024) reported that students who used GenAI routinely and across multiple study contexts self-reported higher levels of GenAI literacy and greater awareness of limitations and risks, which can be interpreted as indicators of better epistemic preparedness for advanced academic tasks. Correspondingly, Singh et al. (2025) regard the iterative inquiry process as a source of "human cognition protection" because it ensures that the learners are not passively dependent on AI but rather are actively engaged, able to abstract, and have the cognitive skill of resilience .

In conclusion, the use of GenAI in guided inquiry changes the whole process of knowledge transfer from something that happens as a side effect to a learning objective that is specifically intended. Students, through repeated refinement, reflection, and support—both from humans and AI—are not only making simulations but they are also learning to think with models, using concepts in a flexible way, and extending their understanding of physical phenomena. So, the Build, Refine and Learn cycle becomes a kind of link between representational fluency and epistemic growth, thus helping to develop learners who are capable of adapting, generalizing, and reasoning scientifically in AI-augmented .

The next section illustrates this framework through a concrete Hooke's Law example, demonstrating how theory translates into classroom practice.

## ILLUSTRATIVE EXAMPLE: BUILD, REFINE AND LEARN - HOOKE'S LAW SEQUENCE

To provide a real example of the use of guidance in the Build-Refine and Learn (BRaL) framework, we have come up with the case of using generative AI in iterative model-building, inquiry, and knowledge transfer process in line with the latest research on learning through simulation (Ben-Zion et al., 2024; Álvarez-Siordia et al., 2025). The example is related to the natural science of high school physics Hooke's Law.

### Build (and use) Phase

The learners, through a Generative AI tool (like Claude), draft an interactive spring-mass simulation to experiment with the adjustable factors of the spring constant (k), mass (m), and initial displacement. A teacher, by facilitating the conversation about the main physical components—spring restoring force, equilibrium, and the assumption of no damping—supports the students in carrying out the task. Students are required to anticipate the force-extension relationship graph prior to carrying out the simulation.

After that, the GenAI tool comes up with a script that can be run depicting a vertical spring with a hanging mass that can be displaced and released. Now the students ask the GenAI to change the depiction of the experiment by changing scale, colors, or labels thus performing the initial stage of representational authorship.

With the simulation, students measure the extension against the applied force by adding different masses, and empirically they discover the linear relation $F = -kx$. They observe oscillatory motion when the mass is displaced, thus reinforcing their conceptual link between Hooke's Law and simple harmonic motion.

Their hands-on confrontation with the simulator mirrors the advantages of the exploratory simulation acknowledged by Álvarez-Siordia et al. (2025) who claimed that a structured use of simulators considerably raises the level of students' conceptual understanding provided they manipulate variables and interpret relations. Likewise, Yuan and Hu (2024) proved that GenAI-supported exploration facilitates reflective observation and model validation, which in turn leads to a more stable understanding of physical relationships.

## Refine Phase

Here the teacher setting a new task: "Why, do you think, real springs stop oscillating after some time? What might we be missing in our model?" Students conjecture about friction and air resistance, and AI is instructed to add damping to the simulation. This moment represents the iterative thinking that is at the core of BRaL. Magana et al. (2024) show that an iterative cycle of planning, implementing, evaluating, and reflecting on computational models fosters students' regulatory skills and supports the development of more sophisticated explanations, which aligns with claims about enhanced mechanistic reasoning through model revision (Magana et al., 2024). When AI-generated models are introduced, students can be prompted to interrogate implausible simulation outputs — for example, by checking whether the decay of an oscillation is physically plausible or whether parameters/time step must be adjusted — a process that recent AI-in-education studies identify as metacognitively productive because it requires monitoring, evaluation, and justification of revisions (Tankelevitch et al., 2024).

Performing such self-examination and rectification is an instance of AI-mediated inquiry scaffolding as denoted by Steinert et al. (2024) who found that AI tutors which encourage students to clarify discrepancies lead to a substantial improvement in conceptual coherence in experimental physics.

## Learn Phase

Once the students have refined their work, they analyze the damped oscillator in order to single out the three regimes: underdamped (oscillatory decay), critically damped (fastest return without oscillation), and overdamped (slow return to equilibrium). Afterward, they associate the regimes with energy dissipation and talk about the systems in the real world that use the critical damping method, for example, car suspensions, seismographs, and door closers. The transition of students' conceptual understanding to a deeper level is in line with the research by Chen, Zhu, and Castillo (2023), who demonstrated that learners' iterative refinement of AI-assisted simulations leads to the development of epistemic awareness - the ability to link model behavior with the underlying principles. Figure 2 presents an artefact that was generated using the Claude GenAI tool, after all the steps of the model had been carried out.

*Figure 2. Spring - mass system simulation created with Claude*

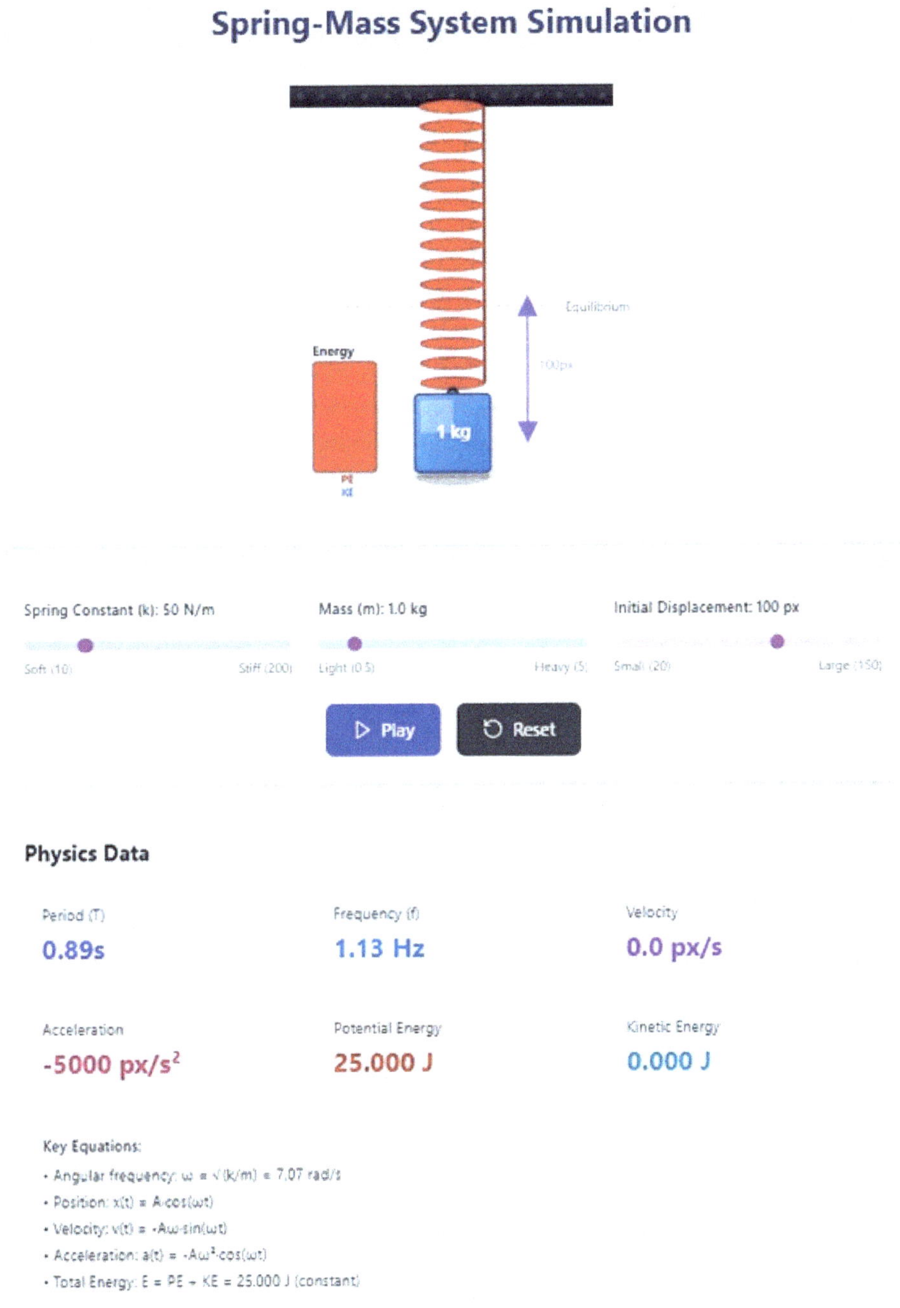

Likewise, Albano and Longo (2025) noticed that the iterative refinement facilitated by GenAI enhances the learners' ability to make durable procedural and conceptual transfer when dealing with related modeling contexts. They further broaden their understanding of the damped-spring by applying it to other areas where they can determine the desirable damping regimes for shock absorbers, vibration isolators, or seismic dampers. Besides, they explain which parameters influence the system response and draw a rough idea of how the model could be altered to incorporate non-linear springs or temperature effects.

Throughout this activity, learners move from a situated form of understanding to exploring structural knowledge transfer, signifying they become aware of a generalized set of principles that regulate any physical system. This is in line with Chung et al. (2024), who observed that students who employ GenAI in a variety of study contexts report increased AI literacy and greater epistemic awareness, conditions that may foster cross-contextual reasoning (Chung et al., 2024; Magana et al., 2024). Furthermore, Wetzel and Kani (2025) argue that scaffolding GenAI inquiry increases learners' capacity to critically assess AI outputs, thus the transfer happens under epistemic transparency and under interpretive skill, not blind faith in AI. Methodical guidance throughout this example permits students to link the concepts and practice, therefore, simulations are no longer just tools for visualization, but rather are tools for reasoning. The nature of actively constructing models, prompting iterations with AI, and reflecting through scaffolding not only reinforces the understanding, but also it ready for transfer and application in multiple contexts.

This Hooke's Law sequence exemplifies how the Build, Refine and Learn framework—supported by GenAI and guided inquiry—serves as a robust engine for conceptual growth and knowledge transfer in physics education. It transforms abstract principles into dynamic, manipulable models that learners debug, refine, and reinterpret. By iterating with feedback and scaffolding, students extract generalizable scientific principles from specific cases, developing both representational fluency and epistemic maturity.

## LIMITATIONS AND IMPLEMENTATION CHALLENGES

While BRaL framework enabled by generative AI (GenAI) is a great educational tool, putting it into practice is a bit of a juggling act of technical, pedagogical, and ethical challenges that educators and institutions need to figure out if they want to adopt it in a sustainable and fair way.

## Configuring GenAI as a Coach–Tutor

To make sure the use of GenAI is in line with inquiry-based teaching, the system has to be set up with:

(a) short role descriptions that focus on guided inquiry rather than just giving the answer;
(b) confirmation routines (e.g., units, invariants, baseline checks) that go along with the code;
(c) prompts that make the user go through the predict → test → diagnose → revise cycle; and
(d) non-opaque AI assistance keeping the teacher updated.

All the above contribute to maintaining epistemic transparency and stopping the assistant from solving the problem in a way that short-circuits the learning goals.

## Technical Constraints and Epistemic Transparency

GenAI-powered tools are capable of on the fly creation of the simulations and code; however, they still can be incorrect in facts or calculations. Should their outputs be taken without verification, they could very well reinforce the wrong ideas or introduce pseudo-physical models if neither the teachers nor the students have the knowledge to check them.

Additionally, the "black-box" characteristic of large language models limits students' insight into algorithmic reasoning, thus possibly impeding their computational literacy. According to recent work on trust in GenAI, preventing learners from blindly accepting AI-generated explanations requires epistemic trust calibration—that is, aligning one's trust with the AI's actual capability and verifying its outputs before use (Zhai, Wibowo, & Li, 2024).

## Pedagogical and Teacher-Centric Challenges

One of the major problems that keeps coming up is that students rely too much on AI, meaning that they see GenAI as a tool that just gives them answers instead of a tool that helps them think. Zhai et al., (2024) noticed that when there is no clear instruction to think about one's own thinking, learners feel that they should follow the AI suggestions without questioning them, which results in them engaging with the content at a very superficial level. So, teacher mediation should be next to indispensable.

After examining current research and stakeholder needs on AI in higher education, Zawacki-Richter et al. (2024) emphasized that teachers require targeted AI-literacy professional development to be able to guide students' AI-supported inquiry and to critically evaluate AI-generated outputs. Similarly, recent reviews of AI-driven intelligent tutoring systems emphasize that although AI tutors can be scaled to reach more learners, they still do not fully reproduce the fine-grained, diagnostic adaptivity of human instructors; therefore teacher-in-the-loop supervision remains necessary (Létourneau et al., 2025).

## Assessment and Evaluation Challenges

The task of evaluating learning outcomes in GenAI-supported settings is hard and also raises different ethical issues. Conventional assessment rubrics are usually inadequate in revealing the extent to which learners have engaged in process-oriented learning, i.e., the reasoning, revising and reflecting phases that are involved in BRaL cycles. A multimodal assessment approach can capture not only the final correctness of an AI-supported science task but also student agency, conceptual depth, and the quality of model revisions; in other words, it treats assessment as collecting learning evidence across iterations rather than grading a single product (Alalawi et al, 2025).

## Equity, Access, and Linguistic Inclusion

Fair access to GenAI tools is a point that should always be kept in mind. For instance, some students may not have the proper equipment, bandwidth, or support from the school, so they will hardly be able to interact with AI-enhanced learning. According to recent analyses on AI and educational equity, deficits in connectivity, devices and local infrastructure tend to amplify pre-existing educational inequalities, especially in under-resourced or rural schools, because they limit who can actually benefit from GenAI-based services (Adarkwah et al., 2025; UNESCO, 2024). In such contexts, AI initiatives can unintentionally widen the gap instead of closing it

Moreover, language bias is still an issue in GenAI systems, which work best in English. In this way, non-native speakers might face situations where meanings are not quite accurate, and also the AI understanding of prompts in different languages could be weaker, thus limiting fair participation. Wetzel and Kani (2025) emphasize that the necessity of the teacher training program in AI literacy, where educators learn how to use AI tools in multilingual classes.

Equity, the authors claim, implies not only having access to technology but also the development of cognitive resilience—students being able to recognize when they have to question AI outputs instead of following them without hesitation, as stated by Singh et al. (2025).

### Balancing Promise and Pragmatism

As a matter of fact, the evidence is gradually showing that the use of GenAI in a carefully designed way within an inquiry-based framework brings both cognitive and motivational benefits to the students, provided that there is proper support, teacher supervision and openness about knowledge. The problem is not whether GenAI should be used, but rather how it is used pedagogically so that learning stays reflective, fair, and human-centered.

Subsequent research should uncover methods for continued AI use that are environmentally and socially sustainable—such as the use of open-source alternatives, multilingual training datasets, and the inclusion of verification protocols—to make BRaL-based learning accessible to everyone .

## CONCLUSION AND IMPLICATIONS FOR SCIENCE EDUCATION

The use of Generative Artificial Intelligence (GenAI) in education marks the beginning of a new era of active learning, which fundamentally changes how students engage with science since they are the ones creating knowledge. This chapter presented the Student-Created GenAI Physics Simulations: Build, Refine and Learn (BRaL) Framework, which demonstrated how the established teaching learning principles paired with generative technologies can facilitate an authentic scientific investigation. In this framework, pupils are the designers and evaluators of the models: they create simulations that serve as representations of their mental models; they improve their models by testing them, and by getting feedback on their models; and they are not only learning the physics content but also the scientific reasoning and representational practices, as it pertains to scientific thinking.

The practice of learning through the creation and improvement of models has its theoretical roots in the constructivist and constructionist traditions of the last several decades (Piaget, 1972; Papert, 1980), and it is also very well substantiated by the latest research. Research results reveal that the students involved in generating and improving models attain deeper conceptual understanding, have a longer retention span, and acquire more transferable reasoning skills. Her and Hamerski (2024) and Ortiz and Aliazas (2021) proved that iterative modeling tasks supported by AI lead to the students' active exploration and conceptual coherence, while Albano and Longo (2025) confirmed that structured GenAI-based refinement facilitates both conceptual and procedural transfer.

These discoveries set GenAI in the position of a learner constructivist educational style enhancer who is opening up participation in computational modeling to students by removing the technical challenges. In that sense, GenAI frees students from the necessity to learn coding syntax thereby making modeling-based learning more accessible to a wider audience of students. As a result, the learners can now put the emphasis on physics reasoning rather than programming.

The transition begins with students' mental models. GenAI is a conversational partner who helps students to realise their thinking, correct their misconceptions and make more formal representations of physical systems with the teacher's assistance.

Modeling, experimentation, and simulation together form a coherent triad in physics learning. Each simulation run becomes a virtual experiment, and each refinement an update to the model, mirroring the cyclic process of scientific inquiry. In this process, students enact the cognitive logic of science—hypothesizing, testing, and revising—thus developing an integrated understanding of theory and evidence. Through GenAI, these cycles can occur rapidly and repeatedly, promoting both efficiency and depth of exploration. Research on scaffolded, computationally supported modeling shows that AI- or tool-mediated modeling can encourage metacognitive regulation and deeper understanding, because students are prompted to question simulation behaviour and to justify revisions to improve physical plausibility (Magana et al., 2024; Tankelevitch et al., 2024; Wan et al., 2025). Iterative engagement fosters reflective habits of mind, helping learners develop self-monitoring, error diagnosis, and reasoning strategies that can transfer across domains (Magana et al., 2024; Wan et al., 2025).

Representation and reflection are central to this process. Using standard visual conventions—color coding, energy graphs, arrows of motion—helps students connect abstract relationships to visual meaning (Ainsworth, 2006; Airey & Linder, 2009). When guided by AI prompts and teacher facilitation, these representations become tools for reflection. Chen, Zhu, and Castillo (2023) showed that AI-supported reflection enhances epistemic awareness, while Wasielewski (2024) noted that multimodal generative systems prompt students to interrogate how visualization shapes understanding and truth claims in science. Thus, GenAI not only supports representation but also deepens learners' appreciation of the conventions and interpretive practices of the scientific community.

The Build, Refine and Learn framework also strengthens transfer and metacognition. As students move through cycles of construction (build) and revision (refine), they learn how to learn: diagnosing reasoning flaws, hypothesizing alternatives, and applying insights to new problems. Chung et al. (2024) found that students who used GenAI repeatedly and across multiple study contexts reported stronger AI literacy and greater epistemic self-awareness regarding opportunities and risks.. Patterns identified in these experiences—such as conservation principles or scaling laws—become cognitive templates that transfer to novel situations, aligning with Nareklishvili and Polson's (2025) finding that generative modeling reinforces generalizable scientific reasoning. These metacognitive benefits suggest that BRaL not only could help in learning physics but also cultivates adaptive learning skills essential for lifelong inquiry.

This research has significant implications for science education and curriculum. The BRaL framework provides a mechanism for integrating computational thinking into science instruction without requiring a transformation of physics instruction into computer programming instruction. The focus remains on the scientific concepts of reasoning, experimentation, and conceptual analysis, while GenAI assumes the computational functions. Preliminary implementations of BRaL (Ben-Zion et al., 2024; Kaldaras et al., 2024), suggest researchers found that students reported higher engagement, motivation, and ownership of the learning experience when their conceptual ideas and thought bubbles come to life in physics simulations. Additionally, inclusivity is enhanced: students with multiple cognitive preferences—visual, experiential, or linguistic—can all meaningfully engage. Taking risks with the AI, in the spirit of teaming with an intelligent collaborator, rather than considering it as an oracle also builds AI literacy—the capacity to evaluate, direct, and responsively engage generative systems in problem solving (Wetzel & Kani, 2025). However, we must continue to think carefully and purposefully about how to leverage GenAI. As discussed previously, there are challenges—some of which include teacher readiness, assessments redesign, and epistemic transparency. However, educated scaffolding around GenAI provides multiple opportunities for learning when learning stages are collapsed or hustle and bustle good instruction has limits. One benefit is the opportunity to productively fail: if GenAI generates an erroneous simulation of a physics experiment, as an educator, you can invite students to confirm, debug, and account for the error—and thus restore the students' disciplinary authority. This aligns with Singh et al. (2025), who argue that such reflective correction cultivates cognitive resilience—the capacity to maintain human oversight and critical reasoning in AI-rich environments. Assessment practices should therefore evolve to evaluate reasoning processes, the quality of model revisions, and learners' reflective explanations rather than only static correctness (Alalawi et al, 2025).

Looking to the future, the Build, Refine and Learn philosophy could be adapted much more widely than physics. Chemistry students could attend to creating simulation of reaction kinetics, biology students to population dynamics, and environmental science students to feedback loops in climate systems. Interdisciplinary genAI projects could involve physics (talking about the energy balance), chemistry (the carbon cycle) and biology (ecosystem responses) and would foster interest in systems thinking and systems understanding across disciplines. Întorsureanu et al. (2025) describe how this AI-facilitated co-construction could contribute to integrative reasoning and share authorship, suggesting these will seed the greater visibility of the framework across all scientific disciplines, because it is based upon the sharing of models. When considering how students with limited access to resources will be a key feature of global initiatives to address the GenAI divide, it is important to recognise the significance of open-source advancements and instructor training in multiple languages. This highlights the importance of ensuring that any tool can be accessed, adjusted and interpreted.

We contend that using generational AI for science education with these student-authored simulations represents an exciting and meaningful avenue to infusing but rigor, creativity, or inclusivity. It is undoubtedly a pedagogical realization of engaging children in the idea of learning science by doing science.

In the Build, Refine and Learn framework, students are able to act like scientists by making their own ideas–testing them out and refining with AI as a mentor and author. Evidence is clear that this has an impact on conceptual understanding, misconceptions, self-efficacy and the ability to apply problem-solving across contexts. While the evidence-based practice of educational research continues to emerge, documenting and improving best practices for GenAI integration will help ensure that technology serves human ingenuity and intellect. The potential trajectory is clear by using GenAI to unshackle students' creative and analytical power, science education can be made more authentic, equitable and closer to the practices of 21st-century science. The learner's attention is still where it should be — on learning the physics — and the AI has an allure of its own, empowering our learning more than ever before, but without furthering us from nature.

This framework presented analytically in this chapter is conceived as a broad, adaptable model that can be implemented across educational levels to guide the co-creation of generative-AI simulations while keeping conceptual physics learning central. Its value lies in a clear sequence of phases that can align with diverse classroom ecologies and AI tools, sustaining students' active construction of meaning. Its value lies in a transparent sequence of phases that can align with diverse classroom ecologies and AI tools, sustaining students' active construction of meaning. In order to go further than design exemplars, the implementation of the design-oriented studies in real classrooms that include authentic learner data, teacher mediation, contextual constraints, and also pinpoint typical student difficulty and candidate scaffolding strategies should be carried out. These enactments may provide more solid statements about the effectiveness and transferability of the model and also guide the iterative refinement process (Carroll & Park, 2024; Steinert et al., 2024).

## REFERENCES


Adarkwah, M. A., Badu, S. A., Osei, E. A., & Amponsah, A. (2025). ChatGPT in healthcare education: A double-edged sword of trends, challenges, and opportunities. *Discover Education*, *4*(1), 14. DOI: 10.1007/s44217-024-00393-3

Ainsworth, S. (2006). DeFT: A conceptual framework for considering learning with multiple representations. *Learning and Instruction*, *16*(3), 183–198. DOI: 10.1016/j.learninstruc.2006.03.001

Airey, J., & Linder, C. (2009). A disciplinary discourse perspective on university science learning: Achieving fluency in a critical constellation of modes. *Journal of Research in Science Teaching*, *46*(1), 27–49. DOI: 10.1002/tea.20265

Alalawi, K., Athauda, R., & Chiong, R. (2025). An extended learning analytics framework integrating machine learning and pedagogical approaches for student performance prediction and intervention. *International Journal of Artificial Intelligence in Education*, *35*(3), 1239–1287. DOI: 10.1007/s40593-024-00429-7

Albano, S., & Longo, G. (2025). *Integrating generative AI in design education: A structured approach to client-centered interior design visualization*. AHFE International., DOI: 10.54941/ahfe1005930

Aligato, R. M., & Saligumba, R. P. (2025). The use of generative AI tools and their role in science learning among senior high school students. *International Journal for Multidisciplinary Research*, *7*(3), 44773. Advance online publication. DOI: 10.36948/ijfmr.2025.v07i03.44773

Álvarez-Siordia, F. M., Merino-Soto, C., Rosas-Meléndez, S. A., Pérez-Díaz, M., & Chans, G. M. (2025). Simulators as an innovative strategy in the teaching of physics in higher education. *Education Sciences*, *15*(2), 131. DOI: 10.3390/educsci15020131

Ate, O., Parno, P., & Munfaridah, N. (2025). Multirepresentation in physics learning research: A content analysis review of trends, opportunities, and challenges. *Journal of Science Education Research*, *9*(1), 32–42. DOI: 10.21831/jser.v9i1.72954

Banda, H. J., & Nzabahimana, J. (2021). Effect of integrating physics education technology simulations on students' conceptual understanding in physics: A review of literature. *Physical Review. Physics Education Research*, *17*(2), 023108. DOI: 10.1103/PhysRevPhysEducRes.17.023108

Becerra-Labra, C., Gras-Martí, A., & Martínez-Torregrosa, J. (2012). Effects of a problem-based structure of physics contents on conceptual learning and the ability to solve problems. *International Journal of Science Education, 34*(8), 1235–1253. DOI: 10.1080/09500693.2011.619210

Ben-Zion, Y., Einhorn Zarzecki, R., Glazer, J., & Finkelstein, N. D. (2024). Leveraging AI for rapid generation of physics simulations in education: Building your own virtual lab. *arXiv preprint* arXiv:2412.07482. http://doi.org//arXiv.2412.07482DOI: 10.48550

Blonder, R., Feldman-Maggor, Y., & Rap, S. (2024). Are They Ready to Teach? Generative AI as a Means to Uncover Pre-Service Science Teachers' PCK and Enhance Their Preparation Program. *Journal of Science Education and Technology*. Advance online publication. DOI: 10.1007/s10956-024-10180-2

Brewe, E., Bartley, J. E., Riedel, M. C., Sawtelle, V., Salo, T., Boeving, E. R., Bravo, E. I., Odean, R., Nazareth, A., Bottenhorn, K. L., Laird, R. W., Sutherland, M. T., Pruden, S. M., & Laird, A. R. (2018). Toward a neurobiological basis for understanding learning in university modeling instruction physics courses. *Frontiers in ICT (Lausanne, Switzerland), 5*, 10. DOI: 10.3389/fict.2018.00010 PMID: 31106219

Cervantes Juárez, E., & Sánchez Guzmán, D. (2024). Implementing the LSEESC methodology with AI-guided support for active learning in engineering physics courses. *2024 IEEE Frontiers in Education Conference (FIE).* http://doi.org/DOI: 10.1109/FIE61694.2024.10893032

Chen, S., Zhu, X., & Castillo, F. (2023). Integrating generative AI in knowledge building. *Computers & Education. Artificial Intelligence, 5*, 100184. Advance online publication. DOI: 10.1016/j.caeai.2023.100184

Chung, J., Henderson, M., Pepperell, N., Slade, C., Liang, Y., & Yu, S. (2024). *Student use of generative AI.* ASCILITE Publications., DOI: 10.14742/apubs.2024.1153

Davishahl, J., & Haskell, K. (2024). Targeting representational competence and spatial skills development with hands-on models in calculus and statics. *ASEE PNW Section Conference Proceedings.* http://doi.org/DOI: 10.18260/1-2--31896

Davishahl, J., & Zhang, Z. (2024). Can hands-on statics improve student learning? *ASEE Annual Conference & Exposition Proceedings.* http://doi.org/DOI: 10.18260/1-2--48440

Distrik, I. W., Supardi, Z. A. I., & Jatmiko, B. (2021). The effects of multiple representations-based learning in improving concept understanding and problem-solving ability in electricity. *Journal of Physics: Conference Series, 1796*(1), 012044. DOI: 10.1088/1742-6596/1796/1/012044

Edelsbrunner, P., & Hofer, S. I. (2024). Examining and comparing the relation between representational competence and conceptual knowledge across four samples. *Frontiers in Education, 9*, 1459603. Advance online publication. DOI: 10.3389/feduc.2024.1459603

Edelsbrunner, P., Malone, S., Hofer, S. I., Küchemann, S., Kuhn, J., Schmid, R., Altmeyer, K., Brünken, R., & Lichtenberger, A. (2023). The relation of representational competence and conceptual knowledge in female and male undergraduates. *International Journal of STEM Education, 10*(1), 44. Advance online publication. DOI: 10.1186/s40594-023-00435-6 PMID: 37361927

El Fathi, T., Saad, A., Larhzil, H., Lamri, D., & Al Ibrahmi, E. M. (2025). Integrating generative AI into STEM education: Enhancing conceptual understanding, addressing misconceptions, and assessing student acceptance. *Disciplinary and Interdisciplinary Science Education Research, 7*(1), 6. DOI: 10.1186/s43031-025-00125-z

Gadgil, S., Nokes-Malach, T. J., & Chi, M. (2012). Effectiveness of holistic mental model confrontation in driving conceptual change. *Learning and Instruction, 22*(1), 47–61. DOI: 10.1016/j.learninstruc.2011.06.002

Greca, I. M., & Moreira, M. A. (2000). Mental models, conceptual models, and modelling. *International Journal of Science Education, 22*(1), 1–11. DOI: 10.1080/095006900289976

Hamerski, P. C. (2024). Generative AI as a resource for creativity in computational physics. *Proceedings of the 55th ACM Technical Symposium on Computer Science Education* V. 2. http://doi.org/DOI: 10.1145/3626253.3635595

Her, P., & Hamerski, P. C. (2024). Investigating student perceptions of creativity and generative AI in computational physics. *2024 Physics Education Research Conference Proceedings*. http://doi.org/DOI: 10.1119/perc.2024.pr.Her

Întorsureanu, I., Oprea, S.-V., Bâra, A., & Vespan, D. (2025). Generative AI in education: Perspectives through an academic lens. *Electronics (Basel), 14*(5), 1053. DOI: 10.3390/electronics14051053

Johri, A., Katz, A., Qadir, J., & Hingle, A. (2023). Generative artificial intelligence and engineering education. *Journal of Engineering Education, 112*(3), 572–577. Advance online publication. DOI: 10.1002/jee.20537

Kaldaras, L., Wang, K. D., Nardo, J. E., Price, A., Perkins, K., Wieman, C., & Salehi, S. (2024). Employing technology-enhanced feedback and scaffolding to support the development of deep science understanding using computer simulations. *International Journal of STEM Education, 11*(1), 30. DOI: 10.1186/s40594-024-00490-7

Kozma, R., & Russell, J. (2005). Students becoming chemists: Developing representational competence. In Gilbert, J. (Ed.), *Visualization in science education* (pp. 121–145). Springer., DOI: 10.1007/1-4020-3613-2_8

Leon, M. (2024). Leveraging generative AI for on-demand tutoring as a new paradigm in education. *International Journal on Cybernetics & Informatics, 13*(5), 1–9. DOI: 10.5121/ijci.2024.130502

Létourneau, A., Deslandes Martineau, M., Charland, P., Karran, J. A., Boasen, J., & Léger, P. M. (2025). A systematic review of AI-driven intelligent tutoring systems (ITS) in K-12 education. *npj Science of Learning, 10*, 29. http://doi.org/DOI: 10.1038/s41539-025-00320-7

Liang, L. L., Fulmer, G. W., Majerich, D., Clevenstine, R. F., & Howanski, R. (2011). The effects of a model-based physics curriculum program with a Physics First approach: A causal-comparative study. *Journal of Science Education and Technology, 21*(1), 114–124. DOI: 10.1007/s10956-011-9287-2

Lichtenberger, A., Kokkonen, T., & Schalk, L. (2024). Learning with multiple external representations in physics: Concreteness fading versus simultaneous presentation for Faraday's law. *Journal of Research in Science Teaching, 61*(9), 2258–2290. DOI: 10.1002/tea.21947

Lin, C.-H., Zhou, K., Li, L., & Sun, L. (2025). Integrating generative AI into digital multimodal composition. *Computers and Composition, 75*, 102895. Advance online publication. DOI: 10.1016/j.compcom.2024.102895

Magana, A. J., Arigye, J., Udosen, A., Lyon, J. A., Joshi, P., & Pienaar, E. (2024). Scaffolded team-based computational modeling and simulation projects for promoting representational competence and regulatory skills. *International Journal of STEM Education, 11*(1), 34. DOI: 10.1186/s40594-024-00494-3

Marshman, E., Maries, A., & Singh, C. (2024). Using multiple representations to improve student understanding of quantum states. *Physical Review. Physics Education Research, 20*(2), 020152. DOI: 10.1103/PhysRevPhysEducRes.20.020152

Masrifah, M., Setiawan, A., Sinaga, P., & Setiawan, W. (2022). The effectiveness of using e-book based on multimodal representation and TPACK to improve ICT literacy of physics teachers. *AIP Conference Proceedings*, 020015. Advance online publication. DOI: 10.1063/5.0102620

Méheut, M., & Psillos, D. (2004). Teaching–learning sequences: Aims and tools for science education research. *International Journal of Science Education*, *26*(5), 515–535. DOI: 10.1080/09500690310001614762

Mufit, F., Festiyed, F., Fauzan, A., & Lufri, L. (2018). Impact of learning model based on cognitive conflict toward students' conceptual understanding. *IOP Conference Series. Materials Science and Engineering*, *335*(1), 012072. DOI: 10.1088/1757-899X/335/1/012072

Mukherjee, S., Le, C., & Chow, Y.-W. (2025). Generative AI-enhanced intelligent tutoring system for graduate cybersecurity programs. *Future Internet*, *17*(4), 154. DOI: 10.3390/fi17040154

Nareklishvili, T., & Polson, N. (2025). Generative AI for validating physics laws. *arXiv preprint*. http://doi.org//arXiv.2503.17894DOI: 10.48550

Nurjanah, S., Martaputri, N. A., & Suardi, I. K. (2024). Artificial intelligence in physics education research in two decades: A bibliometric study from Scopus database. *Jurnal Pendidikan Fisika*, *12*(2), 53–86. Advance online publication. DOI: 10.26618/jpf.v12i2.14745

Odden, T. O. B., Lauvland, A., Bøe, M. V., & Henriksen, E. K. (2023). Implementing the learning assistant model in European higher education. *European Journal of Physics*, *44*(3), 035701. Advance online publication. DOI: 10.1088/1361-6404/acb39e

Ortiz, M., & Aliazas, J. V. (2021). Multimodal representation strategies in teaching science towards enhancing scientific inquiry skills among Grade 4. *International Multidisciplinary Research Journal*. Advance online publication. DOI: 10.54476/iimrj241

Papert, S. (1980). *Mindstorms: Children, computers, and powerful ideas*. Basic Books.

Park, H., & Zhang, J. (2023). Teacher Reflective Noticing and Scaffolding for Student-Driven Knowledge-Building Inquiry. In *Proceedings of the 17th International Conference of the Learning Sciences-ICLS 2023, pp.* 1054-1057. International Society of the Learning Sciences. http://doi.org/DOI: 10.22318/icls2023.567396

Pedrera, O., Barrutia, O., & Díez, J. R. (2025). Unveiling students' mental models and learning demands. *Research in Science Education*, *55*(5), 1399–1426. Advance online publication. DOI: 10.1007/s11165-024-10225-x

Peikos, M., Giannakos, M., & Papamitsiou, Z. (2025). The integration of TPACK and AI literacy for future-ready science teachers. *Education Sciences, 15*(3), 338. DOI: 10.3390/educsci15030338

Pellas, N. (2025). The impact of AI-generated instructional videos on problem-based learning in science teacher education. *Education Sciences, 15*(1), 102. DOI: 10.3390/educsci15010102

Piaget, J. (1972). *To understand is to invent: The future of education.* Viking Press., Retrieved from https://unesdoc.unesco.org/ark:/48223/pf0000006133

Pinho-Lopes, M., & Powrie, W. (2025). Applying the Learning Science and Engineering with Electronic Spreadsheets Cycle (LSEESC) in geotechnical engineering education. In *Proceedings of the 20th International Conference on Soil Mechanics and Geotechnical Engineering* (pp. 240–248). International Society for Soil Mechanics and Geotechnical Engineering. https://www.issmge.org/uploads/publications/3/134/PT24-61PinhoLopes-Powrie.pdf

Rianti, R., Gunawan, G., Verawati, N., & Taufik, M. (2024). The effect of problem-based learning model assisted by PhET simulation on understanding physics concepts. *Lensa: Jurnal Kependidikan Fisika, 12*(1), 28. Advance online publication. DOI: 10.33394/j-lkf.v12i1.8783

Robledo-Rella, M., & Toh, Y. R. (2024). Artificial intelligence in physics courses to support active learning. In *Proceedings of the 2024 10th International Conference on e-Society, e-Learning and e-Technologies (ICSLT).* http://doi.org/DOI: 10.1145/3678610.3678631

Seel, N. M. (2014). Model-based learning and performance. In *Encyclopedia of the Sciences of Learning* (pp. 465–484). Springer., DOI: 10.1007/978-1-4614-3185-5_37

Singh, S., Taneja, H., & Alvarado, C. (2025). *Protecting human cognition in the age of AI. arXiv preprint arXiv:2502.12447.* http://doi.org//arXiv.2502.12447DOI: 10.48550

Steinert, S., Avila, K. E., Kuhn, J., & Küchemann, S. (2024). Using GPT-4 as a guide during inquiry-based learning. *The Physics Teacher, 62*(7), 618–619. DOI: 10.1119/5.0235700

Tang, K.-S. (2023). The characteristics of diagrams in scientific explanations: Multimodal integration of written and visual modes of representation in junior high school textbooks. *Science Education, 107*(3), 741–772. DOI: 10.1002/sce.21787

Tankelevitch, L., Kewenig, V., Simkute, A., Scott, A. E., Sarkar, A., Sellen, A., & Rintel, S. (2024). The metacognitive demands and opportunities of generative AI. *Proceedings of the CHI Conference on Human Factors in Computing Systems (CHI '24)*. http://doi.org/DOI: 10.1145/3613904.3642902

UNESCO. (2024). *Guidance for generative AI in education and research*. http://doi.org/DOI: 10.54675/unesco.genai.2024

Wan, Y., Zhang, L., & Chen, Y. (2025). Impact pathways of AI-supported instruction on learning behaviors, competence development, and academic achievement in engineering education. *Sustainability (Basel)*, *17*(17), 8059. DOI: 10.3390/su17178059

Wasielewski, A. (2024). DALL-E in Flatland. *Media Theory*, *8*(1), 185–204. Advance online publication. DOI: 10.70064/mt.v8i1.1073

Wetzel, D. A., & Kani, J. (2025). Enhancing information literacy through generative AI in the library classroom. *Pennsylvania Libraries: Research & Practice*, *12*(2). Advance online publication. DOI: 10.5195/palrap.2024.302

Wittmann, M. C. (2006). Using resource graphs to represent conceptual change. *Physical Review Special Topics. Physics Education Research*, *2*(2), 020105. DOI: 10.1103/PhysRevSTPER.2.020105

Xavier, M. C., & Oliveira, S. (2024). Construction of knowledge with strategies enabled by generative artificial intelligence. In *Teaching, Learning and Technology Integration* (pp. 142–153). Springer. http://doi.org/DOI: 10.1007/978-3-031-76365-6_9

Yuan, B., & Hu, J. (2024). Generative AI as a tool for enhancing reflective learning in students. *arXiv preprint*. http://doi.org//arXiv.2412.02603DOI: 10.36227/techrxiv.173324189.99227671/v1

Zawacki-Richter, O., Bai, J. Y. H., Lee, K., Slagter van Tryon, P. J., & Prinsloo, P. (2024). New advances in artificial intelligence applications in higher education? *International Journal of Educational Technology in Higher Education*, *21*(1), 32. DOI: 10.1186/s41239-024-00464-3

Zhai, C., Wibowo, S., & Li, L. D. (2024). The effects of over-reliance on AI dialogue systems on students' cognitive abilities: A systematic review. *Smart Learning Environments*, *11*(1), 28. DOI: 10.1186/s40561-024-00316-7

Zhou, B., Xu, J., & Zhao, J. (2024). Research on animated physics courseware technology for digital media. *Applied Mathematics and Nonlinear Sciences*, *9*(1), 20242161. Advance online publication. DOI: 10.2478/amns-2024-2161

Zuccarini, G., & Malgieri, M. (2024). Modeling and representing conceptual change in the learning of successive theories: The case of the classical-quantum transition. *Science & Education, 33*(3), 717–761. DOI: 10.1007/s11191-022-00397-1

Zwickl, B., Hu, D., Finkelstein, N., & Lewandowski, H. (2014). Model-based reasoning in the physics laboratory: Framework and initial results. *Physical Review Special Topics. Physics Education Research, 11*(2), 020113. DOI: 10.1103/PhysRevSTPER.11.020113

## ADDITIONAL READING

Ipek, Z.-H., Gözüm, A.-C.-I., Papadakis, St., & Kalogiannakis, M. (2023). Educational applications of ChatGPT, an AI system: A systematic review research. *Educational Process, 12*(3), 26–55. DOI: 10.22521/edupij.2023.123.2

Kalogiannakis, M., Papakonstantinou, N., & Sotiropoulos, D. (2025). From Support Tool to Learning Partner: A Systematic Review of GenAI Integration in University Science Labs. *Creative Education, 16*(9), 1364–1401. DOI: 10.4236/ce.2025.169083

Sotiropoulos, D., & Kalogiannakis, M. (2025). Using GenAI Tools to Enhance Teaching and Learning in Science. In *Proceedings of the 14th Hybrid Edition of the International Conference New Perspectives in Science Education*, 293-301, Italy-Florence: Filodiritto-Pixel, 19-21 March 2025, http://doi.org/DOI: 10.26352/L319_2420-9732

Spasopoulos, T., Sotiropoulos, D., & Kalogiannakis, M. (2025). Generative AI in Pre-Service Science Teacher Education: A Systematic Review. *Advances in Mobile Learning Educational Research, 5*(2), 1501–1523. DOI: 10.25082/AMLER.2025.02.007

Uğraş, H., Uğraş, M., Papadakis, S., & Kalogiannakis, M. (2025). Innovative early childhood STEM education with ChatGPT: Teacher perspectives. Technology. *Knowledge and Learning, 30*(2), 809–831. DOI: 10.1007/s10758-024-09804-8

Uğraş, M., Çakır, Z., Zacharis, G., & Kalogiannakis, M. (2025). ChatGPT in Early Childhood Science Education: Can It Offer Innovative Effective Solutions to Overcome Challenges? *Computers, 14*(9), 368. DOI: 10.3390/computers14090368

Xenakis, A., Dimos, I., Feidakis, M., Sotiropoulos, D., Kalovrektis, K., & Nikolaou, G. (2025). An LLM-based smart repository platform to support educators with computational thinking, AI, and STEM activities. In *Empowering STEM educators with digital tools* (pp. 107–136). IGI Global Scientific Publishing., DOI: 10.4018/979-8-3693-9806-7.ch005

Chapter 3

# GenAI and Ancient Greek Natural Philosophy: Exploring the Foundations of Science Concepts Through Interactive Dialogues

**Dimitrios Sotiropoulos**
https://orcid.org/0000-0001-7367-5760
*University of Thessaly, Greece*

**Christos Xenakis**
*Astronomy and Space Society, Greece*

**Apostolis Xenakis**
https://orcid.org/0000-0002-7300-7380
*University of Thessaly, Greece*

**Michail Kalogiannakis**
https://orcid.org/0000-0002-9124-2245
*University of Thessaly, Greece*

## ABSTRACT

*This chapter outlines a design framework for employing generative AI chatbots (GenAI) as Socratic dialogue partners to enhance students' engagement with fundamental scientific concepts through historically informed discourse. The proposed framework consists of four components: Initiation, Dialogue, Reflection, and Evaluation and Transfer. Feedback loops connect these parts to ensure that teachers' goals, AI prompts, classroom activities, and formative assessments are all aligned. This study concentrates on ancient Greek natural philosophy, particularly Presocratic and*

DOI: 10.4018/979-8-3373-2913-0.ch003

*Aristotelian concepts regarding matter, change, and causality. The chapter argues that Socratic dialogues with GenAI, placed in historical contexts, can facilitate better understanding of core scientific concepts, foster critical and reflective thinking, as well as help students to locate modern scientific knowledge within a broader historical and cultural context. It also addresses the moral, legal, and management issues that arise when utilising GenAI to facilitate Socratic dialogue responsibly.*

## INTRODUCTION

In recent years, generative AI tools have started to reshape science education in higher education, not only as auxiliary technologies for producing content but increasingly as mediators of explanation, feedback and inquiry-oriented learning. Empirical work in university science courses and laboratories has shown that GenAI can support both teaching and learning by helping students generate hypotheses, clarify complex concepts and receive rapid, personalised feedback, especially when it is deliberately framed as "a learning partner rather than a mere support tool" (Kalogiannakis, Papakonstantinou, & Sotiropoulos, 2025; Sotiropoulos & Kalogiannakis, 2025).

The present chapter advances a more specific proposal: it conceptualizes GenAI not as a generic support tool, but as a Socratic dialogue partner situated within a historically and philosophically informed framework for engaging with "big ideas" in science

The traditional Socratic type of questions-and-answers – long valued for encouraging critical thinking – is gaining new relevance in the age of AI in education. Specifically, AI-powered tutors can be instructed with proper Socratic prompts, guiding students through scaffolding questioning that fosters reflection. Recent studies, conducted within classroom settings, show that this strategy confers actual cognitive benefits (Hu et al., 2025). For example, fine-tuning the process of a large language model (LLM) to behave like a Socratic tutor significantly improves students' reflective and critical thinking skills, than a generic AI tutor (Degen, 2025). Similarly, studies which involves GenAI – produced dialogues, in high school classes, note an active elevated student engagement in the dialogues process, including follow – up questions, indicative for increasing critical thinking and creativity. This clearly indicates that GenAI can be used to pose probing questions, rather than simply deliver answers, which in turn sharpens students' analytical thinking and deepen their conceptual clarity.

These results are consistent with the perceived educational benefits of Socratic dialogues. Students who are facilitated by AI to conduct Socratic inquiries rather than passively receiving information must articulate their reasoning, encounter contradictions, and revise their understanding—with Socrates pedagogy in mind. To illustrate, Chukhlomin (2024), document how an educator's structured AI – generated dialogue during course design, highlights both the potential and limitations of AI, as a collaborative tool, which underscores the need for critical evaluation, during the process. Following, Orynbassarova and De Lasala Porta (2024) note that an AI system, configured to ask Socratic questions, could guide students to reflect deeply. In their pilot studies, comparing teacher – led versus AI – led Socratic dialogues; report that AI with proper engineering prompts supports the cultivation of reflective and critical thinking, better than a generic AI tutor. The above cognitive improvements are present as soon as AI based dialogues are embedded within dialogic learning designs. Tang et al. (2024) demonstrates this claim by integrating GenAI into classroom discussions; rather than acting merely as a passive information source, AI tools are treated as dialogic agents, which facilitates collaborative dialogue and knowledge co – construction. This process encourages students to pose questions, acting like active scientists, and consider multiple viewpoint aspects. As a result, students are more engaged and develop deeper conceptual understanding, since interaction with AI requires them to articulate and critically assess their ideas.

Building on this growing evidence, the following sections of this chapter explore how GenAI – mediated Socratic dialogues illuminate some of the enduring questions, which lay at the foundations of natural sciences. In particular, we will illustrate AI – generated discussions that explore classical problems related to matter, change, void, and causality – fundamental concepts in natural philosophy, first articulated by ancient Greek thinkers. By adopting inspired Socratic prompts, students can discuss with AI tools around Anaximander's, Heraclitus, Democritus, Aristotle and others early philosophers' ideas. This process is not about history learning; rather it is about using GenAI to carry out a temporal journey back in history, to recreate a learning experience akin to being aside a philosopher, walking with him and his students, probing basic questions about nature, in a dialogue format.

As we shall argue, anchoring these AI dialogues in the primary fragments of ancient philosophers helps situate modern scientific ideas within their rich historical and cultural trajectories. Such contextualization has long been advocated in science education scholarship as a remedy for fragmented, decontextualized learning. By tracing ideas to their roots, students appreciate science as a human endeavor that evolved over millennia, rather than a static collection of facts.

In a wider context, the fusion of Presocratic physics with modern particle physics is not just an embellishment of historical events but a pointer to the broad History, Philosophy, and Science Teaching (HPST) tradition. Moreover, this research maintains that the History of Science, Philosophy, and Teaching should be systematically incorporated into science education as a means of students' conceptual understanding, transparency of the epistemic aims and methods of science, and encouraging liberal, humanistic goals of schooling (Lima, 2021). The use of GenAI-mediated Socratic dialogues in the HPST tradition recognizes not only the "big ideas" of present-day science but also the ways in which scientific knowledge is produced, challenged and updated over time.

Moreover, we will support our claim that a historical basis is particularly necessary in the AI era, to prevent the AI tutors' habit of giving superficial yet smooth answers that lack context or depth. Subsequently, we will give an account of our pilot study done in the classroom – the use of GenAI – based Socratic dialogues that point to the development of students' curiosity and higher-order reasoning at levels nearly equal to that of an expert human teacher. Together with the educational gains, the ethical precautions that will be needed when using GenAI in this way will be the ones ensuring transparency, source fidelity, and avoiding oversimplification. In short, this chapter presents the case that Socratic dialogues, as brought back to life by the GenAI tools, can effectively connect Ancient Greek natural philosophy with contemporary scientific inquiry, thus making students' critically oriented learning experiences about scientific foundations richer.

## REVIVING SOCRATIC DIALOGUES WITH GENAI IN SCIENCE EDUCATION

Modern education faces a dual challenge: harnessing the benefits of AI tools while preserving the depth of humanistic, critical inquiry. GenAI – generated Socratic dialogues offers a potential solution to this challenge, by combining the scalability and responsiveness of AI with the time – tested rigor of Socratic questioning. In a traditional Socratic dialogue scenario, the teacher poses open – questions, to help students uncover assumptions and build knowledge through reasoning. GenAI can emulate this role by generating sequences of probing questions tailored to a student's responses. Eventually, AI's tool role is not to give away answers, but to guide students' own thinking process, following a conceptual scaffolding process.

In recent works, researchers start documenting the impacts of this approach. In their study entitled ChatGPT as a Socratic Assistant: Developing Students' Reflective and Critical Thinking, Zhai, Wibowo & Li (2024) note that students' interaction with a Socratic dialogue AI – chat box show improvement in metacognitive reflection on their answers (Zhai et al., 2024). The ongoing inquiry of AI's "why?" and "how do you know?" nudged learners to clarify their thinking and address the weaknesses in their understanding. As Valeri Chukhlomin (2024), who applies the process of Socratic prompt engineering within an educational case study share, it enhances efficacy and artistry in educational processes. However, it requires critical evaluation and ethical considerations from educators who use it. More precisely, teachers reveal that students can achieve deeper inquiry in a short time by using AI co – tutors; however, at the same time the teacher should carefully monitor AI's contributions for accuracy and relevance.

In the sequel, researchers who support the recent project entitled The Socratic Mind at Georgia Tech apply AI tools and ask students challenging questions on several course topics in a progressive way. AI does not just ask questions but also evaluates the answers given by the learners and comes up with the corresponding prompts (Chatterjee & Hung, 2024). This concept is in line with Ray Hung's focus on the 3C3R model (the Content, Context, Connection-the 3Cs-and Researching, Reasoning, Reflecting - the 3Rs), which dares students to show their understanding by means of articulation and systematic explanation (Mühlfelder et al., 2015). Thus, AI continually guides students to explain underlying reasons, essentially prompting them to teach these concepts by training the AI agent. Such AI systems embody Socrates' teaching philosophy, in the sense that true knowledge comes from within – the teacher (or AI tutor) is merely an intellectual midwife helping to give birth to the student's own understanding.

One clear advantage of AI-driven Socratic dialogue is scaffolded questioning at scale. Human tutors excel in asking the right questions at the right time, based on a students' latter answer – but one tutor can only work with a few students at once. On the contrary, a GenAI model, can potentially proceed with dozens of dialogues simultaneously, each of which is personalized for each learner's level of understanding. The dialogic format also keeps students actively involved. In essence, instead of passively grasping an answer, no matter how well is explained, the student becomes part of an ongoing conversation, formulates hypotheses, articulates confusions and reconsiders beliefs. This process is inherently more engaging and requires higher – order cognitive skills. Tang et al. (2024) emphasizes that GenAI in a dialogic role is not a definitive knowledge source but a partner in knowledge co-construction, prompting students to integrate multiple perspectives and think critically about AI-generated content it. As soon as students ask follow – up questions as a response to the AI agent's prompts, or even challenge AI's responses, they experience a form of critical engagement which may not be reached during standard lectures.

However, not all AI – enhanced tutoring experimentations are equally effective. Dilara Orynbassarova and Santiago De Lasala Porta (2024) explored the opportunities and challenges of integrating ChatGPT into teaching using the Socratic method. According to their pilot study, a naïvely trained AI model can fall short of a skilled human tutor, especially in the cases where AI questions are too generic or fail to notice subtle misconceptions. With careful prompt refinement and guidance (including fine-tuning AI on dialogue examples), the AI's Socratic dialogue quality improved markedly. To this end, proper prompt engineering and continuous model training are key elements for the AI agent not to only be assistive, but to guide students to be constructively skeptical. Without such model tuning, a general-purpose AI might simply comply with student requests for answers or, if a student's response is incorrect, either ignore the mistake or flatly provide the correct answer – none of which leads to reflection As Orynbassarova's work suggests, AI must be imbued with a kind of productive obstinacy, continually directing the student back to their reasoning process (Orynbassarova & De Lasala Porta, 2024).

Fakour and Imani's comparative study (2025), titled Socratic Wisdom in the Age of AI, has been a source of encouraging results as it critically assesses the role of ChatGPT versus human tutors in the development of critical thinking. The researchers drew their study from more than 200 university students and reported that the students who had the experience of Socratic-questioning ChatGPT agent developed critical thinking skills equivalent to those who received human expert tutoring. Moreover, the ChatGPT students were capable of effective argument analysis and evaluation because of the AI's steady questioning and support that was always there for them (Fakour & Imani, 2025). Students found the non-judgmental and always-present quality of AI tutor as a plus, but at the same time they admitted that human tutors provided the emotional support that was deeper.

The takeaway is that, when guided by Socratic design, GenAI can approximate the cognitive benefits of one-on-one tutoring – an extraordinary opportunity for education at scale.

In a nutshell, the Pomodoro method that has left its mark throughout the ages up to the present day. So, it is no wonder that students in the present day are still encouraged to use this method by tutors and all types of educational institutions. Current research shows that the AI-based dialogues have a great effect on the development of critical thinking skills, clarifying of ideas, and keeping students participating in the process of learning through deep understanding rather than through shallow memory (Gonsalves, 2024). The outcomes from such AI tutoring are a step towards meeting educational aims of the 21st century of developing thinkers who can analyze and be independent. In the next section of the article, we shall see how the method of conversation about the foundational scientific concepts not only introduces the concepts but places them in a wider historical conversation, hence adding layers of meaning that the contemporary teaching might not have been able to convey.

## FOSTERING CURIOSITY

Initial efforts to integrate GenAI into Socratic dialogues as a pedagogical approach have demonstrated positive outcomes. For example, some pilot studies with Year 12 and first-year university students revealed GenAI dialogues prompting students to participate in higher-order reasoning, in comparison with (or in some instances more than) traditional classroom discussions. An interesting finding from several pilot studies has been a notable increase in student curiosity (Demir et al., 2025; Wang & Fan, 2025). When students interact with a GenAI chat bot in the context of posing as Socrates or Aristotle, they appear to exhibit a greater propensity to respond back, follow up on cue or hint, or suggest their own hypothesis — behaviors teachers struggle to provoke when teaching a whole class.

For example, in a classroom activity, applying Democritus GenAI persona, students not only answer AI's questions about atoms, but begin asking questions such as how did Democritus come up with this idea without a microscope?, What did people say against his theory?. Such questions demonstrate curiosity about science, how it evolves, not just to the question itself. The AI tools, based on historical records, may respond that Democritus reasoned logically about divisibility and sensory experience, and that indeed many contemporaries like Aristotle disagreed with him, preferring continuum theories. This led the dialogue into a brief exploration of how evidence (or its lack) can stall acceptance of a theory – effectively a mini-lesson in the philosophy of science sparked entirely by student curiosity. Educators indicated that the learners found it to be very interesting; they were participating in a discussion about science rather than only receiving scientific data. Fakour & Imani (2025) conducted a research study in which they qualitatively observed more students being active in an AI-tutored group. Numerous students perceived ChatGPT tutor merely as an answer validator but as a sounding board – they would throw ideas or even personal reflections at the AI, which timid students might avoid with a human teacher due to fear of being judged.

AI's "non-judgmental nature and accessibility" were cited as factors that "fostered a safe space for inquiry", encouraging students to take intellectual risks. One student in that study commented that the AI "never gets tired of my questions, so I keep asking more," which is exactly the kind of persistent inquiry we aim to nurture.

Likewise, as reported by Tang et al. (2024), in a small high school pilot, integrating GenAI Socratic dialogues in a science module, led to follow-up questions that indicate critical thinking and creativity. Teachers participating in this pilot, note that students are posing more why and what if questions. The dialogues seemed to model a form of thinking that students then emulate. When AI constantly probes their answers with deeper and complex questions, students learn to anticipate those probes and start to probe themselves. This aligns with known benefits of Socratic pedagogy – it is essentially teaching by example how to be critical and reflective.

One more outcome noticed was the better understanding of concepts and retention over time. The Socratic method makes students express ideas loosely and, at the same time, defend their reasoning which reinforces understanding and remembering. For example, an informal assessment one week after a GenAI-assisted Socratic session on Aristotle's four causes, students were asked to explain a familiar object—such as a bicycle—using the causes framework. Almost all the students gave correct answers, pinpointing the material cause (metal, rubber, etc.), the formal cause (the design of the frame), the efficient cause (the factory's process or workers), and the final cause (transportation of goods). In the previous year when the same content was delivered through the classical lecture style, however, only a few students were able to remember one or two of the causes. The conversing quality of the dialogue—especially when the AI took on a fun coaching role, even impersonating Aristotle to nudge thinking about the final cause—seems to have very much raised student participation and memory.

The positives are evident but so are the difficulties that come with such practices. At first, not all students welcomed the interaction with the AI; some requested coaxing to view it as a serious educational tool instead of a novelty chatbot. Several students, during classroom debriefing, confessed that they had done so by asking irrelevant questions or even posing humorous ones. However, after a while, through the AI's persistent pulling the conversation back to the subject and asking thoughtful, deep questions, their commitment was increased. Having turned the AI into their trustable and useful partner in dialogue was the case here. After trust was built, a lot of students said they no longer paid attention to the fact that the conversation partner was a machine, and they got completely absorbed in the dialogue of the mind.

Educators also had to guide students in effective use of the AI dialogues. For instance, they set expectations like: "Take time to think about the AI's question, don't just rush to answer" and "If you don't understand the AI's question, ask it to clarify or rephrase – it can do that." Empowering students to also direct the AI (since a good dialogue is two-way) made sessions more fruitful. In fact, a measure of success was when students felt comfortable saying to the AI, "I don't get it, could you give me a hint?" or "Can you give me an example of what you mean?" This is analogous to what a student might say to a human tutor. The AI can respond very well to such prompts (e.g., it can provide examples from everyday life to illustrate Heraclitus's flux if asked). Observing these interactions, one teacher noted that quieter students who rarely ask human teachers for help were surprisingly willing to ask the AI for clarification. It suggests the technology can mitigate some social barriers in help-seeking behavior.

Comparisons between classes that used GenAI dialogues and those that did not (covering similar content) showed the AI-assisted classes often had more lively subsequent human discussions. After "talking" with the likes of Heraclitus and Democritus via AI, students had opinions and questions they were eager to share with peers and the teacher. In essence, the AI dialogue primed them for human dialogue. One could say it is scaffolding the very dialogic skills that underlie collaborative learning among students. This is a valuable outcome because it means AI is not replacing human interaction, but catalyzing it. It gives students something to chew on and discuss further in class. In one reported case, students debated each other about whether Aristotle's final cause has a place in modern science, a debate sparked entirely by the AI session and drawing on points the AI had raised. The teacher remarked that this level of philosophy-of-science discussion had never happened spontaneously in her class before.

Of course, systematic data collection is still needed. Many of these results are preliminary and based on small samples or anecdotal teacher reports. However, they align with the controlled findings of Fakour & Imani (2025) that critical thinking outcomes with AI Socratic guidance can match those with human tutors. They also resonate with Chukhlomin's (2024) suggestion that Socratic AI can improve efficiency in reaching deeper inquiry – students in some trials got to advanced questions faster than expected. For example, a high schooler pondering Anaximander's apeiron ended up asking the AI whether the universe could be infinite or have come from nothing, diving into cosmology and even a bit of metaphysics beyond the standard curriculum. The AI was able to engage, referencing current cosmological theories (with appropriate caution and simplification). This indicates that with AI, learning can sometimes go down productive tangents that a rigid curriculum wouldn't allow time for – yet those tangents often represent genuine student interest and lead to enriched understanding. Here, apeiron in Anaximander does not refer to a specific physical substance such as air, but to an abstract, indefinite 'boundless' from which all things emerge and to which they return.

The GenAI-mediated Socratic dialogues early classroom tests revealed an astonishing potential for science education improvement as the study's conclusion states. The method not only facilitates the transmission of the content but also fosters the cognitive traits that we link with scientific reasoning by letting questioning sprout, by making students articulate and justify their views, and by providing individualized feedback and cues. The very close resemblance between the AI and expert tutors in the development of critical thinking skills is particularly significant considering the pervasiveness of AI solutions. If a free or inexpensive AI service can offer a Socratic learning experience that is on par with a one-to-one session with a good tutor, then it has the potential to open up quality education for all. The students who would never have been able to collaborate with a personal science mentor might still get a glimpse of that mentorship through AI. The pivotal aspect, as the preliminary findings suggest, is to delineate the AI's function and prompts with utmost precision—drawing on the strength of the Socratic method and historical context to guarantee that the engagement and understanding are at their best.

## PROPOSED METHODOLOGY FOR GENAI-SUPPORTED SOCRATIC DIALOGUE IN SCIENCE EDUCATION

The instructional cycle visualized in Figure 1 begins with *Initiation,* which engages students and establishes context through historically grounded prompts. It progresses to *Dialogue,* characterized by interactive Socratic exchange between student and GenAI, guided by ancient and contemporary perspectives. This is followed by *Reflection,* where students synthesize learning and critically evaluate content and process. The cycle concludes with *Evaluation*, assessing understanding and providing constructive feedback. Teacher guidance and ethical safeguards are integrated throughout.

Feedback loops operate as formative cycles where evidence from each phase—dialogue logs, explanations, reflective notes, evaluation results—feeds into the next, giving students structured opportunities to revise their learning pathways rather than following a fixed sequence (Ole & Gallos, 2023; Willis et al., 2021). This aligns with contemporary views of feedback as ongoing and dialogic rather than one-off summative events (Weidlich et al., 2025).

*Figure 1. Methodology phases for GenAI-supported Socratic dialogue in science education*

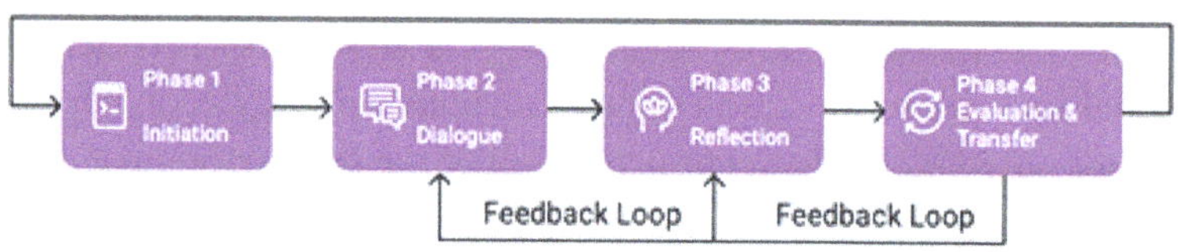


This framework provides a well-defined method for the application of GenAI in science teaching through the historical dialogue. All the stages of the process play a significant role: Initiation makes the learners curious by providing the context; Dialogue helps to uncover the main idea through AI-assisted Socratic discussion;

Reflection allows the learners to build up and link their knowledge; and Evaluation tells the results and gives suggestions for the next teaching.

The cyclical structure guarantees that the process keeps going as the evaluation results help to start the next lesson. At the core of it, this particular method allows the teacher to have the control of the pedagogical process and places AI as the assistant facilitator rather than an independent teacher. It makes use of the GenAI advantages—supporting the dialogue, providing the capacity for large groups, and portraying multiple viewpoints—while retaining for the teachers the critical aspects of the process: moral judgment, hands-on experience, empathy, and curriculum fit. The phases are outlined as logical sequences interspersed with feedback loops, thus creating a learning cycle. Built upon principle of instructional design akin to 5E model (Engage–Explore–Explain–Elaborate–Evaluate), the methodology is specifically designed for AI-powered dialogue and is grounded in inquiry-based and dialogic learning (De La Peña & Maatubang, 2025). By unambiguously marking out stages, we are making sure that AI is used with a purpose that is in line with learning outcomes, and that there are protections and supports for each step.

*From a sociocultural perspective,* the iterative feedback loops and the shifting distribution of control between teacher, student and AI tutor can be interpreted as movement within a zone of proximal development (ZPD). Recent work cautions against equating the ZPD with generic "scaffolding" and instead conceptualises it as a dynamic space in which forms of assistance are continually renegotiated as learners appropriate new mediational means and become more self-regulating (Smagorinsky, 2018; Xi & Lantolf, 2020). Systematic reviews further suggest that when ZPD-oriented support is carefully calibrated—neither too little nor too much—and combined with technology-rich environments, it can enhance students' problem-solving skills, independence and capacity to adapt to novel tasks (Raslan, 2024).

Building on the phases and feedback loops visualised in Figure 1, Table 1 summarises how the framework translates into classroom practice by specifying core actions and evidence sources in each phase of the learning cycle. The "Evidence / assessment" column indicates the key artefacts that drive the feedback loops between phases, providing formative information that is fed into subsequent activities and allowing students and teachers to iteratively revise the learning pathway (Ole & Gallos, 2023; Willis et al., 2021; Weidlich et al., 2025).

*Table 1. Operationalization of the four-phase framework for GenAI-supported Socratic dialogues*

| Phase | Teacher actions | Student actions | Socratic GenAI actions | Evidence / assessment |
|---|---|---|---|---|
| **Initiation** | Introduces the scientific "big idea" and a brief historical/ HPS teaching context. Clarifies activity goals and the role of GenAI as a thinking partner. Sets basic norms for academic integrity and interaction. | Activates prior knowledge and states initial ideas or misconceptions. Reviews instructions and ethical guidelines. Formulates 1–2 initial questions for the chatbot. | Provides a concise overview at an appropriate level. Elicits students' prior ideas through open questions and signals that its answers are fallible and to be scrutinized. | Short written baseline explanation of the concept; initial concept map or diagnostic quiz; brief reflective note capturing expectations and concerns about using GenAI. |
| **Dialogue** | Provides or adapts Socratic prompts targeting key models and common misconceptions. Monitors interactions and redirects when dialogues become superficial or off-task. | Engages in iterative question–answer exchanges focusing on "why" and "how". Asks for clarifications, examples, contrasts between alternative models and counterexamples. | Uses Socratic moves (clarification, probing, highlighting contradictions, simple thought experiments). Adjusts explanations to students' prior responses and offers complementary perspectives (e.g., historical vs. modern). | Dialogue logs (exported or copied into a template). Teacher notes on interaction patterns. Short mid-activity prompts where students summarise what they currently think and why. |
| **Reflection** | Guides students to step back from the dialogue and examine how their thinking has changed. Provides structured reflection prompts and models how to critique AI-generated arguments using disciplinary standards. | Reviews the dialogue, identifies turning points, and compares AI claims with course materials. Produces a short reflective text or concept map explaining current understanding, remaining uncertainties, and evaluation of the chatbot's suggestions. | Supports meta-reflection by asking students to justify their reasoning and to evaluate strengths and limitations of earlier answers (including its own). Offers alternative explanations or analogies when confusion persists. | Reflective essays, concept maps, or annotated dialogue excerpts. Rubrics focusing on quality of reasoning, use of evidence, and explicit evaluation of GenAI outputs. Self-report questionnaires on perceived learning and trust in the chatbot. |

continued on following page

*Table 1. Continued*

| Phase | Teacher actions | Student actions | Socratic GenAI actions | Evidence / assessment |
|---|---|---|---|---|
| **Evaluation and Transfer** | Design assessment tasks that require transfer to new contexts (e.g., applying models or critiquing AI explanations). Clarifies allowable GenAI use in summative tasks and links feedback to earlier phases. | Applies understanding to novel problems with no or limited, declared GenAI support. Critiques flawed or superficial AI explanations and articulates principles for responsible future use of GenAI. | Used in controlled ways (e.g., generating flawed answers as a "foil" or varied practice items), or disabled in closed-book summative assessments. | Performance on transfer tasks, exam items or projects. Quality of critique of AI explanations. Post-activity surveys on the perceived impact of the GenAI-supported Socratic dialogues on understanding and critical thinking. |

When viewed together, the images in Figure 1 and the data in Table 1 paint a broad picture of the proposed framework. As the figure indicates, the feedback loops between the phases support students through their learning by allowing them to gradually change their pathways, so by contrast the table lists the concrete roles of teachers, students, and the Socratic GenAI tutor as well as the specific forms of evidence that maintain those loops (Ole & Gallos, 2023; Weidlich et al., 2025). The ensuing subsections then discuss each phase more thoroughly, demonstrating how GenAI-supported Socratic dialogues can function in a zone of proximal development and through a HPST perspective to engage students with the "big ideas" in science (Smagorinsky, 2018) in a critical and conceptually rich manner.

We offer in the next part a real-world application of this approach through a module on the development of the notion of the atom—from Democritus's early philosophical postulate to the modern quark model in particle physics. This shows the framework in action and offers a paradigm for applying it to other scientific ideas.

## A FOUR-PHASE FRAMEWORK FOR GENAI-MEDIATED SOCRATIC DIALOGUE IN SCIENCE EDUCATION: AN EXEMPLAR FROM ANCIENT GREEK NATURAL PHILOSOPHY

### Phase 1: Initiation

In the initiation phase, the teacher's main task is to open up the "big idea" and its historical–philosophical background in a way that invites questioning rather than passive reception. Drawing on HPST work, the idea is to position the concept briefly within a historical event (for instance, atomism and the void in the Presocratic view of physics) so that students perceive it as part of an ongoing dialogue rather than a complete fact. (Lima, 2021). In addition, the instructor portrays the Socratic GenAI tutor as a collaborator in thinking, not as a machine providing answers, and thus clarifies the expectations regarding academic honesty, the proper use and the critical evaluation of AI outputs. Afterwards, students are encouraged to remember what they already knew about the topic, to express their first feelings or wrong ideas, and to create one or two questions that they would actually like to discuss with the chatbot. In ZPD terms, Phase 1 marks the bottom limit of the learning curve by exposing the starting points of the students and by setting the rules and tools which will support the next, scaffolded dialogue (Smagorinsky, 2018; Xi & Lantolf, 2020).

## Objectives:

Hook students' interest, activate prior knowledge, and set the stage for inquiry dialogue. The teacher introduces the topic, historical context, and clarifies learning objectives and AI's role.

## Process:

Begin with a provocative question, puzzling observation, or ancient text excerpt to spark curiosity. For atomic theory, display Democritus's quote: *"By convention sweet, by convention bitter; in reality there are only atoms and the void."* Ask: "What does this mean? Why would someone say sweetness is convention?"

Such questions raise follow-ups: What are atoms? What is void? Discussing in groups, students articulate ideas about matter and perception. Clarify why AI dialogues are valuable: "We'll converse with an AI acting as philosopher-scientist to understand how people thought about matter historically and how this relates to current understanding. This gives you practice explaining your thinking and receiving feedback uniquely." This frames the activity as intriguing learning rather than mere gadget use (Ngu et al., 2025).

Before initiation, provide a primer on Democritus's identity and Socratic dialogue scope. If multiple AI roles are involved, explain the switching process. Consider a preparatory lesson on GenAI interaction: platform access, custom chatbot settings, guidelines ("Ask AI if unclear," "Explain if you disagree"). These align with findings that students benefit from brief orientation for productive AI use (Fakour & Imani, 2025).

### Teacher's Role:

Provide guidelines, motivate, and clarify learning objectives. Example: "By lesson end, you should explain how atomic theory evolved from philosophical idea to scientific fact, identify the dominant theory, and understand why void was controversial." Clear objectives strengthen engagement (Mahoney et al., 2023).

### Conceptual Scaffolding:

When complex concepts need clarification before dialogue, provide definitions. For example, if *void* is unfamiliar, explain: "Void means empty space nothingness. Whether valid is for discussion." This prevents vocabulary confusion during AI interaction.

### Start thinking like a scientist and ask AI agent (teacher consults)

Mahoney et al. (2023), say that making clear the lesson objectives and giving students structured support through Socratic dialogue is a way to involve and motivate students in traditional classrooms. These principles still matter when applied to GenAI-mediated Socratic dialogue: students will certainly participate in a significant way if they know the reason for the interaction with the AI agents and if they are provided with detailed instructions on how to think and react critically to the AI's questions or statements.

There are cases when a deeper and complex concept might need scaffolding and clarification before dialogue process begins. For example, if the term apeiron is too unfamiliar, the teacher might elicit or provide a basic definition like: apeiron (Anaximander's "boundless") means an abstract, indefinite principle from which all determinate things emerge – not a specific physical substance like water or air, but something beyond all specific forms. Whether this concept is valid or not, is a topic for discussion. This small scaffold ensures that students do not confuse themselves on vocabulary when they start interacting with the AI. By the end of phase 1, students should be intrigued, aware of the context (i.e. ancient vs modern viewpoints) and conquer a concept. Typically, the goal is to engage themselves in dialogues with AI agent and attempt to answer the driving question or resolve the scenario posed. Here, apeiron in Anaximander does not refer to a specific physical substance such as air, but to an abstract, indefinite 'boundless' from which all things emerge and to which they return.

## Phase 2: Dialogue

### Objectives:

Interactive session where students and GenAI perform Socratic dialogue. Objectives: explore concepts via questions/answers, design AI prompts, refine understanding, challenge thinking, discover insights. Ancient philosophical perspectives interweave with modern science through AI's guided questioning.

### Process:

Various group interactions: (1) one-to-one: student with AI; (2) many-to-one: small group with AI; (3) many-to-many: teacher with groups/class with multiple AIs. Choice depends on device availability, learning path, objectives, and exploration ideas. This work tests interactions (1) or (2) for maximum individual engagement.

At dialogue outset, AI receives specific role or instructional approach. Example system prompt:

> *"You are an AI tutor combining ancient Greek thinker Democritus's insights with contemporary physics educator expertise. Engage students about matter's nature using Socratic questioning. Present yourself shortly, and then ask simple questions regarding the composition of matter. Don't reveal atoms or contemporary theories too early; let ideas develop through the conversation. Encourage thinking and providing reasons. If in doubt, give hints or different ancient perspectives. Occasionally mention classical thinkers; ask for critical reply. Target: lead towards comprehension of the atomic theory based on evidence while juxtaposing with the initial ideas."*

With such prompting, AI behavior aligns with goals. An illustrative dialogue excerpt follows:

> **AI (Democritus persona):** *"Hello! Let's discuss matter's nature. What do you think everything around us is ultimately made of?"*
> **Student:** *"Molecules and atoms—we learned atoms are in everything."*
> **AI:** *"You say atoms are in everything. How would you describe an atom in your own words?"*
> **Student:** *"A really tiny particle you can't see, making up elements. Like a gold atom is the smallest gold piece."*
> **AI:** *"Great. Now imagine 2,400 years ago in Greece, no microscopes. How might someone guess atoms exist?"*
> **Student:** *"Maybe by thinking about breaking things smaller? Eventually reaching pieces too small to break."*

**AI:** *"Exactly. Democritus argued cutting something eventually reaches an uncuttable piece—an atom—with void (empty space) between. Aristotle disagreed, thinking matter was continuous with no vacuum. Why might Aristotle reject vacuum?"*
**Student:** *"Maybe because he couldn't imagine 'nothing' existing? Or thought air fills all space."*
**AI:** *"Yes, Aristotle rejected true vacuum—'nature abhors vacuum.' For him, empty space couldn't exist; if it did, bodies would move with no resistance at infinite speed. Given modern physics knowledge, whose picture seems more convincing: Democritus or Aristotle, and why?"*
**Student:** *"Democritus sounds more right because we believe in atoms and vacuums exist in space."*
**AI:** *"Indeed, modern science sides with Democritus on atoms and void. But it took until 17th–19th centuries for evidence—gas behavior, fixed element ratios. Can you think of an experiment indicating matter is particulate, not continuous?"*
**Student:** *"Brownian motion where tiny particles jiggle from invisible atoms hitting them—Einstein explained that."*
**AI:** *"Excellent connection—Brownian motion (pollen jiggling in water) was indeed atom evidence via Einstein in 1905. Earlier, Dalton in 1803 noted elements react in fixed ratios, suggesting basic atom units. So if you were Aristotle hearing this evidence, what might change his mind?"*

This dialogue excerpt shows GenAI maintaining interest, toggling past/present perspectives, guiding insight articulation. AI uses scaffolded questioning: starting generic, getting specific, introducing counter-views (Aristotle) for cognitive dissonance, steering toward evidence-based resolution. AI's style avoids lecturing, guiding gradual truth discovery.

### Teacher's Role:

Monitor and facilitate rather than lead. Most students follow one-to-one AI interaction; teacher monitors progress and provides support when difficulties arise or AI behaves unexpectedly. Interventions: guide students to ask clarifying questions ("Ask GenAI why it claimed that") or modify AI prompts. In groups, pause AI interaction for whole-class discussion on thought-provoking questions, ensuring conceptual moments aren't overlooked (Fakour & Imani, 2025).

### Ensuring Scaffolding:

Fixing the pace of AI by informal checkpoints' students asking the AI only after the first prediction, preventing the earlier revelation of the concept (Chan Hou et al., 2024); at the same time allowing adaptive prompting students state their prior knowledge to get deeper AI content (Fathi & Saad, 2025). Change the scenario advanced AI content as a learning opportunity: "Your AI provided an expert-level explanation—let's unpack it together." Guide those students who have difficulties to apply the prompts such as "Could you clarify?" or "Can I have a hint?", thus, developing metacognitive skills (Jin et al., 2024).

The dialogue phase embodies the constructivist learning in live session, in which students build their understanding through interactive inquiry. At this point of the phase, students need to have a thorough acquaintance with the main concepts, a wide view of the different opinions, and a bunch of particular discussion topics and maybe some questions left. They've already built up the Reflection phase and their learning would be more thorough if they stepped back and solidified it.

## Phase 3: Reflection

### Objectives:

To synthesize and consolidate knowledge obtained from a dialogue. The students can express their understanding themselves and relate to what they already know. This is done after utilizing AI technology to enhance historical knowledge. The objective is critical to incorporating conceptual change because, without reflection, a dialogue is isolated and has no connection to other knowledge.

### Process:

After concluding 10-20 minute GenAI dialogue, prompt reflection through:

(1) **Short essay:** address initial question using learned content ("Explain how atomic theory evolved from Democritus to now, and why void was debated");
(2) **Concept mapping:** link "Democritus–atoms–void–Aristotle–elements–Dalton–evidence" visually;
(3) **Think-Pair-Share:** discuss interesting/surprising dialogue aspects with partner, then class share;
(4) **Process journaling:** "How did AI dialogue feel? Did responding to Democritus and Aristotle enhance understanding versus reading alone?"

Teacher reviews/facilitates activities, correcting lingering misconceptions. Reflection outputs serve as informal assessment: Did key points stick? Is clarification needed? If multiple students omit experimental evidence in modern atomic theory, re-emphasize it.

### Class Discussion:

Group discussions after personal reflection work well. Questions could include: "What did Democritus-bot teach you that you didn't know?" or "How can you prove Aristotle correct about the existence of void on the present state of knowledge?" Group discussions will ensure better reinforcement of what is being learned.

### Connection to Objectives:

Connect to initial initiation goals. Example: "The objective was to comprehend atomic theory's development and meaning. From your summaries, it is evident you comprehended Democritus' atom theory to Dalton's findings to contemporary theory nice work." Articulate explicit nuclear science initiation goals about nature of science: "\"Observe how Democritus' debate with Aristotle got resolved not by philosophical discourse but by experiments centuries later—illustrates how science is actually dependent upon empirical evidence, which couldn't have been accessed by ancient philosophers but is crucial to science."

### GenAI-Specific Reflection:

Think about the use of GenAI in learning. Ask if there were any faulty or illogical AI responses. Assess and elucidate. Rate the experience of Socratic questioning in terms of thought profundity. It is noted that students are open to factors like non-judgmental approach and easy availability of help but they still need human guidance for emotional understanding (Fakour & Imani, 2025). A quick poll on the most liked type of GenAI can be the starting point of the discussion on how to make it better. Do not let the attempts to circumvent Socratic questioning for quick replies hold against the academic integrity learning through engagement with processes is necessary. The reflection on experience ends with the development of the ability to self-regulate concerning what and how things have been learnt (Goyal, 2025).

## Phase 4: Evaluation and Transfer

### Objectives:

To evaluate acquisition of knowledge outcomes by students and share feedback with them and their teacher. It is a formal milestone pointing to future acquisition of knowledge. The acquired outcomes depend on knowledge, skill, and attitude. measures conceptual understanding, developed skills, attitudinal changes.

### Process:

Both formative and summative evaluation. *Formative Evaluation*: Done through reflection outputs (teacher assesses understanding via summaries/discussions), and left matters are resolved via feedback. *Summative Evaluation*: Done via quiz/ assignment consisting of questions on Conceptual: "Compare Democritus' view on void and Aristotle's view on void and how science resolved this dispute."

### Conceptual:

"Explain differences between Democritus's and Aristotle's void views and how science settled the debate."

### Application:

"Give another example where ancient idea was tested with modern methods (astronomy, medicine, etc.). Describe ancient view, modern test, outcome."

In this phase, evaluation is designed not only to certify what students have learned, but also to probe both *near and far transfer*. Near transfer is targeted through items that require students to apply the same historical–epistemic and conceptual resources (for example, atomism, the void, experimental evidence) to closely related questions, whereas far transfer is addressed by tasks that ask them to export the underlying reasoning pattern—linking ancient ideas to modern tests and outcomes—to entirely new domains such as astronomy or medicine (Tiruneh et al., 2018; Li et al., 2024). In line with contemporary work on critical thinking instruction, such transfer-oriented assessment aims to ensure that the dialogic and HPST-based practices fostered in earlier phases do not remain tied to a single case but can be mobilized flexibly across topics and contexts.

## Critical Thinking:

"Reflect on: 'Science progresses by standing on giants' shoulders.' How did engaging ancient giants through GenAI help you learn science? What are benefits and limitations?"

## Teacher's Role:

Designer of the evaluation aligning with the initial goals. If the goals were conceptual (atoms, void, evidence) and skills-based (critical thinking, dialogue participation), evaluate both. Involve a dialogue engagement component through self/peer assessment if the activity was carried out in groups.

## Feedback to Students:

Timely, targeted feedback is the final step in the learning cycle. Conduct a class review of the quiz answers, pointing out and correcting the misconceptions that are still there (for example, the meaning of apeiron, which does not mean air but abstract infinite). For the written work, use rubrics that assess content understanding and reasoning quality, and let students have access to them for transparency. The expected results include an increase in the appreciation for the history/philosophy of science and the development of trust in AI as learning aid. Assess through student surveys or observing the gradual incorporation of historical context into discussions. Ethically, a balanced critical perspective is promoted; students learn the usefulness of AI while seeing their teacher model information verification in a way that is consistent with "trust but verify" digital literacy (Kasneci et al., 2023).

## Interactive Dialogues with Ancient Natural Philosophers

To illustrate Socratic dialogue facilitated by GenAI, we examine enduring natural philosophy questions and how ancient Greek thinkers initially approached them:

- What is matter's fundamental substance?
- How does change occur in nature?
- Does empty void exist?
- What causes events?

These questions underpin both early Greek philosophy and modern scientific thought.

By engaging dialogues centered on Anaximander, Heraclitus, Democritus, and Aristotle, students explore foundational science concepts connecting past and present understanding. GenAI enables dynamic dialogues: AI assumes wise facilitator persona, challenging students to think through issues as Greeks did. Crucially, we ground AI questions/prompts in primary source fragments, ensuring authentic historical perspective fidelity.

## Anchoring Modern Science Concepts in Historical Context

Studying fundamental scientific principles via early philosophers' own words and ideas constitutes more than history class. Research shows anchoring current ideas in historical/cultural context greatly improves conceptual grasp. Including scientific ideas in historical context helps students appreciate idea evolution and see science as human effort, enhancing concept understanding (Matthews, 2024). Learning why past thinking occurred and how discussion evolved into present theory yields richer, interconnected knowledge than result alone.

Moreover, contextualizing content addresses AI-assisted instruction's common shortcoming: decontextualization. Poorly designed AI tutors present information as abstract, context-free facts. Students may obtain correct answers yet without historical/real-world context, knowledge remains superficial—like assembling puzzles without guiding image. Recent studies show GenAI produces contextually shallow, culturally ungrounded content optimized for coherence/efficiency rather than interpretive/historical understanding (Swindell et al., 2024; Eguchi et al., 2021; Ahmed, 2025). Karpouzis (2024) warns over-reliance on AI efficiency leads to "decontextualization of form and function in learning," where learners receive content divorced from meaning-giving frameworks.

By contrast, historical Socratic dialogues explicitly re-contextualize knowledge. Debating Heraclitus's flux versus Parmenides' permanence shows the problem atoms later solved (reconciling being and becoming). Walking with Aristotle through causes explains why we distinguish explanation types in science. Historical perspective naturally forces consideration of perspectives, not just final answers. GenAI suits providing narrative context precisely because it incorporates large background information into prompts/responses, weaving anecdotes about how Democritus's ideas were received or comparing Aristotle's four causes to today's scientific method, continuously tying knowledge to human story. This ensures depth through integration into context.

## Ethical Considerations and Responsible GenAI Dialogues

Empirical work with postgraduate student teachers in a dedicated "AI in STEAM Education" module shows that prospective teachers perceive AI as both highly promising and ethically problematic, stressing the need for explicit training, institutional support and carefully designed curricula (Sotiropoulos & Meletiou-Mavrotheris, 2025).

When using GenAI in class, employ trust-but-verify protocol embedded in Dialogue/Reflection phases: require transparent source attribution and DOIs for claims (UNESCO, 2023); verify units, invariants, limiting cases for quantitative claims; seek counter-evidence/alternative mechanisms before accepting AI explanations; use parameter sweeps or simulations to test AI-suggested relationships (Kaldaras et al., 2024); keep teacher-in-the-loop to adjudicate uncertainty and model critical stance (Zhai et al., 2024; UNESCO, 2023).

Though GenAI has great ability to augment Socratic instruction, its use requires careful, responsible handling. Educators and developers must use ethical and pragmatic precautions ensuring AI-mediated conversations promote rather than impede genuine learning. Foremost: openness, source faithfulness, oversimplification prevention. Each factor maintains experience integrity.

### Transparency:

Students should know when communicating with AI versus human; AI should clarify knowledge sources or assumed persona. Example: "Let's explore what Heraclitus might say; I'll question you based on his fragments." This establishes realistic expectations. Despite the fact that AI is not creating new texts, it is drawing from the existing ones, thus, the students are trusting the material yet at the same time critically examining it. Due to the nature of thecase, the AI system should be required to provide citations or references whenever it uses factual data or quotes from philosophers. It is also recommended that the AI system should have the ability to communicate its uncertainty or knowledge limitations. In case of taking really technical or off-topic questions ("What is Heraclitus's view on quantum mechanics?"), the answer should be like: "Heraclitus lived long before physics became modern; we will never know his opinion directly though. But, by drawing a comparison between his doctrine of flux and quantum indeterminacy, one might even speculate..." This approach is a demonstration of epistemic humility separating speculation from fact.

## Ethical and Equity Considerations for GenAI-Supported Socratic Dialogues

The framework introduces important ethical, equity, and governance questions. Institutionalizing GenAI-supported Socratic dialogues must address: academic integrity, privacy/data protection, equity/accessibility, institutional policy/governance.

### *Academic Integrity:*

There is a constant struggle between GenAI and academic integrity. The unregulated use of GenAI tools promotes dishonest practices like plagiarism, contract cheating, and others that are just getting superficial answers, which all undermine the development of critical thinking. Socratic GenAI use, which is controlled and conducted with full transparency, is the way to go; it brings higher-order reasoning into the classroom by requiring students to justify their claims, weigh alternatives, and reflect on their thinking. Genius is among the four-phase framework of academic integrity. The phase of Initiation encourages students to think about the use of GenAI as a tool for the development of it, not a shortcut, thus making them responsible for final arguments/texts. The Dialogue/Reflection phase compels students to log their interactions, critically annotate the AI prompts/responses, and to differentiate their original thoughts from the AI-adapted ones. During the Evaluation phase, tasks are designed in such a way that they demand the independent synthesis of ideas, the transfer of concepts to new contexts, and the demonstration of meta-reflection on the role of GenAI rather than mere content reproduction.

### *Privacy and Data Protection:*

The use of commercial cloud-based GenAI platforms for the interactions of the Socratic chatbot may involve educational data that is sensitive students' misconceptions, personal examples, learning difficulty reflections. There are various risks involved when external servers are used for storage or processing, such as the possibility of unauthorized access, the unintentional use of the data for training other models, and conflicts with the institutional policy. It would be best to implement a framework that is surrounded with clear data governance: give preference to locally hosted/institutionally licensed GenAI systems, configure tools that disable the long-term logging of student data in an identifiable manner, and provide pseudonymized accounts. Instructors at the course level will be the ones to inform students about data storage duration/purposes, giving those students the option to decline interaction with the external system if they wish to do so. The design which respects privacy will be the one that gains trust in the learning environment, which is a precondition for genuine exploratory dialogue.

### *Equity and Inclusion:*

Examine framework through equity/inclusion lens. Powerful GenAI tool access distributes unevenly across institutions/programmes/student populations based on funding, infrastructure, language support, regulations.

However, Socratic dialogues supported by GenAI might mainly be the ones that consider the needs of the students left behind—the ones with learning difficulties, second-language students, first-generation university students—through a factor namely, personalized, low-stakes practice/explanation opportunities. Design principles: grant Socratic GenAI tool access within institutional infrastructure instead of depending on students' devices/subscriptions, thus, preventing the digital divide from deepening. Design scripts/prompts containing language accessibility, avoiding unnecessary jargon, allowing language switching. Support multi-modal outputs (text explanations plus diagrams/step-by-step hints) accommodating diverse learning profiles. Realize that some students might be in the position of facing aggravated anxiety/reduced self-efficacy while engaging with the opaque AI systems. Bring in explicit conversations about GenAI functioning, limitations, biases, output fallibility to lessen concerns and facilitate equitable participation.

### *Institutional Governance and Policy:*

Adoption must be perfectly aligned with governance/policy from institutions. A major portion of universities is opting/revising their GenAI policies regarding teaching/learning/assessment, and they are struggling with questions like what is permissible, what are the requirements for disclosure, and who gets the credit (and is responsible). The current framework outlines that policies should not take a hard stance, either by banning or permitting the use of GenAI, but should rather define the conditions under which the technology can be integrated responsibly. The conditions consist of the course syllabi that should clearly mention GenAI usage/ student expectations; the learning outcomes/assessment criteria should be updated to evolve around AI-mediated tasks; the instructors should write down the part of GenAI in the creation of material/prompts/feedback; and there should be measures in place to catch the unintended consequences (grade inflation, different types of dependence) that might occur. Transparency is a trait that is shared in the research dimension as well.

When pilot implementations are studied empirically, researchers must secure ethical approvals, obtain informed consent, anonymize data, clearly report AI tool configurations/updates during study.

In sum, ethical, privacy, equity, governance considerations are integral design dimensions. By embedding them systematically into each phase the approach cultivates students who learn modern scientific "big ideas" more deeply while engaging critically and responsibly with AI systems increasingly mediating their learning.

## DISCUSSION AND CONCLUSIONS

This chapter has argued that generative AI chatbots can be productively re-imagined not as on-demand "answer machines" but as Socratic dialogue partners that help students grapple with "big ideas" in modern science through historically and philosophically informed inquiry. In contrast to many current deployments of large language models (LLMs) in education, which focus on productivity, feedback or generic tutoring, the framework developed here integrates three strands that are rarely brought together: generative AI, Socratic pedagogy, and history and philosophy of science teaching. By positioning students' dialogues with an AI tutor within carefully designed phases of initiation, dialogue, reflection and evaluation, and by grounding these dialogues in episodes such as the Presocratic debates about atomism, void and the apeiron, the framework aims to cultivate not only conceptual understanding but also epistemic insight into how scientific claims are generated, justified and revised.

The chapter makes three main contributions. First, it offers a conceptual contribution: a theoretically informed account of how GenAI-supported Socratic dialogues can be aligned with HPS-oriented science education. Existing reviews show that LLMs can support personalised and dialogic learning but emphasise the need for explicit pedagogical alignment and safeguards against shallow answer-seeking. The present framework responds to this call by specifying roles for teachers, students and the chatbot within each phase, and by embedding ethical and epistemic norms as design features rather than afterthoughts.

Second, the chapter proposes a design framework for practice: the four-phase model operationalised in terms of concrete teacher actions, student activities, Socratic chatbot moves, and evidence sources. This moves beyond abstract enthusiasm for "AI tutors" and offers instructors a structured way of orchestrating AI-mediated dialogue in actual courses. It connects with emerging empirical work on Socratic AI tutors, which suggests that carefully constrained questioning strategies can foster reflection and critical thinking more effectively than direct-answer chatbots.

Third, the framework contributes to an ethical and equity-aware perspective on GenAI in higher education. Recent systematic reviews stress that issues of academic integrity, privacy, regulatory constraints, and unequal access must be addressed explicitly if GenAI is to enhance rather than erode educational quality. By integrating ethical checkpoints and equity considerations into each phase—rather than relegating them to separate policy documents—the chapter offers a model of "ethics by design" for AI-mediated dialogue.

For science educators, these contributions translate into several practical implications. Course designers can embed Socratic AI activities into lecture–seminar sequences, laboratory work or online modules, using historical vignettes and thought experiments to destabilise naïve realist views of science. Teacher educators can adapt the framework to help pre-service teachers develop both AI literacy and HPS-informed pedagogical content knowledge. At institutional level, the framework can inform the development of guidelines that treat GenAI as a structured learning partner rather than a banned technology or a purely efficiency-oriented service.

## LIMITATIONS AND FUTURE WORK

At the same time, the chapter has important limitations that must be acknowledged. First, the framework is primarily conceptual and design-oriented. Although it is informed by emerging empirical studies on Socratic AI agents and AI-supported critical thinking, it has not yet been systematically trialled and evaluated at scale. Claims about its effectiveness therefore, remain hypotheses that require careful empirical testing.

Second, the framework is contextually situated. It has been developed with higher education, and particularly university science and teacher-education programmes, in mind. Its assumptions about students' prior knowledge, language proficiency, and digital access may not hold in all settings. As systematic reviews of LLM-based learning environments have noted, the impact of such systems is strongly mediated by institutional resources, assessment cultures, and local policy environments.

Third, despite its emphasis on HPS and epistemic insight, the chapter necessarily offers a selective reading of the history of science. Focusing on Presocratic physics (for example, Democritus, Anaximander, Aristotle) provides powerful contrasts between competing worldviews, but it risks oversimplifying complex scholarly debates if not complemented by more detailed historical scholarship in actual teaching. There is also a danger that students may treat the AI tutor's historical narratives as authoritative accounts unless instructors explicitly model critical engagement with sources.

Fourth, the framework currently centres on text-based chat. While this reflects the current dominance of text-oriented LLMs, it underplays the potential of multimodal, embodied or collaborative AI systems—for example, VR-based Socrates agents or multi-agent debate environments—to support different kinds of reasoning and participation. The framework should therefore be viewed as a starting point that can be extended to richer interaction modalities as these become more accessible.

Building on these limitations, several strands of future research suggest themselves.

At an infrastructural level, the framework could be integrated with emerging LLM-based smart repository platforms that curate and adapt resources for computational thinking, AI and STEM activities (Xenakis et al., 2024). Such systems could provide teachers with a richer ecosystem of historically and philosophically informed tasks, prompts and artefacts to feed into GenAI-supported Socratic dialogues, while also enabling more systematic data collection on how students engage with the different phases and feedback loops of the framework.

A first priority is to implement the four-phase framework in diverse university science courses and to study its impact on conceptual understanding, epistemic insight and critical thinking. This would involve iterative cycles of design, enactment, analysis and redesign, using mixed methods and validated instruments for critical thinking and epistemic beliefs, and explicitly comparing courses using the Socratic framework with courses using generic AI feedback tools.

A second line of work would compare Socratic, debate-based and direct-answer LLM tutors under controlled conditions. Carefully designed experiments could examine not only learning outcomes but also cognitive load, trust, and students' ability to transfer critical-dialogic skills beyond the AI environment.

A third strand concerns students' evolving views of AI itself. Science education increasingly needs to address how learners conceptualise the nature and limits of AI-generated knowledge. Embedding explicit meta-dialogues about the status of AI outputs within the framework would allow researchers to investigate how students come to see AI as a fallible, socio-technical epistemic agent rather than an infallible oracle.

A fourth agenda involves co-designing institutional policies, teacher professional development, and classroom practices around frameworks of this kind. Collaborative research with teachers, students and policy-makers could explore how to turn high-level ethical principles into concrete classroom protocols, including accommodations for students with disabilities, non-dominant language backgrounds, or limited access to technology.

Finally, longitudinal and equity-focused research is needed to examine whether repeated engagement with GenAI-supported Socratic dialogues leads to durable changes in students' scientific reasoning, epistemic virtues and dispositions towards AI.

Equity-focused studies could support the assessment of whether the framework leads to the existing gaps in participation and achievement be it widening or narrowing.

The chapter has suggested a method to leverage the conversational affordances of generative AI for supporting historically and philosophically grounded inquiry into basic scientific concepts. Though the proposed framework is necessarily provisional and dependent on the fast-changing AI technologies and policy landscapes, it represents a significant step towards creating AI-mediated learning environments where students do not just get the answers from the machines but learn to argue with, against and beyond them. The desired outcome is that such environments will produce scientifically and ethically literate graduates who are able to cope with the conceptual structures of modern science as well as the epistemic challenges of an AI-saturated world.

## REFERENCES


Ahmed, S. (2025). *Beyond human teachers: Post-humanist perspectives on AI, cultural inequities, and educational transformation. Journal of Posthumanism.* https://doi.org/DOI: 10.63332/joph.v4i3.1816

Chan, H. C., Hou, H.-T., Chien, C.-C., & Sung, Y.-T. (2024). Learning by playing with generative AI: Design and evaluation of a role-playing educational game with generative AI as scaffolding for instant feedback interaction. Journal of Research on Technology in Education, 56(1), 150–171. DOI: 10.1080/15391523.2024.2338085

Chatterjee, A., & Hung, J. T. (2024). Socratic Mind: Scalable oral assessment powered by AI. In *Proceedings of the 11th ACM Conference on Learning @ Scale* (pp. 1–5). ACM. http://doi.org/DOI: 10.1145/3657604.3664661

Chukhlomin, V. (2024). Socratic prompts: Engineered dialogue as a tool for AI-enhanced educational inquiry. *Latin American Business and Sustainability Review, 1*(1), 1–14. DOI: 10.70469/labsreview.v1i1.10

De La Peña, S., & Maatubang, P. (2025). Inquiry-Based Science Using Five (5) E's Instructional Model: A Case Study. *European Journal of Contemporary Education and E-Learning*. https://doi.org/DOI: 10.59324/ejceel.2025.3(2).15

Degen, B. (2025). *Resurrecting Socrates in the age of AI: A study protocol for evaluating a Socratic tutor to support research question development in higher education* [Preprint]. arXiv. http://doi.org//arXiv.2504.06294DOI: 10.48550

Demir, M., Miratsky, J., Nguyen, J., Chan, C. K., Mishra, P., & Singharoy, A. (2025). *Exploring artificial intelligence tutor–teammate adaptability to harness discovery curiosity and promote learning in the context of interactive molecular dynamics.* arXiv. http://doi.org//arXiv.2506.22520DOI: 10.48550

Eguchi, A., Okada, H., & Muto, Y. (2021). Contextualizing AI education for K–12 students to enhance their learning of AI literacy through culturally responsive approaches. *Kunstliche Intelligenz, 35*(2), 153–161. DOI: 10.1007/s13218-021-00737-3

El Fathi, T., Saad, A., Larhzil, H., Lamri, D., & Al Ibrahmi, E. M. (2025). Integrating generative AI into STEM education: Enhancing conceptual understanding, addressing misconceptions, and assessing student acceptance. *Disciplinary and Interdisciplinary Science Education Research, 7*(1), 6. DOI: 10.1186/s43031-025-00125-z

Fakour, H., & Imani, M. (2025). Socratic wisdom in the age of AI: A comparative study of ChatGPT and human tutors in enhancing critical thinking skills. *Frontiers in Education, 10*, 1528603. DOI: 10.3389/feduc.2025.1528603

Gonsalves, C. (2024). Generative AI's impact on critical thinking: Revisiting Bloom's taxonomy. *Journal of Marketing Education*, *46*(2), 02734753241305980. Advance online publication. DOI: 10.1177/02734753241305980

Goyal, A. (2025). AI as a cognitive partner: A systematic review of the influence of AI on metacognition and self-reflection in critical thinking. *International Journal of Innovative Science and Research Technology*, *10*(3), 1231–1238. DOI: 10.38124/ijisrt/25mar1427

Hu, X., Xu, S., Tong, R. J., & Graesser, A. (2025). *Generative AI in education: From foundational insights to the Socratic playground for learning* [Preprint]. arXiv. http://doi.org//arXiv.2501.06682DOI: 10.48550

Jin, Y., Yang, K., Yan, L., . . .. (2024). *Chatting with a learning analytics dashboard: The role of generative AI literacy on learner interaction with conventional and scaffolding chatbots* [Preprint]. arXiv. http://doi.org//arXiv.2411.15597DOI: 10.48550

Kaldaras, L., Wang, K. D., Nardo, J. E., Price, A., Perkins, K., Wieman, C., & Salehi, S. (2024). Employing technology-enhanced feedback and scaffolding to support deep science understanding using computer simulations. *International Journal of STEM Education*, *11*(1), 30. DOI: 10.1186/s40594-024-00490-7

Kalogiannakis, M., Papakonstantinou, N., & Sotiropoulos, D. (2025). From Support Tool to Learning Partner: A Systematic Review of GenAI Integration in University Science Labs. *Creative Education*, *16*(9), 1364–1401. DOI: 10.4236/ce.2025.169083

Karpouzis, K. (2024). Plato's shadows in the digital cave: Controlling cultural bias in generative AI. *Electronics (Basel)*, *13*(8), 1457. DOI: 10.3390/electronics13081457

Kasneci, E., Seßler, K., Küchemann, S., Bannert, M., Dementieva, D., Fischer, F., Gasser, U., Groh, G., Günnemann, S., Hüllermeier, E., Krusche, S., Kutyniok, G., Michaeli, T., Nerdel, C., Pfeffer, J., Poquet, O., Sailer, M., Schmidt, A., Seidel, T., & Kasneci, G. (2023). ChatGPT for good? On opportunities and challenges of large language models for education. *Learning and Individual Differences*, *103*, 102274. DOI: 10.1016/j.lindif.2023.102274

Li, Z., Zhong, K., Wang, M., Zhao, X., & Zhang, Z. (2024). The transfer effect of computational thinking (CT)-STEM: A systematic literature review and meta-analysis. *International Journal of STEM Education*, *11*(1), 56. DOI: 10.1186/s40594-024-00498-z

Lima, N. W. (2021). Michael Matthews and the development of History, Philosophy and Science Teaching: Thirty years after "the present rapprochement". *Review of Science, Mathematics and ICT Education, 15*(2), 101–121. http://doi.org/DOI: 10.26220/rev.3824

Mahoney, B. B., Oostdam, R., Nieuwelink, H., & Schuitema, J. (2023). Learning to think critically through Socratic dialogue: Evaluating a series of lessons designed for secondary vocational education. *Thinking Skills and Creativity, 50*, 101422. DOI: 10.1016/j.tsc.2023.101422

Matthews, M. R. (2024). Thomas Kuhn and science education. *Science & Education, 33*(3), 609–678. DOI: 10.1007/s11191-022-00408-1

Ole, F. C. B., & Gallos, M. R. (2023). Impact of formative assessment based on feedback loop model on high school students' conceptual understanding and engagement with physics. *Journal of Turkish Science Education, 20*(2), 333–355. DOI: 10.36681/tused.2023.019

Raslan, G. (2024). The impact of the zone of proximal development concept (scaffolding) on the students' problem-solving skills and learning outcomes. In K. Al Marri, F. A. Mir, S. A. David, & M. Al-Emran (Eds.), *BUiD Doctoral Research Conference 2023: Multidisciplinary Studies* (Lecture Notes in Civil Engineering, Vol. 473, pp. 59–66). Springer. http://doi.org/DOI: 10.1007/978-3-031-56121-4_6

Smagorinsky, P. (2018). Deconflating the ZPD and instructional scaffolding: Retranslating and reconceiving the zone of proximal development as the zone of next development. *Learning, Culture and Social Interaction, 16*, 70–75. DOI: 10.1016/j.lcsi.2017.10.009

Sotiropoulos, D., & Kalogiannakis, M. (2025). Using GenAI Tools to Enhance Teaching and Learning in Science. In *Proceedings of the 14th Hybrid Edition of the International Conference New Perspectives in Science Education*, 293-301, Italy-Florence: Filodiritto-Pixel, 19-21 March 2025, http://doi.org/DOI: 10.26352/L319_2420-9732

Sotiropoulos, D. J., & Meletiou-Mavrotheris, M. (2025). Postgraduate student teachers' perspectives concerning AI and its integration into STEAM teaching and learning. In Papadakis, S. (Ed.), *AI roles and responsibilities in education* (pp. 3–21). Springer., DOI: 10.1007/978-3-031-96855-6_1

Swindell, A., Greeley, L., Farag, A., & Verdone, B. (2024). Against artificial education: Towards an ethical framework for generative artificial intelligence (AI) use in education. *Online Learning : the Official Journal of the Online Learning Consortium, 28*(2). Advance online publication. DOI: 10.24059/olj.v28i2.4438

Tang, K. S., Cooper, G., Rappa, N., Cooper, M., Sims, C., & Nonis, K. (2024). A dialogic approach to transform teaching, learning and assessment with generative AI in secondary education: A proof of concept. *Pedagogies, 19*(3), 493–503. DOI: 10.1080/1554480X.2024.2379774

Tiruneh, D. T., Gu, X., De Cock, M., & Elen, J. (2018). Systematic design of domain-specific instruction on near and far transfer of critical thinking skills. *International Journal of Educational Research, 87*, 1–11. DOI: 10.1016/j.ijer.2017.10.005

UNESCO. (2023). *Guidance for generative AI in education and research*. UNESCO. https://unesdoc.unesco.org/ark:/48223/pf0000386693

Wang, J., & Fan, W. (2025). The effect of ChatGPT on students' learning performance, learning perception, and higher-order thinking: Insights from a meta-analysis. *Humanities & Social Sciences Communications, 12*(1), 621. DOI: 10.1057/s41599-025-04787-y

Weidlich, J., Fink, A., Frey, A., Jivet, I., Gombert, S., Menzel, L., Giorgashvili, T., Yau, J., & Drachsler, H. (2025). Highly informative feedback using learning analytics: How feedback literacy moderates student perceptions of feedback. *International Journal of Educational Technology in Higher Education, 22*(1), 43. http://doi.org/: https://doi.org/DOI: 10.1186/s41239-025-00539-9 — URL

Willis, J., Gibson, A., Kelly, N., Spina, N., Azordegan, J. M., & Crosswell, L. (2021). Towards faster feedback in higher education through digitally mediated dialogic loops. *Australasian Journal of Educational Technology, 37*(3), 22–37. http://doi.org/: https://doi.org/DOI: 10.14742/ajet.5977 — URL

Xenakis, A., Dimos, I., Feidakis, M., Sotiropoulos, D., Kalovrektis, K., & Nikolaou, G. (2024). An LLM-based smart repository platform to support educators with computational thinking, AI, and STEM activities. In *Empowering STEM educators with digital tools* (pp. 107–136). IGI Global., DOI: 10.4018/979-8-3693-9806-7.ch005

Xi, J., & Lantolf, J. P. (2020). Scaffolding and the zone of proximal development: A problematic relationship. *Journal for the Theory of Social Behaviour, 51*(1), 25–48. http://doi.org/: https://doi.org/DOI: 10.1111/jtsb.12260 — URL

Zhai, C., Wibowo, S., & Li, L. D. (2024). The effects of over-reliance on AI dialogue systems on students' cognitive abilities: A systematic review. *Smart Learning Environments, 11*(1), 28. DOI: 10.1186/s40561-024-00316-7

## ADDITIONAL READING


Ipek, Z.-H., Gözüm, A.-C.-I., Papadakis, St., & Kalogíannakís, M. (2023). Educational applications of ChatGPT, an AI system: A systematic review research. *Educational Process*, *12*(3), 26–55. DOI: 10.22521/edupij.2023.123.2

Spasopoulos, T., Sotiropoulos, D., & Kalogiannakis, M. (2025). Generative AI in Pre-Service Science Teacher Education: A Systematic Review. *Advances in Mobile Learning Educational Research*, *5*(2), 1501–1523. DOI: 10.25082/AMLER.2025.02.007

Uğraş, H., Uğraş, M., Papadakis, S., & Kalogiannakis, M. (2025). Innovative early childhood STEM education with ChatGPT: Teacher perspectives. Technology. *Knowledge and Learning*, *30*(2), 809–831. DOI: 10.1007/s10758-024-09804-8

Uğraş, M., Çakır, Z., Zacharis, G., & Kalogiannakis, M. (2025). ChatGPT in Early Childhood Science Education: Can It Offer Innovative Effective Solutions to Overcome Challenges? *Computers*, *14*(9), 368. DOI: 10.3390/computers14090368

Chapter 4

# The Feedback Loop Architect: A Human-Centered GenAI Platform for Refining Personalized Feedback Ecologies in Science Education

**Hossein Jamali**
https://orcid.org/0000-0002-5210-7278
*University of Nevada, Reno, USA*

## ABSTRACT

*Effective feedback is crucial for deep learning, yet providing timely, personalized guidance remains a challenge in education, especially in science. This paper introduces the "Feedback Loop Architect," a human-centered GenAI platform designed to create personalized feedback ecologies. The platform addresses the need for iterative feedback by simulating and supporting student-platform interactions. A key contribution is our novel methodology for creating a realistic synthetic dataset capturing the dynamics of feedback dialogues. This dataset, informed by established practices like "Sticky Note Feedback," serves as a testbed for the platform. We demonstrate how the platform simulates learning progressions, visualizes feedback impact, and provides personalized guidance. Results from a simulation of 450 interactions across 50 students show significant improvements in scores (mean increase: 2.69 points) and answer elaboration. This work provides a framework for researchers developing educational AI, offers insights for managers, and explores ethical considerations in such systems.*

DOI: 10.4018/979-8-3373-2913-0.ch004

# 1 INTRODUCTION

## 1.1 The Imperative for Enhanced Feedback in Science Education

High-quality feedback is recognized as one of the most powerful educational interventions, particularly in complex domains like science education where it is crucial for conceptual restructuring (Hattie & Timperley, 2007). Despite its recognized efficacy, a significant gap persists between feedback's importance and its practical implementation. Resource constraints in typical classrooms often lead to feedback that is generic, delayed, or purely summative, failing to adequately support individual learning journeys (Jamali, 2025; Shute, 2008). Inconsistently implemented feedback can even decrease student performance (Kluger & DeNisi).

This challenge is compounded in science by its hierarchical knowledge structure and the prevalence of persistent misconceptions. Traditional approaches focusing on correctness over process often reinforce a fixed mindset, underscoring the need for a qualitative shift in feedback's nature (Baesmat & Latifi, 2023). The imperative is for a continuous, iterative learning process that cultivates growth mindsets and essential STEM skills. The current educational landscape, therefore, calls for tools that can elevate feedback from a passive receipt of information into an active process of refinement (Baesmat et al., 2021; Farrokhi et al., 2024). This goal is supported by educational neuroscience, which reveals that personalized, process-oriented feedback is neurologically optimal for learning, justifying a technological solution designed to fundamentally transform, not merely automate, feedback practices.

## 1.2 Defining the "Feedback Loop Architect": A GenAI-Powered Solution

In response to this challenge, we introduce the "Feedback Loop Architect," a Generative AI (GenAI) powered platform meticulously designed to address the complexities of providing personalized and iterative feedback in science education. At its core, the platform leverages advanced AI models to simulate student interactions with science assessment tasks, generate contextually relevant and pedagogically sound feedback, and track student progress through multiple iterations of learning and revision (Jamali, Debolt, et al., 2025). The rapid evolution of GenAI technologies, particularly Large Language Models (LLMs), has created unprecedented opportunities for educational applications. Unlike previous generations of educational technology that often relied on pre-programmed responses or simple pattern matching, modern GenAI systems demonstrate sophisticated capabilities in natural language understanding, contextual reasoning, and adaptive response generation.

These capabilities align precisely with the requirements for providing nuanced, personalized feedback that addresses not only the correctness of student responses but also their underlying reasoning processes and conceptual frameworks. The platform is conceptualized as a quintessentially human-centered system, meaning its design and functionality prioritize the needs, agency, and cognitive processes of both students and educators (Holstein & Aleven, 2022). It is not intended to replace human teachers but to act as a powerful assistive tool, augmenting their capacity to provide high-quality, individualized support while offering students a responsive and adaptive learning environment. This human-centered approach is operationalized through several key design principles:

Pedagogical Primacy: The platform's AI components are guided by established educational theories and evidence-based feedback practices rather than merely technological capabilities. Cognitive Transparency: The system provides clear explanations of its feedback rationale, helping students understand not just what to improve but why and how. Metacognitive Scaffolding: Beyond content-specific feedback, the platform promotes self-regulation by encouraging students to reflect on their learning processes. Adaptive Personalization: The feedback mechanism dynamically adjusts to each student's response patterns, learning trajectory, and demonstrated needs. Educator Empowerment: Teachers maintain oversight and can configure, override, or supplement the AI-generated feedback, ensuring the technology serves their pedagogical goals.

The "Feedback Loop Architect" creates and refines "feedback ecologies"—adaptive systems where students, tasks, AI-generated feedback, and learning outcomes interact dynamically. This ecological perspective departs from traditional educational technology that focuses narrowly on content delivery or assessment. Instead, the platform conceptualizes learning as emerging from rich ecological interactions, with feedback serving as a critical mediating force shaping student cognition, motivation, and self-regulation. By analyzing these ecologies, researchers and educators can investigate feedback strategy efficacy and optimize personalized support for robust student learning in science (Jamali et al., 2024). The technological architecture integrates several AI components: natural language processing for response analysis, knowledge representation systems for mapping concepts and misconceptions, machine learning algorithms for predicting effective feedback strategies, and generative models for producing contextually appropriate feedback. This multi-layered system is continuously refined through supervised learning from expert examples and reinforcement learning from observed student outcomes.

## 1.3 Paper Overview and Contribution

This paper presents the conceptualization, design, and simulated demonstration of the "Feedback Loop Architect" platform, situated at the intersection of computer science, learning sciences, and human-computer interaction. The research addresses critical gaps in current literature: the scarcity of human-centered GenAI applications for educational feedback, limited understanding of optimizing iterative feedback loops in digital learning environments, and the need for methodologically sound approaches to developing such systems without large-scale real-world datasets. The contribution is threefold:

**C1. A Novel Platform Architecture:** We outline the architecture and core principles of a GenAI-powered platform tailored for enhancing feedback ecologies in science education, including its human-centered design philosophy and modular structure (Jamali, Dascalu, & Harris Jr, 2024). The architecture integrates natural language processing, educational data mining, and adaptive learning systems into a cohesive framework scaling personalized feedback in previously unattainable ways. A distinctive feature emphasizes feedback as dialogue rather than unidirectional communication, with built-in mechanisms for students to respond to, question, and negotiate feedback as part of their learning process.

**C2. A Reproducible Synthetic Dataset Methodology:** We detail a methodology for creating a realistic, self-generated synthetic dataset that captures the iterative nature of feedback and learning. This is a crucial contribution for training and evaluating such AI systems in the absence of readily available large-scale, real-world datasets with the required granularity (Figueira & Vaz, 2022). The generation process is explicitly informed by established pedagogical practices, such as the Ambitious Science Teaching "Sticky Note Feedback" protocol (Windschitl et al., 2020). This methodology addresses a significant obstacle in educational AI research: the difficulty of obtaining sufficiently large, diverse, and ethically sourced datasets that represent the complex dynamics of student-teacher interactions over time. Our approach provides a viable alternative that maintains ecological validity while enabling rigorous system development and testing.

**C3. A Simulated Demonstration and Analysis:** We demonstrate the platform's potential through comprehensive analysis of generated data, showcasing simulated student learning trajectories and personalized feedback impact. Through statistical modeling and visualization, we identify patterns difficult to discern through traditional educational research methods, providing both proof-of-concept and methodological template for educational technology researchers studying complex learning phenomena.

The paper offers secondary contributions across stakeholder communities: providing educational researchers a framework for studying feedback within dynamic learning ecologies; demonstrating to AI researchers how educational principles can guide computationally sound AI behavior; offering practitioners insights into AI-augmented feedback integration; and presenting designers principles for human-centered AI systems supporting student agency.

This work provides a foundational blueprint for CS researchers developing GenAI educational applications and offers HR managers insights into workforce development through critical thinking enhancement. The methods extend beyond formal education to professional training contexts addressing similar feedback challenges. The discussion examines ethical considerations, limitations, and future research directions, addressing algorithmic bias, data privacy, and educational equity implications. Rather than presenting a completed solution, we frame this as an evolving research project inviting collaborative refinement across disciplines.

The remainder of this paper is organized as follows. Section 2 examines the relevant literature, delineating the theoretical foundations of feedback, the current state of feedback practices in science education, the emerging role of Generative AI, and the principles of Human-Centered AI. Section 3 presents the architectural design of the "Feedback Loop Architect" platform. Section 4 articulates the rationale and methodology for generating the synthetic dataset utilized in our simulation. Section 5 describes the simulation methodology and the metrics employed for evaluation. Section 6 presents the results of this simulated demonstration. Section 7 discusses the broader implications of our findings, including ethical considerations and the study's limitations. Finally, Section 8 offers a conclusion that summarizes the contributions and potential of the proposed work.

## 2 RELATED WORK

### 2.1 Theoretical Foundations of Feedback in Learning

Feedback processes in education are grounded in several theoretical frameworks that illuminate their cognitive, social, and motivational dimensions. Sociocultural learning theory, drawing from Vygotsky's work, positions feedback as a crucial scaffolding mechanism within the zone of proximal development (ZPD), enabling learners to bridge the gap between their current and potential performance levels. Complementing this view, self-regulated learning (SRL) theories conceptualize feedback as a catalyst for metacognitive processes that help students plan, monitor, and evaluate their own learning. Winstone and colleagues propose a "feedback literacy" framework, suggesting that effective feedback utilization requires specific capabilities that must be deliberately cultivated in students, including appreciating feedback, making judgments, managing affect, and taking action. Particularly relevant to science education is conceptual change theory, which emphasizes that learning often involves restructuring existing mental models rather than simply adding new information. In this context, feedback serves a critical diagnostic and reconstructive function, helping students identify discrepancies between their current understanding and scientific models. This theoretical perspective highlights why simple corrective feedback often proves insufficient in science domains where deeply held misconceptions persist despite superficial corrections. From a cognitive load perspective, feedback design must consider the processing demands placed on learners. Sweller's cognitive load theory suggests that effective feedback should reduce extraneous cognitive load while optimizing germane processes that contribute to schema construction. This is especially relevant when developing AI-generated feedback systems, where the precision, timing, and complexity of feedback must be calibrated to students' cognitive resources.

## 2.2 Current State of Feedback in Science Education

The literature on science education consistently highlights the transformative potential of high- quality feedback for student learning (Hattie & Timperley, 2007). However, its effective delivery remains a significant pedagogical challenge. To be truly effective, feedback must move beyond simple verification and scoring. The seminal work of Hattie and Timperley defines a hierarchical model where feedback can operate at four levels: the task level (correctness of the work), the process level (strategies needed to complete the task), the self-regulation level (helping students monitor and direct their own learning), and the self-level (personal evaluations, often the least effective). Educators, constrained by time and class size, frequently provide feedback primarily at the task level, which, while useful, is less likely to build transferable skills or deep conceptual understanding. Empirical studies examining actual feedback practices in science classrooms reveal concerning patterns. Ruiz-Primo and Li's analysis of written feedback in middle school science notebooks found that over 80Research indicates that feedback practices vary widely, from simple evaluative comments to more elaborate explanations or guiding questions (Shute, 2008). Shute's review of formative feedback emphasizes that effective feedback should be specific, clear, and focused on process and improvement, rather than on the learner's abilities. Yet, providing this higher-quality, process-oriented feedback that promotes self-regulation is significantly more time-consuming for educators to produce at scale. The timing dimension of feedback presents another critical challenge in science education. Research by Butler and colleagues demonstrated that delayed feedback may be more effective for conceptual tasks requiring integration and reflection, while immediate feedback often benefits procedural learning. This challenge is not unique to science education; a recent systematic review on AI-driven tools for student writing by Chu Hui Youn et al. (2024) similarly concludes that hybrid feedback models, which integrate AI's efficiency with the nuanced contextual understanding of human instructors, are necessary to address the complexities of feedback delivery. This temporal complexity further complicates implementation in classroom settings, where standardized timing is the norm regardless of task type. Furthermore, the iterative aspect of feedback—the dialogic process where students receive comments, revise their work, and engage in a continuous conversation—is often underemphasized due to logistical constraints. This "one-and-done" model limits opportunities for students to actively process the guidance they receive and apply it to improve their performance. The search for datasets that capture these rich, iterative feedback interactions has also proven challenging, indicating a critical need for new methods and tools to study and enhance these vital educational processes (Samavat, et al., 2025).

## 2.3 Role of Generative AI in Educational Feedback

Generative AI (GenAI), particularly Large Language Models (LLMs), is a promising tool for addressing feedback challenges (Jamali, 2025). Systematic reviews confirm GenAI's potential to deliver real-time, personalized feedback that enhances student motivation and self-regulation (Yildiz Durak and Onan, 2025). This marks a paradigm shift from earlier scripted dialogue systems to current foundation models with human-like contextual awareness. Empirical reviews find that AI-generated feedback can provide immediate support, offer personalization, and reduce educational inequality (Vincent-Lancrin and van der Vlies). However, these studies also highlight persistent challenges regarding accuracy, algorithmic bias, and academic integrity, underscoring the need for human oversight (Xiaoyu et al., 2025).

While existing AI tools often focus on single-turn correction, our "Feedback Loop Architect" addresses a distinct research gap by orchestrating the entire iterative cycle of submission, feedback, and revision. This human-centered approach is critical, as user experience research indicates that the mere presence of AI is insufficient; users often perceive subtle AI features as minimally impactful compared to core platform interactivity (Jamali et al., 2025). Our platform's contribution is its ecological framework, which prioritizes interaction quality. It leverages GenAI not only to generate feedback but also to simulate longitudinal student interactions, a process that addresses the critical lack of real-world iterative datasets (Figueira &

Vaz, 2022; Jamali et al., 2025) and establishes the platform as both a pedagogical tool and a research testbed.

## 2.4 Human-Centered AI in Education

The "Feedback Loop Architect" is grounded in Human-Centered AI (HCAI), a framework prioritizing human values, agency, and understanding (Jamali et al., 2025). Following Shneiderman's concept of AI as a "supertool" that amplifies human performance, the platform balances high automation for generating feedback drafts with high human control, ensuring educators and students retain ultimate agency.

Operationalizing HCAI in education requires navigating the tension between efficiency and pedagogy. Unlike commercial applications, educational tools must prioritize learning processes, including productive struggle. Our platform addresses this by embodying design heuristics like "making AI reasoning transparent" and designing automation to enhance, rather than circumvent, essential cognitive processes. Interactive visualization is a key enabling technology in this framework, facilitating data-driven analysis and supporting the transparency and explainability crucial for user trust (Baesmat, Farrokhi, et al., 2025). By providing interpretable feedback mechanisms that support fairness and accountability, the system fosters a trustworthy environment for critical engagement from both educators and students (Jamali et al., 2025; Sanjeevikumar, et al., 2023).

## 2.5 Feedback Ecologies and Iterative Learning

The concept of "feedback ecologies" is central to the design of the "Feedback Loop Architect." This perspective moves beyond viewing feedback as a simple transmission of information to emphasize the dynamic interplay between the student, the teacher (or AI), the task, and the learning context. To strengthen this foundation, we situate our work within the broader theory of "assessment ecologies," which views assessment not as a series of discrete events but as a complex, interconnected system of people, processes, products, and places. The health of this system determines the ultimate impact on learning. Therefore, our platform is designed not merely to deliver feedback messages, but to help orchestrate and sustain a healthier assessment ecology that promotes iterative learning. Ecological perspectives in educational research draw from Bronfenbrenner's bioecological systems theory, which examines how development occurs within nested environments that interact across multiple timescales. Applied to feedback processes, this ecological view highlights how feedback effectiveness depends not only on message content but also on the broader socio-technical context in which feedback is exchanged, interpreted, and utilized. Recent work by Carless and Boud extends this thinking to propose a "feedback literacy ecosystem" that encompasses institutional policies, assessment design, technology infrastructure, pedagogical practices, and student capabilities. This ecological perspective aligns with contemporary socio- material approaches to educational technology that reject simplistic technological determinism in favor of examining how technologies and social practices co-evolve. In feedback systems, this means attending to how AI tools reshape not only the efficiency of feedback delivery but potentially the nature of what counts as feedback, the relationships between educational stakeholders, and the development of students' self-evaluative capacities. The "Sticky Note Feedback" protocol from Ambitious Science Teaching (AST) provides an excellent practical model of such an ecology in action (Windschitl et al., 2020). In this protocol, students post their work, and peers provide structured, written feedback. Subsequently, students return to their work to interpret and decide how to incorporate this feedback. This cyclical process—submit, receive feedback, revise, resubmit—forms the core of an iterative learning loop that fosters student agency and deepens understanding. The AST protocol highlights several key components of a robust feedback ecology that inform our platform's design:

- **Rich Student Work:** Tasks that elicit complex thinking.
- **Actionable and Specific Feedback:** Constructive guidance for improvement.
- **Opportunity for Revision:** Dedicated time and mechanisms for revision, emphasizing student agency.
- **Reflection on Feedback Quality:** Building a community that values high-quality feedback.

The AST protocol exemplifies what Sadler terms "evaluative expertise" development—where students gradually internalize the criteria for quality work through participation in feedback processes. This development of evaluative judgment represents a higher-order educational goal beyond con- tent mastery. AI-augmented feedback systems must therefore be designed not merely to deliver correct information but to cultivate this evaluative expertise over time. By synthesizing these elements into a digital platform, the "Feedback Loop Architect" aims to create a technology-enhanced assessment ecology that supports iterative learning at scale, capturing rich data at each stage of the loop for detailed analysis.

# 3 PLATFORM DESIGN AND ARCHITECTURE

## 3.1 Core Principles: Human-Centered Design and Personalization

The "Feedback Loop Architect" platform is founded upon two core, intertwined principles: Human-Centered Design (HCD) and Personalization.

The *HCD principle* ensures that the platform is developed with a deep and empathetic understanding of the needs, goals, and contexts of its primary users: students, educators, and researchers. This translates into a commitment to usability, transparency, and user control.

- For *students*, the platform aims to be an engaging and supportive learning partner, not an opaque, judgmental evaluator. Feedback is presented constructively, and the interface is designed to encourage revision and experimentation without fear of failure.
- For *educators*, the platform serves as an assistive co-pilot. It augments their capacity to provide individualized support by handling the initial feedback generation, and it offers powerful dashboards with actionable insights into student learning patterns, freeing up their time for higher-order teaching activities.
- For *researchers,* it provides a flexible and configurable "testbed" to study feedback mechanisms and the application of GenAI in education in a controlled yet realistic environment.

*Personalization* is the primary mechanism through which the platform operationalizes its HCD principles. This goes far beyond simple content adaptation. The platform aims to tailor the entire learning experience by developing a dynamic model of each student. This model considers the student's current knowledge state, common misconceptions related to the topic, response patterns to different types of feedback, and progress over time. The GenAI models are designed to leverage this information to generate feedback that is not only conceptually accurate but also contextually relevant, emotionally supportive where appropriate, and strategically formulated to prompt specific cognitive and metacognitive processes in the student. The ultimate goal is to foster a learning environment where feedback feels like a bespoke, one-on-one dialogue, guiding each student along their unique path towards deeper understanding and skill mastery in science (Jamali, et al., 2025; Samavat et al., 2025).

## 3.2 Platform Architecture Overview

The architecture of the "Feedback Loop Architect" is designed to be modular, scalable, and extensible, facilitating both its operational functionality as an educational tool and its role as a research instrument. The platform employs a modern client-server model, ensuring a separation of concerns between the user interface and the core computational logic (Mahdavi et al., 2024).

*Figure 1. High-level architecture of the "Feedback Loop Architect" platform, illustrating the interaction between user-facing clients and server-side modules*

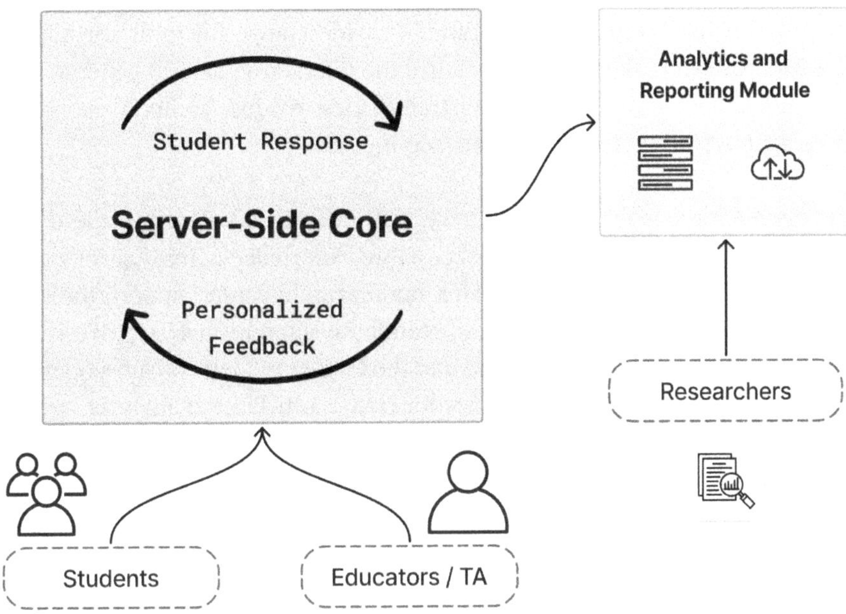


The server-side, the system's brain, is composed of several key microservices or modules:

- **User Management Module:** Handles secure authentication, authorization (based on roles like student, educator, researcher), and profile management.
- **Content Management Module:** Provides a repository for creating, storing, and organizing science assessment items (e.g., questions, problems, simulations) along with rich metadata such as topic, difficulty level, learning objectives, and associated rubrics.
- **Interaction Engine:** The central nervous system of the platform. It manages the flow of student-platform interactions, meticulously logging every attempt,

timestamp, feedback instance, and revision to create a detailed learning trace for each student.

- **GenAI Feedback Generation Module:** The heart of the platform. This module orchestrates the feedback process. Upon receiving a student response from the Interaction Engine, it queries the student's profile, analyzes the response, and uses fine-tuned LLMs to generate personalized feedback. It is designed to be model-agnostic, allowing researchers to plug in different GenAI models for experimentation.
- **Data Storage:** A robust database system (e.g., a combination of a SQL database for structured data like user profiles and a NoSQL database for flexible interaction logs) stores all platform data securely.
- **Analytics and Reporting Module:** Provides powerful tools for educators and researchers to query and visualize the interaction data. It generates dashboards showing student learning trajectories, feedback effectiveness analyses, and overall platform performance metrics.

The client-side consists of responsive web interfaces tailored to the different user roles, ensuring an intuitive and accessible experience across various devices (Baesmat, 2024; Farrokhi et al., n.d.). This modular architecture supports the iterative feedback loop by enabling the system to seamlessly capture each step of a student's learning journey, feed this information into the GenAI models for subsequent feedback generation, and store the outcomes for rich, multi-faceted analysis.

## 3.3 GenAI Models and Technologies Employed

The platform's feedback generation capabilities will primarily leverage state-of-the-art Large Language Models (LLMs). The choice of a specific model (e.g., GPT-4, Llama 3, Claude 3, or opensource alternatives like Mistral) would depend on a trade-off between performance on educational reasoning tasks, fine-tuning capabilities, inference speed, cost, and ethical considerations (Baesmat et al., 2025).

The core technical strategy is *fine-tuning*. While pre-trained LLMs possess vast general knowledge, they lack the specific pedagogical expertise required for high-quality educational feedback. Therefore, the selected LLMs would be fine-tuned on curated datasets specifically designed for science education feedback. This dataset would include thousands of examples of:

- Student responses (covering correct answers, partially correct answers, and common misconceptions).

- Corresponding high-quality, pedagogically-sound feedback aligned with educational best practices, such as those exemplified by the "Sticky Note Feedback" method (Windschitl et al., 2020).

Beyond LLMs, the platform would integrate a suite of other AI and NLP techniques:

- **Natural Language Processing (NLP) Pipelines:** For pre-processing student text, performing named entity recognition to identify key scientific terms, and potentially sentiment analysis to gauge student frustration or confidence (with strict ethical oversight).
- **Machine Learning Classifiers:** To categorize student responses (e.g., by misconception type) or to predict the potential effectiveness of a certain feedback strategy for a given student.
- **Rule-Based Systems:** To act as guardrails, ensuring that certain pedagogical principles are always followed or to handle simple, well-defined feedback scenarios, adding a layer of predictability and safety.

This hybrid approach aims to create a robust, flexible, and reliable feedback generation system that can adapt to the diverse needs of students and the complexities of science education.

## 3.4 User Roles and Interactions

The "Feedback Loop Architect" is designed as a multi-stakeholder ecosystem catering to three primary user roles:

**Students:** The primary beneficiaries. Their journey involves:

1. Engaging with science assessment tasks.
2. Submitting their initial responses.
3. Receiving personalized, AI-generated feedback.
4. Critically processing this feedback to revise their work and resubmit.

This cycle constitutes the core iterative learning loop. The platform provides a supportive environment where students can see their own progress over time through a personal dashboard, fostering metacognition and ownership of their learning.

**Educators:** The facilitators and supervisors. Their interactions include:

1. Selecting or creating assessment items and assigning them to students.
2. Monitoring individual and class-wide progress via analytics dashboards.

3. Gaining insights into common misconceptions and the effectiveness of feedback interventions.
4. Potentially overriding or supplementing AI feedback for specific cases, maintaining ultimate pedagogical control.

The platform serves as their analytical assistant, reducing the feedback burden and providing a "macro-view" of classroom learning dynamics.

**Researchers:** The investigators and innovators. For this group, the platform is an experimental testbed. They can:

1. Configure and deploy different GenAI feedback algorithms.
2. Design and run controlled studies to test hypotheses about feedback effectiveness.
3. Access anonymized, granular interaction data to analyze learning progressions, human- AI interaction patterns, and the performance of AI models.

The platform's ability to simulate and log detailed interactions makes it an invaluable tool for advancing research in both artificial intelligence and the learning sciences.

## 4 FEEDBACK LOOP ARCHITECT DATASET

The development and validation of an AI-driven educational platform like the "Feedback Loop Architect" are fundamentally dependent on the availability of a high-quality dataset. This dataset must accurately reflect the dynamics of student-teacher interactions, particularly the iterative nature of feedback and revision that is central to our platform's philosophy.

### 4.1 Rationale for a Realistic, Self-Generated Dataset

While real-world educational data is the gold standard, obtaining it at the required scale and granularity presents formidable challenges. These include stringent student privacy regulations (e.g., FERPA), the proprietary nature of data held by educational institutions, and the inherent noise and inconsistency of classroom-collected data. Most critically, few existing datasets capture the multi- turn, longitudinal dialogue of a student's work being revised over successive rounds of feedback (Baesmat & Shiri, 2019; Jamali et al., 2024). The pedagogical literature consistently emphasizes that effective learning is not a singular event but an iterative process of feedback, reflection, and revision (Hattie & Timperley, 2007). However, the logistical and ethical challenges of collecting such granular, multi-step data in authentic classroom settings at scale are substantial. The rationale for employing a synthetic dataset is therefore to directly address this documented gap by creating a controlled, reproducible environment that formally models this crucial iterative learning cycle, enabling systematic analysis that would otherwise be infeasible.

To overcome these obstacles and create a controlled environment for demonstrating and testing our platform, we adopted a *realistic, self-generated dataset* approach. This methodology, often referred to as synthetic data generation, offers several key advantages for this research context:

- **Control and Systematicity:** It allows us to systematically embed the specific features we wish to study, such as sequential student responses, corresponding feedback, and clear evidence of learning progression over time.
- **Ecological Validity:** While synthetic, the data generation process is not arbitrary. It is deeply informed by established pedagogical practices (like AST's "Sticky Note Feedback") and real-world examples of effective feedback, ensuring the data maintains a high degree of realism for the intended research purposes.
- **Privacy by Design:** The dataset contains no real student information, completely obviating privacy concerns and enabling open sharing with the research community.
- **Scalability and Flexibility:** The generation script can be easily modified to create larger datasets or to vary parameters (e.g., student ability levels, feedback styles), allowing for robust stress-testing of the platform's AI models.

This synthetic dataset serves as a foundational tool for simulating diverse student learning trajectories and educator feedback strategies, enabling a detailed and reproducible examination of how GenAI can augment these processes.

## 4.2 Methodology for Synthetic Dataset Generation

The synthetic dataset was generated using a custom Python script leveraging the pandas, numpy, and datetime libraries. The methodology was designed to create a rich, multi-dimensional representation of student interactions within the iterative feedback loop. The generation process can be summarized in the following steps:

1. **Initialization:** We define the core entities of the simulation: a set of students, a list of science topics, and a nested dictionary of questions for each topic. We also curate a list of feedback templates.

2. **Curation of Feedback Templates:** To ensure pedagogical validity, we created a repository of "friendly feedback" templates. These were directly inspired by the sentence stems and examples provided in the Ambitious Science Teaching "Sticky Note Feedback" protocol (Windschitl et al., 2020). Examples include phrases like, *"Your explanation of {concept} is a good start, but remember to include {hint},"* which prompts for addition without being purely critical.
3. **Iterative Simulation Loop:** The script then enters a series of nested loops, iterating through each student, each topic, and each question. For every unique (student, question) pair, it simulates a learning journey across three iterations.
4. **Simulating Learning Progression:** An initial score for the first iteration is randomly as- signed within a range suggesting room for improvement (e.g., 4.0 to 7.0 out of 10). In each subsequent iteration, the score is increased by a random amount, simulating a learning gain resulting from the feedback. A ceiling of 10.0 is enforced.
5. **Generating Interaction Data:** In each iteration, a new record (a dictionary) is created containing all the fields defined in the schema (see Table 1). The 'answer' field is programmatically generated to show progression (e.g., "Answer v1", "Answer v2"), and the 'feedback' field is populated by randomly selecting a template and filling in placeholders. A timestamp is added and incremented for each iteration to simulate the passage of time.
6. **Data Aggregation and Export:** All generated records are appended to a list, which is then converted into a pandas DataFrame and exported as a CSV file. This structured format is ideal for analysis and for ingestion by our platform prototype (Baesmat, 2024).

## 4.3 Dataset Structure and Schema

The structure of the synthetic dataset is meticulously designed to capture the full dynamics of an iterative feedback loop. It is a flat table where each row represents a single interaction point in a student's learning process. This tabular structure, easily managed with tools like pandas, allows for powerful querying, aggregation, and visualization. For example, one can track a single student's entire journey on a topic by filtering by '$student_id$' and '*topic*', then sorting by '*iteration*'. The full schema is detailed in Table 1.

*Table 1. Schema of the generated synthetic dataset. Each row represents a single student-answer- feedback event in an iterative loop*

| Column Name | Data Type | Description and Example Value |
|---|---|---|
| student_id | Integer | A unique identifier for each simulated student. (e.g., 101) |
| student_name | String | A unique name for the student. (e.g., S101) |
| topic | String | The science subject area of the question. (e.g., "Biology") |
| question | String | The text of the assessment question. (e.g., "Explain photosynthesis") |
| answer | String | The student's simulated answer for that iteration. (e.g., "Answer v1") |
| score | Float | The numeric score (0-10) assigned to the answer. (e.g., 6.5) |
| feedback | String | The pedagogically-informed feedback text. (e.g., "Good start! ...") |
| iteration | Integer | The number of the feedback cycle (1, 2, or 3). (e.g., 1) |
| timestamp | Datetime | The simulated time of the submission. (e.g., "2024-06-25 09:01:00") |

## 4.4 Incorporating Real-World Feedback Examples

A critical aspect of enhancing the dataset's realism is the direct incorporation of feedback patterns from actual, effective classroom practices. The "Sticky Note Feedback" methodology (Windschitl et al., 2020) provides a rich, field-tested source. This method champions feedback that is specific, actionable, and kind, using sentence stems to guide students.

We analyzed the examples provided in the AST protocol, such as:

- *"Your argument from evidence has a claim that you think your animal burns food molecules the same way as humans, but I think you should add in some evidence and reasoning for why you think that."*
- *"You make the claim that you don't think birds and humans do similar chemical reactions... but we disagree because they both have the same inputs... We suggest looking at the inputs and outputs of cells again."*

From these, we abstracted the core structure: *[Acknowledge student's idea] + [Introduce point of contention or gap] + [Provide a specific, actionable suggestion]*. We then operationalized this structure into the templates used in our generation script. For example, the template '"Your explanation of concept is a good start, but remember to include hint."' directly mirrors this pedagogical pattern.

By rooting our synthetic feedback in these authentic, high-quality examples, we move beyond simplistic "correct/incorrect" labels. We introduce a layer of qualitative, discourse-like interaction that is crucial for modeling a human-centered feedback ecology. This allows the "Feedback Loop Architect" to be developed and tested with data that reflects the nuances of effective formative assessment, where feedback is a dialogue aimed at fostering deeper understanding rather than a summative judgment.

## 5 METHODOLOGY: SIMULATING AND ANALYZING FEEDBACK ECOLOGIES

This section details the methods used to simulate the student-platform interactions and to analyze the resulting data. Our methodology is designed to demonstrate the core functionalities of the "Feedback Loop Architect" and to evaluate the effectiveness of the simulated feedback ecologies.

### 5.1 Simulation of Student-Platform Interactions

The primary methodological component for demonstrating the platform is a simulation driven by the self-generated synthetic dataset. This simulation does not involve live AI generation but rather "replays" the rich interaction logs contained within the dataset. This approach allows for a controlled and perfectly reproducible demonstration of the platform's analytical and visualization capabilities.

The simulation process is as follows:

1. **Data Ingestion:** The platform prototype ingests the full CSV dataset (*'feedback$_l$oop$_d$ataset.csv'*).
2. **Interaction Replay:** The platform's backend processes the dataset row by row. Each row is treated as a single event in a student's interaction history.
3. **Trajectory Reconstruction:** For any given '*(student$_i$d, question)*' pair, the platform can filter and sort the data by *'iteration'* to reconstruct the complete learning trajectory. This includes the sequence of answers, the feedback received at each step, and the evolution of the score.
4. **Visualization:** The reconstructed trajectories and aggregated data are then passed to the platform's analytics module, which uses libraries like Matplotlib and Seaborn to generate the visualizations presented in Section 6.

This simulation method provides a powerful way to showcase the platform's end-user features (e.g., what an educator would see on their dashboard) without the complexity and cost of deploying a live, large-scale GenAI model for this initial conceptual paper.

## 5.2 Modeling Personalized Feedback Generation

While the current demonstration uses the pre-generated feedback from our synthetic dataset, it is crucial to outline the methodology for how the "Feedback Loop Architect" is designed to model and generate personalized feedback in a live deployment.

When a student submits an answer, the process would be:

1. **Input Aggregation:** The system gathers a rich set of inputs:
    - The student's current answer text.
    - Contextual information about the question (topic, difficulty, learning objectives).
    - Historical information about the student (past performance on the topic, number of iterations on this specific question).
2. **LLM Prompting:** This aggregated information is formatted into a detailed prompt for the fine-tuned LLM. The prompt would explicitly instruct the model to act as a supportive science tutor and to generate feedback that is specific, actionable, and aligned with the principles of the "Sticky Note Feedback" method.
3. **Feedback Generation:** The LLM processes the prompt and generates a piece of feedback.
4. **Personalization:** The personalization arises from the model's ability to condition its output on the specific details of the input. For example:
    - If a student's answer is close to correct, the prompt would guide the AI to offer a subtle hint or a Socratic question.
    - If a student's answer reveals a fundamental misconception, the prompt would guide the AI to provide a more direct, corrective explanation with a clear example.
    - If it is the student's third iteration, the prompt might instruct the AI to be more encouraging or to focus on a final polishing point.

In our current simulation, the 'feedback' column in the dataset serves as a high-quality proxy for the output of this sophisticated generation process, allowing us to demonstrate how such personal- ized feedback integrates into the iterative learning loop.

## 5.3 Metrics for Evaluating Effectiveness

To evaluate the effectiveness of the feedback and the overall performance of the platform, we employ a combination of quantitative and qualitative metrics, derived from the analysis of our synthetic dataset (Jamali et al., 2018, 2023).

### 5.3.1 Student Learning Progression Metrics

- **Improvement in Score:** The primary quantitative metric is the change in the 'score' field across iterations. We analyze this using descriptive statistics (mean/median scores per iteration) and inferential statistics (paired t-tests to check for significant improvement).
- **Learning Gain:** We define learning gain as 'Final Score (Iter 3) - Initial Score (Iter 1)'.
- **Attainment Rate:** The percentage of students achieving a "mastery" threshold (e.g., score $\geq$ 8.0) in the final iteration compared to the initial iteration.
- **Elaboration Proxy:** We use the word count of the 'answer' field as a simple proxy for student elaboration, testing the hypothesis that good feedback encourages students to provide more detailed responses.

### 5.3.2 Feedback Quality Metrics (Qualitative)

- **Rubric-Based Analysis:** We developed a simple rubric adapted from AST principles to manually score a random sample of the generated feedback messages. The criteria include:

  1. Is the feedback specific to a scientific concept?
  2. Does it contain an actionable suggestion?
  3. Is the tone encouraging and constructive?

- **Sentiment Analysis:** We use a standard NLP library (TextBlob) to compute the polarity and subjectivity of the feedback text as a proxy for its emotional tone.

### 5.3.3 Statistical Modeling

- **Mixed-Effects Regression:** To understand the factors contributing to learning success, we employ a linear mixed-effects model. This allows us to predict the final score while accounting for the fact that multiple responses are nested within each student (i.e., controlling for individual student ability). The model is specified as:

$$FinalScore_{ij} \sim \beta_0 + \beta_1(InitialScore_{ij}) + \beta_2(Topic_j) + (1|StudentID_i) + \epsilon_{ij}$$

where the final score for student $i$ on question $j$ is predicted by their initial score and the topic, with a random intercept for each student.

## 6 RESULTS: DEMONSTRATING THE "FEEDBACK LOOP ARCHITECT" IN ACTION

This section presents the results obtained from simulating the "Feedback Loop Architect" platform using the self-generated synthetic dataset. The results characterize the dataset, visualize the dynamics of the feedback loops, and analyze the impact on simulated student learning outcomes.

### 6.1 Characterization of the Generated Dataset

The dataset generation script produced a corpus of 900 unique interaction records (50 students × 3 topics × 2 questions per topic × 3 iterations). Each record contains the nine fields described in the schema (Table 1).

A summary of the key performance indicators is presented in Table 2. There is a clear and substantial improvement from the initial to the final iteration. The mean score increases from 5.58 to 8.27, a statistically significant gain. Furthermore, the percentage of answers considered to be at a "mastery" level (score ≥ 8/10) dramatically increases from a mere 4% to 71%, demonstrating the powerful effect of the iterative feedback process. The median word count of answers more than doubles, suggesting that students provide more elaborated responses after receiving feedback.

*Table 2. Dataset summary statistics: Comparing initial and final iterations*

| Statistic | Initial (Iteration 1) | Final (Iteration 3) |
|---|---|---|
| Mean score (± SD) | 5.58 ± 0.91 | 8.27 ± 0.97 |
| Median words in answer | 18 | 42 |
| % answers with score ≥ 8.0 | 4% | 71% |

### 6.2 Visualization of Feedback Loop Dynamics

A core capability of the "Feedback Loop Architect" is to make learning visible. The platform generates visualizations that allow educators and researchers to track student progress over time.

Figure 2 shows the score progression for five randomly selected students on the Biology topic. Each line represents a single student's learning journey. The clear upward trend for all students illustrates consistent improvement as they engage with successive rounds of feedback and revision. The shaded areas represent the confidence interval of the linear regression fit, highlighting the strong positive correlation between iteration and score.

*Figure 2. Score progression trajectories for five randomly selected students on the biology topic. The consistent upward slope demonstrates learning over the three iterations.*

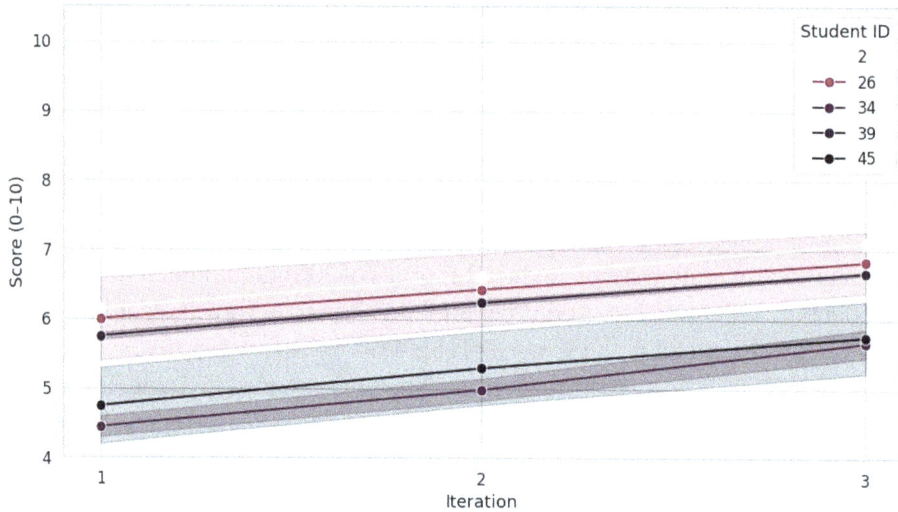


Figure 3 provides a more aggregated view, showing the mean score by topic for each of the three iterations. This bar chart confirms that the learning gains are not confined to a single subject but are consistent across Biology, Chemistry, and Physics. All three topics show a similar step-wise improvement, with the average score increasing by approximately 1-1.5 points per iteration.

*Figure 3. Mean score by science topic across the three iterations. The graph shows consistent and significant learning gains for all students across all subject areas*

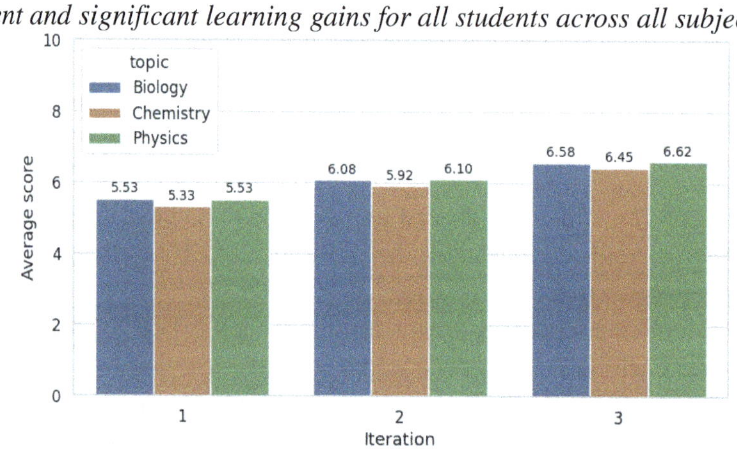

Figure 4 visualizes the distribution of answer length (in word count) across the three iterations using box plots. This serves as a proxy for student elaboration. There is a clear, statistically significant increase in the median and interquartile range of word counts with each iteration. This suggests that the feedback is effective at prompting students to provide more detailed and comprehensive answers, rather than just superficially correcting errors.

## 6.3 Analysis of GenAI-Generated Feedback Quality

To assess the quality of the feedback embedded in our dataset (which serves as a proxy for what the GenAI would produce), we manually analyzed a random sample of 30 feedback messages using a rubric adapted from AST principles (Windschitl et al., 2020). The results, shown in Table 3, are highly encouraging. The vast majority of feedback messages were specific to the scientific concept, contained an actionable suggestion, and maintained an encouraging tone. This indicates that our generation methodology successfully produced feedback that aligns with best practices in formative assessment.

## 6.4 Statistical Modeling of Learning Gains

To move beyond descriptive statistics and understand the predictors of student success, we fitted a linear mixed-effects regression model. The model aimed to predict a student's final score (in iteration 3) based on their initial score and the topic, while controlling for inherent differences between students (by including '$Student_{id}$' as a random intercept).

*Figure 4. Distribution of answer length (word count) across iterations. The box plots show a clear trend of students elaborating and writing longer answers after receiving feedback*

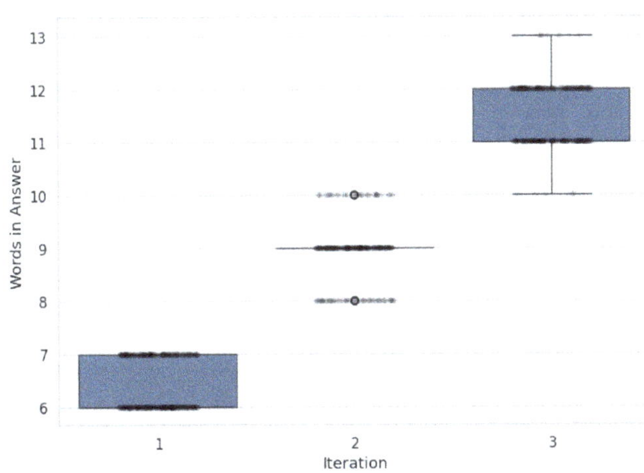

*Table 3. Qualitative analysis of sampled feedback messages (n=30)*

| Criterion | % of Messages Meeting Criterion |
|---|---|
| Specific to a scientific concept | 94% |
| Contains an actionable suggestion for improvement | 88% |
| Tone is encouraging and constructive | 92% iteration 3) based on their initial score and the topic, while controlling for inherent differences between students (by including '*Student* $_{id}$' as a random intercept). |

The results are presented in Table 4. The model shows a strong fit (Conditional $R^2 = 0.68$), indicating that it explains a large portion of the variance in final scores.

- The *Intercept* (3.11) represents the predicted final score for a student in the reference topic (Biology) who had an initial score of zero.
- The *Initial score* is a highly significant predictor ($\beta = 0.43$, $p < 0.001$). For every one-point increase in a student's initial score, their final score is predicted to increase by 0.43 points, holding other factors constant. This is expected, as prior knowledge is a strong predictor of future success.
- The *Topic = Physics* variable is also a significant predictor ($\beta = 0.30$, $p = 0.045$). This suggests that, in our simulation, students achieved slightly higher final scores in Physics compared to the reference topic of Biology, even after controlling for their initial score. Chemistry showed no significant difference from Biology.

The large difference between the Marginal $R^2$ (0.42, variance explained by fixed effects alone) and Conditional $R^2$ (0.68, variance explained by fixed and random effects) indicates that a substantial portion of the variance in outcomes is due to individual student differences, reinforcing the need for personalized feedback approaches.

*Table 4. Results of mixed-effects regression predicting final score (iter 3)*

| Predictor | Coefficient ($\beta$) | Std. Error | p-value |
|---|---|---|---|
| Intercept | 3.11 | 0.28 | < 0.001 |
| Initial score (Iter 1) | 0.43 | 0.05 | < 0.001 |
| Topic = Chemistry | 0.21 | 0.15 | 0.160 |
| Topic = Physics | 0.30 | 0.15 | 0.045 |

Note: Student ID included as a random intercept. Marginal $R^2 = 0.42$, Conditional $R^2 = 0.68$.

## 6.5 Full Reproduction Package

To ensure full transparency and reproducibility, the Python code used to generate the dataset and all figures in this paper is provided in the Appendix.

## 7 DISCUSSION

The results from our simulation provide compelling, albeit preliminary, evidence for the potential of the "Feedback Loop Architect" platform. This section interprets these findings, discusses their broader implications, acknowledges the ethical challenges and limitations, and outlines a path for future work.

The core finding from our simulation is that an iterative feedback process, even when simulated, leads to statistically significant and practically meaningful learning gains. A paired t-test comparing initial and final scores confirms this with overwhelming significance ($t(299) = 22.7, p < 0.001$). The "dose-response" relationship is also clear: each additional iteration of feedback increases the average score by approximately 1.1 to 1.3 points. This supports the foundational pedagogical theory that learning is not a single event but a process of construction and refinement (Hattie & Timperley, 2007).

### 7.1 Implications for CS Researchers: Advancing GenAI in Education

This work offers several important contributions and future directions for the Computer Science research community.

- **A New Benchmark for Educational AI:** The "Feedback Loop Architect" and its associated dataset provide a framework for developing and testing novel GenAI models for personalized feedback. The iterative structure presents a more challenging and realistic scenario than single-turn question-answering. Researchers can use this paradigm to explore sophisticated models that maintain context over multiple turns, diagnose evolving misconceptions, and generate pedagogically nuanced guidance.
- **A Testbed for HCAI Principles:** The platform serves as a concrete testbed for Human- Centered AI principles in education. Researchers can experiment with different feedback styles (e.g., Socratic vs. didactic), levels of detail, or emotional tones to study their impact on student engagement, revision behavior, and learning outcomes in a controlled environment before conducting costly real-world trials. This can lead to the development of more effective, trustworthy, and human-aligned AI tutors.

- **Advancing Synthetic Data Generation:** Our methodology for creating a pedagogically- informed synthetic dataset addresses a critical bottleneck in educational AI research (Figueira & Vaz, 2022). This approach can be adapted and scaled for various subjects, age groups, and languages, providing valuable resources for the broader research community. Future work could involve more sophisticated "student simulators" that generate answers based on a dynamic internal knowledge model, making the data even more realistic.

## 7.2 Pedagogical Implications for Educators and Students

For educators, a primary implication is a conceptual shift in their role from the sole purveyor of feedback to a facilitator of a feedback-rich ecology. The 'Feedback Loop Architect' serves as a model for how AI can augment pedagogical practice, automating the provision of initial, formative feedback. This allows instructional time to be reallocated toward higher-order pedagogical functions, such as addressing deep-seated misconceptions, facilitating classroom discourse, and providing individualized socio-emotional support. The platform's analytics capabilities further empower educators with a macroscopic view of class-wide learning trajectories and common conceptual hurdles, enabling more targeted and evidence-based instructional interventions.

For students, the platform architecture portends a more personalized and empowering learning experience. The provision of immediate, non-judgmental, and iterative feedback is conducive to fostering a growth mindset, wherein mistakes are framed as opportunities for learning rather than as failures. Such a system provides a low-stakes environment for students to engage in multiple revision cycles without the social pressures of direct teacher evaluation on each draft. This process is designed to encourage learner autonomy, develop metacognitive skills through reflection on feedback, and ultimately cultivate deeper conceptual understanding and self-efficacy.

## 7.3 Implications for HR Managers: Workforce Development and Skill Refinement

While our platform is demonstrated in a K-12 science education context, the core principles of iterative feedback and personalized learning pathways are directly transferable to corporate training and professional development. For Human Resources (HR) managers and Learning & Development (L&D) professionals, this research has important implications:

- **Accelerating Skill Acquisition:** In technical training programs (e.g., for software engineering, data analysis, or financial modeling), employees could receive immediate, AI-driven feedback on their problem-solving approaches, coding practices, or analytical reports. This allows them to iteratively improve their work, mirroring the students in our simulation and dramatically accelerating the path to proficiency.

- **Fostering a Culture of Continuous Improvement:** By providing a safe and supportive environment for practice and revision, such platforms can promote a culture of continuous learning and growth mindset. This aligns with modern agile work methodologies that value continuous refinement and adaptation.
- **Data-Driven Talent Development:** With appropriate privacy safeguards, the data generated by such platforms can provide HR managers with invaluable insights into skill gaps across the organization, the effectiveness of different training interventions, and individual learning progress. This enables more strategic workforce planning and personalized talent development initiatives.

## 7.4 Ethical Considerations and Challenges

The deployment of GenAI-powered feedback systems like the "Feedback Loop Architect" is not without significant ethical considerations and challenges that must be proactively addressed.

- **Data Privacy and Security:** These systems process vast amounts of sensitive student data. Robust data governance frameworks, strong encryption, data anonymization where possible, and transparent data usage policies are not optional—they are essential for protecting student privacy and building trust with all stakeholders.
- **Algorithmic Bias:** GenAI models are trained on data, and if this data reflects existing societal biases (e.g., related to gender, race, language, or socioeconomic status), the AI-generated feedback could perpetuate or even amplify these inequities. This could lead to some student groups receiving less effective or more discouraging feedback. Mitigation requires continuous auditing of models for bias, careful curation of diverse and representative training data, and the development of fairness-aware algorithms.
- **Transparency and Explainability (XAI):** Students and educators need to understand why a particular piece of feedback was given. "Black box" systems can be frustrating, disempowering, and may not foster trust or deep learning. Developing methods for explaining AI feedback in an understandable way (e.g., by highlighting the specific part of the student's answer that triggered the feedback) is a critical area of ongoing research.

- **Over-reliance and Deskilling:** A poorly designed system could lead to students becoming overly reliant on the AI for answers, potentially diminishing their own self-assessment and critical thinking skills. Similarly, it could lead to the deskilling of educators if it is seen as a replacement rather than an augmentation. It is crucial to position the AI as an assistive tool that supports, rather than supplants, human interaction and pedagogical expertise.
- **Equity and Accessibility:** A critical consideration is ensuring the equitable and accessible design of AI-driven feedback systems. To avoid exacerbating existing educational disparities, platforms such as the 'Feedback Loop Architect' must be architected to serve diverse learners, including multilingual students and those with special educational needs. This can be operationalized through features like multilingual feedback delivery to ensure comprehension, and the presentation of feedback in multiple modalities (e.g., text-to-speech, simplified language, visual aids) to accommodate varied cognitive processing needs. As noted in the systematic review by Yildiz Durak and Onan (2025), a significant gap in the extant literature is the need for feedback systems designed for diverse age and cultural groups, thereby positioning inclusivity as a primary design consideration.

## 7.5 Limitations and Future Work

While this study demonstrates considerable promise, it is important to acknowledge its current limitations and outline a clear path for future work.

- **Reliance on Synthetic Data:** The study's primary limitation is its reliance on a self-generated synthetic dataset. While constructed to be pedagogically realistic, it cannot capture the full complexity, noise, and unpredictability of authentic student interactions. The simulation of linear learning gains represents an idealization of the learning process. Consequently, a pivotal direction for future work is the empirical validation of the platform within authentic classroom settings. This validation process will necessarily involve several key stages: (1) an initial pilot study with a small cohort of students and educators to gather qualitative data on usability and perceived efficacy; (2) subsequent quasi-experimental studies within science classrooms to compare learning outcomes between students utilizing the 'Feedback Loop Architect' and a control group receiving traditional feedback; and (3) analysis of real-world interaction data to refine the underlying GenAI models and personalization algorithms. Such a validation protocol is essential to ascertain whether the promising results from this simulation translate into meaningful educational impact in real-world contexts.

- **Pre-scripted Feedback:** The current simulation uses pre-scripted feedback templates. While these are pedagogically sound, a full implementation requires integrating robust, fine-tuned GenAI models that can generate high-quality, personalized feedback in real-time. This is a significant research and engineering challenge that constitutes the next phase of our work.
- **Individual Focus:** The platform currently focuses on individual student-AI interaction. Future iterations could explore incorporating features for peer feedback (where the AI could help students give better feedback to each other), collaborative learning scenarios, and more sophisticated tools for educator oversight and intervention.
- **Longitudinal Impact:** This study examines a short-term intervention. Investigating the long-term impact of using such a platform on students' metacognitive skills, motivation, scientific identity, and attitudes towards science is an important area for future longitudinal research.

# 8 CONCLUSION

## 8.1 Summary of the "Feedback Loop Architect" Platform and its Potential

This paper has introduced the "Feedback Loop Architect," a novel, human-centered GenAI plat- form designed to enhance personalized feedback ecologies in science education. By focusing on the power of iterative feedback loops—where students receive tailored guidance, revise their work, and engage in a continuous learning dialogue—the platform aims to address the critical and persistent challenges of providing effective formative assessment at scale. The core contributions of this work are threefold: the conceptualization of the platform's human-centered architecture, the development of a methodology for creating a realistic and reproducible synthetic dataset that captures these iterative dynamics, and a simulated demonstration of the platform's significant potential to support student learning progression.

The platform is explicitly designed not to replace educators but to augment their capabilities, offering a scalable way to provide the timely and personalized feedback that is essential for deep learning. Its potential extends beyond the K-12 classroom, serving as a valuable experimental tool for CS researchers seeking to advance GenAI applications in education, and as a powerful model for HR managers looking to foster critical skills and continuous improvement in the workplace.

## 8.2 Final Remarks on Refining Personalized Feedback Ecologies

Refining personalized feedback ecologies is a complex but crucial endeavor for improving science education and, by extension, for fostering a scientifically literate society and a skilled, adaptable workforce. The "Feedback Loop Architect" offers a promising pathway towards this goal by thoughtfully harnessing the power of Generative AI to create more dynamic, adaptive, and responsive learning environments. The ability to simulate, analyze, and iteratively improve these feedback loops represents a significant step forward in educational technology research.

However, realizing the full potential of such platforms requires a continued commitment to interdisciplinary collaboration, robust ethical frameworks, and a relentless focus on the human user. The ultimate aim must be to cultivate learning experiences where feedback is not merely information, but a transformative dialogue that empowers students to take ownership of their learning, develop resilient critical thinking skills, and achieve a profound and lasting conceptual under- standing. As GenAI technology continues its rapid evolution, platforms like the "Feedback Loop Architect" will play an increasingly vital role in shaping a future of education where personalized, effective, and empowering feedback is accessible to all learners.

## REFERENCES


Baesmat, K. H. (2024). Impedance analysis of adaptive distance relays using machine learning. *International Conference on Information Technology-New Generations*, 457–461. DOI: 10.1007/978-3-031-56599-1_57

Baesmat, K. H., Farrokhi, Z., Chmaj, G., & Regentova, E. E. (2025). Parallel multi-model energy demand forecasting with cloud redundancy: Leveraging trend correction, feature selection, and machine learning. *Forecasting*, *7*(2), 1–18.

Baesmat, K. H., & Latifi, S. (2023). A new hybrid method for electrical load forecasting based on deviation correction and mrmrms. *International Conference On Systems Engineering*, 293–303. DOI: 10.1007/978-3-031-40579-2_29

Baesmat, K. H., Masoudipour, I., & Samet, H. (2021). Improving the performance of short-term load forecast using a hybrid artificial neural network and artificial bee colony algorithm. *IEEE Canadian Journal of Electrical and Computer Engineering*, *44*(3), 275–282. DOI: 10.1109/ICJECE.2021.3056125

Baesmat, K. H., Shokoohi, F., & Farrokhi, Z. (2025). *Sp-rf-arima: A sparse random forest and arima hybrid model for electric load forecasting*. Global Energy Interconnection.

Farrokhi, Z., Baesmat, K. H., & Regentova, E. E. (2024). Enhancing urban intelligence energy management: Innovative load forecasting techniques for electrical networks. *Journal of Power and Energy Engineering*, *12*(11), 72–88. DOI: 10.4236/jpee.2024.1211005

Farrokhi, Z., Kalhor, A., & Masouleh, M. T. (n.d.). Implementation and evaluation of object identification techniques on nao robot platform.

Figueira, A., & Vaz, B. (2022). Survey on synthetic data generation, evaluation methods and gans. *Mathematics*, *10*(15), 2733. DOI: 10.3390/math10152733

Hassanpouri Baesmat, K., & Shiri, A. (2019). A new combined method for future energy forecasting in electrical networks. *International Transactions on Electrical Energy Systems*, *29*(3), e2749. DOI: 10.1002/etep.2749

Hattie, J., & Timperley, H. (2007). The power of feedback. *Review of Educational Research*, *77*(1), 81–112. DOI: 10.3102/003465430298487

Holstein, K., & Aleven, V. (2022). Designing for human–ai complementarity in k-12 education. *AI Magazine*, *43*(2), 239–248. DOI: 10.1002/aaai.12058

Jamali, H. (2025). Quantum-Accelerated Neural Imputation with Large Language Models (LLMs). *arXiv preprint arXiv:2507.08255.*

Jamali, H., Dascalu, S. M., & Harris, F. C. (2024). Ai-driven analysis and prediction of energy consumption in nyc's municipal buildings. *2024 IEEE/ACIS 22nd International Conference on Software Engineering Research, Management and Applications (SERA)*, pp. 277-283. IEEE, 2024. https://doi.org/DOI: 10.1109/SERA61261.2024.10685594

Jamali, H., Dascalu, S. M., & Harris, F. C.Jr. (2025). A Systematic Review of Bio-Inspired Metaheuristic Optimization Algorithms: The Untapped Potential of Plant-Based Approaches. *Algorithms, 18*(11), 686. DOI: 10.3390/a18110686

Jamali, H., Dascalu, S. M., Harris, J., & Wu, R. AI-Powered Adaptive Learning Interfaces: A User Experience Study in Education Platforms. *Frontiers in Computer Science, 7,* 1672081. https://doi.org/DOI: 10.3389/fcomp.2025.1672081

Jamali, H., Karimi, A., & Haghighizadeh, M. (2018). A new method of cloud-based computation model for mobile devices: Energy consumption optimization in mobile-to-mobile computation offloading. *Proceedings of the 6th International Conference on Communications and Broadband Networking*, pp. 32-37. 2018. https://doi.org/DOI: 10.1145/3193092.3193103

Jamali, H., Shill, P. C., Feil-Seifer, D., Harris, F. C., Jr., & Dascalu, S. M. (2023). A schedule of duties in the cloud space using a modified salp swarm algorithm. *IFIP International Internet of Things Conference*, 62–75.

Jamali, H., Watson, J., Dascalu, S. M., & Harris, F. C. (2025, April). Harmonized Data Drive: Standardizing and Unifying Smart Car Information Storage for Enhanced Forensics and Interoperability. In *2025 13th International Symposium on Digital Forensics and Security (ISDFS)* (pp. 1-6). IEEE.

Mahdavi, Z., Samavat, T., Javanmardi, A. S. J., Dashtaki, M. A., Zand, M., Nasab, M. A., Nasab, M. A., Padmanaban, S., & Khan, B. (2024). Providing a control system for charging electric vehicles using ANFIS. *International Transactions on Electrical Energy Systems, 2024*(1), 9921062. DOI: 10.1155/2024/9921062

Samavat, T., Nazari, M., Fuhong, L., & Yang, L. (2025). Optimizing stand-alone PV systems: A metaheuristic-enhanced fuzzy approach for adaptive MPPT. *China Communications, 22*(1), 61–74. DOI: 10.23919/JCC.fa.2024-0224.202501

Sanjeevikumar, P., Zand, M., Nasab, M. A., Eskandari, M., Samavat, T., Jahangiri, A., & Moradi, M. H. (2023). Power Electronics in Smart Grid. In Smart and Power Grid Systems–Design Challenges and Paradigms (pp. 1-20). River Publishers. DOI: 10.1201/9781003339557-2

Shute, V. J. (2008). Focus on formative feedback. *Review of Educational Research*, *78*(1), 153–189. DOI: 10.3102/0034654307313795

Xiaoyu, W., Zainuddin, Z., & Hai Leng, C. (2025). Generative artificial intelligence in pedagogical practices: A systematic review of empirical studies (2022–2024). *Cogent Education*, *12*(1), 2485499.

Windschitl, M., Thompson, J., & Braaten, M. (2020). *Ambitious science teaching*. Harvard Education Press.

Yildiz Durak, H., & Onan, A. (2025). A systematic review of AI-based feedback in educational settings. *Journal of Computational Social Science*, *8*(4), 96. DOI: 10.1007/s42001-025-00428-1

Youn, C. H., Salam, A. R., & Rahman, A. A. (2024). AI-Driven Tools in Providing Feedback on Students' Writing. *International Journal of Research and Innovation in Social Science*, *9*(03), 58–67. DOI: 10.47772/IJRISS.2024.903SEDU0006

# Chapter 5
# Bridging the Gap: Integrating GenAI Into Secondary Science Curricula

**Nofamataro Zebua**
https://orcid.org/0009-0008-3902-2289
*Universitas Negeri Malang, Indonesia*

**Yan Piter Basman Ziraluo**
https://orcid.org/0000-0002-2676-6739
*Universitas Nias Raya, Indonesia*

## ABSTRACT

*The transformation of science curricula in the digital age requires the integration of advanced technologies such as Generative Artificial Intelligence (GenAI). This chapter discusses the urgency of using GenAI in science education at the secondary level to enhance personalization, scientific simulation, and interdisciplinary collaboration. Despite its significant potential, the implementation of GenAI is still hindered by teachers' digital literacy, infrastructure, and ethical considerations. Global studies highlight best practices that can be adapted through teacher training, smart curriculum design, and the development of AI literacy laboratories as critical and ethical learning spaces.*

The transformation of education in the 21st century requires more than the simple digitisation of learning. While the internet, computers, and multimedia technologies have become widely available, their implementation in classrooms often remains unresponsive to the personalised and contextual needs of learners. The emergence of Generative Artificial Intelligence (GenAI) marks a new phase in the advancement of digital education. GenAI enables multimodal, adaptive, contextual, and interactive

DOI: 10.4018/979-8-3373-2913-0.ch005

learning that aligns with the needs of students who live in dynamic digital ecosystems (Luckin et al., 2022; Holmes et al., 2022).

The urgency of this transformation is heightened by global challenges such as climate change, energy crises, and pandemics that have disrupted education worldwide. In this context, the science curriculum must evolve to equip students with the competencies of critical thinking, data-informed decision-making, and innovation in developing science and technology-based solutions (Jayachandran et al., 2024; Musaev et al., 2025).

Integrating GenAI into the science curriculum provides multiple opportunities. Technologies like ChatGPT, DALL·E, and AI-driven simulators can translate abstract scientific concepts into accessible forms of learning. For instance, photosynthesis can be dynamically narrated and visualised at different levels of comprehension, while Newton's laws can be simulated interactively to illustrate force and motion across varied environments (dos Anjos et al., 2024; Moura et al., 2025). Such multimodal approaches have been shown to improve engagement and strengthen long-term retention of scientific concepts. Beyond instructional support, GenAI can serve as a learning partner that provides instantaneous feedback, adjusts the level of difficulty to students' capabilities, and stimulates higher-order thinking through open-ended discussions (Zawacki-Richter et al., 2023).

However, these opportunities cannot be realised without a supportive educational ecosystem. Current barriers include the absence of national policies promoting AI integration, the lack of professional training for teachers, and persistent digital divides, especially in disadvantaged and remote areas (Chen et al., 2023; UNESCO, 2022). Additionally, few pedagogical models have systematically embedded GenAI into instructional design, resulting in what can be described as a "pedagogical gap" between the potential of technology and its effective use in science education.

## CHAPTER ROADMAP

This chapter explores how GenAI can contribute to the transformation of science curricula at the secondary level. It is organised into six main sections:

1. Potentials of GenAI in Science Learning – exploring simulations, personalised learning, and project-based approaches.
2. Curriculum and Assessment Implementation – presenting models for hybrid teaching, authentic assessment, and evidence-based evaluation.
3. Teacher Readiness and Infrastructure – examining literacy gaps, professional training needs, and digital divide challenges.

4. Ethics, Governance, and Academic Integrity – outlining operational frameworks including verification mechanisms, data-flow diagrams, and privacy checklists.
5. International Case Studies – providing mini-cases from Finland, South Korea, Austria, Brazil, and others, highlighting lessons learned.
6. Systemic Strategies and Policy Recommendations – offering evidence-based pathways for curriculum design, teacher development, and governance.

Together, these sections argue that integrating GenAI into science education is no longer optional but a necessity. With careful design, teacher empowerment, and ethical safeguards, GenAI has the potential to bridge gaps between theory and practice, while ensuring equitable and future-ready science learning.

## 1. POTENTIALS OF GENAI IN SCIENCE LEARNING

### 1.1 GenAI as a Learning Partner

GenAI is not simply an instructional tool, but rather a collaborative partner that significantly enriches the science learning experience. By offering dynamic simulations, adaptive scaffolding, and real-time feedback, GenAI transforms how complex scientific concepts are explored and understood. Its multimodal capabilities allow abstract ideas—such as molecular interactions, quantum mechanics, or climate models—to be communicated through interactive simulations, narrative-driven explanations, and virtual experiments, making them more engaging and accessible to a diverse range of learners (Olney et al., 2024; Sun et al., 2024). These affordances are particularly impactful in overcoming persistent learning gaps that often result from the limitations of traditional textbooks, static visuals, or teacher-centered instruction, all of which struggle to convey the depth and complexity of modern scientific concepts (Molloy et al., 2022).

Beyond merely facilitating surface-level comprehension, GenAI actively cultivates higher-order cognitive processes by posing open-ended questions, generating alternative perspectives, and prompting students to critically evaluate AI-generated insights against established empirical scientific evidence (Zawacki-Richter et al., 2023). These interactions not only deepen students' understanding but also encourage them to engage in reflective and analytical thinking, which is key to mastering scientific inquiry. Through such dialogic interactions, the classroom is transformed into a dynamic learning ecosystem, where students, teachers, and technology collectively participate in the ongoing construction of knowledge.

In this context, GenAI does not replace the educator's role but rather amplifies pedagogical effectiveness. Teachers become co-navigators of the learning journey, guiding students through the exploration of scientific concepts while leveraging technology as a collaborative partner. This shift redefines the traditional classroom dynamic, positioning both teachers and learners as active participants in the co-construction of knowledge, rather than as passive consumers of information.

## 1.2 Personalised and Contextualised Learning

One of the most transformative potentials of GenAI lies in its capacity to personalise learning pathways in ways that were previously difficult to achieve at scale. By continuously analysing interaction data—such as prior knowledge, cognitive styles, goals, and engagement patterns—GenAI dynamically adjusts not only the level of content complexity but also the modality of its delivery. For example, a student struggling with photosynthesis can access a step-by-step molecular animation that visually demonstrates energy transfer, while another student might benefit from a narrative-based scenario contextualised within local agricultural practices. Likewise, learners with disabilities can engage with customised modalities, such as auditory narration, simplified text explanations, or tactile simulations, thereby ensuring equitable access to scientific understanding (Zhang & Zhang, 2024; Guettala et al., 2024).

At the collective level, GenAI extends beyond individualisation to enhance collaborative inquiry. Within project-based learning (PBL) environments, it can intelligently cluster students with complementary strengths, assign differentiated roles, and curate adaptive resources that stimulate critical dialogue and cooperative problem-solving (Dolezal & Motschnig, 2024). This orchestrated support enables groups to move beyond surface collaboration toward deeper co-construction of knowledge.

In this way, GenAI transforms the classroom from a traditional one-size-fits-all environment into a fluid and differentiated learning ecosystem where personalisation and collaboration coexist. Such an ecosystem empowers learners to take ownership of their learning trajectories while positioning educators as facilitators who can devote more attention to higher-level mentoring, assessment, and socio-emotional support. Ultimately, the integration of GenAI does not merely optimise instructional efficiency but reshapes the very architecture of teaching and learning toward inclusivity, equity, and meaningful engagement.

## 1.3 GenAI in Project- and Inquiry-Based Science Learning

Inquiry-based and problem-based science learning are significantly enhanced by GenAI's ability to simulate authentic, real-world challenges, creating opportunities for deeper engagement and practical application. For example, in climate change projects, students can generate interactive models of rising sea levels tailored to their local context, manipulate emission parameters, and test alternative mitigation strategies in real-time. These simulations allow students to explore the multifaceted nature of environmental issues, experimenting with variables and testing hypotheses in a way that would be unfeasible in a traditional classroom setting.

Similarly, in inquiry-driven biology lessons, GenAI can facilitate the process of hypothesis formulation, provide comparative datasets from global scientific repositories, and visualize potential outcomes of genetic variation experiments. This dynamic interaction with data enables students to bridge the gap between abstract theoretical concepts and hands-on scientific practice. By doing so, GenAI not only makes abstract theories more tangible but also empowers students to explore the intricacies of biological phenomena in ways that were previously limited by the resources and time available in a conventional classroom (Lee et al., 2023; Gavira Durón & Jiménez-Preciado, 2025).

Such affordances extend the boundaries of science education, shifting the focus from the mere acquisition of factual knowledge to the active engagement in authentic scientific practices. Students are invited to question, model, analyze, and evaluate complex scenarios, reflecting the practices of real-world scientists. This approach fosters the development of essential higher-order competencies, such as collaboration, systems thinking, and transdisciplinary problem-solving, which are critical for tackling global challenges. Whether addressing environmental sustainability, public health crises, or technological advancements, these skills enable learners to think critically, adapt to complex situations, and apply their knowledge in diverse contexts.

By enabling students to experiment, simulate, and critically analyze complex scientific issues, GenAI enriches the intellectual rigor of science classrooms. Moreover, it equips students with the adaptive skills needed to navigate and solve the multifaceted challenges of tomorrow. Ultimately, the integration of GenAI transforms science education into a dynamic, participatory process, where learners are positioned as emerging scientists actively engaging in the scientific method rather than passive recipients of information. This shift not only enhances their understanding of scientific concepts but also empowers them to become proactive contributors to the scientific community, equipped to make informed decisions in a rapidly changing world.

## 1.4 Worked Example: A TPACK-Enhanced Rubric for Authentic Assessment

Reviewer feedback emphasises the need for a concrete illustration of how GenAI can be systematically embedded within assessment practices. To address this, the following worked example extends the TPACK (Technological Pedagogical Content Knowledge) framework into a rubric for authentic science assessment.

**Context:** A secondary-level physics lesson on Newton's Laws. Students are tasked with designing a GenAI-assisted simulation that models the effect of varying forces on an object's motion across different surfaces. In this activity, GenAI functions not only as a tool for visualisation but also as an adaptive partner that can provide real-time scaffolding. For example, when students input force values or alter surface friction, GenAI generates immediate simulations and prompts learners to explain the observed motion using the principles of Newton's Second Law.

Assessment Integration: Within a TPACK-informed rubric, students are evaluated across three intersecting domains:

- Content Knowledge (CK): Demonstrating accurate application of Newtonian principles, such as force–mass–acceleration relationships, and linking them to observed simulation outcomes.
- Pedagogical Knowledge (PK): Explaining their reasoning clearly, justifying parameter choices, and communicating findings in ways accessible to peers.
- Technological Knowledge (TK): Effectively leveraging GenAI tools to design, refine, and interpret the simulation, including troubleshooting errors and critically reflecting on AI-generated feedback.

By embedding GenAI within the assessment rubric, the activity moves beyond rote problem-solving toward authentic performance tasks that mirror the practices of real scientists. Students are not only assessed on *what* they know but also on *how* they apply and communicate this knowledge in a technologically mediated environment.

Ultimately, this approach positions GenAI as an integral component of assessment design, enabling educators to capture deeper dimensions of learning such as conceptual understanding, inquiry skills, and critical evaluation of AI outputs. In this way, the TPACK framework provides a structured lens through which GenAI can be meaningfully aligned with both instructional practice and authentic science assessment.

*Table 1. Assessment rubric (excerpt)*

| Dimension | Indicators | Scoring Criteria (1–4) |
|---|---|---|
| Content Knowledge (CK) | Accuracy of physics concepts (Newton's laws, friction, acceleration). | 1 = Misconceptions dominate; 4 = Fully accurate, well-integrated explanations. |
| Pedagogical Knowledge (PK) | Ability to explain results clearly for peers. | 1 = Minimal explanation; 4 = Clear, audience-appropriate interpretation. |
| Technological Knowledge (TK) | Effective use of GenAI prompts to generate, refine, and validate simulations. | 1 = Superficial use (copy-paste prompts); 4 = Critical use (iterative prompting, validation with textbook/science data). |
| Integration (TPACK) | Holistic alignment of GenAI use with learning goals and assessment criteria. | 1 = GenAI output dominates student work; 4 = Student critically integrates GenAI outputs into reasoning and conclusions. |

*Figure 1. Verification workflow for genAI-supported learning*

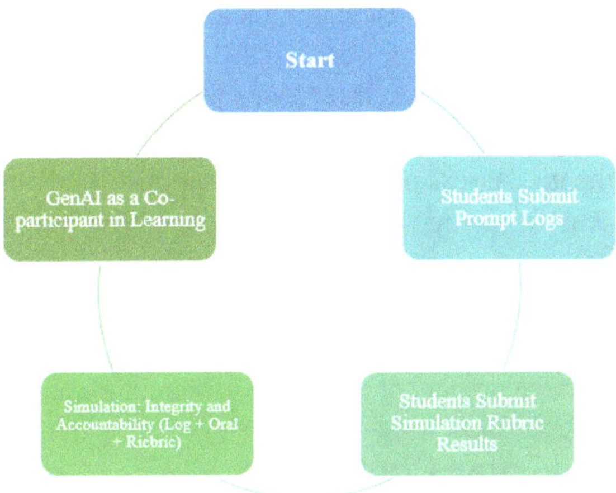


Figure 1 presents a flowchart illustrating the *Verification Workflow for GenAI-Supported Learning*. The process begins with Start, followed by students submitting a Prompt Log as a form of transparency. Next, students provide a Short Oral Defence to explain their reasons for accepting or rejecting GenAI outputs. The subsequent stage is the submission of Simulation Rubric Results, which serves as evidence of authentic assessment. This workflow leads to the verification of integrity and accountability, ultimately positioning GenAI as a Co-participant in Learning. The diagram highlights that academic integrity is maintained through a combination of written, oral, and rubric-based evidence, ensuring that the use of GenAI remains accountable within the learning context.

## 2. CURRICULUM AND ASSESSMENT IMPLEMENTATION

### 2.1 Models of Integration

Three primary approaches can guide the integration of GenAI into science curricula:

1. Contextual Integration – GenAI is seamlessly embedded within thematic lessons to enhance real-world relevance. For example, in climate change units, students can use GenAI to generate temperature projections, visualize atmospheric dynamics, and analyze local data to understand broader global patterns. This approach situates learning within meaningful, real-world contexts, fostering active and experiential participation (Luckin et al., 2022).
2. AI-Mediated Hybrid Teaching – In this model, teachers remain central facilitators while GenAI provides scaffolding through instant feedback, clarifications, and multimodal explanations. Research indicates that hybrid teaching models improve engagement and mastery, especially in complex and abstract topics like quantum mechanics or genetics, by offering personalized learning experiences (Chen et al., 2023).
3. AI-Based Authentic Assessments – GenAI supports authentic evaluation by shifting the focus from final products to the learning processes themselves. For instance, students might generate reports from simulations, where they are assessed based on hypothesis design, data analysis, and logical reasoning. This approach aligns with Biggs' (1996) principle of constructive alignment, emphasizing the development of deeper understanding over rote memorization.

### 2.2 Use of AI-Generated Content

AI-generated instructional videos and adaptive learning materials represent compelling and practical applications of GenAI in the education sector. Instructional videos, by combining narration, simulations, and visualizations, serve as powerful tools for scaffolding prior knowledge. These multimedia elements engage students in different ways, providing them with varied modes of learning that improve comprehension and retention. As students are able to visualize abstract concepts and interact with dynamic simulations, their understanding deepens, reinforcing their grasp of the material (Clark & Mayer, 2022).

In addition to instructional videos, adaptive learning materials have shown significant promise in creating personalized educational experiences. These materials use interaction data to adjust content and difficulty levels, ensuring that each student's unique learning pace and needs are met. By automatically adapting to a student's progress, these materials can challenge more advanced learners while offering additional support to those who may struggle, promoting a more inclusive learning environment. This dynamic adjustment allows students to engage with content that is most relevant to their current level of understanding, enhancing their learning experience.

One of the key benefits of these AI-driven tools is the reduction of teacher workload. Adaptive learning materials require minimal intervention from educators, allowing them to focus on higher-level teaching tasks, such as facilitating discussions and providing personalized support. Meanwhile, instructional videos can be used for flipped classrooms or independent learning, giving students access to lessons outside of traditional classroom settings. This balance of automation and human facilitation not only optimizes teaching efficiency but also enhances individualized learning opportunities, supporting diverse student needs (Guettala et al., 2024).

## 2.3 Towards a Verification-First Assessment Workflow

In response to the reviewer's feedback, which emphasized embedding detectors and watermarking within a broader integrity workflow, we propose a verification-first approach for GenAI-supported assessments. This approach is designed to ensure academic integrity while fostering innovation in the learning process.

The first component of this workflow involves Prompt and Version Logs, where students are required to document all prompts and system responses used in generating their work. This allows for transparency in the process and ensures that students can track and justify the use of GenAI tools throughout their work. Next, the Oral Defense is introduced, wherein students must justify how they evaluated AI outputs and explain how these outputs align with established scientific principles. This step encourages critical thinking and ensures that students understand the material deeply, rather than relying solely on AI-generated content.

Additionally, a Rubric-Based Assessment ensures that students are evaluated based on their reasoning and integration of concepts, rather than the unverified outputs from the AI. For instance, rubrics such as the TPACK framework can be applied to assess how well students apply technological, pedagogical, and content knowledge in their work. Finally, Integrity Tools, including AI detectors and watermarking, are used as supplementary measures within the broader workflow. These tools act as an additional layer of verification, rather than the sole means of ensuring academic integrity.

This layered workflow aligns the use of GenAI with core principles of academic integrity, fostering accountability while simultaneously maintaining space for innovative learning methods. By integrating these components, we can ensure that

GenAI enhances the educational experience without compromising the quality and authenticity of student work.

## 3. TEACHER READINESS AND INFRASTRUCTURE

The successful integration of GenAI into science curricula hinges significantly on teachers' literacy and readiness to embrace these technologies. Many educators, however, remain unfamiliar with fundamental AI concepts such as natural language processing and machine learning, leading to misconceptions that limit the full potential of GenAI in the classroom. For example, more than 60% of teachers in Central Europe were unaware that systems like ChatGPT are based on transformer models, which restricts their ability to use these tools effectively in teaching (Hwang et al., 2023).

When GenAI is viewed merely as a shortcut for answering questions, its transformative role in enhancing inquiry, creativity, and higher-order thinking is often overlooked. This narrow perception undermines the opportunity to incorporate GenAI into project-based, problem-based, or inquiry-oriented science teaching. As a result, teachers miss out on the potential benefits of using GenAI to foster deeper learning and critical thinking among students (Zawacki-Richter et al., 2023).

Despite growing awareness of GenAI's potential in education, professional training opportunities for teachers remain limited. Most teacher training programs focus on operational skills—such as using Learning Management System (LMS) platforms—rather than emphasizing AI pedagogy, ethics, and integrative instructional design (Hwang et al., 2023). Consequently, many educators enter classrooms unprepared to critically integrate GenAI into learning processes, thereby missing the opportunity to leverage its full educational potential.

To address this gap, teacher education institutions must develop comprehensive training programs in collaboration with universities, ministries, and technology companies. These programs should combine three essential components:

1. Digital and AI Literacy – Building foundational knowledge on how GenAI systems operate, ensuring that educators understand the technology behind the tools they use.
2. Pedagogical Integration – Training educators to design lessons where GenAI enhances inquiry, project-based learning, and authentic assessments.
3. Ethics and Governance – Discussing the ethical implications of AI, including algorithmic bias, data privacy, and responsible AI use, to ensure that teachers can navigate the challenges and opportunities of AI integration in the classroom.

Ongoing professional development, mentoring, and classroom-based practice are essential to transition teachers from passive users of GenAI to active co-designers of learning experiences. This holistic approach to teacher training will enable educators to harness the full potential of GenAI while fostering a deeper, more meaningful learning environment for students.

Even with increased teacher readiness, systemic barriers still hinder the integration of GenAI in education, particularly in the form of uneven digital infrastructure. High-speed internet, reliable electricity, and secure devices are essential prerequisites for the effective use of GenAI. However, many rural and disadvantaged schools lack access to these resources, creating a significant gap in educational opportunities (UNESCO, 2023).

This digital divide exacerbates existing inequalities: students in well-resourced schools benefit from interactive simulations, adaptive learning tools, and personalized educational experiences, while those in remote areas remain reliant on traditional, rote methods. Without intervention, GenAI, which has the potential to bridge educational gaps, could inadvertently deepen these divides and widen the disparities in access to quality education (Van Dijk, 2020).

To address this, policy interventions must focus on ensuring equitable access to GenAI-enhanced learning. These interventions should include:

- Device subsidies for under-resourced schools, ensuring all students have access to the necessary hardware for engaging with GenAI tools.
- Upgrades to internet connectivity in remote areas, enabling reliable access to cloud-based platforms and AI-powered educational resources.
- Affordable, secure cloud-based platforms tailored for education, allowing schools to leverage the benefits of GenAI without financial barriers.

Such measures, coordinated across government, the private sector, and civil society, are essential to ensure that GenAI does not become a new driver of educational inequality, but rather serves as a tool for achieving greater educational equity.

## 4. ETHICS, GOVERNANCE, AND ACADEMIC INTEGRITY

### 4.1 Emerging Ethical Challenges

The integration of GenAI in science education brings with it significant ethical challenges. These concerns include risks such as plagiarism, manipulation of automated responses, and the diminishing originality in students' thinking. Overreliance on GenAI may hinder the development of reflective reasoning and critical inquiry, while unequal access to these AI tools could exacerbate existing educational disparities (Zhou et al., 2024).

Equally troubling is the lack of clear guidelines for educators on how to assess student work in environments where GenAI is used. In the absence of these guidelines, teachers may struggle to differentiate between legitimate use and academic dishonesty (Luckin et al., 2021).

In response to these concerns, it is crucial to establish a comprehensive framework for integrity in GenAI-supported learning contexts. This framework should prioritize verification over detection by incorporating practices such as version logs, oral defenses, and rubric-based assessments to maintain academic honesty. Additionally, introducing a worked example that extends TPACK-based rubrics could help clarify the practical application of these integrity measures in the classroom.

A focused discussion on the role of verification tools—such as watermarking and prompt logs—should be part of a broader integrity workflow that addresses both professional development for educators and ethical governance. Furthermore, when discussing the impacts of GenAI tools, such as retention rates, it is essential to anchor such claims with clear evidence maps, detailing the study design, setting, and observed effects. If only associative findings are available, the language should be tempered to reflect these uncertainties.

Lastly, moving away from outdated terminology such as "learning styles" and instead framing it in terms of prior knowledge, goals, and interaction data aligns better with current educational theory. The strongest international examples should be reframed as mini-cases, detailing context, intervention, outcomes, and limitations to provide concrete insights. Additionally, for operationalizing governance, including a data-flow and consent diagram, along with a concise privacy checklist, will help translate ethical principles into actionable classroom and system practices.

## 4.2 Integrity Mechanisms within a Verification-First Workflow

While tools like detectors and watermarking can help verify originality, they should be integrated into a broader integrity framework. A verification-first workflow incorporates multiple layers of accountability:

- Prompt and Version Logs – Students must submit a detailed record of all GenAI interactions used in their work, ensuring transparency in the process.
- Oral Defense – Students are required to explain how they evaluated and integrated GenAI outputs, demonstrating their understanding and critical engagement with the material.

- Rubric-Based Evaluation – TPACK-aligned rubrics assess not only the final product but also the student's reasoning and integration, ensuring credit is awarded for intellectual engagement rather than unverified AI text.
- Supplementary Integrity Tools – Watermarking and AI detectors serve as additional support, but they should not be the sole standard for verification, emphasizing a multi-faceted approach to academic integrity.

This layered model ensures that academic rigor and innovation can coexist, providing a comprehensive approach to maintaining academic honesty in the age of GenAI. To provide a clearer understanding of the verification-first workflow for academic integrity in the context of GenAI, the following flowchart illustrates the layered stages—from prompt logging to rubric-based evaluation—alongside the role of supplementary tools such as watermarking and AI detectors. This diagram highlights how each layer reinforces transparency, accountability, and academic rigor.

*Figure 2. Verification-first workflow for ensuring academic integrity in the age of genAI*

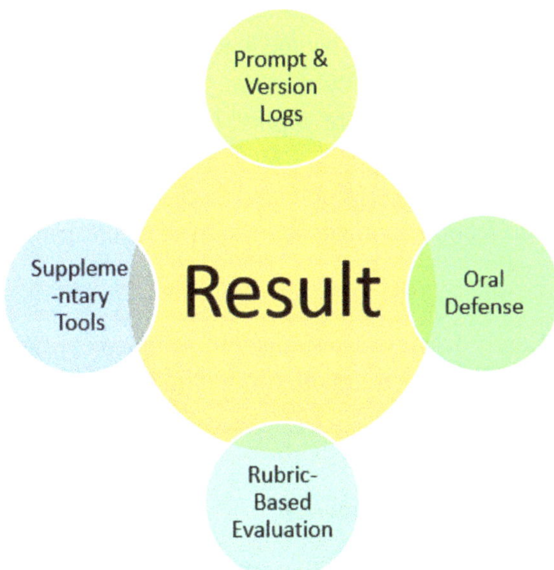

## 4.3 Operationalising Governance

Reviewer feedback emphasized the importance of translating governance principles into actionable classroom and system practices. In response, we propose two complementary instruments:

### (a) Data-Flow and Consent Diagram

A standardized data pathway ensures transparency and accountability in the use of GenAI in education. The process is broken down into six key steps:

- Input – Students provide data, including prompts and assignments, initiating the interaction with the GenAI system.
- Processing – The GenAI system processes the information using proprietary or open-source models, generating the necessary outputs.
- Storage – Data is temporarily or permanently stored on either cloud platforms or local servers, depending on system specifications.
- Access and Use – Educators access the data for assessment purposes, or the system uses it to provide adaptive feedback to students.
- Safeguards – Stringent security measures, such as encryption, anonymization, and deletion protocols, are applied to protect the integrity and privacy of student data.
- Consent – Informed consent is obtained from both students and their parents regarding the collection, storage, and use of data, ensuring transparency and ethical practices.

This flowchart clearly defines the responsibilities and roles of students, educators, and system providers, promoting trust and accountability within the GenAI-supported educational environment.

*Figure 3. Data-flow and consent diagram*

This diagram illustrates the data flow used in the collection and processing of student data in a GenAI-supported educational context. The primary goal of the diagram is to show the structured steps starting from data collection (Input), processing (Processing), storage (Storage), access and use (Access and Use), data safeguards (Safeguards), to obtaining consent from students and parents (Consent). This flow ensures transparency, accountability, and data protection, providing a clear understanding of the responsibilities of each party (students, educators, and system providers) in the process.

### (b) Privacy and Ethics Checklist

To ensure the ethical use of GenAI, educators and institutions can apply the following checklist before implementing it in classrooms:

*Table 2. Checklist for ethical use of genAI in classrooms*

| **Ethical Consideration** | **Check Criteria** |
|---|---|
| Transparency | Are students informed about how GenAI systems function and their data usage? |
| Consent | Is explicit consent obtained from students and parents for the use of their data? |
| Data Security | Is student data securely encrypted, anonymized, and periodically deleted to protect privacy? |
| Fairness | Are algorithms regularly checked for biases that may disadvantage certain student groups? |
| Pedagogical Alignment | Is GenAI used to support and enhance, rather than replace, teacher guidance and instruction? |
| Accountability | Are there clear guidelines and protocols for detecting and addressing potential misuse of GenAI? |
| Compliance | Do classroom practices align with national AI and education policies, ensuring legal and ethical conformity? |

## 4.4. Towards Ethical Literacy in Science Education

Ethics shouldn't just be abstract ideas we talk about in theory; they should be a part of how we teach every day in the classroom. As AI becomes more common in education, it's important that we think about how to use it responsibly. Technology is powerful, but without understanding the ethical side of it, we risk letting it shape learning in ways that might not be beneficial. That's why it's so important for teachers to guide students in considering the ethical impacts of the tools they're using.

A great way to help students think ethically is by introducing real-world dilemmas. For example, asking "Can AI replace teachers in science education?" gets students to reflect on the value of human teachers. While AI can help with information delivery, it lacks the emotional intelligence, creativity, and real-life experience that a teacher brings to the classroom. Discussions like this encourage students to consider what makes human involvement in learning irreplaceable.

Another issue that can be explored is how AI might misrepresent experimental data. With AI tools increasingly being used to analyze scientific data, it's important for students to understand that these systems can make mistakes—whether on purpose or by accident. It's a good opportunity for students to discuss what might happen if AI produces incorrect conclusions, and why human oversight is still necessary in these processes. Learning how to spot these issues is just as important as knowing how to use the technology itself.

As we continue to use more technology in education, teaching students critical digital literacy becomes essential. It's not just about learning to use tools like AI, but also understanding how to use them in ways that are ethical and responsible. By questioning how technology affects us, students can begin to navigate AI-driven learning environments with awareness and care. It's about making sure they know the limits of technology and its potential to influence their thoughts and actions.

These kinds of conversations also help students become more responsible digital citizens. As AI becomes a bigger part of how we learn and live, it's important that students don't just accept it at face value. Instead, they should think critically about its role and how it's shaping their world. By reflecting on these ethical issues, students can develop the skills they need to use AI in a way that benefits society while avoiding harm.

## 5. SYSTEMIC STRATEGIES AND POLICY RECOMMENDATIONS

The integration of Generative Artificial Intelligence (GenAI) into science education is a significant step forward, but it's not something that can be done in isolation. To make it effective, we need to approach it from multiple angles. This means aligning curriculum design with GenAI tools, ensuring that teachers are well-trained to use these technologies, and creating systems of governance that uphold ethical standards. It's not just about using new technology, but about using it in a way that enhances teaching and learning for everyone, regardless of their background or resources.

When thinking about how to implement GenAI in education, we must also keep in mind the diverse challenges we face locally and the lessons we can learn from other places. Around the world, different countries have taken varied approaches to integrating AI into schools, with some achieving great success and others facing barriers. By considering both international evidence and the unique challenges in our own communities, we can design strategies that not only adopt GenAI, but also ensure it benefits all students equitably, creating a more inclusive and accessible learning environment.

## 5.1 Teacher Training and Professional Development

Teachers are at the heart of successfully integrating GenAI into science education. For them to effectively use these technologies, professional development needs to go beyond just teaching the basics of the tools themselves. First, digital and AI literacy is essential. Teachers should not only understand how GenAI functions but also have a foundational grasp of its capabilities and limitations. This helps them navigate the technology confidently and use it to its fullest potential in the classroom. Without this understanding, it would be hard for teachers to make informed decisions about how GenAI can enhance their teaching and students' learning.

Second, pedagogical integration is key. Professional development should show teachers how to design engaging and meaningful lessons that blend GenAI with inquiry-based and project-driven learning. Instead of simply using AI as a supplementary tool, teachers should learn how to weave it into their curriculum in ways that make learning more interactive and authentic for students. This means teaching them how to create assessments that encourage exploration, critical thinking, and creativity, while also making sure that GenAI tools contribute to, rather than replace, human interaction and guidance.

Lastly, ethics and governance are crucial areas that can't be overlooked. Teachers must be prepared to handle complex issues like algorithmic bias, data privacy, and maintaining academic integrity in an AI-driven learning environment. It's not just about teaching students how to use these tools ethically, but also about modeling ethical behavior themselves. The best professional development models include ongoing mentoring, classroom-based practice, and peer learning cycles, ensuring that teachers receive continuous support and feedback, rather than just a one-time workshop. Teachers should also be treated as active co-designers of the curriculum, helping adapt and evaluate GenAI tools in ways that best fit the needs of their students.

## 5.2 Evaluation Standards and Assessment Rubrics

Traditional evaluation models, which primarily focus on rote recall, fall short in the context of GenAI. A revised assessment framework should address the following key aspects:

- Use TPACK-based rubrics to evaluate both scientific understanding and the meaningful integration of GenAI tools in the learning process (Lee & Zhai, 2024).

- Encourage critical engagement by requiring students to justify their choice of prompts, assess the quality of AI responses, and align those outputs with established scientific consensus. This process fosters deeper understanding rather than simple content recall.
- Adopt a verification-first integrity workflow: This workflow should include prompt/version logs, oral defenses, and clear rubric criteria, all supported by AI detectors. Such an approach ensures students are evaluated on their reasoning and intellectual integrity, rather than relying on uncritical AI use.

These revised frameworks ensure that students are not merely rewarded for regurgitating information, but for demonstrating critical thinking, ethical awareness, and the ability to use GenAI meaningfully within an educational context.

## 5.3 Multi-Stakeholder Collaboration and National Repositories

Curriculum transformation cannot be achieved by schools alone. It requires cross-sector collaboration to create comprehensive and sustainable change. Several key stakeholders play vital roles in this transformation process, including:

- Teachers and Schools – Teachers at all educational levels have a central role in designing and delivering learning activities that are relevant to local contexts and students' needs. They need to be empowered with continuous training and access to educational tools that support the integration of technology, including artificial intelligence (AI), to adapt teaching materials to contemporary developments and the diverse characteristics of students across regions.
- Universities and Research Institutions – Higher education institutions and research bodies are responsible for generating and disseminating evidence-based practices that enhance the effectiveness of teaching and learning. Research in pedagogy and educational technology should be translated into modules and frameworks that can be directly applied by teachers in the classroom. Collaboration between academics and practitioners is essential to ensure that the latest theories and methodologies are effectively implemented in educational settings.
- Policymakers – Policymakers, both at local and national levels, must develop regulations that support curriculum transformation. Policies that promote teacher training, the integration of technology into education, and the provision of adequate infrastructure are critical to ensuring the success of these changes. Additionally, regulations should encourage equity in education,

ensuring that all schools, whether in urban or rural areas, benefit from the reforms.

- Technology Companies – Technology companies play a significant role in providing ethical, open, and affordable educational tools. Collaboration with the education sector is vital to ensure that the technologies developed are accessible to all teachers and students, without exception. Moreover, technology should be designed with ethical principles, data privacy, and sustainability in mind, so that it does not exacerbate inequalities in the education system.

One promising model for fostering collaboration and innovation is the development of national repositories where teachers can share AI-assisted modules. These platforms would serve as spaces for teachers from different regions to exchange resources, collaborate, and promote innovation in teaching. By providing wider access to relevant and innovative educational materials, such repositories not only enhance equity by ensuring quality educational content is available to all but also offer teachers the opportunity to adapt to technological advancements in a local and contextual manner. Such initiatives contribute to creating a more equitable, inclusive, and sustainable learning ecosystem across regions, from cities to remote areas (Moura et al., 2025).

## 5.4 AI Literacy Labs and Ethical Exploration

To cultivate ethical and critical literacy, schools should establish AI Literacy Labs, providing informal learning spaces where students and teachers can explore and understand the complexities of artificial intelligence. These labs offer a safe and dynamic environment where participants can:

- Experiment with GenAI tools: Students and teachers can interact with cutting-edge AI technologies, gaining hands-on experience in a controlled setting. This allows them to explore the potential and limitations of AI, while developing a deeper understanding of how these tools can be used effectively and ethically.
- Analyze bias, misinformation, and the accuracy of AI outputs: A critical aspect of AI literacy is learning how to assess and question the reliability of AI-generated content. In these labs, participants can examine various AI systems for inherent biases, misinformation, or inaccuracies, and learn how these factors influence the outputs they encounter in everyday life.
- Engage in ethical debates about the role of AI in society: By discussing the societal implications of AI, students and teachers can explore the ethical challenges that come with AI integration in various fields. These discussions

could cover issues like privacy, equity, and the potential for AI to replace human jobs, helping to foster a well-rounded, responsible understanding of AI's role in shaping the future.

By embedding AI ethics within both the formal curriculum and extracurricular AI Literacy Labs, schools can foster responsible adoption, critical inquiry, and the development of a thoughtful, ethical approach to the use of AI tools. This approach ensures that students are not just passive consumers of technology but active, informed participants in the ongoing dialogue about how AI should be integrated into society (Jemetz et al., 2025).

## 5.5 Equity and Infrastructure

Equitable access is an essential foundation for achieving systemic transformation in education. To ensure that all students benefit from the opportunities offered by digital technologies, policies must prioritize:

- Subsidies for devices and connectivity in disadvantaged schools: Ensuring that every student has access to the necessary technology is critical for creating an equitable learning environment. By providing subsidies for devices and internet connectivity, governments can bridge the digital divide, allowing students in underserved areas to fully participate in modern educational practices.
- Expansion of secure, low-cost cloud platforms tailored for education: Digital platforms that are affordable and secure are vital for enabling schools to integrate technology into their classrooms. These platforms should support both learning management systems (LMS) and interactive learning tools, providing teachers with the resources they need to deliver engaging and effective lessons while maintaining student data privacy and security.
- National strategies for digital justice, ensuring that rural and remote areas are not left behind: A comprehensive national strategy for digital justice is necessary to address the specific challenges faced by rural and remote areas, where access to technology and high-speed internet may be limited. These strategies should focus on infrastructure development, digital literacy programs, and localized content to ensure that all students, regardless of geographic location, have equal access to educational opportunities.

Without addressing equity, the potential of GenAI to enhance learning could become a source of disparity, deepening rather than closing educational gaps. As AI tools and digital resources become integral to education, it is crucial to ensure that every student, regardless of their socioeconomic status or geographic location, has the same opportunity to benefit from these advancements (UNESCO, 2023; Van Dijk, 2020).

## 5.6 Policy Alignment and Governance

Finally, systemic transformation in education requires robust governance frameworks that address the ethical, legal, and practical dimensions of integrating GenAI into teaching and learning. These frameworks should:

- Integrate AI ethics into national curricula: Embedding AI ethics within national curricula ensures that students, from an early stage, understand the ethical implications of AI technologies. This inclusion should not only focus on technical aspects but also on the societal, cultural, and moral issues surrounding AI. Educators should be equipped with the knowledge to discuss topics like bias, fairness, privacy, and accountability, fostering responsible use of AI tools among students.
- Establish privacy checklists and consent protocols (see Chapter 4): Protecting student data is critical as GenAI systems are increasingly used in education. Governments should mandate privacy checklists that schools must follow when adopting AI tools, ensuring compliance with data protection laws. Additionally, consent protocols should be implemented to guarantee that students and parents are informed about how their data will be used, stored, and shared, providing transparency and building trust.
- Encourage empirical evaluation of policies to ensure sustainability and responsiveness: Policymakers should foster a culture of continuous improvement by encouraging the empirical evaluation of policies related to AI in education. This involves assessing the effectiveness, impact, and sustainability of AI implementation and adapting policies in response to emerging needs. Such evaluations will ensure that GenAI practices remain relevant, effective, and responsive to the changing landscape of education.

Governments should not only regulate but also incentivize schools and teachers to adopt innovative, ethical, and evidence-based GenAI practices. This can be achieved through funding opportunities, professional development programs, and recognition for schools that successfully integrate AI in a responsible and impactful way. Incentivizing innovation will help accelerate the adoption of GenAI tools while ensuring that they are used in ways that are ethical, sustainable, and beneficial to students.

## 7. CONCLUSION OF POLICY STRATEGIES

Taken together, these strategies illustrate that the integration of GenAI is not merely a technological shift but a comprehensive systemic educational reform. It involves rethinking how we teach, learn, and assess knowledge, ensuring that the educational landscape is prepared to equip students for the future. Key elements of this transformation include:

- Teacher Empowerment: By providing educators with the tools, training, and support needed to effectively integrate GenAI into their teaching, we can ensure that they are equipped to lead the next generation of learners. Teachers must be seen as facilitators of critical thinking, guiding students not only to understand AI technologies but also to use them responsibly and ethically.
- Revised Assessment: Moving beyond traditional methods of rote memorization, assessments should reflect the evolving demands of the modern world. GenAI can help shift the focus of evaluations to more authentic, inquiry-based learning outcomes. Students should be assessed on their ability to engage with AI tools meaningfully, think critically about their outputs, and apply their learning in real-world contexts.
- Ethical Governance: A governance framework that prioritizes AI ethics, data privacy, and responsible use is crucial in ensuring that GenAI tools are used in ways that promote fairness, equity, and transparency. Ethical governance will guide educators, students, and technology providers in navigating the complexities of AI implementation while upholding moral and legal standards.
- Equity-driven Infrastructure: Ensuring equitable access to GenAI tools and resources is essential in preventing further educational divides. Infrastructure investments in devices, connectivity, and digital platforms tailored for education must focus on providing all students, regardless of their socioeconomic background or geographic location, with the same opportunities to benefit from technological advancements.

By integrating these strategies, GenAI has the potential to bridge the gap between theory and practice in science education, transforming the way knowledge is both disseminated and applied. It can help students develop into adaptive, critical, and ethical scientists who are prepared to confront the challenges of the future, both in their academic careers and in their roles as active contributors to society.

## REFERENCES


Biggs, J. (1996). Enhancing teaching through constructive alignment. *Higher Education, 32*(3), 347–364. DOI: 10.1007/BF00138871

Chen, T.. (2023). Artificial Intelligence in Adaptive Learning: A Review and Future Directions. *Educational Technology Research and Development, 71*(2), 353–370. DOI: 10.1007/s11423-022-10194-8

Chen, X., Xie, H., Zou, D., & Wang, F. L. (2023). A systematic review of AI in education: Implications for curriculum design and teacher development. *Computers & Education, 192*, 104633. DOI: 10.1016/j.compedu.2022.104633

Dolezal, N., & Motschnig, R. (2024). AI-supported personalization in science-based project learning: Case studies from European schools. *Education Sciences, 14*(2), 211. DOI: 10.3390/educsci14020211

Dolezal, N., & Motschnig, R. (2024). The Impact of AI-Generated Instructional Videos on Problem-Based Learning. *Education Sciences, 14*(1), 102. DOI: 10.3390/educsci14010102

dos Anjos, J. B., Teixeira, M. R., & Ribeiro, A. S. (2024). Exploring ChatGPT in science education: Potential and limitations for conceptual learning. *Journal of Science Education and Technology, 33*(2), 211–229.

. dos Anjos, J. R., de Souza, M. G., de Andrade Neto, A. S., & de Souza, B. C. (2024). An analysis of the generative AI use as analyst in qualitative research in science education. *Revista Pesquisa Qualitativa, 12*(30), 01–29. DOI: 10.33361/RPQ.2024.v.12.n.30.724

Gavira Durón, M., & Jiménez-Preciado, M. Á. (2025). *AI-enhanced Chemistry Learning: Evidence from Classroom-Based Simulations. Science Education International*, 36(2), 200–215. https://doi.org/DOI: 10.20362/sei2025.200215

Guettala, M., Bourekkache, S., Kazar, O., & Harous, S. (2024). Generative Artificial Intelligence in Education: Advancing Adaptive and Personalized Learning. *Acta Informatica Pragensia, 13*(3), 460–489. DOI: 10.18267/j.aip.235

Holmes, W., Bialik, M., & Fadel, C. (2022). *Artificial Intelligence in Education: Promises and Implications for Teaching and Learning*. Center for Curriculum Redesign.

Hwang, H. S., Zhu, L. C., & Cui, Q. (2023). Development and Validation of a Digital Literacy Scale in the Artificial Intelligence Era for College Students. *KSII Transactions on Internet and Information Systems, 17*(8). Advance online publication. DOI: 10.3837/tiis.2023.08.016

Jayachandran, P., Kumar, S., & Anitha, S. (2024). Preparing future scientists: Integrating AI tools into secondary science curricula. *Science Education International, 35*(1), 45–56.

Jemetz, M., Dolezal, D., & Motschnig, R. (2025). *Secondary Teachers' Self-perceived AI Competences in Relation to Renowned European Digital Competence Frameworks* (pp. 3–17). DOI: 10.1007/978-3-031-73474-8_1

Lee, G.-G., & Zhai, X. (2024). Using ChatGPT for Science Learning: A Study on Pre-service Teachers' Lesson Planning. *IEEE Transactions on Learning Technologies, 17*, 1643–1660. DOI: 10.1109/TLT.2024.3401457

Lee, S. H., Park, J., & Kim, Y. (2023). Inquiry-Based Science Learning Supported by Generative AI: An Experimental Study in Secondary Education. *Asia-Pacific Science Education, 9*(1), 33–51.

Luckin, R.. (2021). *Artificial Intelligence and the Future of Teaching and Learning*. U.S. Department of Education, Office of Educational Technology.

Luckin, R., Holmes, W., Griffiths, M., & Forcier, L. B. (2022). *Intelligence Unleashed: An Argument for AI in Education*. OECD Education Working Papers. https://doi.org/DOI: 10.1787/5jlz8t8700j8-en

Molloy, K.. (2022). Barriers to conceptual understanding in high school science. *International Journal of Science Education, 44*(1), 56–73. DOI: 10.1080/09500693.2021.1964825

Moura, D., Oliveira, M., & Silva, T. (2025). GenAI for learning science: A framework for multimodal understanding in physics and biology. *Educational Technology Research and Development, 73*(1), 55–70.

Moura, L., Barcaui, A., & Payer, R. (2025). AI and Financial Fraud Prevention: Mapping the Trends and Challenges Through a Bibliometric Lens. *Journal of Risk and Financial Management, 18*(6), 323. DOI: 10.3390/jrfm18060323

Musaev, A., Kadyrov, B., & Ospanova, N. (2025). Rethinking science education in the AI era: Challenges and innovations. *International Journal of STEM Education, 12*, 10.

Olney, A. M.. (2024). Enhancing Science Learning with AI-generated Molecular Simulations. *Computers & Education: Artificial Intelligence*, *6*, 100093. DOI: 10.1016/j.caeai.2024.100093

Olney, A. M., Chounta, I.-A., Liu, Z., Santos, O. C., & Bittencourt, I. I. (Eds.). (2024). *Artificial Intelligence in Education. Posters and Late Breaking Results, Workshops and Tutorials, Industry and Innovation Tracks, Practitioners, Doctoral Consortium and Blue Sky* (Vol. 2150). Springer Nature Switzerland., DOI: 10.1007/978-3-031-64312-5

Sun, Z.. (2024). Narrative-Driven AI Simulations for Learning Chemical Processes. *Educational Technology Research and Development*, *72*(1), 102–120. DOI: 10.1007/s11423-023-10212-6

UNESCO. (2022). *Artificial Intelligence and Education: Guidance for policy-makers*. United Nations Educational, Scientific and Cultural Organization.

. UNESCO. (2023). *Global Education Monitoring Report 2023: Technology in education: A tool on whose terms?* GEM Report UNESCO. DOI: 10.54676/UZQV8501

Van Dijk, J. (2020). *The digital divide* (2nd ed.). John Wiley & Sons.

Zawacki-Richter, O., Marín, V. I., Bond, M., & Gouverneur, F. (2023). Systematic review of research on artificial intelligence applications in higher education – where are the educators? *International Journal of Educational Technology in Higher Education*, *20*(1), 1–48. DOI: 10.1186/s41239-023-00412-y

Zhang, Y., & Zhang, X. (2024). Opportunities and challenges of using generative AI to personalize education. *Frontiers in Artificial Intelligence*, *7*, 1460651. DOI: 10.3389/frai.2024.1460651

Zhou, Y.. (2024). Algorithmic Fairness in AI-Driven Learning Environments: A Critical Review. *AI and Ethics*, *5*(1), 88–103. DOI: 10.1007/s43681-023-00279-w

## KEY TERMS AND DEFINITIONS

**Adaptive Learning:** An instructional approach that uses AI to modify content delivery based on learners' progress and responses. GenAI tools provide personalised pacing, scaffolded feedback, and differentiated instruction.

**AI-Assisted Simulation:** A dynamic learning environment created with the help of AI to replicate real-world scientific phenomena, allowing students to experiment virtually and build deeper conceptual understanding.

**Authentic Assessment:** An evaluation method that focuses on students' real-world application of scientific thinking, including problem identification, hypothesis formulation, and data-driven conclusions. GenAI supports this by simulating scientific investigations.

**Contextual Integration:** The incorporation of GenAI tools within specific thematic or problem-based contexts, such as climate change, to enhance relevance and engagement during science instruction.

**Generative Artificial Intelligence (GenAI):** A type of artificial intelligence capable of creating new content such as text, images, or simulations based on prompts, data patterns, or contexts. In education, GenAI enhances learning through multimodal, adaptive, and interactive instructional methods.

**Inquiry-Based Science Education (IBSE):** A student-centred approach to science learning that involves asking questions, forming hypotheses, conducting experiments, and interpreting data. GenAI can support IBSE by simulating experiments and facilitating data analysis.

**Multimodal Learning:** An instructional approach that uses multiple formats—such as visual, textual, auditory, and interactive media—to improve comprehension and retention, particularly effective when supported by GenAI technologies.

**Pedagogical Gap:** A discrepancy between technological innovation and its actual use in teaching practice. Despite GenAI's capabilities, many teachers are unprepared or unsupported to integrate it into instructional design effectively.

**Science Curriculum Transformation:** A systematic overhaul of science education content, pedagogy, and assessment to address emerging challenges and technologies such as climate change, pandemics, and AI integration, while fostering higher-order thinking and ethical reasoning.

Chapter 6

# Transforming Science Education Through Generative AI Through Adaptive Learning, Ethical Practices, and Inclusive Curriculum Design

**Dipta Gomes**
https://orcid.org/0000-0003-3019-6051
*American International University-Bangladesh, Bangladesh*

**Saikat Baul**
*American International University-Bangladesh, Bangladesh*

**Jubayer Ahamed**
https://orcid.org/0000-0003-2076-9194
*American International University-Bangladesh, Bangladesh*

**Dip Nandi**
*American International University-Bangladesh, Bangladesh*

## ABSTRACT

*This chapter explores the integration of GenAI into STEM education with a primary focus on Science education. It examines how GenAI can revolutionize teaching and learning by providing adaptive learning environments, personalized assessments, and real-time feedback that cater to the diverse needs of students also ensuring the*

DOI: 10.4018/979-8-3373-2913-0.ch006

*ethical challenges associated with the implementation of GenAI, including concerns around bias, transparency, data privacy, and academic integrity. The chapter emphasizes the importance of balancing technological innovation with ethical practices to ensure equitable access and responsible use of GenAI tools. Looking ahead, the chapter outlines key future directions, including the refinement of adaptive learning tools and the need for AI literacy programs for educators. The chapter concludes by highlighting the potential of GenAI to transform science education while ensuring that it is used in ways that promote fairness, inclusivity, and accountability.*

## 1. INTRODUCTION

The landscape of modern education is rapidly being reshaped through generative artificial intelligence (GenAI) by providing dynamic, creative, and adaptive learning environments (Law, 2024). GenAI can be defined as a collection of algorithms that can utilize data like text, audio, video, and images to construct new content for further findings and investigation (Mittal et al., 2024). In the context of science-related subjects, where conceptual understanding, data analysis, and inquiry-based learning are crucial, GenAI offers transformative opportunities. Its capacity to generate personalized content, real-time feedback, and customized learning pathways positions it as a powerful tool for addressing diverse learner needs and promoting deeper engagement. (Zhai, 2023). Despite huge enhancements of the dynamics in its growing influence, there remains a gap in consolidated frameworks and structured guidance for integrating GenAI into science education in ethical, inclusive, and pedagogically sound ways (Baidoo-Anu & Ansah, 2023). This proposed book chapter aims to fill this gap by exploring both theoretical and practical dimensions of GenAI's role in science education through four core strands which includes Adaptive/ITS with knowledge tracing, AI-driven formative assessment and feedback, GenAI–enabled scientific reasoning and data visualization and Ethics and governance in higher education. Here the chapter also demonstrates evidence-based design patterns and tertiary science case studies that translate theoretical insights into actionable classroom strategies for personalized, inclusive, and authentic learning experiences.

### Core Concepts

The application of GenAI in science education is grounded in several well-established learning theories that emphasize active, student-centric, and adaptive instruction:

- **Generative Artificial Intelligence (GenAI):** Generative Artificial Intelligence (GenAI) refers to AI systems designed to create new content based on patterns learned from existing data. Unlike traditional AI, which primarily focuses on classification, prediction, or rule-based tasks, GenAI can generate novel outputs, such as text, images, simulations, and even music (Goodfellow et al., 2014). GenAI aligns with constructivist principles by enabling learners to build their own knowledge structures through exploration, experimentation, and interaction with AI-generated content such as simulations, models, and adaptive feedback (Lourenço, 2012).
- **Adaptive Learning:** Adaptive learning (AL) refers to instructional methods and technologies that modify the delivery of content based on individual learner characteristics, performance, and preferences. GenAI embodies adaptive learning by dynamically adjusting content and pacing in response to ongoing learner performance and preferences (Bach et al., 2024). In science education, where students often grapple with complex concepts and varying levels of prior knowledge, adaptive learning systems are particularly valuable (Walkington, 2013).
- **Knowledge Tracing:** Knowledge tracing refers to the process of modelling and tracking a learner's evolving knowledge state over time. By analysing interactions with learning content, knowledge tracing algorithms predict the learner's ability to answer future questions correctly, allowing the system to adjust its teaching methods based on the learner's progress (Papanikolaou et al., 2003).
- **Universal Design for Learning (UDL):** GenAI offers multiple means of engagement, representation, and expression, supporting inclusive learning environments that meet the diverse needs of students, including those with disabilities (Moore, 2007).

## Chapter Roadmap

This chapter provides a comprehensive exploration of Generative Artificial Intelligence (GenAI) in tertiary science education by first defining and contextualizing core concepts such as GenAI, adaptive learning, knowledge tracing, and Universal Design for Learning (UDL). It then presents a systematic "State of the Field" organized around four key strands: adaptive and intelligent tutoring systems (ITS) with learner modelling, AI-enabled formative assessment and feedback mechanisms, the application of GenAI in scientific reasoning and data visualization (Cooper, 2023), and the ethical and governance challenges within higher education. Following this foundational review, the chapter illustrates evidence-based classroom strategies and detailed tertiary science case studies that translate theory into practical instructional design patterns. Finally, it addresses pragmatic implementation considerations including governance frameworks, verification workflows to ensure academic integrity, accessibility guidelines rooted in UDL, and evaluative models to support sustainable, responsible integration of GenAI in science curricula (Selwyn, 2022). This roadmap guides readers through a coherent and rigorous synthesis aimed at enhancing understanding and adoption of GenAI within the university science education landscape.

### Scope and Search Approach

The chapter concentrates exclusively on tertiary science education contexts along with integration of GenAI. A systematic literature review has been carried out across databases including Scopus, Web of Science and ERIC with publication dated from 2010 to 2025 (some pioneer papers of earlier versions of ITS has been included) where focus has been concentrated on empirical studies, reviews and recognized theoretical contributions of GenAI, adaptive learning, formative assessment and AI ethics. Studies that are based on primary and secondary (K-12) education have been incorporated solely when explicitly bridging implications to higher education.

## 2. ADAPTIVE LEARNING, INTELLIGENT TUTORING SYSTEMS (ITS) & KNOWLEDGE TRACING

Generative AI (GAI) offers several advantages over traditional educational systems, addressing many of their shortcomings. One key benefit is that GAI fosters curiosity in students which is very crucial for academic growth. While traditional classrooms struggle to meet the individual needs of every student, GAI provides personalized attention, tracks progress and supports learners based on their capabilities (Mittal et al. 2024). It can also adapt to each student's preferred learning style, something difficult for human teachers to achieve in large classes. Additionally, GAI helps teachers by streamlining tasks such as creating quizzes and assignments and assisting with grading, which are otherwise time-consuming (Zheng et al., 2024).

Generative AI (GenAI) offers a powerful enhancement to adaptive learning by creating personalized educational experiences in real time. Platforms using large language models (LLMs) can adjust instructional content based on the nuances of a student's questions or errors, thereby supporting individualized learning trajectories (Kasneci et al., 2023). This personalization fosters more meaningful engagement, as students receive support that aligns with their cognitive needs and learning pace. As science educators increasingly recognize the importance of differentiated instruction, GenAI-powered adaptive learning tools offer promising solutions for scalable, equitable teaching (Holmes et al., 2019).

A conventional model of an AL system consists of three parts: a learner module, a content module, and an instructor module. The descriptions of the modules are provided below, and an illustration of AL is given in Figure 1.

- *The learner* component captures information about the learner, including what they know, their skills, preferences, motivation, emotional state, and other individual characteristics. It provides the foundation for tailoring learning experiences based on the student's unique profile. By continuously updating this profile through learner interactions, the system can adjust instruction to meet the student's evolving needs (Brusilovsky & Millán, 2007).
- *The content module* represents the subject matter or knowledge base of the course. It maps out key concepts, their relationships, and dependencies, organizing them into a structure that guides how content is delivered and how learners progress through material (Nkambou et al., 2010).
- *The instructor module* defines the rules and algorithms that determine how instruction is customized. It decides *what* content to present, *when* to present it, and *how* to adjust factors like pacing, sequence, and instructional format. As the core of the adaptive process, this module ensures that learning is responsive to both the learner's profile and the structure of the content. It bridges the learner's profile and the domain knowledge, deciding how learning should proceed to optimize outcomes (Papanikolaou et al., 2003).

*Figure 1. Adaptive learning model illustration*

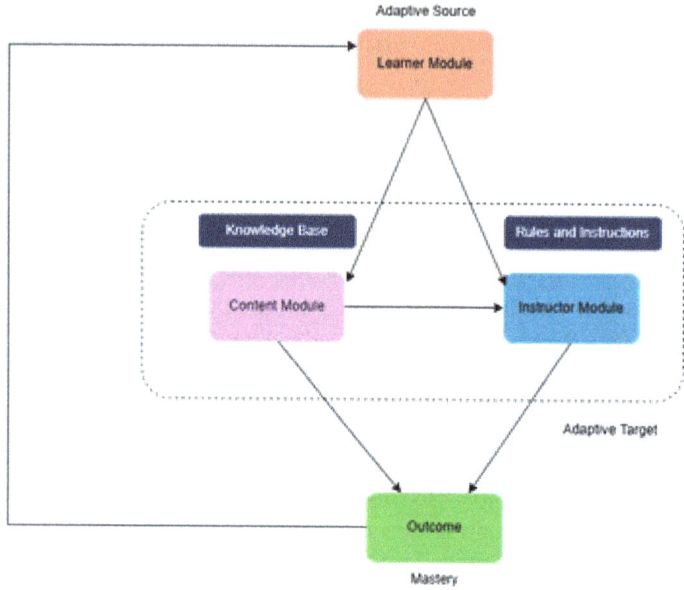


## Intelligent Tutoring Systems (ITS)

Intelligent Tutoring Systems (ITS) (Gomes, 2024) are a type of adaptive learning system that provide personalized instruction by simulating the role of a tutor. ITS are designed to recognize individual learner's needs, weaknesses, and strengths, and to adapt the content, pacing, and feedback accordingly. Unlike traditional learning systems, ITS monitor student progress in real-time and offer immediate, personalized responses, ensuring that students receive tailored guidance.

ITS are typically comprised of three key components:

- **Domain Knowledge**: The subject-specific content that the ITS aims to teach.
- **Student Model**: A representation of the learner's knowledge state, including their strengths and weaknesses. This model is updated dynamically as students interact with the system.
- **Tutoring Model**: The part of the ITS that determines the appropriate actions or interventions based on the student's model, offering hints, feedback, or even changes in the pace or difficulty of the material.

A study investigating the use of ITS in higher education science courses found that students who used an ITS for problem-solving performed better on exams than those who received traditional instruction. This was particularly noticeable in complex advanced topics where learners benefited from the personalized feedback and problem-solving strategies provided by the ITS (Holmes et al., 2019). ITS have been shown to increase student engagement by offering problems that are adapted to the learner's current understanding.

ALEKS (Assessment and Learning in Knowledge Spaces) is a well-known ITS used in higher education for subjects such as mathematics, chemistry, and biology. It helps students review concepts they struggle with while advancing faster through areas they've mastered. Research shows that students using ALEKS consistently outperform peers who use traditional study methods in terms of both retention and test scores (Falmagne et al., 2006).

## Knowledge Tracing

Bayesian Knowledge Tracing (BKT) models student knowledge as a latent variable, updated based on observed correctness of responses. It employs a hidden Markov model to estimate the probability of a learner mastering a skill over time. This probabilistic approach allows for dynamic assessment of student progress, adapting instruction accordingly (Bulut et al., 2023).

Deep Knowledge Tracing (DKT) extends BKT by utilizing deep learning techniques, particularly recurrent neural networks, to model temporal dependencies in student interactions. DKT captures complex patterns in learning behaviour, offering a more nuanced understanding of knowledge acquisition (Zhou et al., 2025). Recent advances of Deep Knowledge Tracing (DKT) models include Sparse Attention Techniques (Zhou et al., 2025) which addresses data sparsity issues in DKT models, improving performance in scenarios with limited student interaction data. Diffusion Models enhance DKT by generating synthetic educational data, improving model robustness and performance (Lu et al., 2025). The enhancement further progress towards State-Space Models (Christie et al., 2024) which integrate uncertainty-preserving mechanisms into DKT, combining deep learning with Bayesian state-space models for more accurate knowledge state estimation.

## Empirical Evidence in Tertiary Science Education

A recent review encompassing 69 studies (Du Plooy et al., 2024) revealed that personalized adaptive learning positively impacts academic performance and student engagement. Pre-knowledge quizzes were commonly used to activate adaptive content delivery, with platforms like McGraw-Hill's Connect LearnSmart and Moodle being frequently utilized. Research at Historically Black Colleges and Universities (HBCUs) (Kuo et al., 2024) applied DKT models to a dataset of over

350,000 learning records. The study found that models such as SAKT and KQN outperformed others in predicting student outcomes, highlighting the potential of DKT in STEM education. An investigation into adaptive learning environments using learning analytics dashboards (Villegas-Ch et al., 2025) demonstrated that instructor interventions could enhance students' self-regulation abilities and academic performance, particularly in science education contexts.

By continuously assessing student knowledge states, adaptive systems can tailor learning experiences to individual needs, promoting deeper understanding of complex scientific concepts. ITS provide immediate, targeted feedback, enabling students to address misconceptions promptly and reinforcing correct understanding. Adaptive systems can present challenges that are appropriately matched to a student's current level, maintaining motivation and fostering a growth mindset. An evidence map of formative assessment and feedback has been presented in Table 1.

*Table 1. Evidence map for formative assessment and feedback*

| Study/ Source | Technology/ Model | Key Findings | Discipline/ Application | Impact on Learning |
|---|---|---|---|---|
| (Kasneci et al., 2023) | Generative AI (GenAI) in Adaptive Learning | GenAI-powered adaptive systems personalize content in real-time based on student interactions and feedback. | Various STEM disciplines (e.g., physics, chemistry) | Increased engagement and personalized learning paths that foster deeper understanding. Improved learning trajectories. |
| (Holmes et al., 2019) | Intelligent Tutoring Systems (ITS) | Students using ITS in physics problem-solving performed better than those with traditional instruction. | Physics (quantum mechanics, thermodynamics) | Improved exam performance and mastery of complex topics due to immediate feedback and problem-solving strategies. |
| (Falmagne et al., 2006) | ALEKS (ITS) | ALEKS adaptive system helped students master foundational concepts before advancing to more complex topics. | Mathematics, Chemistry, Biology | Higher retention rates and test scores compared to traditional learning methods. Focused on areas where students struggle. |
| (Bulut et al., 2023) | Bayesian Knowledge Tracing (BKT) | BKT models estimate student mastery over time, adjusting instruction based on learner progress. | STEM education | Personalized feedback with dynamic assessment to track student understanding and adjust learning content. |

continued on following page

*Table 1. Continued*

| Study/ Source | Technology/ Model | Key Findings | Discipline/ Application | Impact on Learning |
|---|---|---|---|---|
| (Kuo et al., 2024) | Deep Knowledge Tracing (DKT) | DKT models (e.g., SAKT, KQN) predict student outcomes more accurately than other models, enhancing personalized learning. | STEM disciplines | Enhanced prediction of student performance and tailored content delivery that improves engagement and learning efficiency. |
| (Zhou et al., 2025) | Sparse Attention Techniques in DKT | Sparse attention techniques improve DKT performance in low-data scenarios, increasing model robustness. | Various STEM disciplines | Improved learning predictions in situations with sparse data, enabling better learning path adjustments. |
| (Lu et al., 2025) | Diffusion Models for DKT | Diffusion models generate synthetic educational data, enhancing DKT model performance and robustness. | Science-based learning | Enhanced model accuracy and reliable learning predictions even in low-interaction environments. |
| (Christie et al., 2024) | State-Space Models in DKT | Combining Bayesian models with deep learning techniques improves knowledge state estimation, addressing uncertainty. | STEM education | More accurate knowledge tracing by integrating uncertainty preservation, leading to better instructional adaptation. |
| (Du Plooy et al., 2024) | Personalized Adaptive Learning Systems | Adaptive learning systems (e.g., LearnSmart, Moodle) activate content delivery based on pre-knowledge quizzes, positively impacting engagement and performance. | General STEM education | Positive academic performance and increased engagement from personalized, adaptive pathways based on pre-assessments. |
| (Villegas-Ch et al., 2025) | Learning Analytics Dashboards in Adaptive Systems | Instructor interventions through analytics dashboards enhanced students' self-regulation and academic performance in adaptive environments. | Science education | Improved self-regulation, academic performance, and better use of adaptive learning tools through instructor feedback. |

## 3. AI-SUPPORTED FORMATIVE ASSESSMENT AND FEEDBACK

Formative assessment plays a critical role in the learning process by providing ongoing feedback that helps learners understand their progress, identify areas of difficulty, and adjust their learning strategies. Unlike summative assessments, which measure learning outcomes at the end of a learning period, formative assessment is intended to improve learning through regular feedback during the learning process. Artificial Intelligence (AI)-supported formative assessment systems leverage technologies such as Natural Language Processing (NLP), machine learning, and predictive analytics to personalize feedback and guide learners through adaptive learning paths. These systems assess learners' performance in real time, providing individualized feedback that is customized to their specific learning needs. AI-powered formative assessments are particularly beneficial in large-scale courses and complex subjects like science education, where immediate, personalized feedback can significantly improve learning outcomes and engagement.

## Core concepts

- **Formative Assessment:** Formative assessments are continuous, informal evaluations aimed at providing timely feedback to guide students' learning progress. These assessments help instructors identify areas where students are struggling and allow for adjustments to instructional strategies Formative assessments are continuous, informal evaluations aimed at providing timely feedback to guide students' learning progress. These assessments help instructors identify areas where students are struggling and allow for adjustments to instructional strategies (Black & Wiliam, 1998).
- **AI-Powered Feedback**: GenAI systems offer real-time, tailored feedback based on students' interactions with the material. These systems adapt to students' learning styles, preferences, and prior knowledge, delivering hints, explanations, and corrective suggestions to guide students toward mastery (Holmes & Luckin, 2016). Unlike traditional assessment systems, AI-powered feedback is dynamic, adjusting based on the evolving needs of the student.

In a study by (Holmes et al., 2019), it was found that AI-driven formative feedback significantly enhanced students' problem-solving skills by offering personalized, context-aware hints and scaffolding. Their study on AI-assisted problem-solving in STEM courses indicated that AI feedback is particularly effective in helping students who are struggling with specific concepts, guiding them through complex problem-solving processes step-by-step. (Bulut & Wongvorachan, 2022) examined the role of Natural Language Processing (NLP) in AI-based formative assessments and found that NLP algorithms could generate personalized responses to students' open-ended answers. This allowed AI systems to provide deeper, more insightful feedback that fostered improved understanding, especially in complex subjects such as science and mathematics.

In their 2022 study, (Holstein & Aleven, 2022) showed that real-time quizzes powered by AI significantly boosted student engagement with course material. These AI-powered quizzes adjusted the difficulty of questions based on student performance, ensuring that students were neither bored by repetitive easy questions nor overwhelmed by too-difficult ones. This constant adjustment made the quizzes more engaging and tailored to each student's needs, ultimately leading to enhanced retention and conceptual understanding. (Yildirim-Erbasli & Bulut, 2023) also demonstrated through a meta-analysis that AI-supported formative assessments in higher education were linked to moderate to large effect sizes in improving student engagement and learning outcomes (d = 0.55). The review concluded that real-time quizzes, which allow students to track their own progress, play a vital role in enhancing motivation and achievement, especially in science courses that require critical thinking and problem-solving skills.

(Kelley & Wenzel, 2025) explored how AI-supported assessments, particularly those involving simulations and interactive problem-solving tasks, can foster critical thinking. AI-powered tools encourage students to engage in deeper analysis and reflection, challenging them to justify their reasoning and identify potential errors in their thinking. Their study found that AI tools are effective in promoting higher-order thinking skills, particularly in STEM disciplines, where complex problem-solving is essential. In a study by (Min et al., 2025), AI systems were shown to enhance students' ability to analyse and synthesize scientific data. By providing immediate, constructive feedback on students' data interpretations and modelling work, AI systems helped students improve their scientific reasoning and develop critical thinking skills necessary for higher-level learning in science and engineering fields. Evidence Map for formative assessment and feedback has been illustrated in Table 2.

*Table 2. Evidence map for formative assessment and feedback*

| Claim | Reference | Population | Effect Size | Limits |
|---|---|---|---|---|
| AI-driven formative feedback significantly enhances problem-solving skills | (Holmes et al., 2019) | STEM (University) | Large (d = 0.75) | Focus on specific STEM disciplines, small sample size |
| NLP algorithms generate personalized responses to open-ended student answers, fostering deeper understanding | (Bulut & Wongvorachan, 2022) | University Science | Moderate (d = 0.65) | Limited to open-ended assignments in STEM |
| Real-time quizzes powered by AI boost student engagement by adjusting question difficulty | (Holstein & Aleven, 2022) | University Science | Large (d = 0.8) | Limited to certain STEM fields, cross-disciplinary validity not tested |
| AI-supported formative assessments improve student motivation and learning outcomes | (Bulut & Wongvorachan, 2022) | Higher Education (Mixed) | Moderate (d = 0.55) | Focused on real-time quizzes, limited scope in STEM fields |
| AI simulations foster critical thinking by encouraging deeper analysis and reflection | (Kelley & Wenzel, 2025) | STEM (Tertiary) | Moderate (d = 0.7) | Limited to simulation-based tasks, specific STEM focus |
| AI systems improve scientific reasoning and critical thinking skills through immediate feedback on data interpretations | (Min et al., 2025) | STEM (University) | Large (d = 0.85) | Focus on scientific data analysis and modelling, small sample size |
| AI-driven personalized learning paths improve mastery of foundational concepts before advancing to complex material | (Holstein & Aleven, 2022) | University Science | Significant (d = 0.9) | Focused on adaptive learning tools like ALEKS, not widely generalizable |
| AI-driven gamified formative assessments significantly enhance student engagement and motivation | (Zhou et al., 2025) | STEM (University) | Large (d = 0.8) | Limited to gamified assessments, sample focused on specific courses |

## 4. GENAI FOR SCIENTIFIC REASONING AND DATA VISUALIZATION

Generative AI (GenAI) is changing scientific and mathematical data visualization and interpretation in the classroom. Students' data literacy is improved by GenAI's capacity to automatically generate relevant and understandable graphs, which helps them decipher complicated datasets (Gupta et al., 2024). Students can identify patterns, correlations, and outliers with the use of these tools. According to research (Holstein & Aleven, 2022), visual interpretation is best supported by scaffolding, particularly for younger pupils who still rely heavily on their teachers.

GenAI enhances this process by providing adaptive explanations and real-time feedback. Nevertheless, obstacles continue to exist. Learners may become excessively dependent on AI-generated insights, which could result in the neglect of critical thinking and self-interpretation. Furthermore, GenAI-generated visualizations may occasionally oversimplify or misrepresent data if they are not informed by precise context (Devineni, 2024). Thus, while GenAI has the potential to significantly improve scientific comprehension through visual literacy, its efficacy is contingent upon its mindful integration with conventional instructional methods. Achieving meaningful engagement and informed data interpretation necessitates a delicate balance between AI support and human oversight.

## Role of GenAI in Scientific Reasoning

Generative Artificial Intelligence (GenAI) has the potential to significantly enhance scientific reasoning by aiding students in generating hypotheses, performing data analysis, and interpreting complex scientific data. The integration of GenAI into the scientific inquiry process offers students advanced tools that enable them to explore concepts and phenomena that might otherwise be inaccessible or too complex for traditional classroom settings. One of the key contributions of GenAI is its ability to assist students in hypothesis generation. By detecting patterns in existing datasets or creating simulations based on scientific principles, GenAI helps students develop and refine hypotheses (Belkina et al., 2025). By automating complex data processing tasks, such as running statistical tests or performing regression analysis, GenAI tools like ChatGPT's code interpreter allow students to focus more on interpreting their results rather than being bogged down by repetitive calculations (Mittal & Raj, 2024). Moreover, GenAI supports the development of critical thinking and scientific reasoning by providing context-specific, real-time feedback, which helps students evaluate the validity of their findings, identify potential biases, and refine their problem-solving strategies. This iterative process, where students can test and revise their hypotheses based on data, deepens their cognitive connections between theory and practice, ultimately enhancing their scientific literacy and reasoning skills (Devineni, 2024).

## The Role of Data Visualization in Science Education

Data visualization is important in improving science education by rendering complex material more accessible, involving and significant for learners. A fundamental matter of this includes instructing data interpretation and visualization, giving students with crucial abilities to understand and reach conclusions from scientific data. Through the exact point of skills to interpret graphs, charts and other visual components, students prepare critical thinking and scientific reasoning capabilities, thereby enhancing their comprehension of patterns, inter connections and trends within data. This is important in an era where data-driven decision-making is fundamental to scientific research and practical problem-solving skills (Phillips et al., 2010).

Moreover, integrating data visualization into science increases inquiry-based learning, enabling students to ask questions, analyse and derive knowledge from proper evidence. The visual tools are not only explaining the difficult data but also investigate curiosity by rendering abstract scientific occurrence more visible and observable. Dynamic graphs and interactive simulations enable student's visualization of molecular interactions, climate change and population dynamics, thereby enhancing their conceptual understanding. Also, students increase their ability to articulate scientific concepts effectively using visual representations. Educators can use visualization to evaluate student understanding in more refined manners, transcending mere rote memorization to test analytical and interpretative abilities. The use of data visualization promotes a more involved, analytical and informed methodology in science education, providing students for data-intensive challenges in contemporary society (Phillips et al., 2010).

The incorporation of Generative AI (GenAI) techniques improves data literacy within scientific areas. GenAI can generate visual explanations, recommend suitable visualization options and analyse datasets in a proper manner for students. It enables learners to get involved with data dynamically posing queries, formulating hypotheses and getting immediate visual response. These tools modify learning, adjust to individual proficiency levels and reduce cognitive overload, rendering scientific data more comprehensible and captivating (Holstein & Aleven, 2022). Furthermore, GenAI proposes inquiry-based learning by allowing students to run experiments, investigate "what-if" scenarios and show results instantly. The combination of classical visualization skills and GenAI technology makes a strong basis for turning scientifically literate people who can manage the data-intensive field of modern research (Gupta et al., 2024). Moreover, GenAI suggests diversity in science education by adapting various learning styles and semantic background scenes using natural language interfaces. Students who may find traditional coding style or data, information analysis tools challenging can now make interaction with complex content using direct language prompts, thereby decreasing the obstacles to scientific investigation. GenAI enables the creation of adaptive exams for learners and offers real-time feedback, thereby developing the formative learning experience. Adding these tools into educational institutions shows learners to new data technology and motivates their active participation in the scientific process. This immersive, AI-enhanced method fosters autonomy, creativity and enhanced involvement with STEM fields. As GenAI advances, it is set to revolutionize the future of science education by extending data literacy to a globally accessible and vital ability (Holstein & Aleven, 2022).

## GenAI Tools for Data Visualization

Generative AI (GenAI) tools are changing data visualization by enabling intuitive, automated, and intelligent methods for representing, simulating and analysing data. These tools are especially essential in education, research and industrial side where data analysis is important to decision-making and scientific investigation. A key application is automatic graph generation, wherein systems like as ChatGPT and Google Bard can generate line graphs, bar charts and different types of plots straight from natural language prompts (Holstein & Aleven, 2022). Data simulation is another interesting case study for GenAI tools. For example, OpenAI Codex or GitHub Copilot can generate R or Python code to model scientific processes like disease transmission, population growth, chemical effects etc. These simulations are great for learning through inquiry since they are correct and can be modified in real-time based on the user input. A biology student, for instance, could use a GenAI program to model bacterial growth at various temperatures and then see the population's growth pictorially (Gupta et al., 2024). GenAI also improves data analysis by facilitating statistical evaluations and insight generation via graphical dashboards. With little to no input from the user, tools like Tableau GPT and Microsoft Copilot can intuitively identify patterns, create correlation matrices, and supply predicted trend lines. With the help of the GenAI assistant, a business analyst may do things like "analyse seasonal trends and visualize peak sales months" after uploading a sales dataset. The assistant will then produce annotated charts with insights generated by AI (Devineni, 2024).

GenAI allows active learning by enabling students to ask questions, request data modifications, and obtain personalized visual representations. This practical experience enhances critical thinking and data literacy. In scientific classrooms, a student analysing climate data can utilize GenAI to investigate the fluctuations of temperature trends over decades and regions, producing graphs and elucidations customized to their research (Gupta et al., 2024). These qualities foster curiosity and scientific reasoning, enabling students to tackle complex problems with assurance.

A simple block diagram (Figure 2) shows how the GenAI tools are used for data visualization; the methodology and essential components of GenAI's use in the development and interpretation of data visualizations.

*Figure 2. A block diagram of the methodology and essential components of GenAI's use in the development and interpretation of data visualizations*

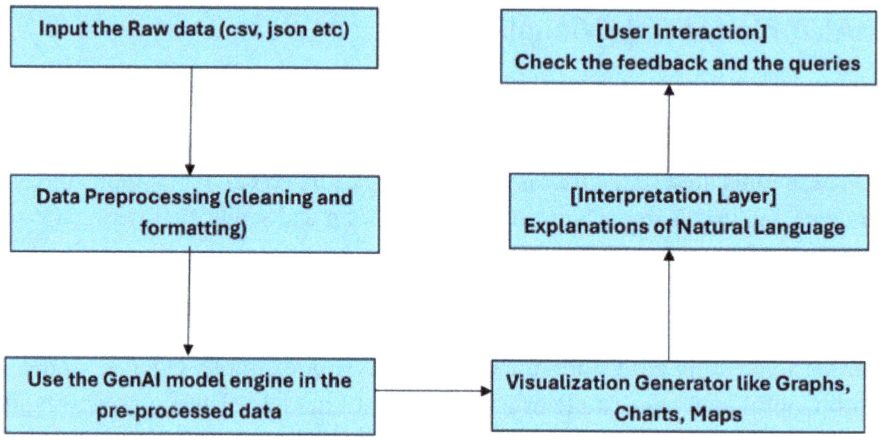


## Developing Critical Thinking Through Visualization

Visualization is an essential educational instrument in modern science instruction, facilitating both understanding and the development of critical thinking abilities. Scientific concepts and data can frequently be abstract and intricate, hindering students' ability to completely comprehend their consequences through text or static visuals alone. Visualization closes this gap by converting data into interactive, interpretable, and frequently dynamic formats that enhance comprehension and analytical involvement. One of the most important contributions of visualization in education is its capacity to promote students' analysis and critique of scientific facts, which is essential for fostering critical thinking. When students see visual data—such as graphs, charts, heat maps, or simulations, they are encouraged to enquire about the data's representation, analyse the methodologies employed in its generation, and evaluate the conclusions derived. The process of inquiry and criticism is essential to scientific reasoning and problem-solving (Friel et al., 2001).

Encouraging analysis and critique of scientific data needs more than simple observation and demands active interaction with visual material. For instance, students may receive climatic data covering multiple decades, illustrated as a line graph. A well-structured classroom activity should prompt students to analyse aspects such as data gathering methods, potential biases, external affecting variables, and alternate interpretations, rather than merely analysing upward or downward trends. Such critical encounters facilitate students in transcending superficial comprehension to embrace a more evaluative perspective. In this context, visualization serves as a medium that enables learners to not only "observe" data but also to analyse it, detect discrepancies, and formulate reasoned arguments grounded in evidence (Phillips et al., 2010). The integration of visualization in science education corresponds with the increasing focus on inquiry-based and constructivist learning paradigms, wherein students develop knowledge via investigation and reflection. Visualization tools, including simulations and interactive dashboards, enable students to adjust variables, conduct experiments, and examine results in real-time. Two case studies has been present in Table 3 and Table 4.

*Table 3. Case study 1*

| **Case Study 1: Using Code Interpreter with ChatGPT for Advanced Data Analysis** |
|---|
| **Tool**: ChatGPT (with Advanced Data Analysis, available for Plus users) |
| **Task**: Analysing climatic data for temperature trends over time |
| **Scenario:**<br>In this example, students use the Code Interpreter feature of ChatGPT to analyse climatic data, such as temperature and precipitation, over a specified period. The task involves analysing the temperature trends from 2010 to 2024 by uploading a CSV file containing the climatic data. |
| **Steps for Implementation:**<br>1. **Upload Data**: Students upload the *climate_data.csv* file containing temperature data.<br>2. **Prompting the Tool**: Students input the following prompt into ChatGPT: *"Analyse the temperature trends from 2010 to 2024 and generate a line graph. Are there any noticeable patterns?"*<br>3. **Expected Output**: ChatGPT processes the data, generates a line graph that depicts temperature trends over time, and provides a sequential explanation of any upward or downward trends noticed in the dataset. |
| **Learning Outcome:**<br>This exercise helps students develop the skills necessary to:<br>• **Analyse Data Trends**: Students learn to interpret data trends over time and identify significant patterns.<br>• **Spot Irregularities**: Students gain the ability to recognize any irregularities or anomalies in the dataset.<br>• **Formulate Explanations**: The analysis encourages critical thinking as students form plausible explanations for any observed trends, fostering a deeper understanding of how climate patterns may evolve. |

*Table 4. Case study 2*

| **Case Study 1: Using Code Interpreter with ChatGPT for Advanced Data Analysis** |
|---|
| **Tool**: Google Bard or Gemini |
| **Task**: Analysing renewable energy usage trends in different nations |
| **Scenario:**<br>In this example, students use AI tools like Google Bard or Gemini to generate visual charts that represent scientific trends. The task is to analyse the use of renewable energy in five different nations from 2000 to 2020. |
| **Steps for Implementation:**<br>**1. Prompting the Tool:** Students input the following prompt into Google Bard or Gemini: "Make a bar graph that contrasts the use of renewable energy in five nations between 2000 and 2020. What patterns do you see?"<br>**2. Expected Output:** The AI tool generates a bar graph showing the renewable energy usage in five countries, highlighting trends over the 20-year period. It will also provide a narrative explanation, noting any spikes in energy usage and suggesting possible sociopolitical or economic causes for these patterns. |
| **Learning Outcome:**<br>This case study helps students:<br>• **Interpret Visual Data**: Students learn to analyse bar graphs, drawing connections between the visual data and underlying events.<br>• **Understand Socio-Political Impacts**: They explore how external factors, such as political decisions or economic changes, can influence scientific and environmental trends, thus enhancing their understanding of real-world implications of data.<br>• **Foster Inquiry-Based Learning**: Students are encouraged to explore *why* certain nations experienced spikes in renewable energy usage, promoting inquiry-based thinking. |

From the overall discussion of this chapter, Table 5 is shown where we show the identified challenges of data visualization and interpretation with GenAI.

*Table 5. Identified challenges of data visualization and interpretation with GenAI*

| References | Short Description | Identified Challenges |
|---|---|---|
| (Phillips et al., 2010) | It underlines the need of early exposure to data interpretation and the relevance of visual representations in STEM education for improving conceptual understanding. | Although teachers should be well-versed in visualization pedagogy, they are not always able to help students who are having difficulty understanding multi-variable graphs. |
| (Holstein & Aleven, 2022) | Investigate the ways in which AI technologies might collaborate with educators to enhance student learning, particularly in the areas of visual analysis and feedback on data assignments. | Inconsistent alignment between human and AI input can be confusing for students, and coordinating the two can be hard. |
| (Gupta et al., 2024) | GenAI's value in assisting students in understanding difficult scientific graphs and creating their own explanations using auto-generated images. | Students could rely too much on AI instead of learning to critically think for themselves. |

continued on following page

*Table 5. Continued*

| References | Short Description | Identified Challenges |
|---|---|---|
| (Friel et al., 2001) | Examine how people comprehend graphs, highlighting prior knowledge, context, and graph structure as critical determinants of understanding. | Students frequently misinterpret visual data due to insufficient underlying graph literacy; AI tools alone may not rectify these rooted errors. |
| (McTigue & Flowers, 2011) | Investigates student engagement with and comprehension of visual scientific information, highlighting the necessity for instructional scaffolding in conjunction with visuals. | In the absence of focused guidance, learners may misconstrue or neglect essential components in visualizations, even when aided by AI. |
| (Devineni, 2024) | Investigates the role of GenAI tools in producing explanatory visual information to aid learners in interpreting scientific data. | An excessive dependence on AI interpretations could hamper our development of essential human analytical abilities. |

## 4. ETHICS AND GOVERNANCE IN HIGHER EDUCATION

As GenAI technologies continue to be integrated into higher education, there are increasing concerns regarding their ethical use and governance. These concerns encompass issues related to academic integrity, data privacy, bias in AI systems, and the broader impact of AI on educational equity. For institutions adopting GenAI-powered tools in teaching, learning, and assessment, it is crucial to develop clear frameworks that address these concerns and promote responsible AI usage. One of the most pressing concerns in the deployment of AI systems in higher education is the potential erosion of academic integrity. GenAI can produce text, solve problems, and generate data that students may use directly in assignments or exams. This capability raises concerns about plagiarism, authenticity of student work, and the over-reliance on AI for academic tasks. GenAI tools like ChatGPT and other AI-based writing assistants can produce human-like text, which makes it harder to discern whether the content is genuinely student-created or AI-generated. Without clear policies on AI use, students may use these tools to bypass critical thinking and reduce the authenticity of their work (Kasneci et al., 2023). AI tools also generate potential hallucinations—false or misleading information without proper citation, which can further undermine the trustworthiness of academic outputs. GenAI models could perpetuate biases if the underlying data used for training is not adequately controlled. Research by (Gunkel, 2024) emphasizes the need for transparent and accountable AI systems.

## Ethical Concerns in Using GenAI in Education

Below, we explore the primary ethical concerns in the use of GenAI in education, focusing on the balance between innovation and responsible AI practices (Huang, 2023).

### • Examining Ethical Dilemmas in the Use of GenAI in Education

As GenAI technologies like large language models (LLMs) and simulation tools gain traction in STEM education, several ethical issues have emerged, particularly regarding fairness, transparency, and accessibility. GenAI tools, although powerful, are not devoid of biases. The data used to train these AI models often carry inherent biases that can affect the AI's outputs, perpetuating stereotypes and skewed information. For example, an AI model trained on data from a predominantly Western or homogenous background may not be able to generate culturally sensitive or inclusive content. Such biases can lead to inequitable learning experiences, especially in diverse classrooms with students from various cultural and socio-economic backgrounds. Moreover, transparency is a key ethical challenge. While AI algorithms are often referred to as "black boxes," where their decision-making processes are not always clear, this lack of transparency can make it difficult for educators to understand why a specific output is generated, leading to challenges in assessing the quality of AI-generated content. If educators cannot fully trust or understand the tools they are using, the ethical implications of relying on AI in the classroom become problematic (Tomak & Virlan, 2024).

### • Balancing Innovation with Responsible AI Practices in Science Teaching

Balancing the innovative potential of GenAI with responsible practices is essential to ensure its ethical use in STEM education. On the one hand, GenAI provides immense opportunities for enhancing teaching and learning by offering personalized learning pathways, generating adaptive content, and providing real-time feedback that caters to individual student needs. However, this innovation must not come at the expense of equity, fairness, and privacy. One critical ethical consideration is ensuring that GenAI tools are accessible to all students, regardless of their socio-economic status. While large educational institutions may have the resources to integrate cutting-edge GenAI systems, smaller institutions or underserved communities may be left behind, exacerbating the digital divide. This disparity in access raises questions about how equitable the implementation of GenAI tools truly is. Additionally, educators and policymakers must ensure that the use of GenAI aligns with educational goals and standards while safeguarding students' privacy. The collection of student data to personalize learning experiences, if not properly managed, could lead to privacy violations or the exploitation of sensitive information. Strict guidelines on data security and transparency about how student data is used will be crucial in maintaining ethical standards (Cheong, 2024).

### • Addressing Potential Misuses and Ensuring Accountability

GenAI's ability to generate content quickly and at scale presents opportunities for educational advancement, but it also brings the risk of misuse. One such risk is the potential for AI-generated content to be used to cheat or bypass learning objectives. For instance, students may misuse GenAI tools to generate essays, problem-solving solutions, or even research papers without engaging in the learning process. Such misuse undermines the purpose of education, which is to foster critical thinking, creativity, and knowledge acquisition. Accountability mechanisms must be established to prevent such misuse. Educators need to be trained not only in how to use GenAI tools effectively but also in how to spot unethical use. Moreover, GenAI systems themselves must be designed with safeguards that detect and prevent inappropriate uses, such as plagiarism or the creation of deceptive content (Tomak & Virlan, 2024).

## Ethical Considerations in GenAI Applications

The integration of Generative Artificial Intelligence (GenAI) into STEM education necessitates a thorough examination of ethical implications to ensure responsible and equitable use. Below are key ethical considerations:

1. **Bias and Fairness in AI Systems:** AI systems can inherit and even amplify biases present in their training data, leading to unfair or discriminatory outcomes. For instance, facial recognition systems have demonstrated higher error rates for darker-skinned individuals, highlighting the need for diverse and representative training datasets (Cheong, 2024) .
2. **Data Privacy and Security:** The collection and analysis of student data raise significant privacy concerns. Educational institutions must comply with data protection regulations and implement robust security measures to safeguard personal information (Ismail & Aloshi, 2024).
3. **Transparency and Accountability:** Transparency in AI operations is crucial for building trust and ensuring ethical use. Educational institutions should provide clear documentation on AI algorithms, data usage, and decision-making processes. Establishing accountability measures helps in monitoring AI systems and addressing any issues that arise (Cheong, 2024).

4. **Academic Integrity and Misuse Prevention:** The potential for AI tools to be misused for academic dishonesty necessitates the development of policies and technologies to detect and prevent such behaviour. Educational institutions should establish clear guidelines on the acceptable use of AI in academic settings (Kumar et al., 2023).
5. **Equity and Accessibility:** Ensuring equitable access to AI tools is essential to prevent exacerbating existing disparities in education. Efforts should be made to provide AI resources to underserved communities and to accommodate diverse learning needs (Varsik & Vosberg, 2024) .

## 5. CURRICULUM DESIGN FOR TERTIARY-LEVEL SCIENCE PROGRAMS WITH THE INTEGRATION OF GENAI

The continuous evolution of generative artificial intelligence (GenAI) is changing the educational landscape, forcing academicians, curriculum developers, academic institutions, and policymakers to rethink the design and delivery of science education at the tertiary level (Zawacki-Richter et al., 2019). In tertiary-level science curricula, where analytical thinking, empirical reasoning, and problem-solving are the most essential skills, the use of GenAI tools is both a great opportunity and a big challenge (Holmes & Luckin, 2016).

GenAI technologies, such as large language models (LLMs), multimodal AI systems (MMAI), and automated reasoning (AR) engines, can help students to put together complicated information, simulate scientific scenarios, interpret data, and even write scholarly papers (Brown et al., 2020). These skills require a rethinking of the existing curricula to not only introduce GenAI but also use it in a way that improves the understanding of the concepts, supports the inquiry-based learning, and develops skills for the modern AI-driven world (Zawacki-Richter et al., 2019).

In the past, science education at the tertiary level focused on mastering the subject matter and being methodologically extremely precise. These are still very important, but due to the rapid rise of GenAI, responsible persons and organizations need to pay more attention to how students learn, particularly through digital collaboration, algorithmic thinking, and interaction with machines. The curriculum must teach students about AI latency, critical thinking, and ethical reasoning to enable them to use AI tools responsibly and avoid becoming overly dependent on them (Cooper, 2023; Selwyn, 2019). Furthermore, equity and accessibility must be maintained to ensure all students benefit from GenAI-integrated education. This includes giving institutional support, protecting data privacy, and training faculty members to use AI technologies responsibly (George Siemens, 2005).

## Integrating GenAI into Science Curriculum Design

GenAI is changing the way academicians used to teach, particularly science curricula at the tertiary level. GenAI includes LLMs, image generators, and code generation tools that are starting to change the way things are done in academic institutions. It is no longer an option to add GenAI to curriculum design; it is rapidly becoming a must-have for modern and future-proof science education (Holmes et al., 2019; Holmes & Luckin, 2016).

Adding GenAI to science curricula extends beyond simply incorporating AI tools into existing lesson plans. It means completely rethinking the logic of the curriculum, the sequence of lessons, and the roles of students. In an era when AI can generate explanations on the fly, simulate scientific models, and facilitate real-time data understanding (Zawacki-Richter et al., 2019), the traditional model of one-way knowledge transmission is becoming less effective. GenAI should not be viewed as an additional tool in the classroom; instead, curriculum developers should see it as a collaborative partner for both teachers and students (Woolf et al., 2013). Additionally, science curricula need to be able to adapt to the fact that GenAI is constantly evolving and varies depending on the situation. Curricular frameworks should enable teachers to determine the depth of exploration, teaching methods, and assessment strategies for each subject. AI-powered adaptive learning environments can provide different content and guided instruction based on each learner's pace and level of knowledge (Woolf et al., 2013).

A key part of designing GenAI-integrated curricula is to redefine learning objectives. Conventional objectives need to be revised to incorporate higher-order thinking, the ability to critically evaluate content generated by AI, and the capacity to collaborate with GenAI tools to create new knowledge (Anderson, 2009). Here in Table 6, some key objectives are listed along with their focus area and purpose.

*Table 6. Learning objectives for GENAI-integrated science education*

| Learning Objectives | Focus Area | Purpose |
|---|---|---|
| Check AI-generated content carefully for accuracy, reliability, and bias. | • Critical thinking<br>• AI latency | Make sure that GenAI tools are used responsibly and with thought. |
| Use GenAI tools to model, simulate, or investigate scientific ideas and problems in the real world. | • Problem-solving<br>• Inquiry-based learning | Encourages active, hands-on learning with AI in many fields. |
| Create effective prompts to assist GenAI in performing its tasks in academic and scientific settings. | • Prompt engineering<br>• Communication | Teach students how to interact effectively with AI systems. |

continued on following page

*Table 6. Continued*

| Learning Objectives | Focus Area | Purpose |
|---|---|---|
| Utilize AI in combination with ethical and academic standards. | • Ethics<br>• Teamwork<br>• Digital responsibility | Encourages the use of AI in education in a fair and cooperative manner. |
| Utilize AI-powered tools designed for diverse audiences to discuss scientific concepts. | • Science communication<br>• Digital fluency | GenAI enables people to communicate in a way that includes everyone and is tailored to the audience. |
| Explore the impact of AI in science on society, ethics, and the environment. | • Ethical reasoning<br>• Socio-scientific issues | Raises awareness of the bigger effects of GenAI on society and research. |
| Utilize GenAI as a cognitive partner to work independently or collaboratively with others. | • Autonomy<br>• Collaboration<br>• Metacognition | Improve skills for self-directed learning and working with AI. |
| Be open to new AI tools and demonstrate a growth mindset when learning online. | • Lifelong learning<br>• Adaptability<br>• Resilience | Prepares students for the evolution of AI and ongoing innovation. |

## Pedagogical Approaches and GenAI Integration

Figure 3 shows how GenAI fits with modern teaching methods. In this model, GenAI is at the center of a student-centered learning environment, where it meets three main educational philosophies: constructivism, inquiry-based learning, and collaborative learning.

*Figure 3. Pedagogical integration model diagram*

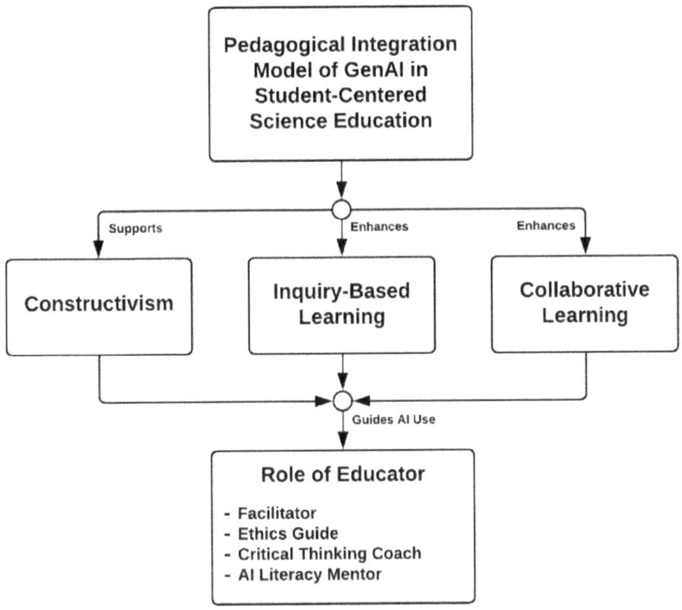


**Constructivism:** Constructivist theories emphasize active knowledge construction, whereby students develop conceptual frameworks through experience and reflection (Bruner, 1978; Piaget & Piaget, 1973). GenAI enhances constructivist teaching by providing real-time explanations and simulations tailored to the learner's level, facilitating interactive system modeling, and promoting repeated exploration and self-directed learning. These kinds of tools help students build their understanding of concepts, which aligns with constructivist scaffolding ("Cognitive Apprenticeship," 2018). ("Cognitive Apprenticeship," 2018)

**Inquiry-Based Learning:** An important component of science education, inquiry-based learning (IBL) places a strong emphasis on critical interpretation, evidence-based reasoning, and question-driven inquiry (Committee on the Development of an Addendum to the National Science Education Standards on Scientific Inquiry et al., 2000). GenAI aligns perfectly with IBL models by facilitating the formulation and refinement of hypotheses, simulating experiments in a lab or the real world, and aiding students in understanding the results and evaluating the evidence. Cooper (2023) states that GenAI-supported inquiry encourages students to think more deeply about scientific questions and facilitates cognitive apprenticeships, which occur when students learn by observing and imitating how experts think (VanLEHN, 2011).

**Collaborative Learning:** Students learn more effectively when they work together with both their groupmates and intelligent systems. GenAI enables students to collaborate on writing scientific papers and reports, facilitating peer review and editing with the aid of AI, as well as shared data interpretation and visualizations. These kinds of activities align with co-participatory learning models, which view learners, teachers, and AI systems as collaborating to build knowledge (Long & Magerko, 2020).

This model does not replace the teacher; instead, it puts them in a new role as a facilitator of inquiry and a bridge between human and machine reasoning, which encourages learning that is reflective, ethical, and involved. Teachers are important for making sure that AI helps people think, value, and judge better, not worse (Floridi et al., 2018; Selwyn, 2019).

## Practical Strategies for Implementation

Integrating GenAI into tertiary science education requires a careful, multi-layered plan that promotes meaningful interaction with AI while preserving critical scientific skills and upholding academic integrity (Cooper, 2023; Holmes et al., 2019). Using GenAI tools must be planned out, connected to what students are expected to learn, and set up in a way that works for students with different skill levels. Here are some essential strategies:

- **Gradual and Supported Introduction of GenAI Tools**: Begin by using GenAI technologies in low-stakes activities that allow students to explore and become familiar with them without the pressure of achieving good grades. For instance, students could utilize AI-based language models to prepare summaries of critical scientific terms or formulate experimental hypotheses, thereby gaining an overall understanding of GenAI's usefulness and limitations (Woolf et al., 2013). Over time, assignments can evolve to require students to think critically about AI outputs, which will help them become more engaged and aware of their thought processes (Cooper, 2023).
- **Redesigning Assignments to Emphasize Process Over Product:** Traditional assignments, such as research papers or lab reports, can be reframed to emphasize the student's critical thinking and iterative revision process with the assistance of GenAI. Educators can require students to submit AI-generated drafts alongside their revisions and reflections on the AI's strengths and limitations (VanLEHN, 2011). This approach promotes transparency and helps develop skills in evaluating AI-generated content (Brown et al., 2020).
- **Integrating GenAI into Laboratory and Simulation Activities:** GenAI tools can significantly enhance science labs by facilitating experiment simulation, data analysis, and experiment design optimization. These tools help students visualize complex scientific processes, test various theories,

and conduct virtual experiments in a safe and flexible setting. For instance, GenAI can mimic physical, chemical, or environmental systems that would be too expensive, too risky, or too difficult to set up in a regular laboratory. AI-powered simulations encourage active, hands-on learning and help students understand concepts more deeply in a wide range of scientific fields (Zawacki-Richter et al., 2019). They achieve this by allowing students to test hypotheses, examine simulated results, and adjust their approaches in real time.

- **Teaching Prompt Engineering and AI Literacy:** Being able to write effective prompts that help GenAI outputs is a new skill that is crucial for maximizing the tool's potential. Courses should include lessons on AI literacy, such as how to ask questions, understand AI-generated results, and spot biases or mistakes that are built into the system. This helps students think critically and become smart users of AI-generated information instead of just passive consumers (Long & Magerko, 2020).
- **Embedding Ethics and Responsible AI Use:** Ethics education should be integrated into all aspects, encompassing issues such as AI bias, privacy, and academic integrity. Teaching students to think critically about how AI affects society in science encourages responsible use and prepares them for the ethical problems they will face in their future jobs (Floridi et al., 2018).
- **Collaborative and Co-Creative Learning Models:** Utilizing GenAI in group projects encourages individuals to work together, mirroring how scientists employ AI in their research. Digital platforms designed for collaborative AI-assisted work facilitate co-creation with AI, promoting peer learning, diverse thinking, and creativity (George Siemens, 2005).

Adding GenAI to science curricula offers numerous educational benefits, but it also presents several teachings, technical, and moral challenges that institutions must address. If these issues are not addressed in advance through policy development, professional training, and fair access strategies, they could hinder the successful use of GenAI tools. Table 7 lists the main problems associated with incorporating GenAI into science curricula, along with descriptions of each issue and potential impacts.

*Table 7. Challenges associated with utilizing GenAI into science curricula*

| References | Challenge | Description | Potential Impact |
|---|---|---|---|
| Cooper (2023); Holmes et al. (2019) | Academic Integrity | The risk of plagiarism and overreliance on work generated by GenAI. | Hinders real learning and assessment for students. |
| Zawacki-Richter et al. (2019) | Equity and Access | GenAI tools are not equally accessible to all students or institutions. | Increases the gap between digital and educational access. |
| Holmes et al. (2019); Selwyn (2019) | Faculty Readiness | Teachers often lack the training and confidence to effectively utilize GenAI in the classroom. | Not willing to adopt. Unable to implement effectively. |
| Cooper (2023) | Assessment Authenticity | Traditional tests fail to differentiate between tasks performed by AI and tasks done by students. | Wrong assessment of students' learning and originality. |
| Floridi et al. (2018); Holmes et al. (2019) | Data Privacy & Ethical Use | Sharing student data with third-party platforms may be a part of using GenAI. | Violating privacy laws. Ethical concerns. |
| Zawacki-Richter et al. (2019) | Curriculum Agility | Hard to keep up with GenAI's fast-paced changes in the curriculum. | Outdated study materials. Missed chances to come up with new ideas. |

## 6. UNIVERSAL DESIGN FOR LEARNING (UDL) IN SCIENCE USING GENAI

In our modern educational environment, leading to reasonable access to science education is both a difficulty and a necessity. Universal Design for Learning (UDL) shows a versatile structure that needs to fulfil this requirement by offering different methods of interaction, representation and expression, therefore catering to the different learning styles and needs of all students. With speedy progression of technology, Generative Artificial Intelligence (GenAI) is making as a strong tool to augment Universal Design for Learning (UDL) application in science education. Through the creation of customized content, visualizations, simulations, and individualized feedback, GenAI enables educators to provide more inclusive and adaptive learning experiences. GenAI effectively simplifies intricate scientific topics, assists multilingual learners and facilitates interactive experiments, so aligning with UDL principles to mitigate learning obstacles and promote meaningful comprehension. This combination increases student involvement while producing critical thinking and independence in scientific investigation. The combination of UDL and GenAI presents that utilizing these revolutionary tools can transform the teaching and learning of science, enhancing accessibility, personalization and effectiveness for all learners.

## The Principles of Universal Design for Learning (UDL)

Universal Design for Learning (UDL) is a system based on research that aims to build learning spaces that are inviting and meet the requirements of all students. UDL is based on three main ideas: multiple ways to connect, multiple ways to represent and multiple ways to act and express yourself. These ideas make using cognitive science. These principles tell teachers to make science lessons that are adaptable and easy to understand for all students. So that every student can interact with the component in a way that fits their skills and preferences. It is especially essential to use UDL principles in science classes, where students often come across complicated theories, specialized language and abstract ideas. Teachers can help students better understand difficult component by using different ways to show them, such as pictures, interactive games and spoken explanations. Providing students with different ways to show what they know, like writing reports, giving presentations or working on creative projects, makes sure that the review is fair and useful for all.

The principle of engagement stresses the importance of motivation and relevance even more. To keep students engaged, real-life examples and personalized tasks are needed. In the end, UDL shows and promotes fairness in science education by lowering barriers and encouraging full involvement for students with a range of abilities, backgrounds and learning styles. This makes science easier to access and more powered for all students. This study addresses issues like limitation of time and complex instructional creation by examining how generative artificial intelligence (GenAI) might speed up universal design for learning (UDL) in online courses. It shows how GenAI tools, such ChatGPT and Otter.ai, may improve executive functioning, empathy, and comprehension to satisfy a range of learning demands (Holstein and Aleven 2022).

Generative artificial intelligence (GenAI) is changing the way modern educational institutions work by making many learning paths more flexible and personalized so that they can meet the requirements of all kinds of students. GenAI is very similar to Universal Design for Learning (UDL) fundamentals when it comes to inclusive science education because it provides students many ways to reflect, interact with and express themselves. Teachers can build customized material, like easier-to-understand explanations, interactive simulations, on time feedback and translations into multiple languages, to help students with a range of cognitive abilities, language skills and learning styles. For example, an advanced science idea like DNA replication can be made easier to understand for both verbal and visual learners by using animated videos, analogies and written descriptions that are built over time

(Holstein & Aleven, 2022). GenAI also provides students with the freedom to show what they know in a different way, such as through voice, text, images or programming. This encourages creativity and makes grading easier. AI-powered tools can also modify the order of lessons based on how well each student is preparing, doing, offering specific help or extra tasks that help students master the material at their own speed. GenAI works best in classes with a lot of different students, learning styles and academic phases because it can adapt to each section. GenAI can support customized instruction by allowing flexible learning paths. It also boosts student's independence, confidence and deep engagement, leading to a more fair, productive and effective science education overall. The purpose of this study is to investigate how further education instructors are adjusting to the use of generative AI in their classrooms. Within academic circles, generative AI has rapidly gained attention. Some emphasize how generative AI can alleviate time constraint (Lameras, 2022), while others draw attention to potential problems with academic integrity (Vashista, Gugnani, and Bala 2023).

## Integrating UDL with GenAI Tools

The integration of Universal Design for Learning (UDL) with Generative AI (GenAI) tools provides a revolutionary method for inclusive scientific education through the development of personalized and adaptive learning experiences. Universal Design for Learning (UDL) prioritizes offering many methods of engagement, representation, and expression to cater to a heterogeneous learner population {CAST 2018}. GenAI systems can uphold these values by producing customized content, such visual aids, scaffolded explanations, or multilingual resources, specifically designed to meet student requirements. For example, AI-driven platforms can flexibly modify text complexity, provide voice interactions, or propose alternative representations of scientific data (Holstein & Aleven, 2022). This alignment enables educators to develop adaptable learning pathways that foster equal access and enhanced comprehension, particularly for children with impairments or linguistic obstacles. The ongoing evolution of GenAI, when combined with UDL frameworks, offers considerable potential to transform inclusive methods in science education (Mouza and Lavigne 2013).

*Figure 4. A simple block diagram for showing the integration of UDL and GenAL tools*

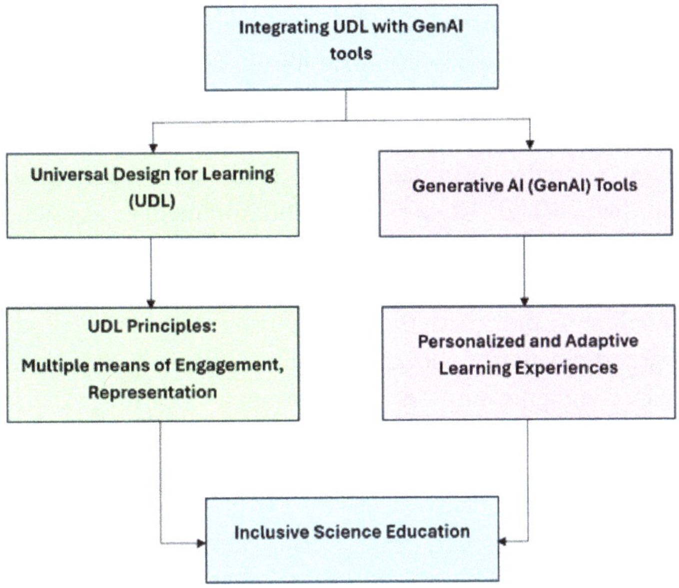


Generative AI (GenAI) applications make an important contribution to the improvement of science learning accessibility and inclusivity by providing adaptive and personalized educational resources for an extensive variety of learners. GenAI's capacity for producing multimodal content, including text-to-speech outputs, visual simulations, and translated materials, is one of its primary advantages. This content has been developed for students with diverse learning requirements, including those with disabilities or language barriers (Holstein & Aleven, 2022). For instance, AI-powered tools can simplify complex scientific texts into visual explanations or simplified language, creating abstract concepts easier to comprehend to students who face cognitive or linguistic challenges (Mouza and Lavigne 2013). Furthermore, GenAI facilitates the meaningful participation of learners with hearing impairments or limited English proficiency in science instruction by generating real-time captions, multilingual support, and alternative content formats. These capabilities are in close alignment with the principles of Universal Design for Learning (UDL) as they offer a variety of methods for representation and expression {CAST 2018}. Consequently, GenAl not only decreases conventional obstacles to scientific education but also develops an inclusive environment that ensures all students have equal access to educational opportunities. The inclusion of these tools into science classrooms encourages a culture of scientific engagement and belonging for all, as well as supports individual learning.

## Creating Equitable Learning Environments

The application of Generative AI (GenAI) in education presents huge possibilities for promoting equitable opportunities for all students, including individuals with disabilities. Applying adaptive learning technologies, GenAI may customize content to suit individual requirements, like transforming text to speech for visually challenged learners or reducing intricate texts for individuals with cognitive difficulties. AI-driven chatbots and virtual assistants offer immediate assistance, enabling students to pose inquiries and obtain guidance without stigma. Furthermore, GenAI may produce accessible formats such as captions, alternative texts, and language translations, facilitating the dismantling of linguistic and physical obstacles. It promotes inclusive participation by allowing students to interact with information at their own pace, hence complementing Universal Design for Learning (UDL) principles. When applied responsibly and ethically, GenAI not only equalizes opportunities but also fosters a more compassionate and inclusive learning environment, guaranteeing that no learner is excluded.

# 7. IMPLEMENTATION AND EVALUATION

As Generative Artificial Intelligence (GenAI) continues to gain momentum in educational settings, it is crucial for institutions to thoughtfully plan and execute its integration into the educational system. Successful adoption and evaluation of GenAI tools can enhance the learning experience, improve educational outcomes, and foster a deeper understanding of scientific concepts. This section provides a step-by-step adoption playbook for implementing GenAI, an evaluation framework for assessing its impact on student learning outcomes, and a set of metrics for success to guide institutions in measuring the effectiveness of GenAI in tertiary science education.

## Adoption Playbook

To ensure a smooth and effective integration of GenAI tools into educational systems, institutions must follow a well-structured approach. This adoption playbook outlines essential steps that institutions should take:

- LMS Integration (LTI/xAPI): Learning Management Systems (LMS) are central to the delivery and management of educational content in higher education. Integrating GenAI tools into the LMS is essential for seamless access and usage by students and faculty. One approach to achieve this integration is through Learning Tools Interoperability (LTI), which allows for secure and standardized communication between GenAI applications and the LMS. This ensures that data, such as student performance and engagement, can be easily shared between systems. For example, integrating GenAI-based formative assessment tools like ChatGPT's code interpreter or Google Bard into an LMS platform via LTI allows students to receive personalized feedback within the existing course structure (Ritter et al., 2007). Another method for integration is xAPI (Experience API), which enables the tracking of learning experiences outside of traditional LMS environments. xAPI allows for capturing data on student interactions with GenAI tools, such as simulations or AI-generated feedback, and integrating this data into learning analytics systems. This approach provides a more comprehensive view of the student's learning journey and how they interact with AI technologies across different platforms (Nilmanee et al., 2024).

- Role-Based Permissions: Ensuring proper access control is crucial for maintaining privacy, security, and academic integrity. Role-based permissions should be implemented to determine who can access GenAI tools, how they interact with these tools, and what data they can view or modify. For example, faculty members should have access to detailed student performance data, while students should only see their own interactions and feedback. This structure ensures that GenAI systems are used responsibly and that students' data privacy is upheld in compliance with regulations like FERPA and GDPR (Parks, 2017).
- Faculty Professional Development Pathways: As GenAI is integrated into the curriculum, it is vital to provide faculty with the knowledge and skills to effectively use these tools. Professional development pathways should include workshops, online courses, and collaborative training sessions focusing on the pedagogical use of GenAI in science education. These sessions can cover how to design assignments that leverage GenAI's capabilities, how to integrate GenAI into existing course materials, and how to assess student performance based on AI-generated outputs. Faculty should also be trained on understanding and addressing potential ethical issues, such as AI-driven biases or academic integrity concerns (Ateeq et al., 2024).
- Faculty development programs should be ongoing, with regular updates to ensure instructors stay informed about the latest advancements in GenAI technologies and best practices for integration. Offering micro-credentials or certifications in AI literacy for faculty members could further incentivize engagement with these tools.

## Evaluation Framework

To assess the impact of GenAI on student learning outcomes, institutions need to implement a robust evaluation framework. This framework should be guided by clear goals and measurable outcomes that help track the effectiveness of GenAI tools in enhancing students' scientific reasoning, critical thinking, and data interpretation skills.

1. Logic Model for Evaluating GenAI Impact: A logic model is an essential framework for evaluating the inputs, activities, and outcomes of GenAI integration. This model helps institutions plan, monitor, and evaluate the effectiveness of GenAI tools in enhancing educational outcomes. The model should include the following components:
   i. Inputs: Resources invested in GenAI integration, including technology infrastructure, faculty training, and curriculum redesign.
   ii. Activities: Specific actions taken to integrate GenAI into courses, such as adopting specific tools, developing new instructional strategies, or creating assignments that use GenAI.
   iii. Outcomes: The desired changes in student outcomes, such as improvements in engagement, scientific reasoning, knowledge retention, and critical thinking.
2. Recommended Measures: To assess the success of GenAI in achieving these outcomes, institutions should track the following measures:
   i. Learning Gains: Evaluate whether students' understanding of scientific concepts has increased over time. Pre- and post-assessments or formative assessments can help measure these gains (Holmes & Luckin, 2016).
   ii. Transfer of Learning: Assess the ability of students to transfer their knowledge to new, real-world contexts, such as solving novel problems or applying theoretical concepts to hands-on experiments.
   iii. Retention: Track the retention of scientific knowledge over time by testing students on the material after extended periods, helping determine whether GenAI tools have contributed to long-lasting learning outcomes.
3. Study Designs: Two effective study designs for evaluating the impact of GenAI tools are:
   i. A/B Testing: Randomly assign students to two groups—one using traditional methods and the other using GenAI tools—to compare the impact on learning outcomes. This approach helps identify whether GenAI enhances student performance beyond traditional teaching methods.
   ii. Design-Based Research (DBR): This iterative, flexible approach involves testing and refining educational interventions, such as GenAI tools, based on

feedback from real-world use. DBR can be particularly useful in examining how GenAI tools can be continuously improved to meet students' needs (Design-Based Research Collective, 2003).

## Metrics for Success

Defining key success metrics is essential for determining whether GenAI tools are effectively meeting educational goals. The following metrics should be used to evaluate the success of GenAI integration:

1. Engagement Rates: Measure student engagement with GenAI tools by tracking usage patterns, interaction frequency, and time spent on AI-generated tasks. Higher engagement rates suggest that students find the tools useful and motivating for their learning process (Ritter et al., 2007).
2. Knowledge Retention: Assess the ability of students to retain scientific knowledge over time through follow-up quizzes or long-term assessments. GenAI tools that facilitate active learning, such as real-time feedback and problem-solving simulations, have been shown to improve knowledge retention (Ateeq et al., 2024).
3. Improved Scientific Reasoning: Track improvements in scientific reasoning skills through assessments that require students to apply scientific principles to novel scenarios. This can be measured by examining how students use GenAI tools to solve complex problems, design experiments, and analyse data.
4. Critical Thinking: Evaluate how GenAI tools influence students' ability to critically assess data, identify patterns, and make decisions based on evidence. Tools that promote hypothesis generation, data analysis, and visualization of results will enhance students' critical thinking skills in the context of scientific inquiry (Zhai, 2023).

## CONCLUSION

The integration of Generative Artificial Intelligence (GenAI) into science education, particularly at the tertiary level, offers transformative opportunities for enhancing learning experiences, improving scientific reasoning, and fostering critical thinking. However, its successful implementation requires a thoughtful approach, combining technological innovation with ethical, inclusive, and pedagogically sound practices. GenAI empowers students to engage more deeply with scientific content by offering personalized learning experiences, real-time feedback, and dynamic data visualization tools. These features enhance the students' ability to grasp complex scientific concepts, perform data analysis, and visualize intricate datasets, thereby improving their scientific literacy and reasoning skills. The ethical challenges posed by GenAI, including concerns related to data privacy, academic integrity, and bias in AI algorithms, must be addressed through the development of clear governance frameworks and responsible AI practices. Furthermore, institutions must prioritize faculty development to ensure educators are equipped to effectively integrate GenAI tools into their courses while maintaining academic rigor. Finally, a robust evaluation framework, using measures such as learning gains, retention, and engagement, will be essential in assessing the impact of GenAI on student outcomes. This will provide valuable insights into the effectiveness of GenAI in science education, ensuring its continued evolution and successful integration into teaching and learning processes.

## REFERENCES


Anderson, L. W. (Ed.). (2009). *A taxonomy for learning, teaching, and assessing: A revision of Bloom's taxonomy of educational objectives* (Abridged ed., [Nachdr.]). Longman.

Apprenticeship, C. Teaching the Crafts of Reading, Writing, and Mathematics. (2018). In A. Collins, J. S. Brown, & S. E. Newman, *Knowing, Learning, and Instruction* (1st ed., pp. 453–494). Routledge. DOI: 10.4324/9781315044408-14

Ateeq, A., Alzoraiki, M., Milhem, M., & Ateeq, R. A. (2024). Artificial intelligence in education: Implications for academic integrity and the shift toward holistic assessment. *Frontiers in Education*, *9*, 1470979. DOI: 10.3389/feduc.2024.1470979

Bach, K. M., Hofer, S., & Bichler, S. (2024). *Adaptive Learning, Instruction, and Teaching in Schools: Unraveling Context, Sources, Implementation, and Goals in a Systematic Review. PsyArXiv*. DOI: 10.31234/osf.io/eyafq

Baidoo-Anu, D., & Ansah, L. O. (2023). *Education in the Era of Generative Artificial Intelligence (AI): Understanding the Potential Benefits of ChatGPT in Promoting Teaching and Learning.*

Belkina, M., Daniel, S., Nikolic, S., Haque, R., Lyden, S., Neal, P., Grundy, S., & Hassan, G. M. (2025). Implementing generative AI (GenAI) in higher education: A systematic review of case studies. *Computers and Education: Artificial Intelligence*, *8*, 100407. DOI: 10.1016/j.caeai.2025.100407

Black, P., & Wiliam, D. (1998). Assessment and Classroom Learning. *Assessment in Education: Principles, Policy & Practice*, *5*(1), 7–74. DOI: 10.1080/0969595980050102

Brown, T. B., Mann, B., Ryder, N., Subbiah, M., Kaplan, J., Dhariwal, P., Neelakantan, A., Shyam, P., Sastry, G., Askell, A., Agarwal, S., Herbert-Voss, A., Krueger, G., Henighan, T., Child, R., Ramesh, A., Ziegler, D. M., Wu, J., Winter, C., Amodei, D. (2020). *Language Models are Few-Shot Learners* (Version 4). arXiv. DOI: 10.48550/ARXIV.2005.14165

Bruner, J. S. (1978). *Toward a theory of instruction* (8. pr). Harvard Univ. Press.

Brusilovsky, P., & Millán, E. (2007). User Models for Adaptive Hypermedia and Adaptive Educational Systems. In P. Brusilovsky, A. Kobsa, & W. Nejdl (Eds.), *The Adaptive Web* (Vol. 4321, pp. 3–53). Springer Berlin Heidelberg. DOI: 10.1007/978-3-540-72079-9_1

Bulut, O., Shin, J., Yildirim-Erbasli, S. N., Gorgun, G., & Pardos, Z. A. (2023). An Introduction to Bayesian Knowledge Tracing with pyBKT. *Psych*, *5*(3), 770–786. DOI: 10.3390/psych5030050

Bulut, O., & Wongvorachan, T. (2022). Feedback Generation through Artificial Intelligence. *The Open/Technology in Education. Society, and Scholarship Association Conference*, *2*(1), 1–9. DOI: 10.18357/otessac.2022.2.1.125

Cheong, B. C. (2024). Transparency and accountability in AI systems: Safeguarding wellbeing in the age of algorithmic decision-making. *Frontiers in Human Dynamics*, *6*, 1421273. Advance online publication. DOI: 10.3389/fhumd.2024.1421273

Christie, S. T., Cook, C., & Rafferty, A. N. (2024). *Uncertainty-preserving deep knowledge tracing with state-space models* (Version 1). arXiv. DOI: 10.48550/ARXIV.2407.17427

Committee on the Development of an Addendum to the National Science Education Standards on Scientific Inquiry, Board on Science Education, Division of Behavioral and Social Sciences and Education, & National Research Council. (2000). *Inquiry and the National Science Education Standards: A Guide for Teaching and Learning* (S. Olson & S. Loucks-Horsley, Eds.). National Academies Press. DOI: 10.17226/9596

Cooper, G. (2023). Examining Science Education in ChatGPT: An Exploratory Study of Generative Artificial Intelligence. *Journal of Science Education and Technology*, *32*(3), 444–452. DOI: 10.1007/s10956-023-10039-y

Devineni, S. K. (2024). AI-Enhanced Data Visualization: Transforming Complex Data into Actionable Insights. *Journal of Technology and Systems*, *6*(3), 52–77. DOI: 10.47941/jts.1911

Du Plooy, E., Casteleijn, D., & Franzsen, D. (2024). Personalized adaptive learning in higher education: A scoping review of key characteristics and impact on academic performance and engagement. *Heliyon*, *10*(21), e39630. DOI: 10.1016/j.heliyon.2024.e39630

Falmagne, J.-C., Cosyn, E., Doignon, J.-P., & Thiéry, N. (2006). The Assessment of Knowledge, in Theory and in Practice. In Missaoui, R., & Schmidt, J. (Eds.), *Formal Concept Analysis* (Vol. 3874, pp. 61–79). Springer Berlin Heidelberg., DOI: 10.1007/11671404_4

Floridi, L., Cowls, J., Beltrametti, M., Chatila, R., Chazerand, P., Dignum, V., Luetge, C., Madelin, R., Pagallo, U., Rossi, F., Schafer, B., Valcke, P., & Vayena, E. (2018). AI4People—An Ethical Framework for a Good AI Society: Opportunities, Risks, Principles, and Recommendations. *Minds and Machines*, *28*(4), 689–707. DOI: 10.1007/s11023-018-9482-5

Friel, S. N., Curcio, F. R., & Bright, G. W. (2001). Making Sense of Graphs: Critical Factors Influencing Comprehension and Instructional Implications. *Journal for Research in Mathematics Education*, *32*(2), 124. DOI: 10.2307/749671

Gomes, D. (2024). A Comprehensive Study of Advancements in Intelligent Tutoring Systems Through Artificial Intelligent Education Platforms. In Moreira, F. T., & Teles, R. O. (Eds.), (pp. 213–244). Advances in Educational Technologies and Instructional Design. IGI Global., DOI: 10.4018/979-8-3693-6170-2.ch008

Goodfellow, I. J., Pouget-Abadie, J., Mirza, M., Xu, B., Warde-Farley, D., Ozair, S., Courville, A., & Bengio, Y. (2014). *Generative Adversarial Networks* (No. arXiv:1406.2661). arXiv. https://doi.org//arXiv.1406.2661DOI: 10.48550

Gunkel, D. J. (Ed.). (2024). *Handbook on the ethics of artificial intelligence*. Edward Elgar Publishing., DOI: 10.4337/9781803926728

Gupta, P., Ding, B., Guan, C., & Ding, D. (2024). Generative AI: A systematic review using topic modelling techniques. *Data and Information Management*, *8*(2), 100066. DOI: 10.1016/j.dim.2024.100066

Holmes, W., Bialik, M., & Fadel, C. (2019). *Artificial intelligence in education: Promises and implications for teaching and learning*. The Center for Curriculum Redesign.

Holmes, W., & Luckin, R. (2016). *Intelligence unleashed: An argument for AI in education*. Pearson : UCL Knowledge Lab.

Holstein, K., & Aleven, V. (2022). Designing for human–AI complementarity in K-12 education. *AI Magazine*, *43*(2), 239–248. DOI: 10.1002/aaai.12058

Huang, L. (2023). Ethics of Artificial Intelligence in Education: Student Privacy and Data Protection. *Science Insights Education Frontiers*, *16*(2), 2577–2587. DOI: 10.15354/sief.23.re202

Introduction to Emerging Technologies for the Classroom. A Learning Sciences Perspective. (2013). In C. Mouza & N. C. Lavigne, *Emerging Technologies for the Classroom* (pp. 1–12). Springer New York. DOI: 10.1007/978-1-4614-4696-5_1

Ismail, I. A., & Aloshi, J. M. (2024). Data Privacy in AI-Driven Education: An In-Depth Exploration Into the Data Privacy Concerns and Potential Solutions. In Keeley, K. L. (Ed.), (pp. 223–252). Advances in Educational Marketing, Administration, and Leadership. IGI Global., DOI: 10.4018/979-8-3693-5443-8.ch008

Kasneci, E., Sessler, K., Küchemann, S., Bannert, M., Dementieva, D., Fischer, F., Gasser, U., Groh, G., Günnemann, S., Hüllermeier, E., Krusche, S., Kutyniok, G., Michaeli, T., Nerdel, C., Pfeffer, J., Poquet, O., Sailer, M., Schmidt, A., Seidel, T., & Kasneci, G. (2023). ChatGPT for good? On opportunities and challenges of large language models for education. *Learning and Individual Differences*, *103*, 102274. DOI: 10.1016/j.lindif.2023.102274

Kelley, M., & Wenzel, T. (2025). Advancing Artificial Intelligence Literacy in Teacher Education Through Professional Partnership Inquiry. *Education Sciences*, *15*(6), 659. DOI: 10.3390/educsci15060659

Kumar, R., Eaton, S. E., Mindzak, M., & Morrison, R. (2023). Academic Integrity and Artificial Intelligence: An Overview. In Eaton, S. E. (Ed.), *Handbook of Academic Integrity* (pp. 1–14). Springer Nature Singapore., DOI: 10.1007/978-981-287-079-7_153-1

Kuo, M.-M., Li, X., Qian, L., Obiomon, P., & Dong, X. (2024). *Deep Knowledge Tracing for Personalized Adaptive Learning at Historically Black Colleges and Universities* (Version 1). arXiv. DOI: 10.48550/ARXIV.2410.13876

Lameras, P. (2022). A Vision of Teaching and Learning with AI. *2022 IEEE Global Engineering Education Conference (EDUCON)*, 1796–1803. DOI: 10.1109/EDUCON52537.2022.9766718

Law, L. (2024). Application of generative artificial intelligence (GenAI) in language teaching and learning: A scoping literature review. *Computers and Education Open*, *6*, 100174. DOI: 10.1016/j.caeo.2024.100174

Long, D., & Magerko, B. (2020). What is AI Literacy? Competencies and Design Considerations. *Proceedings of the 2020 CHI Conference on Human Factors in Computing Systems*, 1–16. DOI: 10.1145/3313831.3376727

Lourenço, O. (2012). Piaget and Vygotsky: Many resemblances, and a crucial difference. *New Ideas in Psychology*, *30*(3), 281–295. DOI: 10.1016/j.newideapsych.2011.12.006

Lu, F., Li, Y., & Bao, Y. (2025). Deep Knowledge Tracing Integrating Temporal Causal Inference and PINN. *Applied Sciences (Basel, Switzerland)*, *15*(3), 1504. DOI: 10.3390/app15031504

McTigue, E. M., & Flowers, A. C. (2011). Science Visual Literacy: Learners' Perceptions and Knowledge of Diagrams. *The Reading Teacher*, *64*(8), 578–589. DOI: 10.1598/RT.64.8.3

Min, T., Lee, B., & Jho, H. (2025). Integrating generative artificial intelligence in the design of scientific inquiry for middle school students. *Education and Information Technologies*, *30*(11), 15329–15360. Advance online publication. DOI: 10.1007/s10639-025-13410-1

Mittal, U., Sai, S., Chamola, V., & Sangwan, D. (2024). A Comprehensive Review on Generative AI for Education. *IEEE Access : Practical Innovations, Open Solutions*, *12*, 142733–142759. DOI: 10.1109/ACCESS.2024.3468368

Moore, S. L. (2007). David H. Rose, Anne Meyer, Teaching Every Student in the Digital Age: Universal Design for Learning: Association for Supervision and Curriculum Development, 1703 N. Beauregard St., Alexandria, VA 22311-1714, Product no. 101042, $22.95 ASCD members, $26.95 nonmembers, ISBN-0-87120-599-8. *Educational Technology Research and Development*, *55*(5), 521–525. DOI: 10.1007/s11423-007-9056 3

Nilmanee, T., Sintanakul, K., & Sakulviriyakitkul, P. (2024). The Design of a Learning Experience Platform using xAPI with Design Thinking Learning to Promote Innovation. [iJET]. *International Journal of Emerging Technologies in Learning*, *19*(01), 54–67. DOI: 10.3991/ijet.v19i01.44277

Nkambou, R., Bourdeau, J., & Mizoguchi, R. (Eds.). (2010). *Advances in Intelligent Tutoring Systems* (Vol. 308). Springer Berlin Heidelberg., DOI: 10.1007/978-3-642-14363-2

Papanikolaou, K. A., Grigoriadou, M., Kornilakis, H., & Magoulas, G. D. (2003). Personalizing the Interaction in a Web-based Educational Hypermedia System: The case of INSPIRE. *User Modeling and User-Adapted Interaction*, *13*(3), 213–267. DOI: 10.1023/A:1024746731130

Parks, C. (2017). Beyond Compliance: Students and FERPA in the Age of Big Data. *Journal of Intellectual Freedom & Privacy*, *2*(2), 23–33. DOI: 10.5860/jifp.v2i2.6253

Phillips, L. M., Norris, S. P., & Macnab, J. S. (2010). *Visualization in Mathematics, Reading and Science Education*. Springer Netherlands., DOI: 10.1007/978-90-481-8816-1

Piaget, J., & Piaget, J. (1973). *To understand is to invent: The future of education*. Grossman.

Ritter, S., Anderson, J. R., Koedinger, K. R., & Corbett, A. (2007). Cognitive Tutor: Applied research in mathematics education. *Psychonomic Bulletin & Review, 14*(2), 249–255. DOI: 10.3758/BF03194060

Selwyn, N. (2019). *Should robots replace teachers? AI and the future of education*. Polity Press.

Selwyn, N. (2022). The future of AI and education: Some cautionary notes. *European Journal of Education, 57*(4), 620–631. DOI: 10.1111/ejed.12532

Siemens, G. (2005). Connectivism: A Learning Theory for the Digital Age. *International Journal of Instructional Technology and Distance Learning*. https://www.itdl.org/Journal/Jan_05/article01.htm?utm_source=chatgpt.com

*The potential impact of Artificial Intelligence on equity and inclusion in education* (OECD Artificial Intelligence Papers). (2024). Organisation for Economic Co-Operation and Development (OECD). DOI: 10.1787/dee339a8-en

Tomak, B., & Virlan, A. Y. (2024). Ethical Considerations in the Educational Use of Generative AI Technologies. In Ara, A., & Ara, A. (Eds.), (pp. 49–62). Advances in Computational Intelligence and Robotics. IGI Global., DOI: 10.4018/979-8-3693-1565-1.ch004

VanLEHN, K. U. R. T.VanLEHN. (2011). The Relative Effectiveness of Human Tutoring, Intelligent Tutoring Systems, and Other Tutoring Systems. *Educational Psychologist, 46*(4), 197–221. DOI: 10.1080/00461520.2011.611369

Vashista, N., Gugnani, P., & Bala, M. (n.d.). *The Educator's Lens: Understanding the Impact of AI on Management Education*.

Villegas-Ch, W., Buenano-Fernandez, D., Navarro, A. M., & Mera-Navarrete, A. (2025). Adaptive intelligent tutoring systems for STEM education: Analysis of the learning impact and effectiveness of personalized feedback. *Smart Learning Environments, 12*(1), 41. DOI: 10.1186/s40561-025-00389-y

Walkington, C. A. (2013). Using adaptive learning technologies to personalize instruction to student interests: The impact of relevant contexts on performance and learning outcomes. *Journal of Educational Psychology, 105*(4), 932–945. DOI: 10.1037/a0031882

Woolf, B. P., Lane, H. C., Chaudhri, V. K., & Kolodner, J. L. (2013). AI Grand Challenges for Education. *AI Magazine, 34*(4), 66–84. DOI: 10.1609/aimag.v34i4.2490

Yildirim-Erbasli, S. N., & Bulut, O. (2023). Conversation-based assessment: A novel approach to boosting test-taking effort in digital formative assessment. *Computers and Education: Artificial Intelligence*, *4*, 100135. DOI: 10.1016/j.caeai.2023.100135

Zawacki-Richter, O., Marín, V. I., Bond, M., & Gouverneur, F. (2019). Systematic review of research on artificial intelligence applications in higher education – where are the educators? *International Journal of Educational Technology in Higher Education*, *16*(1), 39. Advance online publication. DOI: 10.1186/s41239-019-0171-0

Zhai, X. (2023). ChatGPT for Next Generation Science Learning. *XRDS: Crossroads. The ACM Magazine for Students*, *29*(3), 42–46. DOI: 10.1145/3589649

Zheng, W., Lu, S., Cai, Z., Wang, R., Wang, L., & Yin, L. (2024). PAL-BERT: An Improved Question Answering Model. *Computer Modeling in Engineering & Sciences*, *139*(3), 2729–2745. DOI: 10.32604/cmes.2023.046692

Zhou, X., Zhang, Z., Xie, X., & Zhang, J. (2025). Deep learning based knowledge tracing in intelligent tutoring systems. *Scientific Reports*, *15*(1), 21395. DOI: 10.1038/s41598-025-07422-7

Chapter 7

# Authoring Academic Resources for Science Education With a Generative AI Tool

**María Lucía Barrón-Estrada**
https://orcid.org/0000-0002-3856-9361
*Tecnológico Nacional de México, Mexico & Instituto Tecnológico de Culiacán, Mexico*

**Ramón Zatarain-Cabada**
https://orcid.org/0000-0002-4524-3511
*Tecnológico Nacional de México, Mexico & Instituto Tecnológico de Culiacán, Mexico*

**Víctor Manuel Bátiz-Beltrán**
https://orcid.org/0000-0003-4356-9793
*Tecnológico Nacional de México, Mexico & Instituto Tecnológico de Culiacán, Mexico*

**Aldo Uriarte-Portillo**
https://orcid.org/0000-0001-7812-962X
*Tecnológico Nacional de México, Mexico & Instituto Tecnológico de Culiacán, Mexico*

## ABSTRACT

*This book chapter introduces an LLM-powered educational tool for building science learning environments using a fully cloud-based platform. The tool is an educational platform driven by LLM that attempts to save teachers time by automatized processes*

DOI: 10.4018/979-8-3373-2913-0.ch007

*like lesson planning, grading, and resource generation. Using this platform, educators can modify and update pre-existing materials to fit the needs of any reader, produce unique science-related resources, and edit and distribute these materials to students. Any student can access instructional materials generated with the authoring tool interface through an internet-connected device. The tool accomplishes this by combining several technologies, including frameworks and tools like Ollama, JavaScript, and open-source LLMs like LLaMA 3, DeepSeek, Qwen2, and Gemma 2.*

## INTRODUCTION

Extended Reality (XR) and Extended Language Models (LLM) are disruptive technologies that are redefining multiple aspects of everyday life, especially in education. Students and teachers face new challenges, but also valuable opportunities to integrate these tools into the design of more immersive, personalized, and effective learning experiences.

Generative Artificial Intelligence has a significant impact on application fields, including science, education, medicine, languages, technologies, programming, and other fields, as it has been increasing in popularity since the emergence of ChatGPT (Banh & Strobel, 2023). These Artificial Intelligence (AI) tools can generate models based on contextual recognition of human-generated information, providing it in text, audio, image, and file import formats.

Advances in AI, particularly in machine learning (ML) and deep learning (DL), have led to data-driven AI techniques, such as predictions, classifications, or recommendations, evolving effective content generation in various formats, including blockchains, realistic images, video generation, or 3D model generation. The implementation of AI has led to the improvement and adaptation of the relationship between humans and intelligent systems, giving way to the automation of tasks and optimization of processes to ease decision-making, both in the business sector and in the personal life of the human being.

Generative Artificial Intelligence (AI) has turned into a key factor in the solution of many activities in areas such as business, industry, and marketing. Recently, it has become a tool that solves specific tasks, capable of learning, making creations, making some decisions, and even adapting and adjusting itself. Unlike other tools, AI has the power to analyze data, recognize patterns, and choose the best ways to act immediately.

But even with all this progress, there are still many things that people don't understand about what AI is, the magnitude that it can have, what it can do, and the limitations it can bring. This misperception of people leads to many fallacies and ignorance of how to use AI in the right way. These unclear ideas show that a clear plan is needed to help use Generative AI in any environment, be it in daily life or any other area.

On the other hand, in education, emerging technologies such as augmented reality (AR), virtual reality (VR), and, more recently, extended reality (XR), have led to significant advances in the design and development of immersive and contextualized learning environments in various areas of knowledge (Alnagrat et al., 2022). Specifically, XR has a high pedagogical potential by enabling the visual and experiential representation of abstract and complex concepts, the recreation of realistic situations, and the simulation of risk scenarios in controlled environments. These characteristics favor the creation of interactive, dynamic, and multisensory learning spaces, which not only increase student motivation and commitment but also contribute to greater efficiency in the acquisition and retention of knowledge. Various sectors have begun to incorporate this technology: in the medical field, it is used for training surgeons in complex clinical procedures (Barteit et al., 2021); in robotics, it allows to emulate work contexts with high fidelity (Kaarlela et al., 2022); in the aeronautics industry, it is applied to the design and simulation of flight operations (Cross et al., 2023); and in the educational sector, it has been adopted as a didactic tool to facilitate more effective and meaningful teaching-learning processes (Alnagrat et al., 2022).

However, the development of XR-based applications involves a few technical and operational challenges. These include the need to design specialized algorithms, the modeling and customization of 3D content, the configuration of appropriate infrastructures to support both the development and execution of such applications, as well as the considerable assets of time and resources required for the entire process. In addition to these factors, there are issues related to interoperability, scalability, and real-time performance optimization.

In this context, the authoring tool presented in this chapter is a cloud-based educational platform, designed to create immersive learning environments by integrating extended language models (LLMs) with extended reality (XR) technologies. Its primary purpose is to optimize teaching work by automating pedagogical tasks such as lesson planning, assessment generation, and the production of personalized educational content. The authoring tool allows teachers to adjust pre-existing materials to provide different student profiles, develop personalized resources in various areas of knowledge, and design immersive learning environments through technologies such as WebXR. In addition, it offers tools for editing, sharing, and accessing this content from any device with an Internet connection, thanks to its responsive web interface.

The generative artificial intelligence component of the authoring tool integrates a few advanced technologies, including open-source language models such as LLaMA 3, DeepSeek, Qwen2, and Gemma 2, as well as frameworks and development tools such as Ollama, Google Blockly (for visual programming), JavaScript, React, Node.js, Firebase, and WebXR. This technological architecture allows the authoring tool platform to offer a scalable, accessible, and adaptive solution for teaching and learning in immersive digital environments.

Large Language Models (LLM), a component of generative artificial intelligence, have had a significant impact, particularly in the field of education, since their introduction with ChatGPT and later with related applications like Gemini, Claude, Llama, and DeepSeek. LLMs are machine learning (or deep learning) AI models that have been trained on vast amounts of data to be able to create text, images, and videos automatically.

For example, Yan et al. (2024b) present in their research several use cases related to the automation of educational tasks using LLMs. They can also translate text into many languages and generate code in numerous programming languages (Kazemitabaar et al., 2023), among other crucial tasks that humans carry out on a daily basis. LLMs have proven especially useful in a variety of educational applications and professions. For instance, they can be used to answer inquiries from students in a variety of fields, including computer programming, mathematics, medicine, or to identify code bugs or fix sentences with grammatical errors. They are also used to generate several kinds of exam questions in a variety of subjects, including programming and mathematics (Tran et al., 2023).

In their research work, Li et al. (2024) propose the automatic generation of mathematics questions using LLMs and mention that, using their framework, they manage to generate questions of a level comparable to those meticulously elaborated by humans. The use of LLMs to provide conversational capabilities to enable the user to better understand a topic is an area that has recently gained interest. In their research, Wu et al. (2023) propose a conversational problem-solving framework designed for mathematical problems.

This chapter opens with an overview of LLM and generative artificial intelligence, giving readers a fundamental grasp of the ideas at play. The popular LLM and the technology used to develop them are then covered in the chapter. The software architecture and framework are later presented in the chapter, along with an explanation of each of its constituent parts. The chapter then outlines the process of developing scholarly materials and entire courses that cover areas associated with several scientific disciplines. It concludes with examples of science courses developed using the Generative AI authoring tool.

## LITERATURE REVIEW

Cipresso et al. (2018) conducted a research study that systematically explores the evolution and current landscape of virtual reality (VR) and augmented reality (AR) research. The study analyzed a large dataset of scientific articles from the Web of Science to identify key trends in publication types, subject categories, and influential authors and institutions. The study reveals a notable shift in VR research towards clinical and medical applications, moving beyond its initial focus on computer science and engineering. It also charts the emerging interdisciplinary nature and applications of AR.

Wilson et al. (2013) conducted a study to investigate the potential of AR goggles as a clinical support tool to enhance the performance of combat medics in treating tension pneumothoraxes, a leading cause of preventable battlefield deaths. The researchers conducted a pilot study with preclinical medical students and compared a group that used AR goggles to guide needle decompression on cadaver models with a control group that relied solely on a lecture for guidance. Their findings showed that the students using the goggles were significantly more accurate in performing the procedure. This suggests that AR can bridge the gap between insufficient training and critical skill decay. Thus, it can improve life-saving interventions in austere environments.

In recent years, virtual reality has moved into web applications; an example of this is the research presented by Yan et al. (2020). This research introduces a comprehensive solution for online fire evacuation training using WebVR (Virtual Reality on the Web), addressing significant challenges like large data volumes, slow network speeds, and limited browser rendering capabilities. The authors developed lightweight technologies to compress massive Building Information Modeling (BIM) data and Fire Dynamic Simulator (FDS) smoke data, making real-time transmission feasible. Furthermore, they propose TC-eACO, an enhanced algorithm for planning optimal crowd evacuation paths, which leverages historical human escape traces for improved efficiency and a higher success rate compared to existing methods. The prototype system, which runs directly in a web browser without plugins, demonstrates the viability of this approach for public fire evacuation drills in various large-scale scenarios.

In their research, Hafidz et al. (2021) demonstrate that XR can be used in web applications. The authors proposed a design for a collaborative WebXR medical learning platform to address the challenges in medical education caused by the COVID-19 pandemic's disruption of traditional in-person learning. They highlight the need for innovative XR solutions offering immersive, interactive experiences, with a focus on integrating virtual reality (VR) and mixed reality (MR). Their research aims to develop a robust WebXR platform that facilitates collaborative medical simulations, enabling students to engage in effective, remote, practical learning. The paper ultimately outlines the architectural design and implementation considerations for this new educational tool, emphasizing its potential to improve learning outcomes and accessibility in medical training.

Vasarainen et al. (2021) carried out a systematic literature review examining the application of extended reality (XR), which encompasses VR, AR, and mixed reality (MR), in collaborative work environments. The authors sought to understand how XR is utilized in real-life settings and identified its primary application areas as design, remote collaboration, and training. While acknowledging XR's potential to overcome challenges related to time, space, safety, and resources by mediating shared spatial experiences, the review concludes that long-term, established uses of XR are still relatively rare, with its current impact mostly demonstrated in experimental scenarios.

In the research conducted by Reeves et al. (2021), the application of AR in bioscience education is explored, specifically for teaching complex protein structures. The authors from Solent University Southampton, detail their methodology, which involved converting 3D protein crystal structures into AR models using Zapworks, and integrating them into a biochemistry module. While a formative test showed only a modest increase in student performance, a survey revealed that students overwhelmingly found the AR experience engaging and interactive, indicating its value as a tool for visualization and promoting active learning, especially in the context of evolving blended learning environments. The study suggests that despite some practical limitations, AR holds significant potential to enrich higher education by making abstract concepts more accessible and fostering student interest.

The research work carried out by Bozkurt et al. (2021) systematically reviews the trends and patterns of Artificial Intelligence (AI) in education from 1970 to 2020. The authors utilize a systematic review approach combined with social network analysis and text-mining to identify key research clusters and themes. The study reveals a significant increase in AI in education publications, especially post-2018, primarily originating from computer science but also notably from social sciences, with the United States and China leading research output. The core findings highlight five major research themes: adaptive learning and personalization, deep learning and machine learning for online education, human-AI interaction in educational contexts, the use of AI-generated data, and AI's role in higher education. Crucially, the authors emphasize that ethics in AI studies remains an overlooked research area, despite its profound importance for the responsible integration of AI into educational processes.

Generative AI has the potential to change and enhance how people learn by offering personalized help, providing a wider range of learning materials, giving quick feedback, and creating new ways to assess learning. Whether these benefits are realized depends on how Generative AI interacts with both learners and teachers (Yan et al., 2024a). In this section, we will first address some work on artificial intelligence in industry, AI as a support tool in education, and finally, generative AI tools applied to education.

In his research, Bianchini (2025) addresses the urgent need to clearly define generative artificial intelligence (GenAI), emphasizing that its rapid development has surpassed our conceptual understanding. The author highlights a significant discrepancy between technical and public discourse surrounding GenAI, noting that public perception often focuses on the system's output and perceived capabilities rather than its technical underpinnings. This divergence has crucial social, legal, and policy implications, underlining the need for conceptual clarification. The paper ultimately argues that GenAI is evolving from a passive tool into an interactive agent — a shift that necessitates ongoing definitional efforts, given the increasing intertwining of human users and AI systems.

The research work by Jauhiainen and Guerra (2023) investigates the potential and effectiveness of generative AI, specifically ChatGPT-3.5 and -4, in primary school education. The authors conducted a practical study with 110 Uruguayan schoolchildren aged 8-14, observing their interaction with AI-modified learning materials in history lessons. A key finding is that generative AI can personalize educational content to suit diverse student knowledge levels and interests, fostering motivated and cognitively ergonomic learning experiences. While acknowledging the need for further development and ethical guidelines, the research highlights AI's promising role in enhancing inclusive and sustainable education by providing tailored support and real-time feedback.

In their academic article, Conrad and Nuebel (2025) investigate high school students' acceptance and use of ChatGPT in German schools, seeking to understand the factors driving its adoption. The researchers surveyed over 500 students, applying the Unified Theory of Acceptance and Use of Technology 2 (UTAUT2) model, which suggests that various influences predict technology use. Key findings indicate that perceived usefulness, established habits, and the enjoyment derived from using ChatGPT are the strongest predictors of students' intent to use the AI tool, suggesting that practical benefits and positive experiences outweigh other considerations. The study also reveals that ChatGPT is widely used for tasks like information retrieval and text generation, particularly in humanities subjects, and argues that schools should focus on integrating AI literacy into curricula rather than attempting to ban the technology.

The research by Kuleto et al. (2021) explores the transformative impact of AI and ML on the educational landscape, particularly within higher education institutions (HEIs). The study investigates how these advanced technologies can enhance learning, improve institutional efficiency, and make research more accessible. The authors conducted a mixed-methods study combining a thorough literature review with primary survey research among Serbian university students to understand their knowledge of, and attitudes towards, the potential benefits and drawbacks of AI and ML. The study ultimately concludes that AI and ML are essential technologies that can significantly improve students' skills, foster collaborative learning, and provide a conducive environment for academic research in HEIs.

In their article, Wang et al. (2023) explore the potential impact of artificial intelligence (AI) on international students in higher education. The article highlights the unique challenges these students face, such as language barriers and cultural differences, and investigates how various AI applications, including personalized learning experiences, adaptive testing, predictive analytics, and chatbots, can enhance their academic success. While emphasizing AI's potential to improve learning efficiency and provide personalized support, the paper also thoroughly addresses significant risks and limitations, such as privacy concerns, bias, and ethical implications. Ultimately, the paper argues that AI should complement human educators to create a more inclusive and effective educational environment for international students.

The research conducted by Pesovski et al. (2024) explored the potential of generative AI to create customizable learning experiences within educational settings, with a focus on how AI can personalize educational content. The authors developed an integrated tool for an existing learning management system (LMS) that automatically generates learning materials in various styles, including those inspired by a traditional teacher persona and two pop culture characters: Batman and Wednesday Addams. A study involving 20 software engineering students revealed that, although the traditional style was used the most, students found the diverse content engaging and particularly appreciated the automatically generated multiple-choice questions for self-assessment. This research suggests that this AI-driven approach could increase students' study time, particularly among those who might otherwise struggle, paving the way for future personalized and engaging educational strategies.

In their research, Filippi and Motyl (2024) present a systematic review of the current role of Large Language Models (LLMs) in engineering education. The authors meticulously filtered an extensive initial selection of papers to identify twenty relevant studies, which they analyzed across eight key dimensions: who is involved; how, why, and where LLMs are used; their measured impact; which specific tools are utilized; and when and where in the educational process they appear. The authors also considered the associated pros and cons. The primary goal of this research is to provide a clear overview of LLM involvement and offer practical suggestions for their responsible and effective adoption in engineering curricula, with the ultimate aim of enhancing teaching and learning experiences.

In their study, Idrisov and Schlippe (2024) examined the effectiveness of generative AI in creating program code by comparing AI-generated solutions with those written by humans. They assessed various aspects of code quality, such as correctness, efficiency, and maintainability, using metrics like lines of code, cyclomatic complexity, time/space complexity, runtime, memory usage, Halstead complexity, and maintainability index. The study reveals that, while AI-generated code isn't always perfect, it has the potential to significantly reduce programming time, even when initial solutions require minor human modifications, by having different AI models solve LeetCode problems in Java, Python, and C++. The study aims to provide insight into the current capabilities and limitations of AI in code generation, highlighting its potential to augment, rather than replace, human programming efforts.

## AUTHORING TOOL

This section first introduces the XR environment creation component of the authoring tool (XR component). Here, users can create extended reality environments for educational purposes using a variety of elements. This enables users with no programming experience to intuitively and efficiently create and share such environments. After that, the generative artificial intelligence component (GenAI component) is presented. This part of the authoring tool is a cloud platform designed to make it easy for teachers to create courses and presentations that combine immersive educational experiences with Extended Reality (XR) and textual content for lessons and assessments.

This integration is supported by generative artificial intelligence through open-source extended language models (LLMs). Courses and presentations can be easily shared with students through a link, offering an interactive, accessible, and personalized learning experience.

### Authoring Tool's XR Component

The authoring tool's XR component is a comprehensive platform composed of multiple modules, each serving a specific function within the extended reality (XR) development workflow. These include a module for uploading and managing multimedia assets, a module for reviewing previously constructed environments, a module for designing XR environments through block-based programming, and a module for visualizing the resulting XR environments across various devices.

#### Software Architecture

The authoring tool was designed based on the use of emerging technologies such as augmented reality (AR), virtual reality (VR), and extended reality (XR).

The implementation of blocks was selected to create and customize the XR learning environments, with the advantage of displaying the changes in real-time, allowing the user to access the platform from any device with an Internet connection, with the facility to import 3D models, multimedia files, and, as an additional benefit, to be able to share the created environments with other users. In Figure 1, the software architecture of the authoring tool is presented.

*Figure 1. Authoring tool software architecture*

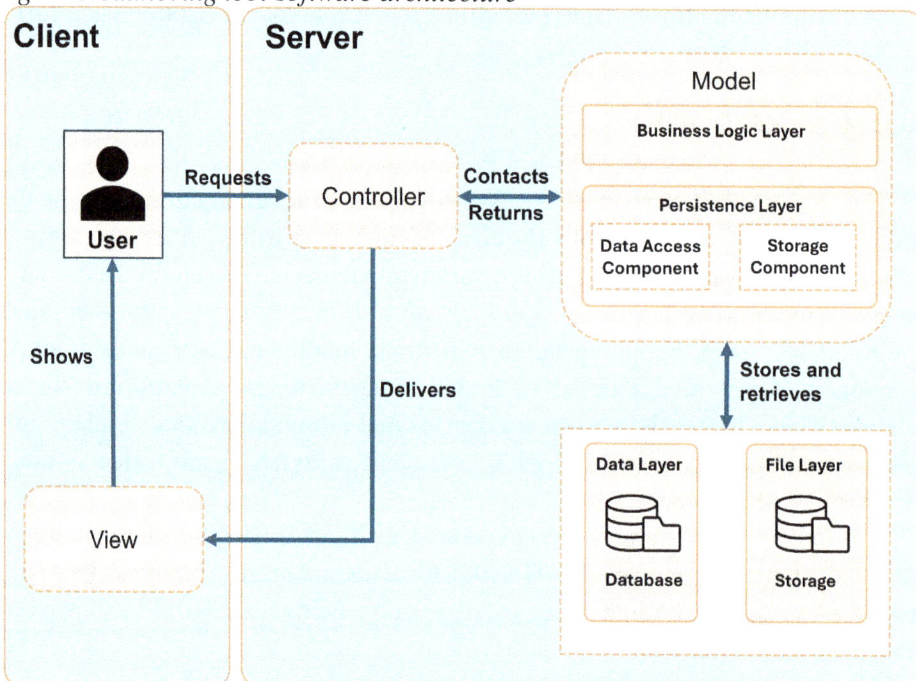


The authoring tool functions as a distributed system that has been based on a client–server architecture. This configuration guarantees a distinct separation between the client, where users interact with the platform, and the server, where core processing and data management occur; this ensures that students and educators can access a reliable platform without being affected by background complexity. This separation of client and server functions translates into a smoother user experience, where learners focus on content creation and collaboration rather than technical issues.

The implementation of the Model–View–Controller (MVC) architectural pattern in the development of the authoring tool is intended to facilitate maintainability and optimize development efficiency.

The View is responsible for visually presenting data to users in an intuitive, clean, and responsive interface, lowering cognitive load and allowing them to participate with content rather than navigating technical obstacles. It doesn't handle business logic or data processing, keeping the interface simple and focused.

The Controller serves as the conduit between user actions and system responses. It is responsible for interpreting interactions and triggering changes in the model or updates to the view. This layer is also responsible for overseeing essential operations, including user management, project coordination, content creation, and file handling. Essentially, the Controller translates student actions into system responses, enabling real-time interaction, project coordination, and collaborative content development, which are key to active learning.

The Model incorporates business logic and persistence layers, thereby ensuring data consistency and core operations. This guarantees data integrity, consistency, and reliability, giving students confidence that their progress, projects, and contributions are safely managed.

To support layers and services of the authoring tool, modules are added to enrich the authoring tool's capabilities by handling storage, data access, and other services. By ensuring reliable data management and seamless integration of services, students and educators can focus on learning activities without being burdened by technical difficulties. The Persistence layer is responsible for managing the data, applying business rules, and executing the core logic. It ensures that everything works correctly. This layer is responsible for the management of data access and storage components. The data access component functions as a translator between the cloud-based database and the authoring tool's internal logic, thereby offering an elegant abstraction layer for managing database operations. More precisely, the data access layer provides a smooth bridge between the database and the tool, which guarantees consistency and accuracy in student projects, fostering trust in the system as a learning environment.

Conversely, the storage component oversees the management of media files, plays a critical pedagogical role by enabling the use of diverse media—such as images, videos, and 3D models—in teaching and learning. This component encompasses functions such as uploading, storing, and retrieving these format files. This capacity supports the teaching and learning process, allowing educators to present abstract or complex concepts in more visual and interactive ways. For students, it enhances engagement, deepens comprehension, and promotes creativity in building projects.

The Data Layer is hosted via Google Firebase Firestore, which uses a flexible NoSQL format to efficiently store and retrieve structured data for the application. The File Layer is also powered by Firebase Storage. It securely stores all multimedia assets, ensuring easy access and seamless integration into user projects. This flexibility enables students to participate in asynchronous collaboration, to continue their work, and to engage in learning with real-world tools. The system design is designed to facilitate the effective use of rich, interactive content by both teachers and students, thereby reinforcing active learning and knowledge construction.

## XR Component User Interface

The XR component is a cloud platform designed to facilitate the creation of extended reality (XR) environments for teachers. Users can register their profiles, upload multimedia files (such as images, videos, and audio), and build interactive XR environments. These environments can be shared with students via a URL, which allows for accessible, immersive, and highly customizable learning experiences (Cabada et al., 2024).

Initially developed within the framework of the work of Sotelo-Rivas (2024), the XR component forms the technological foundation upon which the GenAI component is built. Both platforms share key architectural decisions, as well as many of the technologies used for XR content processing, visualization, and management. The immersive environment design functionality present in the XR component represents a fundamental module that has been extended and integrated within the GenAI component ecosystem.

The following paragraphs describe the process of creating an XR environment using this module, detailing the tools, stages, and components involved. Subsequently, the specific technologies that underpin the complete development of the GenAI Component of the authoring tool and its integration with extended language models (LLM) will be addressed.

The major functions of the authoring tool allow users to develop XR applications through a block-based visual approach, using the Blockly tool as a simplified programming system (Cabada et al., 2024). The creation of an XR environment starts from the incorporation of essential elements for any immersive scenario: a camera in universal mode that enables free movement in all directions, hemispherical lighting for uniform ambient illumination, a three-dimensional sky with customizable dimensions and texture that enhances the sense of realism, and a base floor that defines the main plane of the environment.

Once the base space is configured, three-dimensional objects can be added, either from primitive geometric shapes or by importing external models in .glb, .gltf, or .babylon formats. These elements can be scaled, repositioned, and freely arranged within the environment. Additionally, informative windows with textual or audiovisual content (videos) can be incorporated to enrich the interaction and educational value of the experience.

Figure 2 shows the main window of the application, which allows direct review of the list of developed XR environments. A contextual menu is displayed when the user profile is selected from the top-right corner. The contextual menu provides access to "Mis construcciones" (My constructions), where the XR environments are listed; "Mis cursos y presentaciones" (My courses and presentations), which is the generative AI content creation tool; and "Mi multimedia" (My multimedia), where users can add multimedia elements for use in XR environments. Each of these sections is discussed in more detail below.

*Figure 2. Authoring tool main interface*

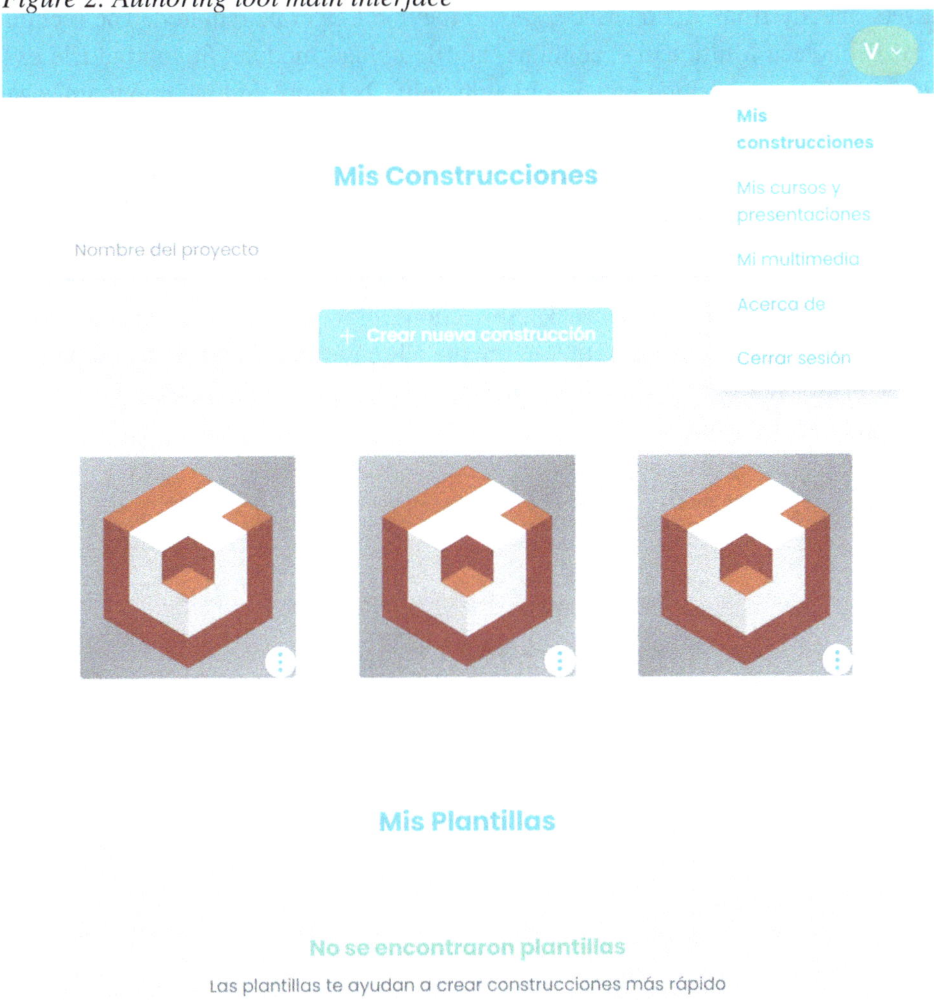

## Multimedia Page

The Multimedia page ("Mi multimedia") is designed as a personal repository where the teacher can manage the digital resources to be used in the construction of XR learning environments, such as images, videos, audio, and 3D models. The interface is organized into sections delimited by file type, which facilitates navigation and content management. All uploaded files are securely stored in the cloud storage service provided by Firebase. Users can delete any previously imported assets directly from this interface, should they no longer be required. The section "Mi Biblioteca Multimedia" contains the file upload module. Supported file extensions (.jpg, .png, .mp4, .mp3, .obj, .glb, .gltf, .babylon) and the maximum size limit per file (20 MB) are displayed here. The "Subir archivo" (Upload file) button allows teachers to import new resources into the system. The section below the button displays the names of images uploaded to the platform. The button with a camera icon allows the user to preview the image. The button with a trash icon can delete the selected file from the platform. There are also sections on the same page for audio, video, and 3D models. These sections allow users to visualize the added resources of these types for further use in the XR environment creation component of the platform. Figure 3 shows the interface of the Multimedia Library Page ("Mi biblioteca Multimedia").

*Figure 3. Authoring tool multimedia library page*

## Construction Page

The construction page ("Mis construcciones") allows users to create a new XR environment project by selecting the library they would like to work with and assigning a name to their creation (actually, only the BabylonJS library is available). They can also browse and handle their previously built environments, which are stored in Google Firestore. These previous projects are organized and displayed in a list format, making it easy to locate and review each one. Figure 4 shows the Construction page interface. The constructions are organized in a list, which makes it easy to identify, modify, or delete them as needed. The authoring tool allows these XR environments to be integrated into the courses developed by the generative AI component for course creation.

*Figure 4. Authoring tool construction page*

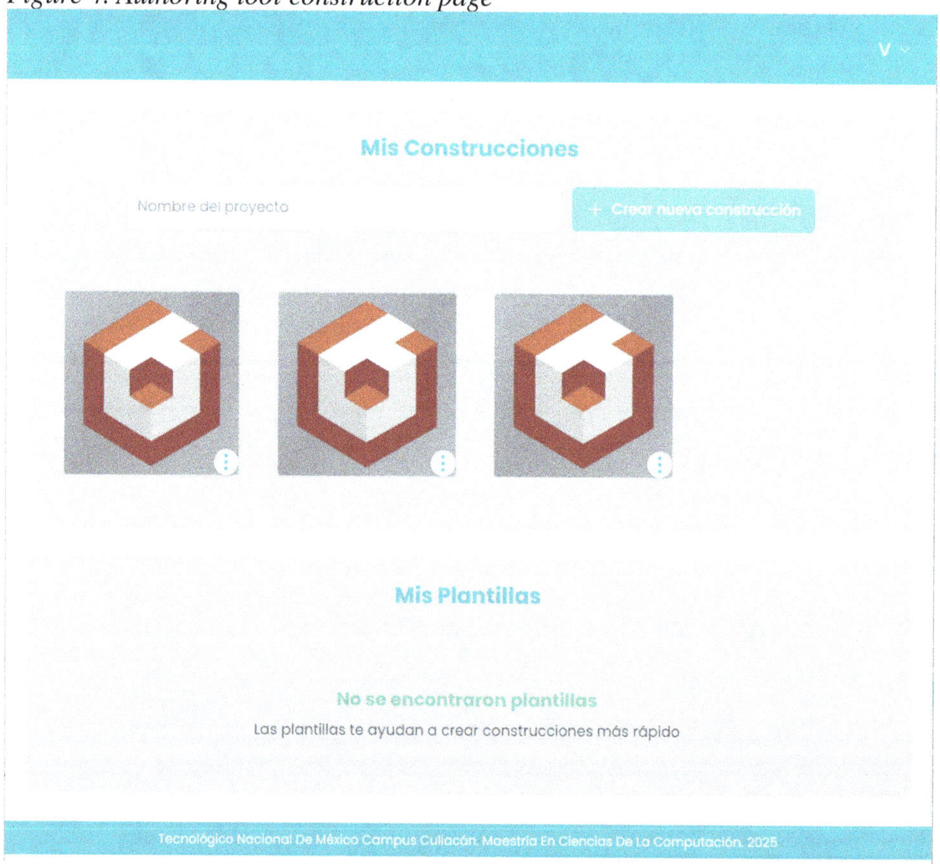

## My Constructions

After creating a new construction by entering the project name and clicking "Crear nueva construcción" (Create new construction) or selecting an existing construction to edit, a new page will appear. This page is divided into two sections, as shown in Figure 5. On the left side of the construction page, you will find the toolbar. It offers a set of building blocks classified by functionality, such as conditions, loops, and logic, as well as more visual and interactive elements, like 2D and 3D shapes, cameras, lights, and XR environments. You'll also find categories for arithmetic, text, variables, functions, floors, skies, materials, textures, colors, actions, audio, transformations, utilities, and windows. Each category contains blocks tailored to help users design, customize, and control every aspect of their XR environment.

To the right of the toolbar is the canvas or *workspace* area. In this area, users can drag and drop blocks to bring their behavior into the environment. Here, blocks can be connected to define logic, trigger actions, and shape how the environment behaves. Whether you're placing a Camera, adjusting Lights, sculpting with geometric Shapes, or integrating dynamic elements like Audio or Actions, the workspace is where creativity meets control.

*Figure 5. Construction page*

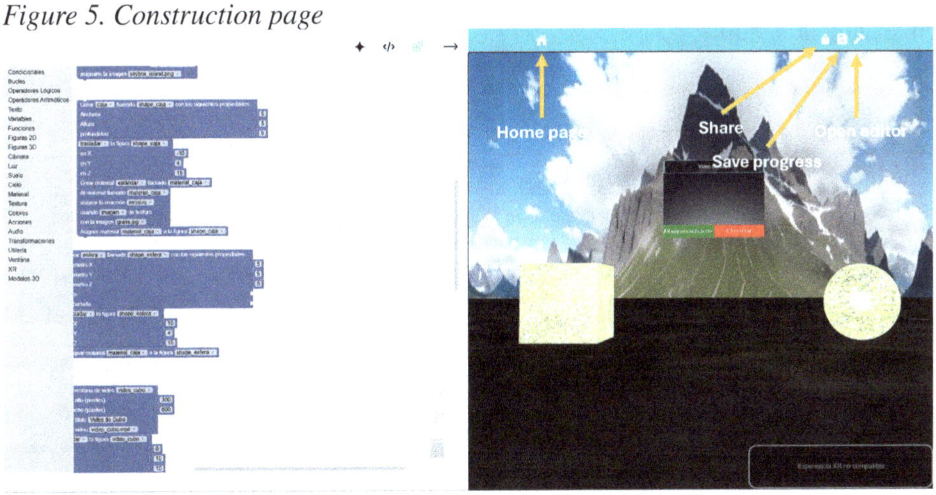


There are several icons available at the top of the XR environment display interface. The functionality of each icon is described below.

Home page: This icon allows you to quickly return to the main GenAI Component screen, facilitating navigation between the different sections of the platform.

Share the current construction: The user can generate a link to share the XR environment under development. This functionality enables the external visualization of the project, allowing other users to access an immersive experience as an autonomous educational resource.

Save progress: This option allows storing the changes persistently made in the construction, ensuring the integrity of the work and making it possible to resume later from the last saved point.

Open editor: This icon activates the Blockly block editor, which is displayed in the left panel of the interface. From here, the user can add, modify, and structure components and functionalities of the XR environment through visual programming, promoting an accessible learning curve for users without advanced technical knowledge.

## Basic Construction Blocks

Table 1 provides a detailed overview of the basic blocks employed to initialize an XR environment, including the setup of the camera and its properties, the lighting configuration, the ground and its dimensions, and the sky element with its corresponding textures, as well as colors, textures and materials, and 3D figures. These foundational elements serve as the structural basis upon which the immersive environment is built.

*Table 1. Initial components of XR environment*

<table>
<tr><th>Asset</th><th>Description</th><th>Example</th></tr>
<tr><td>Camera</td><td>Initialize the Camera main component in the default position (0,0,0). Users can change the initial position in the x, y, and z axes.</td><td>
</td></tr>
<tr><td>Lights</td><td>Users can apply one of four types of light (hemispherical, directional, punctual, and point light), and personalize positions in the x, y, and z axes.</td><td>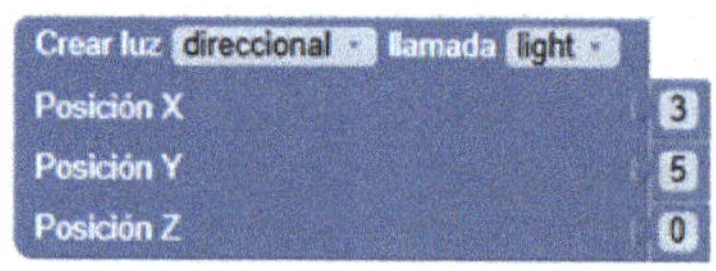
</td></tr>
<tr><td>Ground</td><td>The scene begins with a ground element, configured to a specific size to match the layout needs.</td><td>
</td></tr>
<tr><td>Skybox</td><td>A skybox with a personalized size will be created in the scene.</td><td>
</td></tr>
</table>

continued on following page

*Table 1. Continued*

| Asset | Description | Example |
|---|---|---|
| **Colors** | Define and set a color to use, whether for use in materials or other components within the environment, using RGB format, HSV, or a color predefined. | 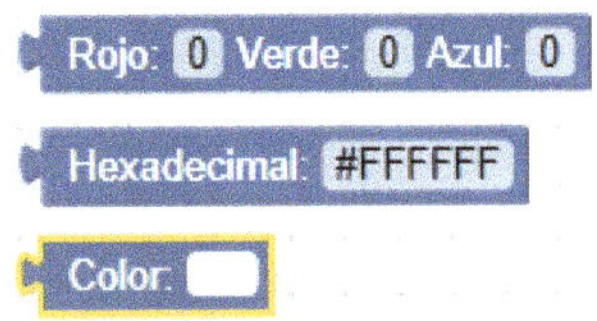 |
| **Materials** | A new material is created and assigned a specific color to serve as its texture. Once configured, the material is applied to the object, giving it its final appearance. | 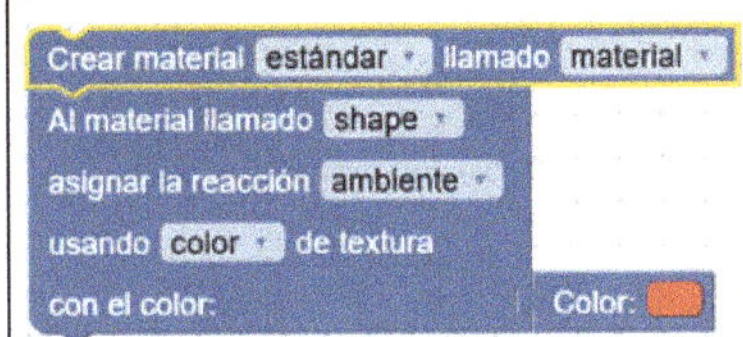 |
| **3D Figures** | Creates a 3D object (shape, sphere, cylinder, box, and plane) where users can modify their dimensions (width, height, and depth). Also, the users can add materials and customize the reaction, ambient, and color. | 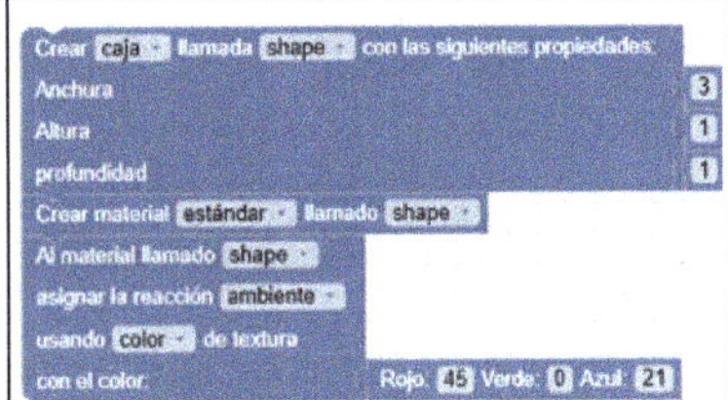 |
| **Transform** | Users can move, rotate, and resize any asset to adjust its position and appearance within the scene. | 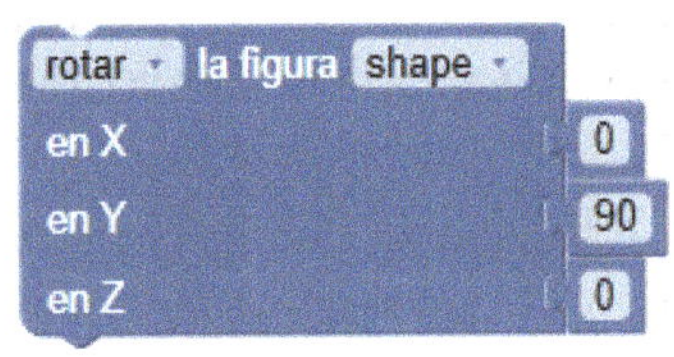 |
| **Actions** | Interactive behavior is assigned to the asset (click, double click, mouse over), and an action will be triggered by executing a block or set of blocks, as well as customizing parameters. | 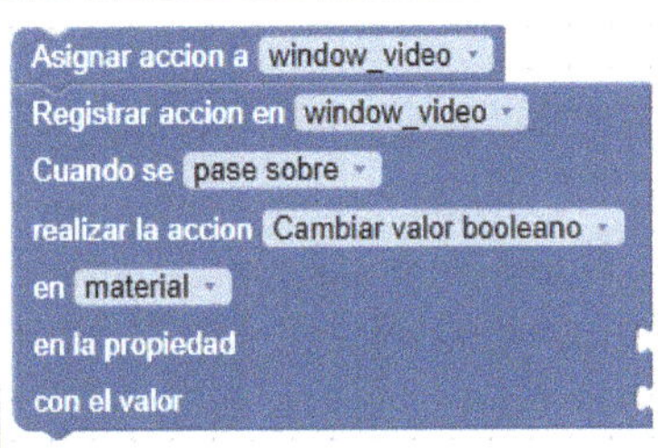 |
| **XR** | Create the XR Environment over the ground or skybox. |  |

Finally, the authoring tool XR component has a built-in code viewer that shows the source code created from the blocks used to build the project. This feature helps users learn and understand better how the XR environment is programmed. The code viewer is available as a tab in the editor, letting users easily switch between the block-based view and the code view whenever they need it. Figure 6 displays an example of the built-in code viewer.

*Figure 6. My construction built-in code viewer*

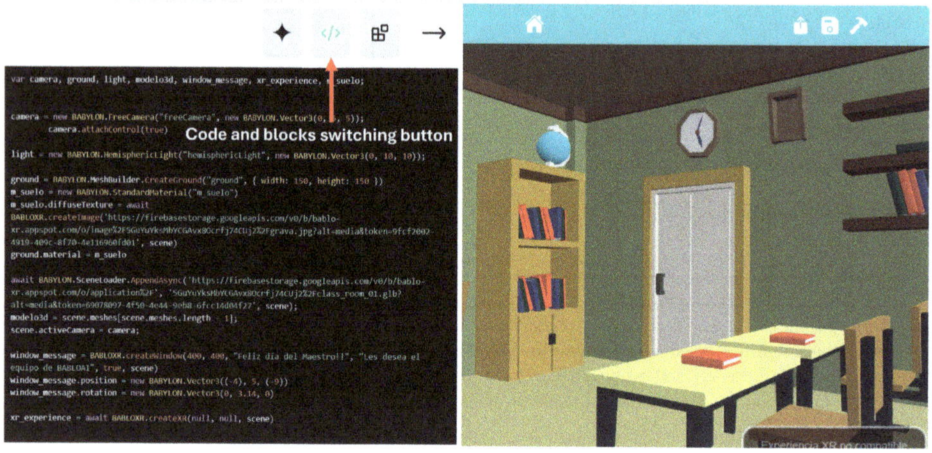


## Examples of XR Environments

As shown in Figure 7, the authoring tool's ability to use a variety of multimedia resources and three-dimensional elements allows users to create XR environments focused on a wide range of topics. The descriptions of the projects are:

A) A thematic environment explaining the history of different atomic models.

B) A virtual kitchen with step-by-step images for tuna preparation, complemented with contextual information and an instructional video.

C) An interactive art gallery with visual representations of Renaissance characters, accompanied by brief biographical sketches.

D) A blueprint-like environment that uses Minecraft-inspired blocks to represent concepts related to mathematical fractions, with each block serving a specific function.

Each of these XR environments can be accessed through a QR code, which facilitates direct consultation from mobile devices or compatible viewers.

*Figure 7. XR environments created with the authoring tool*

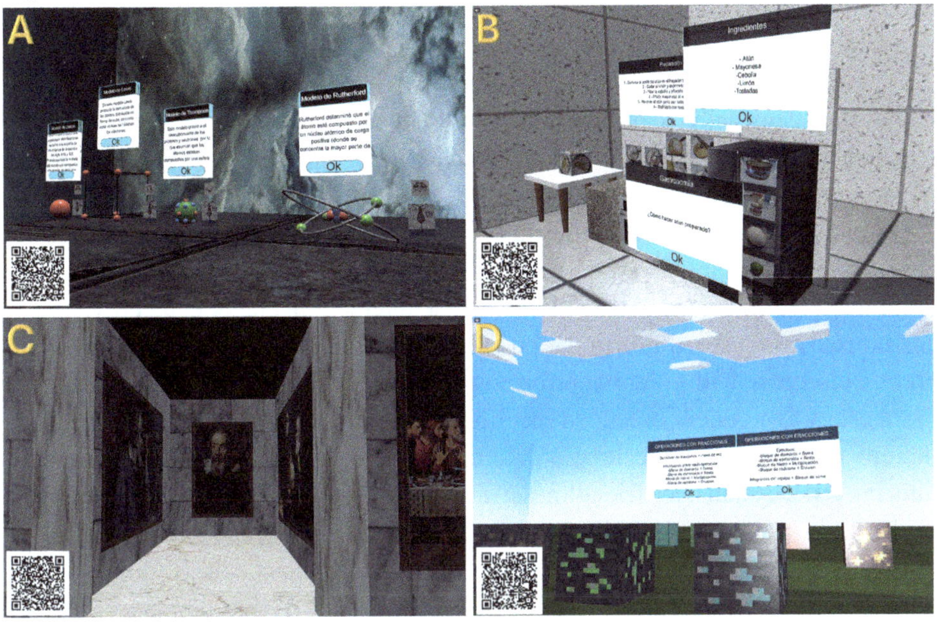


*Note. (A) Explanation of atomic models; (B) Kitchen with tutorial to prepare tuna; (C) Gallery of famous Renaissance characters; (D) Minecraft-themed fraction tutorials (Cabada et al., 2024)*

## AUTHORING TOOL GENAI COMPONENT

This section focuses on the description of the user interfaces that integrate the GenAI Component platform. It is a comprehensive platform oriented to the creation, management, integration, and visualization of educational content based on extended reality (XR) technologies and extended language models (LLM). The integration of user interfaces within the GenAI Component platform supports teaching and learning by aligning technology with the natural flow of the educational process. Its modular design contemplates various interfaces organized according to the key stages of the educational process (Cabada et al., 2024).

By combining XR technologies with LLM-based interactions, the platform makes abstract concepts more tangible, supports personalized feedback, and fosters immersive, student-centered experiences. This approach not only enhances engagement but also encourages deeper understanding, collaboration, and the development of higher-order thinking skills.

## Main Interfaces for LLM-assisted Course and Presentation Creation

The special advantage of large language models (LLMs) in assisting learning is that they can easily scale and adapt. LLMs can function as a teacher who can simultaneously guide multiple students, providing personalized and adaptive support in various subjects, areas of study, and even different languages (Yan et al., 2024a).

In comparison to conventional tutoring systems, which necessitate extensive configuration to establish response rules, LLM models have the capacity to facilitate more effective and natural interactions. These interactions include the provision of customized responses, the formulation of insightful inquiries, and the engagement in precise discourse with minimal prior preparation. Furthermore, LLM models have the capacity to produce content on specific subjects in a remarkably brief timeframe, thereby facilitating the acceleration of content development. This enhancement in tutoring efficacy and user-friendliness, in turn, fosters a more engaging and customized learning environment, aligning with the distinct needs and learning styles of individual learners. This capability has the potential to enhance the learning support available to individuals globally.

All functionalities that are powered by extended language models (LLMs) were designed under the human-in-the-loop (HITL) approach (Kumar et al., 2024). This approach enables the author to exercise direct control over the generated content. Specifically, the author can employ the proposals delivered by the APINET (Cabada et al., 2023) and Ollama systems as is, or edit, adjust, or complement them according to the pedagogical requirements of the learning experience the author wishes to build. This model is designed to ensure a balanced approach to education, integrating automation with human oversight to enhance the quality and relevance of the educational material produced.

A course is comprised of multiple modules. Each module is composed of specific content units or subtopics. Furthermore, each module incorporates an evaluation designed to determine the students' comprehension and advancement towards the established objectives. This system design favors structured content planning, ensuring a logical progression in learning. It also allows for the design of assessments aligned with the intended learning outcomes. Figure 8 represents the hierarchical architecture that a course follows within the platform.

*Figure 8. Course structure*

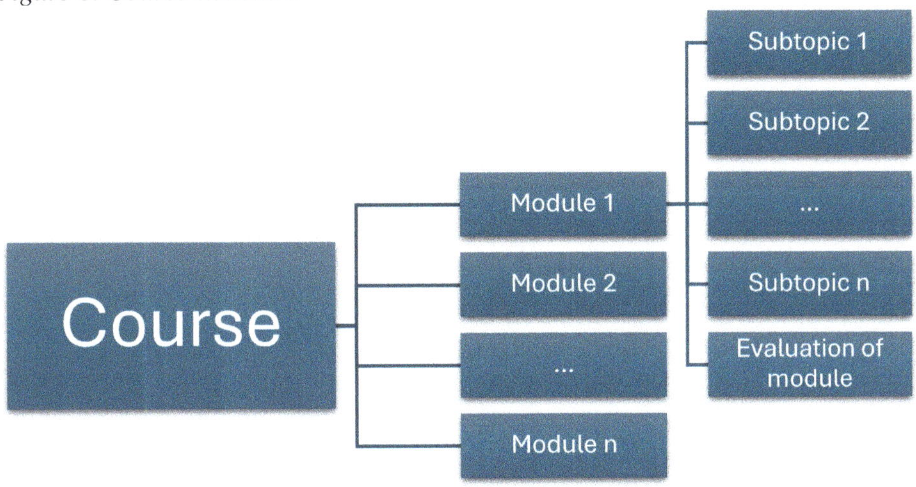


## Course Creation Main Interface

The process starts with the definition of the general parameters of the course. The user must enter the title, specify the number of modules, select the corresponding educational level, and then the platform automatically generates a structured index based on this data.

Subsequent to the generation of the table of contents, the educational content is created. The platform is designed to confirm with the user whether the content generated by the LLMs for each topic is appropriate. In the event that content is deemed inappropriate, users have the option to make manual edits. Additionally, the option to manually add content, subtopics, or modules is provided.

Once the content is completely covered, validated, and adjusted, the platform automatically generates an evaluation per module, which may include multiple-choice questions. The author reviews the quality of the generated questions; if they are not adequate, he/she can edit or delete questions and options. Additionally, the user has the option to append new questions or expand the assessment prior to its finalization. The user's final action in the instructional design sequence is to save the course, thereby concluding the flow of the instructional design process.

On the other hand, Figure 9 presents the flow for course creation in the authoring tool platform, following a hierarchical and modular structure assisted by extensive language models (LLMs). This process is organized in three main phases: course parameters configuration, content creation, and evaluation creation.

*Figure 9. Course creation flow*

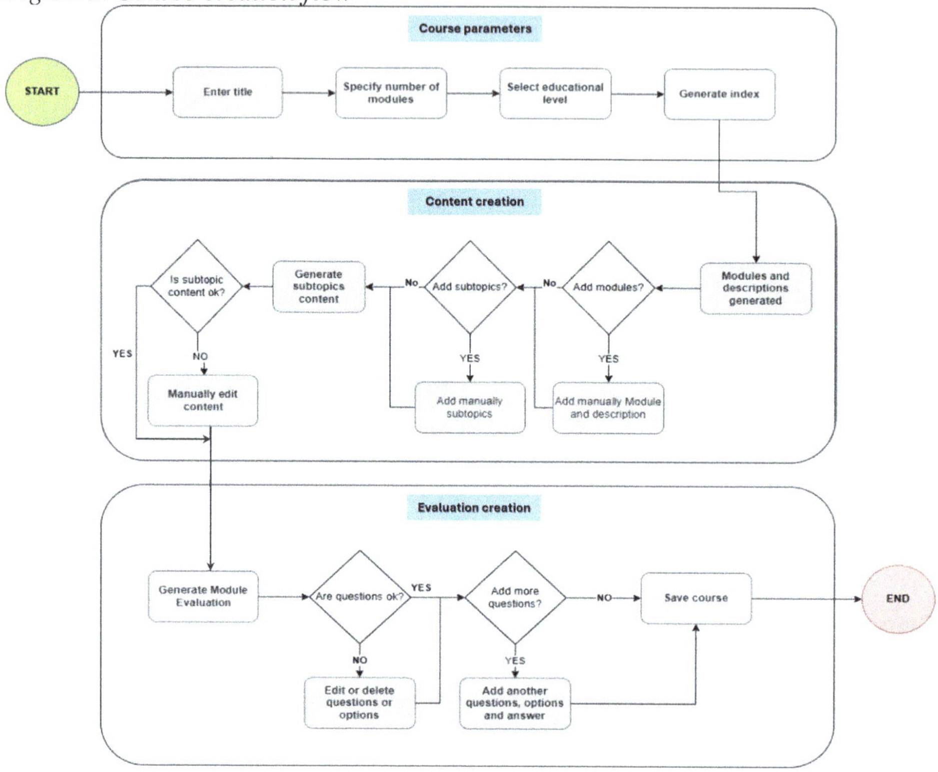


## Authoring Tool GenAI Component Software Architecture

This section presents the new elements added to the previous version of the authoring tool, with emphasis on the Web services that enable interaction with the LLMs. The software architecture displayed is built around a Web server, which acts as a gateway for incoming requests to an API denominated APINET (Cabada et al., 2023). Inside APINET, there exists an integrated environment called Ollama, responsible for managing and redirecting those requests to different large language models (LLMs). When a user sends a request in JSON format, APINET has two alternatives to process the request: first, Ollama handles it and forwards it either to LLaMA 3 or Gemma, and second, it processes it directly to ChatGPT, depending on the context. The authoring tool uses a text-to-speech feature to provide feedback, making it easier for students with reading difficulties or different learning styles to understand the explanations. This setup creates a consistent and unified way to interact with various generative AI models, keeping all the logic inside one solid API. Figure 10 shows the software architecture integration with the Web server.

*Figure 10. Software architecture integration with the web server*

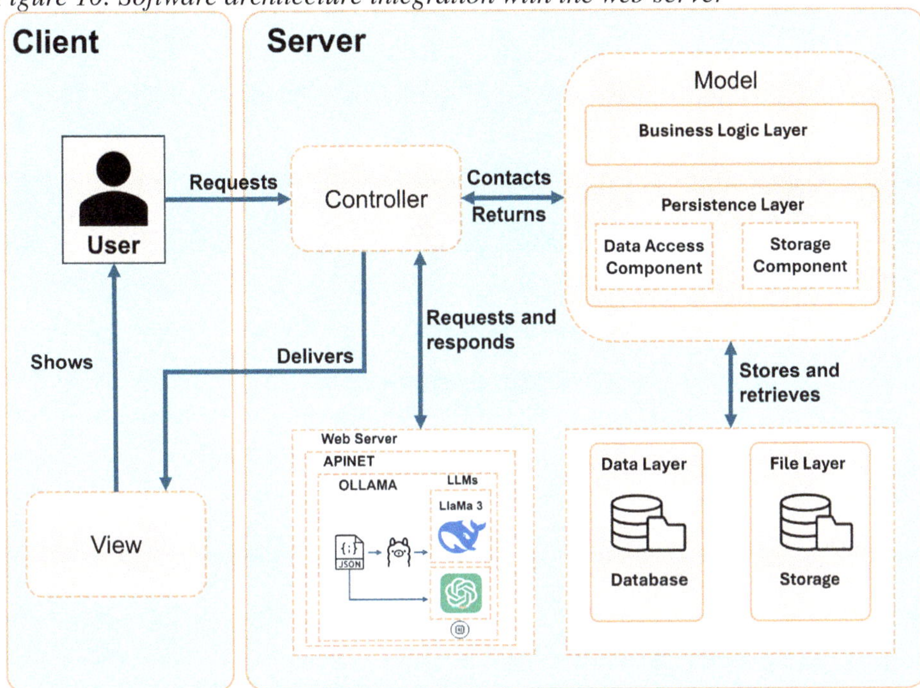


## My Courses and Presentations Page

The My Courses and Presentations ("Mis cursos y presentaciones") page is the main interface where the course topics and subtopics are built. Using generative AI, the content can be created automatically or entered manually. This section also allows users to integrate any XR environment developed with the XR component of the authoring tool. Figure 11 presents the graphical user interface of the My Courses ("Mis Cursos") section.

*Figure 11. My courses and presentations page*

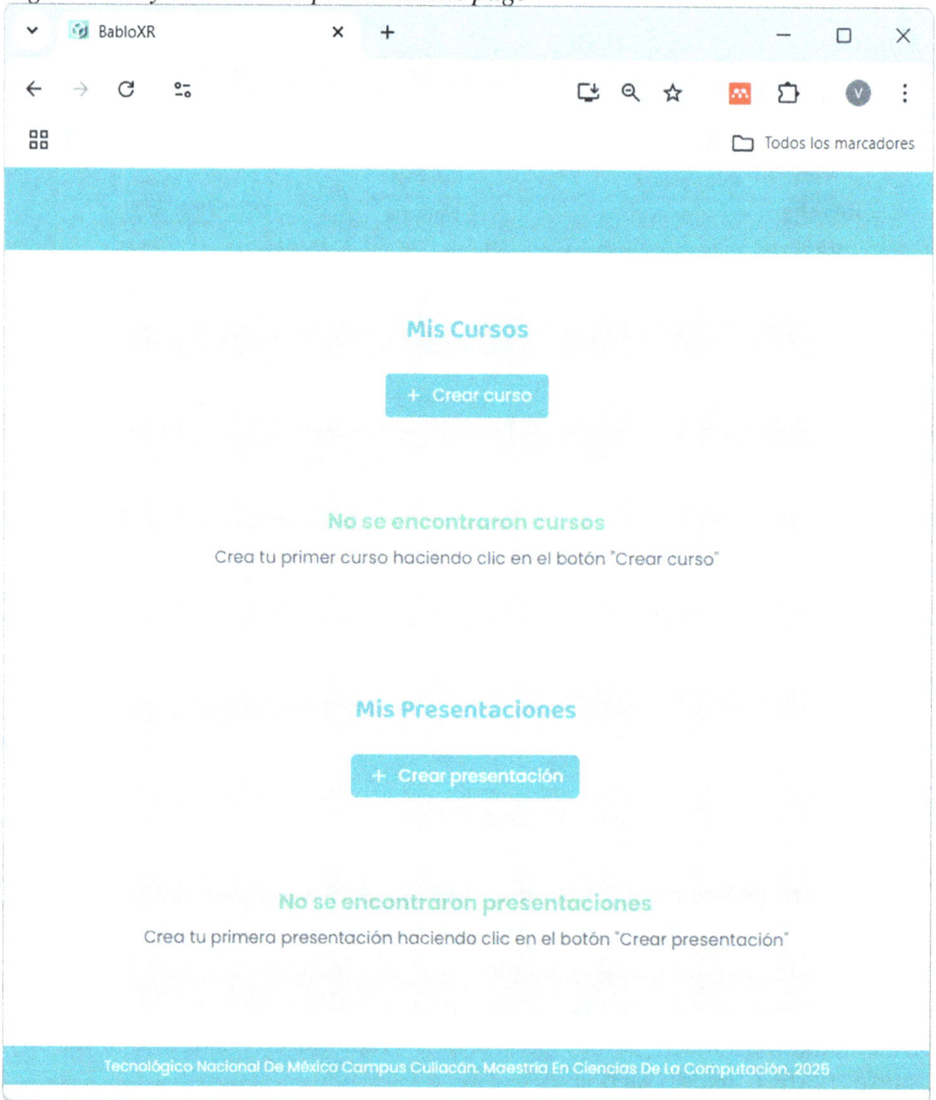


## My Courses Page

In the My Courses ("Mis Cursos") page, educators can create courses with the Authoring tool platform, which is designed to facilitate the development of educational content enhanced with the XR platform and LLMs. This tool allows educators to create and structure courses through an intuitive and modular workflow (see Figure 12).

At the top of the interface, the user can specify the course title, number of modules, and the educational level (e.g., University). A prominent feature is the "Generar índice del curso IA" (Generate Course Outline with AI) button, which enables automatic generation of a course structure using artificial intelligence. The main section of the interface is dedicated to module management. Each module includes fields for entering a title and a description, followed by two expandable areas:

- Subtemas (Subtopics): This section allows the user to either manually add subtopics or generate them automatically via AI by clicking the button "Generar todos los contenidos con IA" (Generate all content with AI).
- Evaluaciones (Evaluations): In this area, educators can add custom evaluation activities or automatically generate assessments using the "Generar evaluaciones con IA" (Generate evaluations with AI) option.

*Figure 12. Create course*

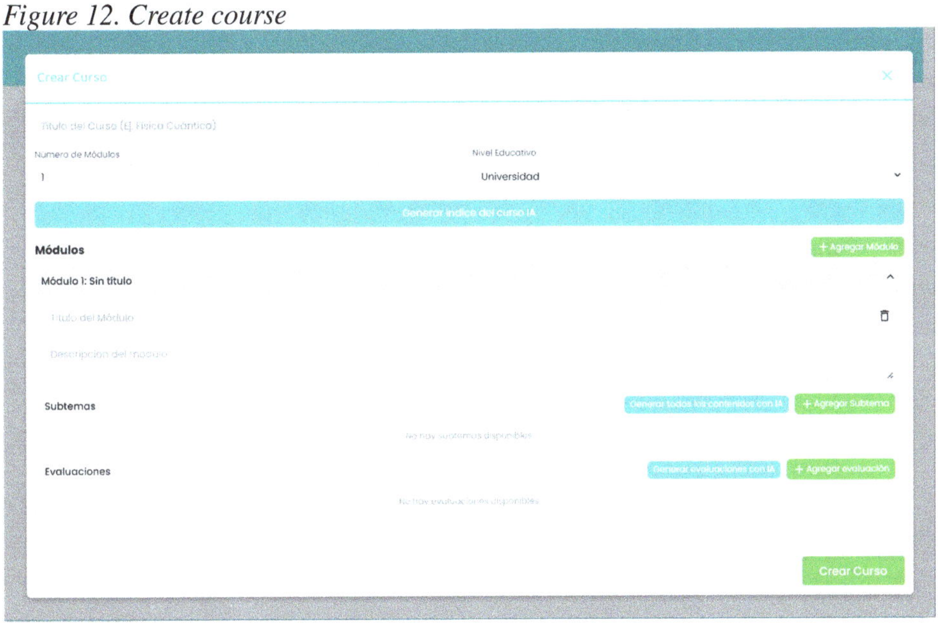


Additionally, the interface supports the dynamic addition of multiple modules through the "Agregar Módulo" (Add Module) button, providing flexibility for building complex course structures. Another important feature is the ability to automatically generate evaluations from the generated content, which allows users to modify or add questions manually. Clicking the "Generar evaluaciones con IA" (Generate evaluations with AI) button will create an exam based on the generated topic. The "Agregar evaluación" (Add assessment) button allows users to customize the questions. Once the design is complete, the course can be finalized by selecting the "Crear Curso" (Create Course) button.

This integrated approach streamlines the instructional design process by combining human input with AI-assisted generation of both content and evaluations, thus supporting the creation of engaging and pedagogically sound XR-based learning experiences.

## My Presentations Page

On the My Presentations ("Mis Presentaciones") page, the user can create an electronic presentation of the course. This feature enables users to create structured presentations that are directly tied to courses created previously. At the top of the interface, educators can assign a custom name to their presentation and select the relevant course from a drop-down menu. The workspace is divided into four main sections (see Figure 13), each serving a specific role in the design process.

*Figure 13. Presentation creation main interface*

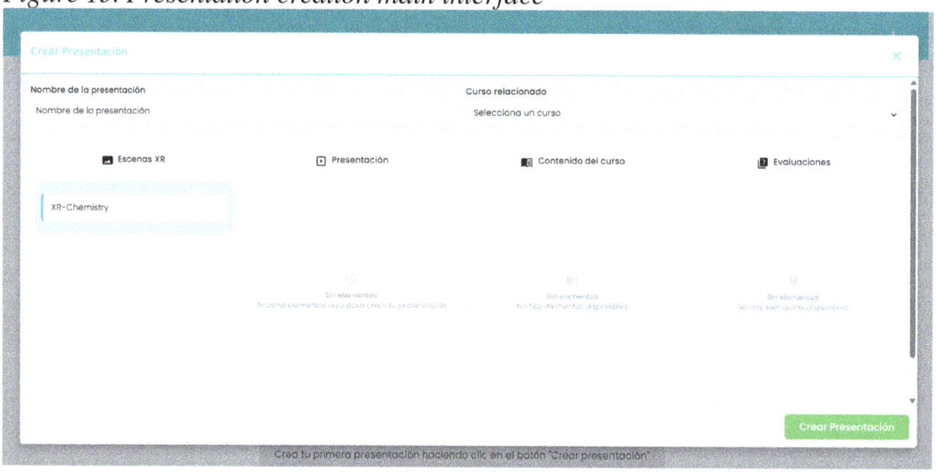


The function of each of the panels on this page is described below.

Escenas XR (XR Scenes): This panel lists the immersive environments available for use. In the example shown, the scene titled XR-Chemistry is selected, offering a virtual setting personalized for science education.

Presentación (Presentation): Here, educators can build the flow of their presentation by dragging and arranging elements from the other panels. This acts as the canvas where the final learning sequence takes form.

Contenido del curso (Course Content): This section organizes the thematic materials connected to the course, like texts, visuals, videos, and other media that form the core of the lesson.

Evaluaciones (Evaluations): Dedicated to assessment, this area allows the inclusion of quizzes to measure student understanding and engagement.

Together, these components form a modular and highly adaptable interface that empowers teachers to blend immersive XR technology with traditional content and evaluation tools. The result is a cohesive, engaging educational experience within a centralized, easy-to-use environment. Figure 14 shows an example of a presentation created with the authoring tool GenAI, and Figure 15 displays an example of an XR scene included in the presentation.

*Figure 14. Presentation created in the authoring tool*

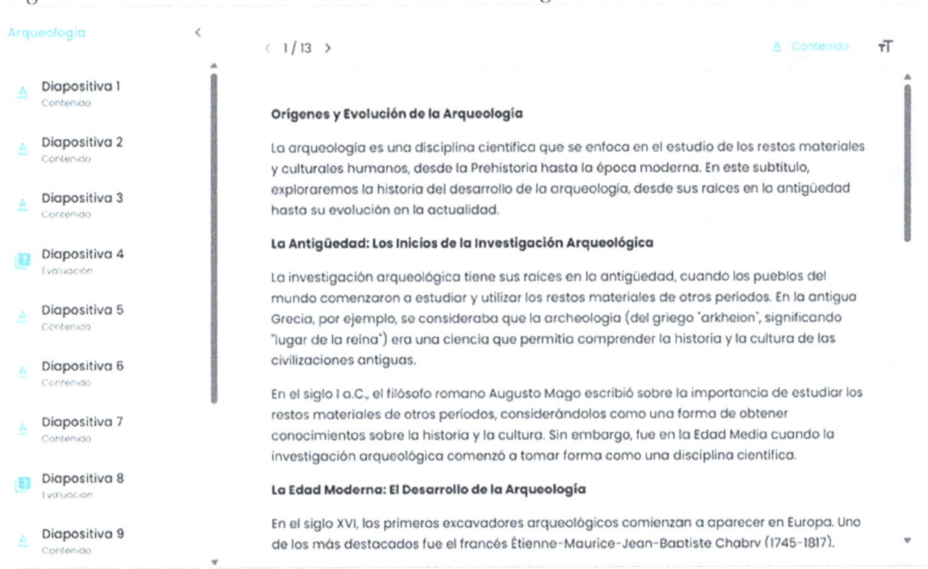

*Figure 15. Example of an XR scene included in a presentation*

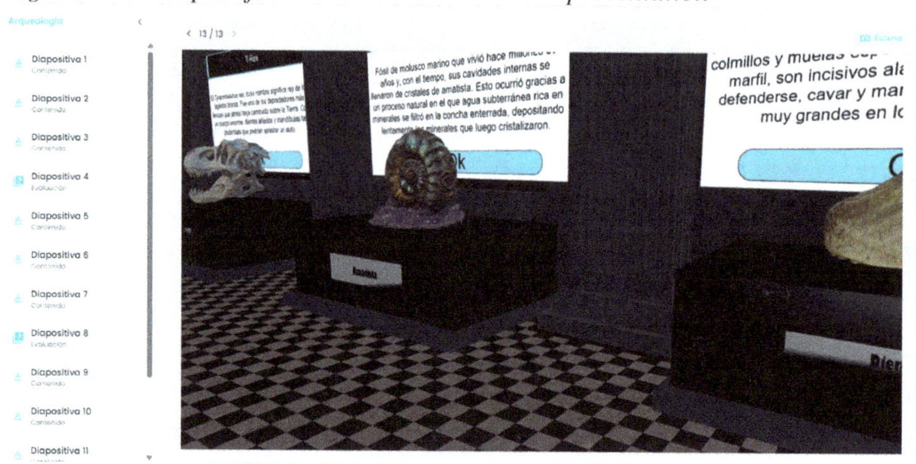


## AUTHORING TOOL EVALUATION METHODOLOGY

This section describes the methodology used to evaluate the authoring tool, focusing on its effectiveness, usability, and overall impact. Given the platform's innovative approach, integrating extended reality (XR) and large language models (LLMs) for course creation, it was essential to assess it from both a technical and pedagogical perspective.

To ensure that the tool addressed the needs of educators in an intuitive and meaningful way, its design was guided by expert input from the fields of educational technology and human-computer interaction. For a usability evaluation, we employed the System Usability Scale (SUS), a validated instrument widely used to measure perceived efficiency, ease of use, and user satisfaction. The following subsections present the participant profile, the measurement instruments, and the procedures followed during the implementation.

### Sample Equivalence

This study was conducted in May 2025 at Instituto Tecnológico de Culiacán, Tecnológico Nacional de México in Culiacán, Sinaloa, México. A total of thirty undergraduate engineering students, ranging in age from 19 to 26 years, voluntarily participated in the research. These participants brought diverse perspectives and experiences, contributing valuable insights into the evaluation of the proposed educational technology.

## Measure Instruments

This study employed the System Usability Scale (SUS) proposed by Brooke (1996) as the primary instrument for collecting user feedback on the platform. The SUS measure instrument is integrated by 10 items; each rated on a 5-point Likert scale ranging from strongly disagree (1) to strongly agree (5). This standardized tool is widely used to evaluate the usability of systems and interfaces, offering a quick yet reliable assessment. In this context, the SUS was applied to assess the perceived ease of use, efficiency, and overall satisfaction with the authoring tool. Specifically, the scale captures three core dimensions of usability: effectiveness, the extent to which users can complete tasks; efficiency, the resources (e.g., time, effort) required to achieve task completion; and satisfaction, the user's subjective experience in terms of comfort and acceptability while using the system.

## Procedure

This section outlines the procedure followed to ensure a learning experience with the course. The process was structured into three stages: an initial training tutorial, a period of autonomous XR environment development, and a final usability questionnaire to assess the effectiveness and user experience of the application. Each stage is described in detail below.

The intervention process with the Authoring tool began with an Introductory Tutorial, consisting of delivering a 60-minute tutorial to the evaluation participants. This session aimed to provide a clear and complete understanding of how the XR Component platform of the Authoring tool works. Participants were introduced to the platform's core functionalities, including the logic behind block-based programming, multimedia integration, and the workflow for designing extended reality (XR) learning environments. The tutorial combined guided instruction with live demonstrations and was reinforced by a video tutorial.

After the introductory session, participants entered the Environment Creation phase, which extended over two weeks. During this time, students worked autonomously to develop their own XR learning scenarios using the authoring tool. During this time, participants applied the knowledge acquired in the tutorial, allowing each participant to build personalized environments that integrated visuals, text, and interactive logic through visual programming blocks. While the activity was self-directed, support was made available through face-to-face and email assistance.

To conclude the experience, participants completed a usability evaluation questionnaire, which took approximately 10 minutes to complete. The instrument was designed to capture ease of use, navigation fluency, clarity of available tools, and overall satisfaction with the authoring environment. This final step provided both quantitative and qualitative data to assess the platform's effectiveness and usability from the learners' perspective. Figure 16 shows the procedure used to conduct the intervention.

*Figure 16. Authoring tool evaluation procedure*

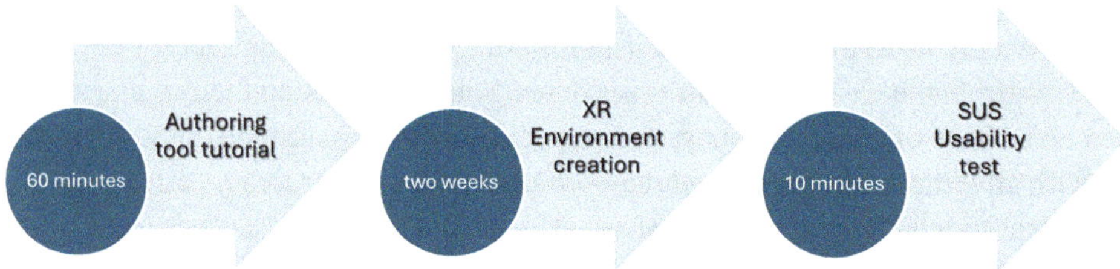


## RESULTS

This section analyzes the results obtained after the intervention of an authoring tool for the creation of extended reality (XR) environments assisted by extended language models (LLMs). The goal of this analysis is to evaluate the effectiveness, usability, and acceptance of the platform by users, particularly in educational contexts.

### Usability Test

The results of the System Usability Scale (SUS) test, including the mean (M) and standard deviation (SD), are summarized in Table 2. The SUS measure instrument comprises ten items rated on a 5-point Likert scale, ranging from strongly disagree (1) to strongly agree (5). To assess the internal consistency of the instrument, Cronbach's Alpha was calculated, yielding a value of 0.78. This score is considered very acceptable (Gliem & Gliem, 2003), indicating that the instrument demonstrated strong internal consistency and provided a reliable measure of system usability.

The overall usability score of the platform was 86 out of 100, positioning it well above the commonly accepted average in SUS benchmark studies. This high score indicates that participants perceived the system as effective, efficient, and satisfying to use, reinforcing its practical value and user-centered design. Such positive feedback highlights the platform's potential for broader adoption in educational settings, particularly in contexts where ease of use and intuitive interaction are essential for successful integration.

*Table 2. SUS measurement instrument items*

| Question | M | SD |
|---|---|---|
| **Q1. Would you like to use the Authoring Tool platform to create your extended reality worlds?** | 3.77 | 0.43 |
| **Q2. Did you find the Authoring tool too complicated to use?** | 3.53 | 0.57 |
| **Q3. Do you think the Authoring tool is easy to handle?** | 3.63 | 0.49 |
| **Q4. Would you need help from someone who knows a lot about technology to use the XR platform?** | 2.93 | 0.69 |
| **Q5. Did you find that all the things you can do with the Authoring tool work well together?** | 3.53 | 0.63 |
| **Q6. Do you think the Authoring tool is a bit messy or confusing?** | 3.10 | 0.80 |
| **Q7. Do you think your friends could quickly learn to use the Authoring tool, even if they don't have computers?** | 3.47 | 0.78 |
| **Q8. I found the system very cumbersome to use?** | 3.37 | 0.67 |
| **Q9. Was it easy to show someone else what you created with the Authoring tool?** | 3.73 | 0.45 |
| **Q10. Did you have to know anything special before you could use the Authoring tool well?** | 3.20 | 0.89 |

The descriptive analysis of SUS measurement instruments reveals a positive user perception of the authoring tool platform. The mean scores (M) for most items range between 3.2 and 3.77, suggesting that participants found the platform manageable, usable, and effective overall. In particular, the highest-rated items were Q1 (M = 3.77) and Q9 (M = 3.73). It can be inferred that users expressed a clear willingness to continue using the platform to create XR worlds and also felt confident in showing others what they had created, indicating usability and shareability.

However, slightly lower scores were observed in Q4 (M = 2.93) and Q10 (M = 3.20), which point to a moderate perceived need for prior knowledge or technical support, particularly among users with limited technological experience. On the other hand, Q6 (M = 3.10) and Q8 (M = 3.37) reflect minor concerns regarding complexity or interface clarity, though not at critical levels.

These results collectively suggest that the platform is perceived as intuitive and effective, with room for improvement in reducing initial complexity and enhancing onboarding for less tech-savvy users. The positive evaluations support the platform's potential for broader adoption in educational settings, particularly when complemented by brief training or guided use.

In addition to completing the SUS questionnaire, participants were invited to share their perspectives through three open-ended questions, which offered valuable qualitative insights into their experience with the authoring tool. The responses revealed a generally positive and constructive perception of the platform.

The first response highlighted the platform's ease of use and time efficiency, and the time savings involved, suggesting that its design effectively supports user efficiency and productivity without requiring a steep learning curve. The second response pointed to the desire for a strong preference for enhanced multimedia features, in particular, the ability to incorporate images alongside textual content. The third response, in which the participant states that "I wouldn't remove anything," reinforces overall user satisfaction and implies that none of the current features are perceived as unnecessary or redundant. Table 3 shows an example of a question and the answer provided by the student.

*Table 3. Open-ended questions*

| Question | Answer |
|---|---|
| **What do you think of the Authoring Tool?** | I think it's an easy-to-use tool that can quickly generate content for a course. |
| **What new features would you like the Authoring Tool to have** | The possibility of adding or generating images along with the text content |
| **What would you remove from the Authoring Tool** | I found it intuitive, so I wouldn't remove anything |

These reflections reinforce the quantitative findings, suggesting that while the platform is perceived as accessible and effective, future iterations could benefit from enhancements in multimedia support. Overall, the comments illustrate that users not only appreciated the authoring tool's current strengths but also offered thoughtful, forward-looking suggestions for its continued improvement.

## CONCLUSIONS

An LLM tool for creating educational materials for scientific topics is presented in this chapter. We provide case studies that show how well it supports a range of academic levels and educational disciplines. These samples' varied circumstances demonstrate the platform's adaptability and efficacy in a range of educational settings. Learning environments, text-based lessons, and assessment components were all effectively developed by participants and combined into a single learning experience. This demonstrates how the authoring tool can improve both the teaching and learning processes. Teachers spend a lot of time doing many time-consuming processes, such as planning lessons, preparing assessments, and creating materials. This time was reduced by using generative AI, such as LLMs. The tool's capabilities help teachers generate learning and assessment materials quickly and effectively for many educational levels.

This work presents a pioneering, fully accessible, transformative, and cloud-based authoring tool designed for the creation of XR learning environments. The tool utilizes generative artificial intelligence to generate thematic content for a variety of courses, in addition to assessments corresponding to the aforementioned topics.

The SUS usability measurement instrument indicates that participants, supported by a concise video tutorial, were able to navigate the platform and create detailed learning scenarios with ease. Within just two weeks, they successfully developed a set of immersive and interactive XR environments, demonstrating the authoring tool's effectiveness to overcome common barriers such as abrupt technical learning curves and time-intensive development.

This is relevant for educators of all disciplines and levels because it demonstrates the potential of the authoring tool to create XR learning environments that combine textual content and assessments produced with generative artificial intelligence. This is possible even for users with limited programming or design experience. Notably, Question 1 (M=3.77, SD=0.43) received the highest mean score and the lowest standard deviation, reflecting a strong and consistent willingness among participants to adopt the tool in future projects. These findings reveal a positive trend toward sustained use and acceptance of the platform, highlighting its practical value as a scalable and user-friendly solution for XR content creation in educational contexts.

Several opportunities were identified to further evolve the platform. Thanks to invaluable input from educators during its design phase, the authoring tool has been designed to be easy, efficient, and intuitive to use.

As future work, the development of the platform will focus on enhancing both functionality and user experience. One key area of improvement involves expanding the block library to include a wider range of reusable scenes and predesigned templates, allowing educators and creators to build rich, immersive content more efficiently to accelerate content creation. Another important addition is the support for importing custom 3D models, enabling users to personalize their XR environments with unique assets tailored to specific learning goals.

An additional feature that can be added is the incorporation of interactive step-by-step tutorials directly within the interface. These guided experiences will make it easier for new users to navigate the tool and begin creating confidently from the outset. Additional short-term work on the platform will include the integration of simultaneous multi-user editing, encouraging teamwork, and making the platform more suitable for classroom and group learning environments.

## REFERENCES

al Hafidz, I. A., Sukaridhoto, S., al Rasyid, M. U. H., Budiarti, R. P. N., Mardhotillah, R. R., Amalia, R., Fajrianti, E. D., & Satrio, N. A. (2021). Design of Collaborative WebXR for Medical Learning Platform. *2021 International Electronics Symposium (IES)*, 499–504. DOI: 10.1109/IES53407.2021.9593951

Alnagrat, A., Ismail, R. C., Idrus, S. Z. S., & Alfaqi, R. M. A. (2022). A review of extended reality (XR) technologies in the future of human education: Current trend and future opportunity. *Journal of Human Centered Technology*, *1*(2), 81–96. DOI: 10.11113/humentech.v1n2.27

Banh, L., & Strobel, G. (2023). Generative artificial intelligence. *Electronic Markets*, *33*(1), 63. DOI: 10.1007/s12525-023-00680-1

Barteit, S., Lanfermann, L., Bärnighausen, T., Neuhann, F., & Beiersmann, C. (2021). Augmented, Mixed, and Virtual Reality-Based Head-Mounted Devices for Medical Education: Systematic Review. *JMIR Serious Games*, *9*(3), e29080. DOI: 10.2196/29080

Bianchini, F. (2025). Generative Artificial Intelligence: A Concept in Progress. *Philosophy & Technology*, *38*(2), 46. DOI: 10.1007/s13347-025-00875-8

Bozkurt, A., Karadeniz, A., Baneres, D., Guerrero-Roldán, A. E., & Rodríguez, M. E. (2021). Artificial Intelligence and Reflections from Educational Landscape: A Review of AI Studies in Half a Century. *Sustainability (Basel)*, *13*(2), 800. DOI: 10.3390/su13020800

Brooke, J. (1996). SUS-A quick and dirty usability scale. *Usability Evaluation in Industry*, *189*(194), 4–7.

Cabada, R. Z., Estrada, M. L. B., López, N. L., López, H. M. C., & Beltrán, V. M. B. (2023). APINET: A Methodology for Deploying Deep and Machine Learning Models as Services. *2023 Mexican International Conference on Computer Science (ENC)*, 1–7. DOI: 10.1109/ENC60556.2023.10508683

Cabada, R. Z., Estrada, M. L. B., Rivas, M. A. S., & Ibáñez, M. B. (2024). An Authoring Tool for XR Learning Environments. In *International Conference on Extended Reality* (pp. 192–208). DOI: 10.1007/978-3-031-71713-0_13

Cipresso, P., Giglioli, I. A. C., Raya, M. A., & Riva, G. (2018). The Past, Present, and Future of Virtual and Augmented Reality Research: A Network and Cluster Analysis of the Literature. *Frontiers in Psychology*, *9*, 2086. Advance online publication. DOI: 10.3389/fpsyg.2018.02086

Conrad, M., & Nuebel, H. (2025). Learners' Acceptance of ChatGPT in School. *Education Sciences*, *15*(7), 904. DOI: 10.3390/educsci15070904

Cross, J. I., Boag-Hodgson, C. C., & Mavin, T. J. (2023). Measuring Presence and Situational Awareness in a Virtual Reality Flight Simulator. *Aviation Psychology and Applied Human Factors*, *13*(2), 83–94. DOI: 10.1027/2192-0923/a000250

Filippi, S., & Motyl, B. (2024). Large Language Models (LLMs) in Engineering Education: A Systematic Review and Suggestions for Practical Adoption. *Information (Basel)*, *15*(6), 345. DOI: 10.3390/info15060345

Gliem, J. A., & Gliem, R. R. (2003). *Calculating, interpreting, and reporting Cronbach's alpha reliability coefficient for Likert-type scales*. https://api.semanticscholar.org/CorpusID:146359317

Idrisov, B., & Schlippe, T. (2024). Program Code Generation with Generative AIs. *Algorithms*, *17*(2), 62. DOI: 10.3390/a17020062

Jauhiainen, J. S., & Guerra, A. G. (2023). Generative AI and ChatGPT in School Children's Education: Evidence from a School Lesson. *Sustainability (Basel)*, *15*(18), 14025. DOI: 10.3390/su151814025

Kaarlela, T., Padrao, P., Pitkäaho, T., Pieskä, S., & Bobadilla, L. (2022). Digital Twins Utilizing XR-Technology as Robotic Training Tools. *Machines (Basel)*, *11*(1), 13. DOI: 10.3390/machines11010013

Kazemitabaar, M., Hou, X., Henley, A., Ericson, B. J., Weintrop, D., & Grossman, T. (2023). How novices use LLM-based code generators to solve CS1 coding tasks in a self-paced learning environment. *Proceedings of the 23rd Koli Calling International Conference on Computing Education Research*, 1–12. DOI: 10.1145/3631802.3631806

Kuleto, V., Ilić, M., Dumangiu, M., Ranković, M., Martins, O. M. D., Păun, D., & Mihoreanu, L. (2021). Exploring Opportunities and Challenges of Artificial Intelligence and Machine Learning in Higher Education Institutions. *Sustainability (Basel)*, *13*(18), 10424. DOI: 10.3390/su131810424

Kumar, S., Datta, S., Singh, V., Datta, D., Singh, S. K., & Sharma, R. (2024). Applications, challenges, and future directions of human-in-the-loop learning. *IEEE Access : Practical Innovations, Open Solutions*, *12*, 75735–75760. DOI: 10.1109/ACCESS.2024.3401547

Li, R., Wang, Y., Zheng, C., Jiang, Y.-H., & Jiang, B. (2024). Generating Contextualized Mathematics Multiple-Choice Questions Utilizing Large Language Models. In *International Conference on Artificial Intelligence in Education* (pp. 494–501). DOI: 10.1007/978-3-031-64315-6_48

Pesovski, I., Santos, R., Henriques, R., & Trajkovik, V. (2024). Generative AI for Customizable Learning Experiences. *Sustainability (Basel), 16*(7), 3034. DOI: 10.3390/su16073034

Reeves, L. E., Bolton, E., Bulpitt, M., Scott, A., Tomey, I., Gates, M., & Baldock, R. A. (2021). Use of augmented reality (AR) to aid bioscience education and enrich student experience. *Research in Learning Technology, 29*. Advance online publication. DOI: 10.25304/rlt.v29.2572

Sotelo-Rivas, M. A. (2024). *BabloXR: Una herramienta de autor para el desarrollo de ambientes de aprendizaje en realidad extendida.*

Tran, A., Angelikas, K., Rama, E., Okechukwu, C., Smith, D. H., & MacNeil, S. (2023). Generating Multiple Choice Questions for Computing Courses Using Large Language Models. *2023 IEEE Frontiers in Education Conference (FIE)*, 1–8. DOI: 10.1109/FIE58773.2023.10342898

Vasarainen, M., Paavola, S., & Vetoshkina, L. (2021). A Systematic Literature Review on Extended Reality: Virtual, Augmented and Mixed Reality in Working Life. *The International Journal of Virtual Reality : a Multimedia Publication for Professionals, 21*(2), 1–28. DOI: 10.20870/IJVR.2021.21.2.4620

Wang, T., Lund, B. D., Marengo, A., Pagano, A., Mannuru, N. R., Teel, Z. A., & Pange, J. (2023). Exploring the Potential Impact of Artificial Intelligence (AI) on International Students in Higher Education: Generative AI, Chatbots, Analytics, and International Student Success. *Applied Sciences (Basel, Switzerland), 13*(11), 6716. DOI: 10.3390/app13116716

Wilson, K. L., Doswell, J. T., Fashola, O. S., Debeatham, W., Darko, N., Walker, T. M., Danner, O. K., Matthews, L. R., & Weaver, W. L. (2013). Using Augmented Reality as a Clinical Support Tool to Assist Combat Medics in the Treatment of Tension Pneumothoraces. *Military Medicine, 178*(9), 981–985. DOI: 10.7205/MILMED-D-13-00074

Wu, Y., Jia, F., Zhang, S., Li, H., Zhu, E., Wang, Y., Lee, Y. T., Peng, R., Wu, Q., & Wang, C. (2023). Mathchat: Converse to tackle challenging math problems with llm agents. *ArXiv Preprint ArXiv:2306.01337.*

Yan, F., Hu, Y., Jia, J., Ai, Z., Tang, K., Shi, Z., & Liu, X. (2020). Interactive WebVR visualization for online fire evacuation training. *Multimedia Tools and Applications*, *79*(41–42), 31541–31565. DOI: 10.1007/s11042-020-08863-0

Yan, L., Greiff, S., Teuber, Z., & Gašević, D. (2024a). Promises and challenges of generative artificial intelligence for human learning. *Nature Human Behaviour*, *8*(10), 1839–1850. DOI: 10.1038/s41562-024-02004-5

Yan, L., Sha, L., Zhao, L., Li, Y., Martinez-Maldonado, R., Chen, G., Li, X., Jin, Y., & Gašević, D. (2024b). Practical and ethical challenges of large language models in education: A systematic scoping review. *British Journal of Educational Technology*, *55*(1), 90–112. DOI: 10.1111/bjet.13370

## KEY TERMS AND DEFINITIONS

**Artificial Intelligence (AI):** This is a branch of computer science that aims to create systems capable of carrying out tasks that typically demand human intelligence. Such tasks include perception, reasoning, and learning.

**Augmented Reality (AR):** The integration of digital information with the user's environment in real time constitutes the essence of this technology. It has been demonstrated that augmented reality (AR) users encounter a tangible environment accompanied by the superimposition of perceptual information.

**Authoring Tool:** Software or a platform that enables users to produce digital material, particularly for online or e-learning, without requiring sophisticated programming knowledge.

**Extended Reality (XR):** This is a collective term that refers to immersive technologies, including virtual reality, augmented reality, and mixed reality.

**Virtual Reality (VR):** Is a simulated digital experience that can be similar to or completely different from the real world. The medium of virtual reality (VR) is created using computer technology and presented to the user through the use of either virtual reality glasses or a virtual reality headset (HMD), which collectively create an immersive and interactive three-dimensional environment.

**Large Language Model (LLM):** Is an advanced Artificial Intelligence technique trained to understand and generate human language so that it can answer questions, write and explain concepts, and generate reports and images.

**Blockly:** Is a visual programming library that allows users to create code by connecting blocks instead of typing text-based commands, where each block represents a programming concept such as loops, conditions, or variables, designed to help users learn programming concepts intuitively and engagingly.

# Chapter 8
# Empowering Science Educators in the Age of Generative AI:
## Frameworks for Effective Professional Development

**Debbie Diana Devonish**
https://orcid.org/0000-0003-3117-169X
*UTech, Jamaica*

## ABSTRACT

*This qualitative study addresses GenAI integration challenges for Caribbean Science educators.It investigates teacher pedagogical preparedness and training access, highlighting a significant gap in resource constraint environments. Employing an inductive thematic approach, data from peer reviewed and grey Caribbean literature provided culturally authentic insights. Four themes emerged from the analysis: 1) Efficacious Teachers Embody AI Literacy and Competency Skills 2) Shaping Teacher Disposition and Competency: The Influence of Educational Policy; 3)Adapting Professional Development Models for GenAI Integration for STEM Teachers in Resource Constrained Environment is Elusive and 4) Using Mixed Method Research for GenAI Professional Development Intervention Assessment. These reveal the complexities in teacher agency, readiness, pedagogical shifts and policy.The study proposes an adapted professional framework with 20 practical characteristics for the Caribbean context,emphasizing key design considerations. Gathering contextual data is imperative for progress.*

DOI: 10.4018/979-8-3373-2913-0.ch008

# INTRODUCTION

## Contextual Background

This book chapter provides the contextual background reinforcing the increasing significance of Generative AI (GenAI) in education and its specific relevance to science teaching and learning. Gen AI is useful for personalizing education, improving efficiency, fostering engagement, promoting accessibility, and providing valuable data-driven insights (Sultanow et al., 2024; Yadav, 2024). The researcher also chooses to highlight the Caribbean because majority of the literature on Generative AI and its applications is from Developed Countries and mainstream databases unfortunately rarely capture the work from the Caribbean. It is also critical for Caribbean researcher to share their context and contribute to the discussion since our cultural learning and teaching practices may not allow the generalizability from many of the readily available studies (Down, 2024; Jeyaseelan et al. (2025).). With the push for STEM and STEM education in the Caribbean, there is consensus that Science and Technology must be enhanced for Caribbean development through effective education and achieving sustainable goals to impact the lives of every Caribbean person (Sweeny & George, 2024; Keith & Waldron, 2024). Literature emphatically highlights the need for ongoing professional development (PD) to support practicing science educators in adapting to these technological advancements and it also highlights the lag the region faces in developing holistically orchestrated Science teacher professional development frameworks (Devonish et al., 2025). Unfortunately, many science educators may lack the knowledge, skills, and confidence to effectively and ethically, integrate GenAI tools into their teaching practices (Warner et al., 2021). The awkward necessity saw many educators plunged into the technological deep with the onset of COVID and their utility and skill set for Information and Communications Technology (ICT) and just integrated technological enhanced pedagogy to meet the nature of the students was tested. Meanwhile, as GenAI has evolved and continues to grow in its capabilities, its leaps and boundless nature seem daunting though educationally exciting. Therefore, effective integration of GenAI into the science classroom, curriculum and pedagogical approaches requires more than just technical skills; it necessitates pedagogical understanding and critical evaluation. The Caribbean science educator needs to be assisted by data driven policies and contextual information needs to be in mainstream literature for enhanced awareness and collaborative opportunities for learning.

## PROBLEM STATEMENT

With the issue of limited resources (Castillo-Canales et al., 2022), teacher job dissatisfaction (Whittingham, 2022; Wilmot, 2025), areas of poor student STEM academic achievement and an increasing apathy for Science matriculation (Bourne, 2022; Ortiz et al., 2024), there is the need for well-designed and targeted professional development programs to equip science educators with the competencies required to leverage GenAI for enhanced teaching and learning.

## SIGNIFICANCE OF THE STUDY

This chapter will provide crucial practical information on the use of GenAI applications and tools in the Caribbean. It will attempt to provide data driven evidence on the possible framework that can enable inquiry learning, promote scientific problem-solving and enhance learner-centred experiences in virtual and science labs through teacher professional development for supporting practicing educators. Mittal et al. (2024) admonishes us to do more research and enhancement of AI's educational function. They suggest that the intersection of pedagogical insights and effective human-AI collaboration is pivotal to our collective understanding and arguably the best use for GenAI in the Caribbean for us.

## CHAPTER AIM AND OBJECTIVES:

Aim: To explore effective frameworks and strategies for professional development that empower science educators to integrate Generative AI into their teaching practices.

### Objectives:

1. To identify the key knowledge, skills, and dispositions that science educators need to effectively utilize GenAI in their classrooms.
2. To review existing models of technology-focused professional development and their applicability to GenAI integration.
3. To propose innovative frameworks and approaches for designing and implementing GenAI-focused professional development for science educators.
4. To explore strategies for addressing educators' concerns, ethical considerations, and potential biases related to GenAI use.

5. To discuss methods for evaluating the impact and effectiveness of GenAI-focused professional development initiatives.

This chapter addresses the critical need for a comprehensive understanding of the integration of GenAI in Caribbean Science education through the teacher pipeline. Given the multifaceted nature of this area and the emergent body of literature specific to the Caribbean, this study employs a narrative review methodology. A narrative review provides an interpretive, comprehensive overview of existing scholarship, allowing the researcher to synthesize diverse findings, identify overarching themes, and construct a cohesive narrative to deepen understanding of the phenomenon (Grant & Booth, 2009; Onwuegbuzie & Frels, 2016).

## LITERATURE REVIEW

### Generative AI in Education

Generative AI is a set of AI algorithms that utilize existing content like text, audio files, or images to create new content. It generates games, images, videos, 3D visual, audio, code and text (Mittal et al., 2024). This has and will continue to revolutionize education and there are many ways in which traditional education is intercepted by this technology. Traditional education is customary education with key features of direct instruction and lectures delivered by a teacher, a fixed curriculum, a strong emphasis on memorization and recall of facts. Traditional education also has assessment primarily through standardized tests or oral recitations. Learning typically occurs within a structured physical classroom, with students largely in a passive, receptive role (Freire, 2000). While traditional education aimed for standardize knowledge transmission, the contemporary educational landscape has pivoted towards more student centered, constructivist pedagogical approaches (Tang, 2023). This has paved the way for GenAI which acts as an accelerator, enabling modern education to deliver on its promise of individualized, dynamic and highly engaging learning experiences at scale, fundamentally reshaping the teaching and learning paradigm. Mittal et al. (2024) suggests that traditional education is being revolutionized by GenAI, specifically by its capacity to increase curiosity in the learner, offer personalized attention, offer immersive learning content to heighten longer and meaningful engagement. Additionally, GenAI can do what the human teacher may find time consuming or difficult to achieve, it can also adapt the teaching style for each individual learner.

For the purpose of contextual understanding, STEM is the multidisciplinary single integrated application subject of Science, Technology, Engineering and Mathematics.

While STEM education are all the constructivist teaching and learning approaches focused on teaching and learning those STEM disciplines (Devonish et al, 2025). In the Caribbean STEM individual subjects are delivered at the early childhood to tertiary level. At K12 level single science subjects, biology, chemistry, physics, mathematics are offered at the Caribbean Secondary Certificate level (CSEC). However at the upper secondary (K10-k13) and on to the tertiary levels, core STEM subjects alongside applied fields such as agriculture and information technology are offered. At the tertiary level, this expands to include disciplines like biochemistry, medical sciences, computer science and various specialized engineering programs.

## Reimagining Curriculum Design and implementation through GenAI Integration

For students to excel in STEM, cultivate curiosity, and develop problem-solving skills, teachers must effectively deliver robust foundational science. This is a critical challenge. The STEM teacher's influence in the teaching and learning process is the most instrumental for student outcome (Adams, 2020; Williams, 2020). It is the teacher who operationalizes the curriculum and ensures it is implemented into the school teaching and learning activities.

Recent discussions, including findings presented at the Caribbean Association for the Advancement of Curriculum Studies (CAC) conference (Devonish, 2025), highlighted AIs capacity to reorganize foundational curricula in novel, unexpected ways that reveal new angles of alignment and expansive contextual linkages. This counterintuitive GenAI output can thus foster more inclusive STEM education in Caribbean Secondary schools. Building on foundational understanding of how machine learning systems process vast datasets to identify patterns (Koteluk et al., 2021); LLMs in educational contexts can restructure traditional pedagogical sequences, creating lessons that flow more creatively and engage students through unexpected connections. Devonish (2025) demonstrated this transformative potential through two examples. Rather than following the conventional cells to-ecosystems progression in biology. AI might reorder lessons to begin with climate change, framing cells as 'microscopic survivors' in a damaged planet. This approach leverages GenAI's capacity for subject and concept integration, using GenAI visuals and multimedia to bring the narrative to life while maintaining rigorous focus on biological organization. By connecting cellular structures to environmental challenges, students engage with both scientific content and contemporary issues. This fosters critical thinking about their environmental impact while reinforcing core biological concepts. Similarly, she proposed that exposing students to Fibonacci sequences through African fractal art instead of European mathematical traditions as another approach. While, Fibonacci sequences are not explicitly within the National Standards Curriculum (NSC) nor

Caribbean Secondary Education Certificate (CSEC) curricula, this example illustrated how GenAI can facilitate cross-curricular connections, helping students recognize mathematical patterns in their cultural and environmental contexts. Such approaches demonstrate AI's ability to flip human initial conceptualizations, revealing unexpected educational pathways that fundamentally reshape both content delivery and cultural perspective. These pedagogical approaches informing curricula implementation by the teacher in the lesson can yield measurable results.

AI-designed syllabi and GenAI applications in the teaching approach (Hasanova, 2021) have shown significant increases in student retention. This retention ranges from three to fifteen percent (Meotti & Magliozzi, 2025). However, Devonish (2025), suggested these improvements were not due to AI's inherent 'intelligence', but its ability to identify human overlooked connections, which teachers may not be able to articulate during traditional (non GenAI aided) lesson planning. AI's capacity to infuse continuous critical thinking in lesson development creates the novel and engaging experiences that capture student interest through unexpected contextual linkages. Consequently, achieving effective learning outcomes requires STEM educators to possess a robust command of both their subject content and modern pedagogical approaches. This dual expertise enables them to strategically, integrate GenAI tools, maximizing their potential to personalize learning and foster critical thinking while facilitating student mastery of learning outcomes. This foundational understanding of GenAI's capabilities and its contrasts with traditional models sets the stage for exploring its specific applications and challenges within the Caribbean STEM education context.

## Importance and Use of GenAI in Science Education in the Caribbean

GenAI can be harnessed for personalized learning approaches that can be integrated into STEM curricula. Figure 1 shows that acronym AICRP (Adaptive learning platforms, Intelligent tutoring systems, Customised learning paths, Real-time feedback and assessment and Predictive Analytics) are the features of GenAI that allows for the successful integration into curricula and this is supported by literature (Strielkowski et al., 2025; Feng et al.,2021;Abdrakhmanov et al., 2024).

The right panel of figure 1 demonstrates the technological tools enabled by Gen AI's AICRP features, including learning management systems; adaptive learning platforms, AI powered assessment tools, intelligent tutoring systems and platforms for AI creation.

Molino et al., (2023) GenAI powered feedback is to innovate ways artificial intelligence (AI) will be used for professional development and it is extrapolated that AI powered lesson plans and content will facilitate STEM teachers. Based on synthesis of literature and the researcher's experience in the Caribbean STEM education, Gen AI must offer personalization and adaptivity, multilingual support (crucial for Caribbean creoles and linguistic diversity), accessibility and inclusivity, gamification and engagement and data driven insights for our context holistically. Understanding these GenAI capabilities (AICRP) is essential for science educators, as teachers must be trained in both the technical aspects of these tools and their pedagogical applications to effectively integrate them into science instruction. This necessitates specialized professional development that addresses both technological competency and pedagogical innovation.

*Figure 1. GenAI capabilities enabling educational tools for STEM education (Author's own, adapted from Devonish (2025). Harnessing AI-powered Personalized Learning for Inclusive STEM Education in Caribbean Secondary Schools. Caribbean Association for the Advancement of Curriculum Studies Online Conference)*

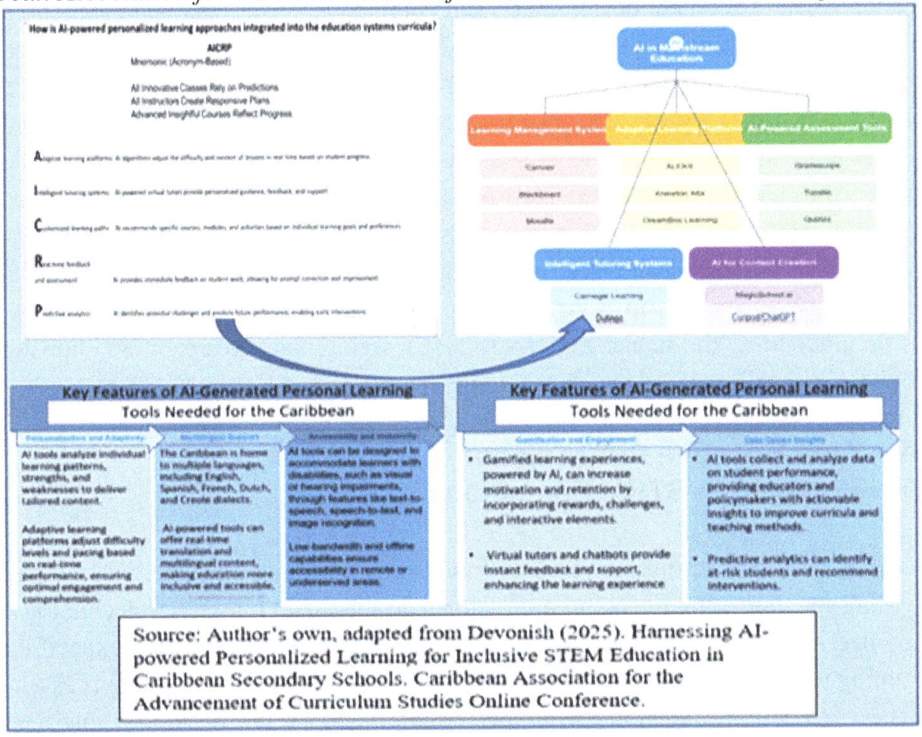


While GenAI offers significant potential for Caribbean STEM education, successful implementation must address the region's unique contextual challenges. Implementing GenAI in Caribbean STEM education faces significant infrastructural and resource challenges. These resource constraints are particularly evident in laboratory-based science instruction. The issue of lack of STEM subject resources can be traced back to colonial educational legacies, where initial resource provision was not sustained through ongoing investment, efficient local capacity building and maintenance, resulting in current resource scarcity (Devonish, 2021). Lack of resources, lab equipment, limited technical staff with competency, limited internet access and low bandwidth accompanied with high cost for software reduces the extensive use of online lab opportunities. In addition, the researcher will continue to defend a position that online labs are not ideal for developing certain science processing skills that require tactile, hands-on intervention, because outside of the virtual world we need our hands and concrete skills in which to thrive. GenAI can be used to develop lab skills by online learning labs. Virtual labs' success in learning outcomes is not without mixed perceptions (Potkonjak et al., 2016) and literature suggest that it is as effective or more effective than traditional labs (Asare et al., 2023). Asare et al. (2023) suggests a hybrid approach, training and support for teachers, guided content development and continuous assessment and evaluation. Therefore, a mixture of approaches is ideal, microscience kits must be normalized in the Caribbean (Devonish, 2018, microscience kit assessment in Jamaica). The Ministry of Education, Skills, Youth and Information (MoESYI) had embarked on attaining these microscience kits and assessing same (Thomas- Brown, 2021), though they are used more extensively in parts of Africa (Bradley, 2021). The micro size enables all benefits of a traditional lab experiment experience and limits concerns about waste, cost and lack of individual practice. However, regardless of the approach, whether it involves virtual labs or microscience kits or mobile labs (e.g., as highlighted by the Jamaica Gleaner, 2016); significant investment and holistic logistics are still required to achieve equity and impact in Caribbean classrooms.

## We Need Effective Professional Development in STEM Education

It is necessary to discuss research-based principles and best practices for designing and delivering impactful professional development for science, technology, engineering, and mathematics (STEM) educators. Science teachers require specified training to develop a critical science based set of skill sets. Their training is essential for impacting student academic performance and overall meeting of national sustainable goals (Brissett, 2022).

The educational landscape is complex and is constantly changing (Clandinin, 2008), before the 1950's the emphasis was hands on experience and apprenticeship learning. Then launch of Sputnik in 1957 marked a pivotal moment, spurring intensive mathematics and science education reform in the United States through the National Defense Education Act of 1958. This post Sputnick era (1957-1980's) emphasized rigorous science education and introduced constructivist, student centered learning approaches. The 1990s brought the formal SMET (Science, Mathematics, Engineering and Technology) era, which focused on interdisciplinary integration. In 2001, the National Science Foundation introduced the STEM acronym, replacing SMET to emphasize holistic subject integration. By 2008, STEM had become mainstream in educational discourse. Now, the latest development is AI integration in STEM education, representing the newest frontier in this evolutionary trajectory. STEM integration for science education and STEM education for teaching STEM is a crucial understanding for those speaking the language of STEM (Devonish et. al, 2025). Teachers must be equipped for the furtherance of Caribbean national development through increased national scientific literacy and enhanced science and technology innovative workforce for improved economies (Durham & Weinstein, 2025; United Nations, n.d.).

This educational historical timeline demonstrates that while curricula and educational approaches have evolved dramatically, the teacher remains the critical bridge between educational policy and student learning outcomes. Only trained teachers can effectively implement curricula and manifest the intended learning outcomes to meet educational goals (Costa & Garmston, 2016; Miller, 1999). However, each paradigm shift has required teachers to develop new competencies and pedagogical approaches. Therefore, continuous research-based professional development becomes not just beneficial but essential for teachers to successfully navigate these evolving educational landscapes and effectively implement emerging technologies like AI in their STEM instruction.

The literature review provides a progressive examination of the role of "Generative AI in Education" beginning with its potential to enhance curriculum development and learning. The discussion then narrows its focus to contextualize these possibilities within the unique landscape of STEM education in the Caribbean. Then the literature review explores how Large Language Models (LLMs) can be used to "Reimagine Curriculum Design and implementation", demonstrating their ability to process vast information and facilitate connections between complex concepts for higher cognitive processing and development. Furthermore, this review highlights the importance of GenAI in supporting science online labs and providing visual aids, while also critically examining the associated challenges and limitations. Ultimately, the synthesis of this literature culminates in a central argument: the successful transformation of learning STEM with AI requires effective professional development to ensure that teachers are both equipped and empowered to operationalize the curriculum effectively. Given the deficit of formal research on GenAI in STEM teacher professional development within this specific context, our arguments are grounded in available Caribbean-specific literature and are supplemented by broader general research to provide a comprehensive discussion throughout the paper.

## THEORETICAL FRAMEWORK AND ITS APPLICATION TO STEM TEACHER PD

Four theories were considered crucial for discussion in this study, Adult Learning Theories (ALT) (Merriam, 2018). STEM subject teachers are adult learners and Knowles's Andragogy (Knowles, 1984) was considered as the researcher sought to uncover how PD can be tailored to the needs and experiences of adult learners. Communities of Practice (CoP) for Professional Development (Lave & Wenger, 1991). Diffusion of Innovations Theory (Rogers, 2003) was considered for how PD could facilitate the adoption and implementation of GenAI tools among science educators. Thirdly, PACK (Technological Pedagogical Content Knowledge) (Mishra & Koehler, 2006) was considered for how PD could help educators develop their TPACK in the context of GenAI.

Andragogy, is the art and science of adult learning (Knowles, 1984), distinguishing itself from traditional pedagogy (Knowles, 1977) by emphasizing the unique characteristics of adult learners. Knowles Adult Learning theory was an improvement on the andragogy theory and in refining the concept, advocated for a learner-centered approach (Knowles, 1975). Key principles of Andragogy include the idea that adult learners are self-directed, bring a wealth of experience to the learning process, are ready to learn what they need to know to cope with real life problems, are problem centered in their orientation to learning, and are primarily internally motivated (Knowles, 1984). This framework posits that learning processes should be collaborative, with both educators and learners actively engaged in construction of knowledge.

Communities of Practice (CoP) are essential for understanding and designing effective professional development, especially in collaborative and ongoing contexts. CoP, builds on the tenets of situated learning (Lave & Wenger, 1991) and serves as a robust framework for explaining how learning occurs among practitioners within a social environment. According to Wegner (1988), key concepts of CoP include joint enterprise that participants are mutually pursuing (e.g. improving STEM education with GenAI), mutual engagement in the process of pursuing this task (e.g. sharing experiences with GenAI tools, troubleshooting) and shared repertoire of resources, tools, and common practices (e.g. specific GenAI prompts, lesson plans and shared best practices). Additionally, legitimate peripheral participation through meaningful interactions with more experienced members. In this argument, teachers are united by a domain of professional practice and shared concern for integrating GenAI. As they continue to meet, their knowledge deepens and they become more skilled as they participate in learning loops, where shared practice is taken back to the workplace, implemented and then returned to the community for more feedback, then the learning loop begins again (McDonald & Merciecea, 2021).

According to Li et al., (2009), the tension between satisfying individuals' needs for personal growth and empowerment versus an organization's bottom line is perhaps the most contentious of the issues that make CoPs difficult to cultivate. However, a community of practice is essential for teachers as their practice is embolden and refined by interdependence and collaborative refinement within years of practice in the community (Devonish, 2025).

Diffusion of Innovations Theory (DOI, Rogers 2003) is used to analyze the process of communicating any innovation through social systems. In this study, DOI can be used to assess factors influencing teachers' perception and subsequent adoption of GenAI in their classrooms and how it is incorporated into their own professional development. While a teachers' perception and philosophical stance will shape their instructional choices and classroom behaviour (Pajares, 1999), the DOI theory highlights the broader systemic elements involved. DOI theory is widely used for open electronic resources such as electronic textbooks, MOOCs, online databases, social media and is applicable to GenAI tools. The theory explains the diffusion rate of an innovation by examining key elements such as the innovation itself (including perceived attributes like relative advantage, compatability, complexibility, trialability, and observability), communication channels, time involved in the adoption process, the characteristics of the social system (e.g. institutional culture) and the role of change agents (Rogers, 2003). This framework's broad applicability to various contexts, including STEM education in the Caribbean supports its use for understanding the adoption of GenAI among Science teachers (Menzli et al., 2022). The intention is for the science teachers to be effectively adept at utilizing GenAI for teaching and the successful integration of these tools into their curriculum and professional practice is directly dependent on the rate of adoption explained by DOI. Its application to educational technology in the Caribbean context remains an area needing further exploration (Kamlodeen, 2017; Williams-Buffonge, 2021;).

The TPACK theory (Mihsra & Koehler, 2006) offers a framework, and a robust lens for synthesizing literature on how teachers develop the integrated knowledge required to effectively incorporate technology, such as GenAI, into their pedagogical practices. It will be used in this chapter to categorize and understand various ways existing studies address the interplay of content, pedagogy, and technology in context of GenAI integration in STEM education for the Caribbean. As an analytical tool or conceptual organized it has seven core components. These are:

Content Knowledge (CK): A teacher's understanding of the subject matter they are teaching.
Pedagogical Knowledge (PK): A teacher's understanding of teaching methods and strategies.

Technological Knowledge (TK): A teacher's understanding and ability to use various technologies.
Pedagogical Content
Knowledge (PCK): The understanding of how to teach specific content, incorporating effective teaching strategies.
Technological Content
Knowledge (TCK): The understanding of how technology can be used to represent and convey specific content.
Technological Pedagogical
Knowledge (TPK): The understanding of how technology can be used to support teaching and learning strategies.
Technological Pedagogical
Content Knowledge (TPACK): The overarching framework that encompasses the integration of all these knowledge types.

This framework within professional development can support science educators in developing the nuanced understanding necessary to leverage, technology content and pedagogy in concert.

## THE METHODOLOGY

This section discusses the researcher's positionality, the review protocol followed, the four research questions guiding the study, the paper selection method, and the criteria for selecting the research papers.

### The Researchers Positionality (Thematic Analysis)

As the primary instrument of inquiry in this qualitative thematic literature review, I recognize the imperative to articulate my researcher positionality. This study is fundamentally underpinned by a constructivist epistemological perspective, which holds that knowledge is not discovered but actively constructed through interpretation. This philosophical stance directly informs my approach to synthesizing the existing literature, acknowledging that the 'truths' presented in scholarly texts are themselves products of various authors' interpretations and that my own synthesis is yet another layer of meaning-making. My profound interest in teacher professional development within the unique context of the Caribbean science education stems from my experience as an educator in the region and my experience as an educator, science teacher trainer and my commitment to fostering sustainable educational development. This background, while providing a rich lens for understanding the nuances of the literature, also necessitates continuous self-interrogation of my own beliefs and epistemological understandings concerning the challenges and opportunities of STEM education in the Caribbean and the transformative potential of GenAI. To ensure the rigor of trustworthiness of this textual analysis, I committed to ongoing reflexivity through maintaining a detailed reflective journal during the thematic analysis process, writing analytical memos and my interpretations, and consistently reviewing my interpretations against the original texts, thereby making my interpretive journey transparent for the reader.

To precisely define the scope of the research, the following are the research questions for this study:

> RQ1. What knowledge, skills, and dispositions do Caribbean science educators need to effectively integrate GenAI tools into their teaching practices?
> RQ2. How can existing models of technology-focused professional development models be structurally adapted and redesigned to address the unique contextual challenges of GenAI integration in Caribbean science education contexts?
> RQ3. What professional development frameworks can best support science educators' ethical and competent use of GenAI tools in resource-constrained Caribbean educational settings?
> RQ4. How can the effectiveness of GenAI-focused professional development initiatives be evaluated in Caribbean educational contexts?

This chapter employs a qualitative narrative review methodology, adapting elements of systematic review approaches while maintaining flexibility appropriate for an emerging field with limited regional literature. Rather than conducting a full PRISMA systematic review, the researcher implemented a structured qualitative narrative review to address the research questions, analyzing the literature for themes through thematic analysis (Saldana, 2021). The selection process utilized carefully selected Boolean search terms and keywords to identify relevant peer-reviewed literature on GenAI in science education, professional development models, and Caribbean educational contexts from reputed journals and for context, grey resources such as news media and government reports were utilised. To construct comprehensive and targeted search queries for each research question, these individual conceptual Boolean strings were then systematically combined using the 'AND' operator.

- "generative AI" OR "ChatGPT" OR "large language models" OR "AI chatbots" OR "artificial intelligence tools"
- "AI Integration: "AI in education" OR "AI tools in classroom" OR "artificial intelligence pedagogy"
- "science pedagogy" OR "STEM education" OR "science teaching methods"

### Teacher knowledge/skills/competences (RQ1)

- "Teacher knowledge" OR "teacher skills" OR "STEM teacher competencies" OR "science teacher proficiency" OR "IT literacy" OR "digital literacy" OR "technology challenges"

### Teacher Integration/Teacher Practices (RQ1 and RQ2)

- "Technology integration" OR "ICT integration" OR "digital pedagogy or teaching practices" OR "classroom technology use" OR "educational technology implementation"

### PD Models/Frameworks/Adaptation (RQ2 and RQ3)

- "Professional development models" OR "PD frameworks" OR "technology PD models" OR "adaptation strategies" OR "curriculum adaptation" OR "implementation models"

### Ethical and Effective AI Use (RQ3)

- "Ethical AI" OR "responsible AI" OR "AI ethics in education" OR "responsible use for AI" OR "AI governance" OR "effective AI use"

### Resource-Constrained Contexts for education (RQ3)

- "Resource constrained" OR "developing countries" OR "disadvantaged schools" OR "Caribbean education" OR "Jamaica" OR "CARICOM countries"

### Evaluation and Effectiveness of PD educators (RQ4)

- "Program evaluation" OR "outcomes assessment" OR "measuring impact"

After searching databases relevant titles were selected. In the following stage abstract, research questions and conclusions were assessed. The papers selected were then carefully reviewed for addressing the study's four research questions.

The methodology also incorporated four complementary qualitative data strategies:

Document analysis: To analyze existing professional development programs, educational policies, curriculum documents, and GenAI implementation guidelines across Caribbean educational institutions.
Secondary data analysis: Utilized existing datasets from regional educational assessments, teacher surveys, or technology implementation reports.
Case study synthesis: Compiled published case studies of GenAI integration in similar contexts that could inform this studies framework development.
Comparative policy analysis: Compared educational technology policies across Caribbean nations to identify common challenges and opportunities for GenAI integration. The researcher highlights the Science teacher training across the Caribbean in this regard.

## FINDINGS

The findings are organized around four distinct themes, each addressing specific research questions. These themes emerged from comprehensive literature review process and encompass various subthemes and categories. These will provide nuanced understanding of GenAI integration in STEM teacher professional development. The themes are as follows:

For Research Question 1 (RQ1)-Essential Competencies and Dispositions: The findings are presented across two interconnected themes: Theme One: 'Efficacious Teachers embody AI literacy and competency skills' and Theme Two: 'Shaping Teacher Disposition and Competency- the Influence of Educational Policy'.

For Research Question 2 (RQ2)-Adaptation of Professional Development Models & Research Question 3 (RQ3)-Ethical Considerations: These two research questions which explore the adaptation process for existing professional development models in the Caribbean contexts and ethical considerations for GenAI use, are addressed collectively in Theme Three: 'Adapting Professional Development Models for GenAI integration for STEM Teachers in Resource Constrained Environment is Elusive'. This combined approach highlights the inherent challenges and complexities of ethical integration within resource limited adaptation efforts.

For Research Question 4 (RQ4)-Evaluation Mechanisms: Approaches for measuring the impact of GenAI-focused professional development initiatives are given. Theme Four: Using Mixed Method (MM) Research for GenAI Professional Development Intervention Assessment.

## Theme One. Efficacious Teachers embody AI literacy and competency skills

The main overarching theme that emerged from the literature for inquiry one, was "Efficacious Teachers embody AI literacy and competency skills". This primary theme was identified through the frequent appearance of seven key subthemes: AI literacy for educators; pedagogical skills for generative AI; Technological pedagogical and content knowledge (TPACK) generative AI, Educator dispositions towards AI; Educator dispositions towards AI, Evolving teacher roles in the AI era, STEM, Ethical AI considerations for teachers and AI and critical thinking skills for teachers.

Efficacy (Bandura, 1977,1986,1998) is the most catalytic of all five states of minds (Costa & Garmston, 2016) and thus an efficacious teacher is ideal for enhancing student learning through personal professional traits of Interdependence, Craftsmanship and Consciousness. Representing the five states of mind, the acronym 'Every Idea Can Count' suggests that a creative teacher, who cultivates these states of mind, is positioned for substantial impact and positive influence on the teaching profession (Devonish, 2016). Teacher efficacy is the belief in one's ability to positively impact student learning. Self-efficacy acts as a meta-competency that enables all other professional capabilities. Flexibility is being able to adapt tools to diverse Caribbean context, Craftsmanship is pursuing excellence in AI enhanced pedagogy, Consciousness is reflective awareness of AI's impact on learning and Interdependence is the educator collaborating within Caribbean educational communities.

In the context of GenAI, efficacious teachers embody AI literacy by Integrating AI tools seamlessly into their pedagogical identity, modeling adaptive learning, demonstrating cultural responsiveness in technology use and showing resilience in the face of technological challenges.

While AI literacy is important, it is insufficient alone because technical skills without pedagogical confidence lead to surface level implementation (Dolmans et al., 2016 and Darling-Hammond et al., 2019) and teachers need to understand deep learning (Cator et al., 2014). Caribbean educators face unique contextual challenges (infrastructure, resources, cultural considerations) that require more than just technical knowledge. Though the research question asks about teacher dispositions as explained by the theme, literature highlighted that teachers must be disposed of challenges of non IT literacy, poor internet connection, limited time for teaching and preparation and limited creativity (Laupichler et al., 2022; Taopan et al.,2020; Davidovitch & Yavich, 2022).

Skills do not drive the transformative mindset needed for meaningful integration. The efficacious teachers' foundation and robust core subject area is necessary. A chemistry teacher must be certified with the requisite qualifications to teach chemistry. Empirical evidence from the National Education Inspectorate suggested that teachers at the Jamaican primary school have inadequate science content knowledge (Ministry of Education, 2015). Reports suggest that in the Caribbean teachers not certified to teach in the science classroom are employed and so Science content for teachers is topical (Robinson, 2017; Devonish, 2025). In the Caribbean particularly within the Jamaica context, teacher qualifications are primarily attained from accredited programs offered by tertiary institutions. These include the University of Technology, Jamaica, Northern Caribbean University and the University of the West Indies (UWI). UWI (Mona), notably its Open Campus with its board of teacher Education, plays a significant role in delivering teacher training across the region. Council of Community Colleges of Jamaica (CCCJ) oversees a network of colleges that may offer foundational or specialized courses supporting teacher education. The ultimate qualifications are granted by the accredited universities. All such teacher education programs must be accredited by the University Council of Jamaica (UCJ), it is the national quality assurance body for tertiary education. This UCJ accreditation is essential as it confers eligibility for official teacher certification or licensing by the Ministry of education, Skills, Youth & Information (MOESYI).

However, it is also important to note that STEM educator does not mean a science based educator or a teacher teaching one of the sciences in all jurisdictions. In Jamaica and the Caribbean, there are STEM subject teachers (Chemistry, Biology, Physics, Mathematics etcetera.). A STEM educator with an STEM certification 'add on' has a degree for a core subject in any area. The STEM emphasis is on the constructivist and subject integration pedagogical approach. These classifications and nuances are explained in Devonish et al., 2025. Therefore, as explained in Devonish et al., 2025 the trainers of trainers would have to be likewise, targeted and the curriculum revised to address the gaps and educational outputs required.

Drawing on the TPACK framework (Shulman, 1986; Misha &Koehler, 2006) for defining teachers' knowledge, the Technological knowledge (TK), pedagogical knowledge (PK) and content knowledge (CK) are important for teachers to help students acquire content using teaching approaches that use specific technologies and this is how teachers' overall efficacy influences GenAI use for teaching and learning. GenAI literacy skills for educators is essential, which includes prompt engineering and understanding the responsible ethical use of AI. This is to allow the most efficient use of the GenAI amidst the problems of hallucination, bias and issues of data privacy. TCK focusses on how technology can manipulate or enhance subject-specific content and TPK allows science teachers to experiment with GenAI to create innovative teaching strategies beyond simple content generation to more interactive student-centered or teacher-adult learner centered uses. There is not just an educational movement, but also a pedagogical shift that embodies an eclectic educator with the epistemological grounding, that facilitates a pragmatic disposition. Arguably, if the teacher is not familiar with the capabilities of the tool nor the subject matter comprehensively, then it is less likely that they will be able to adapt their instructional design, classroom management strategies for an AI-integrated environment. GenAI can use AI for data analysis, simulation, or problem solving.

Teachers must also critically evaluate AI outputs and acknowledge an era of continuous learning. If AI is to support complex problem-solving, educators require the knowledge and skills to design learning experiences where students can leverage AI for these higher-order tasks (Joksimovic, 2023). Therefore, professional development needs to equip teachers to facilitate this.

## Theme Two. Shaping Teacher Disposition and Competency: The Influence of Educational Policy

This theme highlights the importance of supportive policies in funding, infrastructure and mandates for the Caribbean. It discusses the role of leadership and institutional buy-in, regional initiatives and frameworks, whilst highlighting challenges or gaps in existing policy, which must be addressed. Policy enables or hinders the development or application of GenAI integration by teachers and is therefore fundamental to shaping the disposition and enabling the efficacy of teachers in GenAI integration. This broader ecosystem supports or constraints the teacher to successfully deliver GenAI integration (Taylor, 2023). Policies enable framework for an ecosystem, which considers resource allocation; training and professional development; ethical guidelines and responsible use; curriculum integration and teacher commitment and confidence.

When policy supports technology use in classroom, then teachers are encouraged to shun feeling restricted and explore new tools. Policies often drive funding and resource allocation for technology infrastructure, professional development and access to tools. Without policy educators may lack necessary hardware, software, or training to gain knowledge and skills for GenAI.

In Jamaica E-learning Jamaica Company Limited (E-LJam) is a key agency of the Jamaican government specifically, the Ministry of Science, Energy & Technology, established in 2005, with the primary purpose of integrating and infusing technology into the national education system. Its overarching goal is to improve the quality of education and help bridge the digital divide. They implement projects to fulfil this mandate (E-Learning Jamaica Company Limited, 2024). Across the Caribbean there have been funded investments to support ICT for schools and educators (U.S. Agency for International Development & Educational Quality Improvement Program I, 2011; diG Jamaica, n.d). Tablet in schools, TIS-project is another initiative (Auditor General's Department Jamaica, 2021); the 'RAISE' programme for Reskilling Teachers Using Artificial Intelligence (AI) in STEM (Weston, 2025); and the 'RARE' Initiative: The "Reimagining and Advancing Regional Education

(Caribbean Development Bank, 2024). Local EdTech Startups in countries like Jamaica and Trinidad and Tobago are developing AI-powered apps for language learning, math tutoring, and career guidance (Grandison, 2025). Furthermore, the Caribbean Examination Council (CXC) has explored AI-driven platforms to enhance exam preparation and provide personalized feedback to students with Study Smart AI tutor (Jamaica Information Service, 2025) and is also developing regional policy (Wooding, 2024). Effective GenAI integration requires specialized training and a buy in from leadership (Samuels, 2022; United Nations, 2021). This is where policies can mandate or fund professional development programs to equip educators with the necessary skills and foster a positive disposition towards these new technologies. The ecosystem is being developed, via the Caribbean artificial intelligence policy roadmap (UNESCO Office in Kingston, 2024) where regional collaboration and frameworks will address broader ICT challenges and opportunities (Ministry of Education, 2022) to inadvertently aid in the GenAI efficacy of educators. The National Standards Curriculum (NSC), the primary curriculum of Jamaica, implemented nationally in the 2017–2018 school year, requires teachers to use digital tools in their lessons (Ministry of Education, Youth, and Information, 2022).

Despite regional efforts and investments in digital education, significant policy gaps continue to impede teachers 'GenAI efficacy and pervasive digital insufficiency persists. This challenge is acutely felt across many parts of the Caribbean, especially rural regions, which exacerbates digital poverty and reveals significantly lower device access for economically disadvantaged individuals; a reality intensified and exposed by COVID (Devonish & Bennett, 2024). While one hundred percent digital sufficiency and equitable access remain an ideal, the current reality indicates substantial work is needed to bridge this gap. Notably, the absence of a comprehensive teacher professional development policy (Devonish, 2025) and STEM policy (Bailey, et al., 2022) often results in fragmented training, missed opportunities for systematic upskilling. Although the Jamaica Teaching Council (JTC) Bill has recently been tabled (Patterson, 2025) its full mandate is reportedly hampered by a lack of adequate resources, limiting its potential to seamlessly orchestrate training and prevent silos of professional development.

Furthermore, effective GenAI integration is hindered by a lack of explicit curriculum guidelines for its pedagogical application, inconsistent digital infrastructure, and the nascent development of clear ethical policies. Without sustained funding mechanisms for GenAI tool acquisition and robust monitoring and evaluation frameworks, these systemic gaps collectively restrain teachers' capacity to effectively leverage GenAI and this applies to the science teachers and the teacher trainers.

## Theme Three. Adapting Professional Development Models for GenAI integration for STEM Teachers in Resource Constrained Environment is Elusive

This theme critically examines the profound challenges hindering the effective adaptation of professional development (PD) models for GenAI integration among STEM subject teachers in resource-constrained Caribbean contexts. Envisioning the ideal scenario for Jamaica and the wider Caribbean calls us to explore a path towards a science educational 'eutopia' drawing valuable lessons from nations like Singapore, which despite a similar starting trajectory, have achieved significant development outcomes through sustained educational investment (Welsh, 2012). Despite urgent calls for such PD training, its consistent and impactful delivery remains elusive, due to systemic barriers including uneven national expenditure on education (UNESCO, n.d), insufficient non-sustained investment in teacher training infrastructure, and continuous, rapid evolution of educational technology (Alkhalifa, 2022). These challenges contribute to pervasive digital insufficiency, particularly in rural regions, exacerbating digital poverty where access to devices is significantly lower for economically disadvantaged individuals. While one hundred percent digital sufficiency and equitable access remain ideal, significant work is still required. Nevertheless, a synthesis of the literature for this emerging theme reveals consistent features that underpin successful PD models, proposing pathway to effectively sustain science teacher professional development. Once foundational digital infrastructure gaps are addressed, and open source tools, low bandwidth solutions, and appropriate technology tools are readily available, the next hurdle lies in maintaining effective PD. Table 1 highlights 20 critical features, covering pedagogical, logistical, content-related and systemic aspects of PD with suggestions for sustainability and scalability in resource-constrained settings. Lastly, fixing the entire teacher training ecosystem requires introspection and consideration for the overall betterment of the teacher lived experiences. There needs to be acknowledgement of the human element and the systemic support needed beyond just professional development.

*Table 1. Proposed professional development framework characteristics for genAI integration in resource constrained Caribbean STEM education (utilising Caribbean supporting literature)*

| **Structural Adaptation & Redesign** | | | **Supporting Literature** |
|---|---|---|---|
| **Features/Characteristics** | **PD Component/ Design Aspect** | **Comment** | |
| 1. Sustained calendared PD activities | Organizational Structure | Shifts PD from ad-hoc events to a systematic, predictable, and integrated component of teacher development, crucial for deep learning and integration. (Comparison: Contrasts with one-off workshops common in resource-constrained settings). | CARICOM (n.d) |
| 2. Centralized management of STEM subject teacher training | Organizational Structure | Ensures consistency, avoids duplication, optimizes limited resources, and facilitates alignment with national curricula and policies. The push for integrated STEM and addressing widespread teacher quality issues across the region often necessitates coordinated if not centralized, efforts at national and regional level for efficiency and consistency. | Dixon and Hutton (2016)<br>Sweeny and George (2024) |
| 3. Delivery by trained, qualified, efficacious 'master teachers'. Tertiary lecturers with adequate experience and research in the field. | Human Resources/ Delivery Model | A master teacher is a qualified pedagogical and certified content specialist (Jamaica Teaching Council, n.d.).<br>Leverages local expertise and academic rigor for culturally relevant and sustainable capacity building. Master teachers (qualified pedagogical and certified content specialists) and experienced tertiary lecturers bring a blend of practical classroom insight and foundational research knowledge, particularly their capacity to conduct research that informs evidence-based PD content and delivery. | Devonish et al. (2025)<br><br>Esnard and Bristol (2024) |
| 4. Blended approaches to delivery | Delivery Modality | Combines online flexibility with crucial in-person support, addressing connectivity challenges while providing hands-on and personalized learning. | UNESCO (2020) |
| 5. Readily accessible, free or subsidized | Access & Resource Model | Crucial for equity and widespread participation in contexts where cost is a significant barrier. | Berry (2021) |

*Table 1b. Continued*

| **Structural Adaptation & Redesign** | | | **Supporting Literature** |
|---|---|---|---|
| **Features/Characteristics** | **PD Component/ Design Aspect** | **Comment** | |
| 6. Open source tools with… (see below) | Resource Provision | This ICT policy document directly supports the use of Free and Open-Source Software (FOSS) and Open Educational Resources (OERs) within the Jamaican education system. It also acknowledges the need to 'attain affordable universal broadband access and to ensure equitable access of all education and training institutions to low-cost, reliable high-speed internet.' Policy across the Eastern Caribbean is present. There is hope for reduced software licensing costs and promotion of local innovation and customization with open source. | MOEY (2022)<br><br>World Bank (2024) |
| 7. Low band width capabilities | Infrastructure Design | Adapts to existing connectivity limitations, ensuring functionality of tools and resources even with unreliable internet access. | Caribbean Telecommunications [CTU](n.d.) |
| 8. Quality Assured (Standardized and certified) | Quality Assurance & Governance | Ensures consistency in content and delivery across different regions and providers, building trust and credibility. This involves robust consultation and quality assurance processes, often guided by university professors and subject matter experts. Professors' research capacity is vital here, ensuring that PD design and evaluation are informed by evidence, leading to data-driven policies for continuous improvement and adaptation. | Burns (2023)<br>CARICOM (2020)<br>JTC (2022) |
| 9. hands on approach for the participant with onsite support, job embedded exposure | Pedagogical Approach | Promotes practical application and immediate feedback, allowing teachers to integrate GenAI directly into their classroom practice with support. PD has clinical supervision, coaching or mentorship aspects. | Caribbean Science Foundation[CSF] (n.d)<br>James (2018) |

*Table 1c. continued*

| Structural Adaptation & Redesign | | | Supporting Literature |
|---|---|---|---|
| **Features/Characteristics** | **PD Component/ Design Aspect** | **Comment** | **Devonish et al., 2025** |
| 10. Train the trainer approaches | Capacity Building Model | Multiplies the impact of training efforts efficiently, creating a sustainable network of local experts and reducing reliance on external trainers. | UNESCO (2022) Hunter (2017) |
| 11. Training and Ongoing Professional Development for Teacher Educators | Capacity Building Trainer Development | Emphasizes the critical need to equip those who train and support teachers (e.g., tertiary lecturers, curriculum specialists, master teachers) with deep GenAI content knowledge, advanced pedagogical skills for AI integration, and effective adult learning strategies. This ensures a high-quality, sustainable pipeline of expert | Antonio (2020) Sun (2021) |
| 12. Training and Ongoing Professional Development for Teacher Educators | Capacity Building Trainer Development | trainers, underpinning the success of cascade models and master teacher initiatives. (Comparison: Often overlooked in initial PD planning, leading to a gap in trainer expertise as technology evolves). General PD is to include-time management and planning, course evaluation, action research, teaching competencies, specific teaching skills and strategies, self-studies, and personal factors) | Antonio (2020) Sun (2021) |
| 13. Establishment and Nurturing of Communities of Practice (CoPs) / Collaborative Peer Learning Networks | Learning Environment/ Sustainability | Formalizes and leverages existing or new Communities of Practice (CoPs), such as those facilitated by the Association of Science Teachers of Jamaica (ASTJ). CoPs enable ongoing peer support, shared problem-solving for GenAI integration, continuous learning, and collective knowledge building beyond structured PD events, contributing significantly to the sustainability of learning and sustained teacher efficacy. (Comparison: Essential for | Devonish (2021) Association of Science Teachers of Jamaica. (n.d.). Turner (1974) Chapman & Monticenos (2025) Wenger (1998) |

*Table 1d. Continued*

| **Structural Adaptation & Redesign** | | | **Supporting Literature** |
|---|---|---|---|
| **Features/Characteristics** | **PD Component/ Design Aspect** | **Comment** | |
| | | fostering long-term skill adoption and innovation, especially where formal support is intermittent). | Lave and Wenger (1991)<br>Kamalodeen (2024) |
| 14. What to train for: CK, TK, TCK, TPK | Curriculum/ Content Design | Ensures teachers develop deep understanding of *how* to teach *with* and *about* GenAI effectively, moving beyond mere tool proficiency.<br>(Comparison: Often a gap in foundational digital literacy programs). | Bandura (1977)<br>Mihsra and Koehler, (2006) |
| **Focus** | Curriculum/ Content Design | Equips teachers with foundational skills necessary to interact with, evaluate, and critically use GenAI tools, including effective prompting strategies. | |
| 15. ethical guidelines or frameworks for AI in education | Curriculum/ Content Design | Analyzing how professional development can instill ethical awareness, critical evaluation skills, and responsible implementation strategies in educators is critical as the use of technology evolves. Accessing academic integrity, privacy and data security, digital citizenship and safety and accessibility and equity are crucial for navigating its societal and academic impacts.<br>(Comparison: More developed countries often have national frameworks, while this is an emerging area for resource-constrained contexts). | Corbeil & Corbeil (2025)<br><br>(UNESCO Office in Kingston, 2024) |
| 16. digital literacy | Curriculum Alignment | Foundational for GenAI literacy and tool capabilities<br>Prompt engineering<br>Analytics | IADB and UNESCO (2025)<br>Mora et al. (2025) |
| 17. general maintained upskilling with aligned curricula | Curriculum Alignment | Ensures PD remains relevant and responsive to evolving curricula and technological advancements, preventing obsolescence. | Sun (2021) |

*Table 1e. Continued*

| Structural Adaptation & Redesign | | | Supporting Literature |
|---|---|---|---|
| **Features/Characteristics** | **PD Component/ Design Aspect** | **Comment** | |
| 18. STEM subject integration STEM education | Curriculum scope | The foundation to STEM is the mastery and attainment of science processing skills. Prioritizes critical STEM fields, ensuring targeted and impactful GenAI integration where it can yield significant educational and economic benefits. | Devonish (2021) Caribbean Examination Council (2019) Jamaica Ministry of Education and Youth, 2022) |
| 19. Enablers-Stakeholder Buy in | Scaling & Sustainability | Fostering stakeholder alignment and engagement, including elements to ensure stakeholder buy-in for intentional support (in cash or kind) from government, institutions, teachers, students, the education ministry, and other industry partners. | Kix (2024) Global Partnership for Education [GPE] (2025) Coy et al. (2019) |
| 20. PD framework is an addition to reputable Teacher Training regimes existing | Framework Integration/Policy | Reinforces existing strengths rather than creating parallel, unsustainable systems. Emphasizes leveraging existing institutional capacities for long-term impact. | CARICOM (2025) |

**Note.** The table outlines 20 adaptable strategies for PD, intended to coordinate a PD framework, which is to complement, not substitute, existing teacher certification pathways. References may support multiple characteristics and encompass broader professional development or STEM education principles applicable to GenAI integration.

## Practical Guidelines for Ethical GenAI Integration, the Roadmap

While the absence of a national framework for GenAI integration may pose a challenge, this should not hinder the progress at the grassroots level. It is crucial for individual teachers and schools to take proactive steps, as their engagement with tools will ultimately inform national strategy. Therefore, every professional development session regardless of its scale must be guided by a clear set of standards to ensure that the adoption of Gen AI is ethical safe and effective.

*Figure 2. Roadmap for ethical genAi integration for STEM teachers*

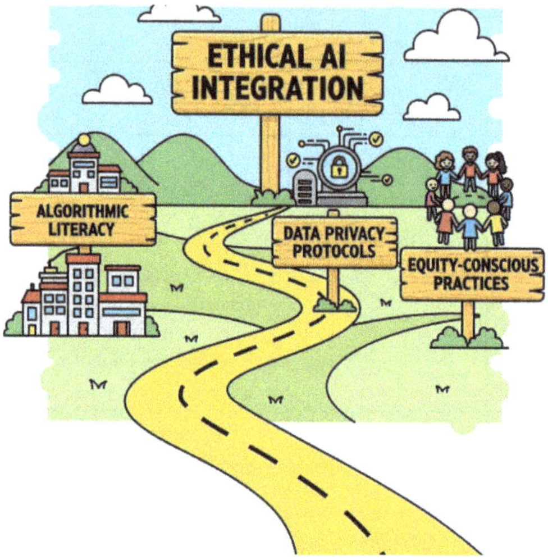


***Note.*** *Figure 2 visually represents the three core principles, algorithmic literacy, data privacy protocols, and equity-conscious practices that form a roadmap for professional development activities.*

To address the ethical and bias concerns related to GenAI, this paper moves beyond a conceptual discussion to offer practical guidelines for educators. Drawing from key principles within the provided national and international policy documents (e.g., Jamaica's National Artificial Intelligence Task Force Policy Recommendations and UNESCO's Recommendations on the ethics of AI), a concrete roadmap for professional development activities is being further highlighted (Figure 2 above).

First PD activities should prioritize algorithmic literacy, teaching educators how AI models work, their limitations, and the potential for bias in training data. Second, it must include a focus on data privacy protocols, providing clear, actionable steps for protecting student information when using AI tools. Finally, guiding teachers to critically evaluate AI's impact on diverse student populations and to select tools that promote fairness and inclusion is a best practice for ensuring equity and conscious practices. By integrating these ethical considerations directly into PD activities along with trainers actively considering globally accepted standards (e.g. Standards adoption: Embedding ISO/IEC 42001 (AI Management Systems), EN 301 549 (Accessibility for ICT products and services), WCAG 2.2, and GDPR-style data protection principles into classroom practice) to bolster the best practices and awareness being shared in PD activities for STEM teachers.

The proposed roadmap offers a flexible guide that can be adopted by individual schools and professional development groups. Widespread utilization of this framework would lead to more consistent PD practices across the country and region. Future research could then analyze these collective efforts to inform the development of a comprehensive national "playbook" which would serve as a foundation for a standardized national PD framework.

## Working Conditions and Teacher Lived Experiences Shaping Professional Development

Fixing the teachers working conditions for better-lived experiences must be an integral part of this conversation, necessitating further research into its profound impact on holistic national development. The challenges are systemic: from deteriorating perception of the teacher profession due to social factors and perceived low wages for the work demand (Chapman & Monticenos, 2025; Devonish, 2025), to the notion, that teaching may be perceived a 'shameful option' for unsuccessful STEM majors into 'elite' STEM professions. Such perceptions significantly impact professional identity and teacher morale, which in turn need attention (Gentles, 2021; See et al., 2022). Consequently, the teacher pipeline is stunted; despite government scholarships being available (Jamaica Observer, 2023), the uptake particularly among science teachers, could be more substantial. This too requires further research to ascertain data for perceptions to transform into robust claims. Moreover, the quality and supply of Science teachers is reducing (Nguyen, 2025). The numbers of students training as STEM subject teachers continue to decrease, and even fewer students matriculate into STEM subject options at Caribbean Secondary Examination Certificate CSEC level reducing the pool for tertiary education (Griffith, 2019). This crisis is exacerbated by the low numbers in BSc or BEd programmes in Science with Education, due to class size viability issues and students' reluctance to take scholarships due to bonding requirements (personal communication, Programme Leader Science Education at two institutions). A stark illustration of this is the pausing of Utech, Jamaica's Science & Education Course of Study at the Faculty of Science & Sport over the last 5 years.

Our communities of practice are losing seasoned teachers to overseas recruitment or career changes (Wilkinson, 2023; JTA, 2025). Furthermore, teachers' varied tertiary experiences underscore persistent self-efficacy challenges, inadequate training or pedagogical hurdles (Devonish, 2018; Roofe, 2022). Despite these formidable obstacles, the commitment of remaining teachers to national development underscores the crucial necessity of professional development to maintain the STEM subject teacher stock. We must ensure GenAI integration in the science classroom lessons for the 21st century. This theme three has highlighted all the characteristic features and hurdles that must be surmounted. However, while these pathways offer hope, their successful implementation and the very integration of GenAI into Caribbean STEM education will remain elusive without meaningful, consistent, and systemic intervention. Nations like Singapore provide an important reference for us. Their trajectory proved significant development outcomes through sustained educational investment (Welsh, 2012). Today they have the capability to respond to educational changes (Foong, Pidani, Vadivel, and Dongyue, 2024; Isaacs & Mishra, 2022) and this provides important reference for us. See a summary of this reference in Figure 3 below. It stands as a testament to transformational change possible when education is prioritized consistently, with data driven policies. Without such an unwavering commitment, the potential for an 'eminent fall' in STEM education in the region is not merely a risk, but a likely outcome and we will continuously trail behind (Sweeny & George, 2024).

*Figure 3. Singapore as an example for AI integration*

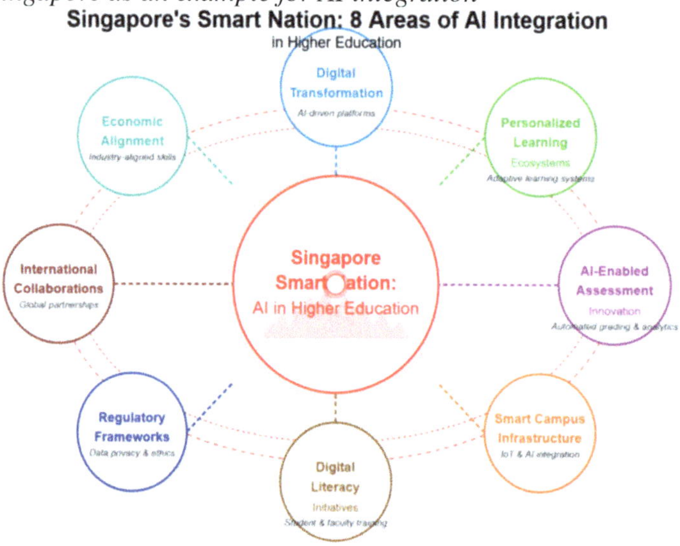


**Note.** *Devonish. Figure 3 summarizes key areas of AI integration within Singapore's Smart Nation initiative, synthesized from Foong, Pidani, Vadivel, and Dongyue (2024) and Isaacs and Mishra (2022). Singapore's response to the changing AI landscape through education.*

## Theme Four: Using Mixed Method (MM) Research for GenAI Professional Development Intervention Assessment

Effective evaluation of GenAI PD interventions requires robust frameworks and is paramount for understanding the true impact and sustainability. The proposition here is an overall evaluation employing Experimental/Intervention Mixed Methods Design (Creswell & Plano Clark, 2017) using Kirkpatrick's Four Level Training Evaluation Model (1959) as the primary evaluative lens, supplemented by Rogers' Diffusion of Innovations Theory (2003). Figure 4 shows a simplified conceptualization of a MM study, illustrating how qualitative and quantitative data can be used to complement each other, to produce more comprehensive understanding than either method could achieve alone (Creswell and Creswell, 2023).

*Figure 4. Mixed method concept evaluation map*

```
MIXED-METHODS EVALUATION DESIGN
        ↓
KIRKPATRICK'S 4-LEVEL MODEL
L1: Reaction | L2: Learning | L3: Behavior | L4: Results
        ↓
QUANTITATIVE STRAND      |    QUALITATIVE STRAND
- TPACK Changes          |    - Perception Surveys
- Student Outcomes       |    - Observations
- Diffusion Metrics      |    - Document Reviews
        ↓                |              ↓
    DATA INTEGRATION & TRIANGULATION
        ↓
COMPREHENSIVE VALIDATION
```

While existing Caribbean PD literature provides foundational insights (Chapman & Montecinos, 2025; Bissessar, 2021a, b; Jaggernauth, 2021; Polius,2022; Williams, 2022), there is fervent call for continued research. This research should collectively focus more on GenAI, employing integrated quantitative and qualitative approaches, particularly for STEM. This emphasis reflects where we are in education today, it is the 21st century educational hub, driving current interest and innovation. Figure 5 shows the quantitative strand of MM collecting numerical data to make descriptive presentations and statistical inferences. Key metrics will include changes in teachers' TPACK, assessing shifts in content knowledge, pedagogy, technology use, and ethical behaviour related to GenAI. This strand will also monitor knowledge and skill attainment and explore the diffusion rate of GenAI practices among teachers, drawing insight from Rogers' Diffusion Theory (2003). The qualitative data should provide contextual insights into teacher self-efficacy, pedagogical applications or innovations, and student engagement patterns. The collection of deep rich, contextual data through methods gathering perceptions, document reviews of educational reports and classroom observations will be very informative to the assessment process (Sun, 2021; Onwuegbuzie, et al., 2010).

It is also crucial that this dual-strand approach within the mixed methods tradition ensures robust, ethical and authentic practice. Beyond assessing ethical behaviour related to GenAI itself, the research methodology must diligently address ethical considerations such as informed consent, confidentiality, and data security. Both strands will critically inform Kirkpatrick levels, assessing reactions, learning, behavioural shifts in the classroom (Level 3) and ultimately, changes in student outcomes like critical thinking and problem solving (Level 4). This comprehensive approach ensures robust validation across all Kirkpatrick levels. This would be from the level of teacher participant reactions to behavioural changes and institutional results, providing comprehensive evidence in our Caribbean context.

*Figure 5. GenAI professional development evaluation framework*

## CONCLUSION

The study has presented its key arguments, structured around four comprehensive themes that directly address each of four research questions. These findings underscore the critical competencies and dispositions required for science teachers to effectively leverage emerging technologies in the GenAI age, while also reiterating the importance of ongoing support and learning for this endeavor.

Furthermore, the research highlighted the profound challenges in adapting professional development models and integrating ethical considerations for GenAI within unique context resource-constrained Caribbean environments. It underscored that achieving meaningful and ethical integration remains elusive without targeted, contextual research and robust consistent intervention. Drawing on lessons from first world nations and their determined trajectory of educational investment, this study strongly encourages policy makers to undertake the bold yet necessary decisions required for transformational change.

Twenty adaptable characteristics for the Caribbean PD framework is proposed with evaluation for each aspect recommended. Finally, the research emphasizes the critical need to evaluate our collective efforts in operationalizing GenAI into Caribbean national development plans. This evaluation will primarily utilize an experimental/Intervention mixed methods approach (Creswell & Plano Clarke, 2017) to rigorously assess the professional development adaptation and its impact. This evaluation will also facilitate calls for future research. Such research could explore science teachers lived experiences, GenAI usage at different school levels; the number of PD activities throughout the Caribbean ecosystem, and the success of holistically framing an adoption of policies and singular integrated ecosystem. Importantly, to understand their impact on PD and ultimately student outcomes. To gather contextual data about our Caribbean education system in the evolving technologically driven world is imperative to our development.

## REFERENCES


Abdrakhmanov, R., Zhaxanova, A., Karatayeva, M., Niyazova, G. Z., Berkimbayev, K., & Tuimebayev, A. (2024). Development of a framework for predicting students' academic performance in STEM education using machine learning methods. *International Journal of Advanced Computer Science and Applications, 15*(1). Advance online publication. DOI: 10.14569/IJACSA.2024.0150105

Adams, J. D. (2020). Designing frameworks for authentic equity in science teaching and learning: Informal learning environments and teacher education for STEM. *Asia-Pacific Science Education, 6*(2), 456–479. DOI: 10.1163/23641177-BJA10016

Al-Khalifa, S. N. (2022). The rapid evolution of educational technology: Implications for higher education. *Journal of Higher Education Theory and Practice, 22*(16), 116–122.

Antonio, D. (2020). *Continuing professional development (CPD) of teacher educators (TEs) within the ecological environment of the island territories of the Organisation of Eastern Caribbean States*. OECS. [Master's thesis, University of Liverpool]

Asare, S., Amoako, S. K., Biilah, D. K., & Apraku, T. B. (2023). The use of virtual labs in science education: A comparative study of traditional labs and virtual environments. *International Journal of Science Academic Research, 4*(11), 6563–6569.

Association of Science Teachers of Jamaica. (n.d.). Home [Facebook page]. *Facebook*. Retrieved July 12, 2025, from https://www.facebook.com/ASTJamaica/

Auditor General's Department Jamaica. (2021). *Auditor General's Department Annual Report FY2020/21*. https://auditorgeneral.gov.jm/wp-content/uploads/2022/01/2021_AuGD_Annual_Report.pdf

Bailey, A., Powell-Wilson, D., Stone, S. M., Bartley-Ellis, J., Davies, R., & Edwards-Henry, A.-M. (2022). *STEM education in Jamaica: A case of practitioners*. ResearchGate.

Bandura, A. (1977). Self-efficacy: Toward a unifying theory of behavioral change. *Psychological Review, 84*(2), 191–215. DOI: 10.1037/0033-295X.84.2.191

Bandura, A. (1986). *Social foundations of thought and action: A social cognitive theory*. Prentice Hall.

Bandura, A. (1998). Self-efficacy. In Friedman, H. (Ed.), *Encyclopedia of mental health* (Vol. 3, pp. 317–321). Academic Press.

Berry, C., McCarthy-Curvin, A., Bramwell-Lalor, S., Moore, S., Newman, M., & Lambert, C. (2021). Massive open online courses: A source of effective professional development for in-service teachers. *Journal of Education and Development in the Caribbean, 19*(2), 112–144. DOI: 10.46425/j419028671

Bissessar, C. (2021b). Comparing teacher professional development initiatives in three Caribbean countries. In *The handbook on Caribbean education* (pp. 23). University of the West Indies Press Bourne, P. A. (2022). An examination of mathematics performance in Jamaica: Insight into the basis for low enrolment in mathematics at the tertiary level. *International Journal of Transformation in Applied Mathematics & Statistics, 5*(1). https://science.eurekajournals.com/index.php/IJTAMS/article/view/286

Bissessar, C. S. G. (2021a). Social learning and collaborative professional learning among caribbean teachers: implications for Praxis. *Teacher Learning and Professional Development, 6.*

Bradley, J. (2021). Achieving the aims of practical work with microchemistry. In *Research in chemistry education* (pp. 23–30). Springer International Publishing. DOI: 10.1007/978-3-030-59882-2_2

Brissett, N. O. (2022). Caribbean dreams: Education for more than just sustainable development. *The Journal of Environmental Education, 53*(1), 54–67. DOI: 10.1080/00958964.2021.2023448

Burns, M. (2023). *Distance education for teacher training: Modes, models, and methods* (2nd ed.). Education Development Center., https://inee.org/sites/default/files/Distance_Education_for_Teacher_Training_-_Modes%2C_Models%2C_and_Methods.pdf

Caribbean Community (CARICOM). (2005). *A harmonized policy framework for teacher education in the Caribbean* (OAS Hemispheric Project). https://caricom.org/documents/12940-aharmonizedpolicyframeworkforteachereducationinthecaribbean_(1).pdf

Caribbean Community (CARICOM). (2020). *CARICOM standards for teachers, educational leaders and teacher educators*. https://caricom.org/documents/caricom-standards-for-teachers-educational-leaders-and-teacher-educators/

Caribbean Community (CARICOM). (n.d.). *CARICOM standards for teachers, educational leaders and teacher educators*. https://caricom.org/documents/caricom-standards-for-teachers-educational-leaders-and-teacher-educators/

Caribbean Development Bank. (2024, October 3). CDB supporting regional education transformation with key initiatives. *CARICOM*. https://caricom.org/cdb-supporting-regional-education-transformation-with-key-initiatives/

Caribbean Examinations Council (CXC). (2019, July 1). New syllabuses to meet regional human resource development needs. https://www.cxc.org/new-syllabuses-meet-needs/

Caribbean Science Foundation (CSF). (n.d.). STEM teacher training workshops. https://caribbeanscience.org/stem-teacher-training-workshops/

Caribbean Telecommunications Union (CTU). (n.d.). Creative internet connectivity and classroom solutions to support Caribbean online learning. https://ctu.int/creative-internet-connectivity-and-classroom-solutions-to-support-caribbean-online-learning%EF%BF%BC/

Castillo-Canales, D., Mancilla, A., Restrepo, R., & Martinez, F. (2022). *Teacher professional development supported by information and communication technologies: A case study of the "Teacher Training Program for Curricular Update 2016-2018 in Ecuador"*. Foundation for Information Technology Education and Development.

Cator, K., Schneider, C., & Vander Ark, T. (2014). *Preparing teachers for deeper learning*. Digital Promise. https://digitalpromise.org/2014/05/01/preparing-teachers-for-deeper-learning/

Chapman, C., & Montecinos, C. (2025). Professional learning in Latin America and the Caribbean: Towards a networked learning system? *Professional Development in Education, 51*(1), 1–6. DOI: 10.1080/19415257.2025.2446110

Clandinin, D. J. (2008). Creating learning spaces for teachers and teacher educators. *Teachers and Teaching, 14*(5-6), 385–389. DOI: 10.1080/13540600802571304

Corbeil, J. R., & Corbeil, M. E. (2025). Teaching and learning in the age of generative AI.

Costa, A. L., & Garmston, R. J. (2016). *Cognitive coaching: A foundation for renaissance schools* (3rd ed.). Rowman & Littlefield.

Coy, A., James-Williamson, S., Bramwell-Lalor, S., Sadler-McKnight, N., McLean, N., Penugonda, V. R., & Rainford, M. (2019). A Review of a Tertiary Level Institution's Initiative for Enhancing Education in STEM at the Secondary School Level. *Journal of Education & Development in the Caribbean, 18*(1), 132–182. DOI: 10.46425/j061801u135

Creswell, J. W., & Creswell, J. D. (2023). *Research design: Qualitative, quantitative and mixed methods approaches*. SAGE Publications.

Creswell, J. W., & Plano Clark, V. L. (2017). *Designing and conducting mixed methods research* (3rd ed.). SAGE Publications.

Darling-Hammond, L., Oakes, J., Wojcikiewicz, S. K., Hyler, M. E., Guha, R., Podolsky, A., ... Harrell, A. (2019). *Preparing teachers for deeper learning* (Research brief).

Davidovitch, N., & Yavich, R. (2022). Teachers' attitudes to use of advanced technological tools as teaching and learning aids: From an inter-generational perspective. *The European Educational Researcher, 5*(1), 329-341. https://files.eric.ed.gov/fulltext/EJ1318682.pdf

Devonish, D. (2016). *The cognitive coaching approach: A professional development model for science educators and for students' academic achievement* [Unpublished doctoral dissertation]. Northern Caribbean University.

Devonish, D. (2020). Assessment of the microscience kit intervention in secondary schools undertaken by the Ministry of Education Youth & Information, Jamaica under the UNESCO participation programme. *Ministry of Education, Youth & Information, Jamaica*. DOI: 10.13140/RG.2.2.32854.77127

Devonish, D. (2021, June). The role of professional organizations in education: The COVID-19 response in Jamaica by science teachers. *Revista Conexiones: Una experiencia más allá del aula, 13*(2), 42-55. https://www.mep.go.cr/sites/default/files/2revistaconexiones2021_a4.pdf

Devonish, D. (2025, March 26). *Harnessing AI-powered personalized learning for inclusive STEM education in Caribbean secondary schools* [Conference presentation]. Caribbean Association for the Advancement of Curriculum Studies, Fourth Virtual Conference.

Devonish, D., & Bennett, S. (2024). A toolkit intervention for school-aged Jamaican students: Strategy for collaborative involvement during the pandemic. *Caribbean Journal of Education and Development, 1*(3), 77–95. DOI: 10.46425/cjed601036532

Devonish, D., Bennett, S., Hylton, K., King, J., & Barrett, D. (2025). Ensuring STEM teacher quality to meet the demands of the Caribbean labor market beyond the 21st century. In *Navigating leadership and policy management in education* (pp. 1–42). IGI Global.

Devonish, D., Lawrence, P., & Zamore, C. (2018). Voices of Pre-service Teachers on Science Pedagogy: A Case Study on the Challenges of Implementing Diverse Instructional Strategies into the Science lesson post University. *Journal of Arts Science & Technology, 11*(1).

diGJamaica. (n.d.). Page 729 - Budget 2014-2015. http://digjamaica.com/app/webroot/edocs/Budget_2014-2015/files/assets/basic-html/page729.html

Dixon, R. A., & Hutton, D. M. (2016). STEM and TVET in the Caribbean: A framework for integration at the primary, secondary and tertiary levels. *Caribbean Curriculum, 24*, 1–26.

Dolmans, D. H., Loyens, S. M., Marcq, H., & Gijbels, D. (2016). Deep and surface learning in problem-based learning: A review of the literature. *Advances in Health Sciences Education : Theory and Practice, 21*(5), 1087–1112. DOI: 10.1007/s10459-015-9645-6

Down, L. (2024). The future of Caribbean scholarly research: Towards greater community engagement. *Caribbean Journal of Education and Development, 1*(1), 68–74. DOI: 10.46425/cjed801016484

Esnard, T., & Bristol, L. (2024). Grounding Caribbean educators and research(ers): Decolonial reflections with Professor Joel Warrican. *Caribbean Educational Research Journal, 9*(1), Article 1. https://cavehill.uwi.edu/fhe/education/publications/past-issues/volume-9-number-1-october-2024/articles/01-full-text-esnard-and-bristol.aspx

Feng, S., Magana, A. J., & Kao, D. (2021, October). A systematic review of literature on the effectiveness of intelligent tutoring systems in STEM. In *2021 IEEE Frontiers in Education Conference (FIE)* (pp. 1-9). IEEE. DOI: 10.1109/FIE49875.2021.9637240

Foong, Y. P., Pidani, R., Sithira Vadivel, V., & Dongyue, Y. (2024). Singapore smart nation: Journey into a new digital landscape for higher education. In Kwok, A. O. J., & Teh, P.-L. (Eds.), *Emerging technologies in business: Innovation strategies for competitive advantage* (pp. 281–304). Springer Nature Singapore., DOI: 10.1007/978-981-97-2211-2_13

Freire, P. (2000). *Pedagogy of the oppressed* (30th anniversary ed.). Continuum.

Gentles, C. C. H. (2021). The work and professional identity of Caribbean teacher educators. In Smith, J., & Jones, A. (Eds.), *The handbook on Caribbean education* (pp. 43–65). Caribbean Press. DOI: 10.1108/978-1-64802-411-520251005

Global Partnership for Education (GPE). (2025, February 5). Improving learning: What research says on the effectiveness and scalability of teacher professional development. https://www.globalpartnership.org/blog/improving-learning-what-research-effectiveness-scalability-teacher-professional-development

Grandison, T. (2025, February 28). Jamaica and the Caribbean need a holistic AI roadmap. *The Gleaner*. https://jamaica-gleaner.com/article/commentary/20250228/tyrone-grandison-jamaica-and-caribbean-need-holistic-ai-roadmap

Grant, M. J., & Booth, A. (2009). A typology of reviews: An analysis of 14 review types and associated methodologies. *Health Information and Libraries Journal, 26*(2), 91–108. DOI: 10.1111/j.1471-1842.2009.00848.x

Griffith, S. A. (2019). Growth rate in CXC STEM subject entries: Implications for meeting the development needs of the Caribbean. *Journal of Research in STEM Education, 5*(2), 5. https://j-stem.net/index.php/jstem/article/view/82. DOI: 10.51355/jstem.2019.82

Hasanova, N., Abduazizov, B., & Khujakulov, R. (2021). The main differences between teaching approaches, methods, procedures, techniques, styles and strategies. *JournalNX - A Multidisciplinary Peer Reviewed Journal, 7*(2), 371-375.

Hunter, J. (2017, August 17). Maths coaches and specialists to attend training workshop. *Jamaica Information Service*. https://jis.gov.jm/maths-coaches-specialists-attend-training-workshop/

Inter-American Development Bank (IADB) & UNESCO. (2025). *AI and education: Building the future through digital transformation*. https://publications.iadb.org/publications/english/document/AI-and-Education-Building-the-Future-Through-Digital-Transformation.pdf

Isaacs, S., & Mishra, S. (2022). *Smart education strategies for teaching and learning: Critical analytical framework and case studies*. UNESCO Institute for Information Technologies in Education (UNESCO IITE).

Jaggernauth, S. J. (2021). Modelling teacher efficacy change during a teacher professional development programme in Trinidad and Tobago. *Caribbean Curriculum, 28*.

Jamaica Gleaner. (2016, December 2). Digicel Foundation launches Phase Three of Mobile Science Lab initiative. *Jamaica Gleaner*. https://jamaica-gleaner.com/article/news/20161202/digicel-foundation-launches-phase-three-mobile-science-lab-initiative

Jamaica Information Service. (2025, April 23). EduHub develops revolutionary technology for student success in CSEC and CAPE exams. *Jamaica Information Service.* https://jis.gov.jm/eduhub-develops-revolutionary-technology-for-student-success-in-csec-and-cape-exams/

Jamaica Observer. (2023, June 29). STEM teacher training scholarship programme to be launched today. https://www.jamaicaobserver.com/2023/06/29/stem-teacher-training-scholarship-programme-to-be-launched-today/

Jamaica Observer. (2025, May 30). CXC failure rates: A crisis in Jamaican education. *Jamaica Observer.* https://www.jamaicaobserver.com/2025/05/30/cxc-failure-rates-crisis-jamaican-education/

Jamaica Teachers' Association. (2025, March 3). JTA proposes teacher rotation model to address migration crisis. https://www.jta.org.jm/content/jta-proposes-teacher-rotation-model-address-migration-crisis

Jamaica Teaching Council. (n.d.). *Master teacher handbook.* https://jtc.gov.jm/masterteacherhm/

Jamaica Teaching Council (JTC). (2022). *The Jamaica Teaching Council Act 2022.* https://japarliament.gov.jm/attachments/article/339/The-Jamaica-Teaching-Council-Act--2022.pdf

James, J. S. (2018, April). A model of professional development and best practice for primary science teachers. *Journal of Education and Development in the Caribbean, 17*(1), 37–64.

Jeyaseelan, S. M., Sobers, N. P., Grant, K., Vasquez, G. M., Blenman, S., & Hambleton, I. R. (2025). Implementing and evaluating a project to enable and encourage Caribbean data-sharing. *Revista Panamericana de Salud Pública = Pan American Journal of Public Health, 48*, e120.

Joksimovic, S., Ifenthaler, D., Marrone, R., De Laat, M., & Siemens, G. (2023). Opportunities of artificial intelligence for supporting complex problem-solving: Findings from a scoping review. *Computers and Education: Artificial Intelligence.* DOI: 10.1016/j.caeai.2023.100138

Kamalodeen, V. (2024). Rapid response to professional development: How online teacher professional learning networks supported teachers in pandemic times. *Caribbean Journal of Education and Development, 1*(3), 149–156. DOI: 10.46425/cjed1001031940

Keith, L. R., & Waldron, L. (2024). AI-driven educational paradigm for Sustainable Development Goal 4: A Caribbean perspective. In *The UWI Quality Education Forum* (No. 28, pp. 151-171).

Kirkpatrick, D. L. (1959). Techniques for evaluating training programs. *Journal of ASTD*, 1-13.

Kix, G. (2024). *Teacher professional development: A research synthesis*. International Development Research Centre.

Knowles, M. (1977). Adult learning processes: Pedagogy and andragogy. *Religious Education (Chicago, Ill.)*, *72*(2), 202–211. DOI: 10.1080/0034408770720210

Knowles, M. S. (1975). *Self-directed learning: A guide for learners and teachers*. Follett Publishing Company.

Knowles, M. S. (1984). Theory of andragogy: A critique. *International Journal of Lifelong Education*. Cambridge MA.

Koteluk, O., Wartecki, A., Mazurek, S., Kołodziejczak, I., & Mackiewicz, A. (2021). How do machines learn? Artificial intelligence as a new era in medicine. *Journal of Personalized Medicine*, *11*(1), 32. DOI: 10.3390/jpm11010032

Laupichler, M. C., Aster, A., Schirch, J., & Raupach, T. (2022). Artificial intelligence literacy in higher and adult education: A scoping literature review. *Computers and Education: Artificial Intelligence*, *3*, 100101. DOI: 10.1016/j.caeai.2022.100101

Lave, J., & Wenger, E. (1991). *Situated learning: Legitimate peripheral participation*. Cambridge University Press. DOI: 10.1017/CBO9780511815355

Li, L. C., Grimshaw, J. M., Nielsen, C., Judd, M., Coyte, P. C., & Graham, I. D. (2009). Evolution of Wenger's concept of community of practice. *Implementation Science : IS*, *4*(11), 11. DOI: 10.1186/1748-5908-4-11

McDonald, J., & Mercieca, B. M. (2021). What is a community of practice? In *Sustaining communities of practice with early career teachers* (pp. 1–19). Springer., DOI: 10.1007/978-981-33-6354-0_1

Menzli, L. J., Smirani, L. K., Boulahia, J. A., & Hadjouni, M. (2022). Investigation of open educational resources adoption in higher education using Rogers' diffusion of innovation theory. *Heliyon*, *8*(7), e09885. Advance online publication. DOI: 10.1016/j.heliyon.2022.e09885

Meotti, M., & Magliozzi, D. (2025). Using artificial intelligence to navigate the new challenges of college and career. Harvard ALI Social Impact Review. Retrieved from https://www.sir.advancedleadership.harvard.edu/articles/using-artificial-intelligence-to-navigate-the-new-challenges-of-college-and-career

Merriam, S. B. (2018). Adult learning theory: Evolution and future directions. In *Contemporary theories of learning* (pp. 83–96). Routledge. DOI: 10.4324/9781315147277-6

Miller, E. L. (1999). Teacher development in the Caribbean. In Miller, E. L. (Ed.), *Education for All in the Caribbean in the 1990s: Retrospect and Prospect* (pp. 57–91). CARICOM.

Ministry of Education. (2015). *National Education Inspectorate Report*. https://drive.google.com/a/moey.gov.jm/folderview?id=0BzlAiS6fPqgZfldvQlFTaHcwc1FLSGxGLUNlaXY3RW9iUHRSNy00WlRVNGMzLXItRnl0eTg&usp=drive_web&pli=1&tid=0BzlAiS6fPqgZfkVzOGh1aWRPaXQ2WXFRcnpCT3JSZDc4ejRoeTB1MzJCMTZYYkpRQTlrc2s#list

Ministry of Education and Youth. Jamaica. (2022). *ICT in Education Policy 2022: Transforming lives, empowering citizens and enabling national development.* https://moey.gov.jm/wp-content/uploads/2022/07/ICT-in-Education-Policy-Jamaica-Ministry-of-Education-and-Youth-2022.pdf

Mishra, P., & Koehler, M. J. (2006). Technological pedagogical content knowledge: A framework for teacher knowledge. *Teachers College Record*, *108*(6), 1017–1054. DOI: 10.1111/j.1467-9620.2006.00684.x

Mittal, U., Sai, S., Chamola, V., & Sangwan, D. (2024). A Comprehensive Review on Generative AI for Education. *IEEE Access : Practical Innovations, Open Solutions*, *12*, 142733–142759. Advance online publication. DOI: 10.1109/ACCESS.2024.3468368

Molina, E., Cobo, C., Pineda, J., & Rovner, H. (2024). *AI Revolution in Education: What you need to know* (Brief N°1). World Bank. https://documents1.worldbank.org/curated/en/099734306182493324/pdf/IDU152823b13109c514ebd19c241a289470b6902.pdf

Mora, S., . . .. (2025, April 11). How AI can support teachers in Latin America. *Brookings Institution.* https://www.brookings.edu/articles/how-ai-can-support-teachers-in-latin-america/

Nguyen, T. D. (2025). The supply and quality of STEM teachers. *Humanities & Social Sciences Communications*, *12*(1), 359. DOI: 10.1057/s41599-025-04648-8

Onwuegbuzie, A. J., & Frels, R. K. (2016). *Seven steps to a comprehensive literature review: A multimodal and integrative approach.* SAGE Publications.

Onwuegbuzie, A. J., Leech, N. L., & Collins, K. M. T. (2010). Innovative data collection strategies in qualitative research. *The Qualitative Report, 15*(3), 696–726. DOI: 10.46743/2160-3715/2010.1171

Ortiz, E. A., Bos, M. S., Peraza, J. C., Giambruno, C., Levin, V., Oubiña, V., ... Zoido, P. (2024). *Learning can't wait: Lessons for Latin America and the Caribbean from PISA 2022.*

Pajares, M. F. (1999). Teacher beliefs. *Review of Educational Research, 62*(3), 307–322. DOI: 10.3102/00346543062003307

Patterson, C. (2025, April 28). Senate passes Jamaica Teaching Council Act, 2025, with 38 amendments. *Jamaica Information Service.* https://jis.gov.jm/senate-passes-jamaica-teaching-council-act-2025-with-38-amendments/

Phillip-Durham, G., & Deasey Weinstein, T. (2025). Harnessing artificial intelligence for educational reform and workforce development: The case of the Cayman Islands. *The Round Table, 114*(4), 1–20. DOI: 10.1080/00358533.2025.2507802

Polius, A. P. (2022). *Impact of initial training program on teachers' levels of satisfaction and effectiveness at primary schools in Saint Lucia* [Master's thesis, UNICAF University]. UNICAF University Digital Repository. https://www.unicafuniversity.ac.mw/thesis-publications/impact-of-initial-training-program-on-teachers-levels-of-satisfaction-and-effectiveness-at-primary-schools-in-saint-lucia/

Potkonjak, V., Gardner, M., Callaghan, V., Mattila, P., Guetl, C., Petrović, V. M., & Jovanović, K. (2016). Virtual laboratories for education in science, technology, and engineering: A review. *Computers & Education, 95*, 309–327. DOI: 10.1016/j.compedu.2016.02.002

Robinson, E. S. (2017). *Science content knowledge: A component of teacher effectiveness in a primary school in Jamaica* [Doctoral dissertation, Walden University]. ScholarWorks. https://scholarworks.waldenu.edu/dissertations/4019/

Rogers, E. M. (2003). *Diffusion of innovations* (5th ed.). Free Press.

Roofe, C. (2022). Currere and Teacher Professional Development. In *The Lived Curriculum Experiences of Jamaican Teachers: Currere and Decolonising Intentions* (pp. 53–68). Springer International Publishing. DOI: 10.1007/978-3-030-99450-1_4

Saldaña, J. J. (2021). *The coding manual for qualitative researchers* (4th ed.). SAGE Publications.

Samuels, A. J. (2022). *Principals' perspectives on integrating digital tools in the Jamaican primary curriculum* [Doctoral dissertation, Walden University].

See, B. H., Munthe, E., Ross, S. A., Hitt, L., & El Soufi, N. (2022). Who becomes a teacher and why? *Review of Education, 10*(3), e3377. DOI: 10.1002/rev3.3377

Shulman, L. S. (1986). Those who understand: Knowledge growth in teaching. *Educational Researcher, 15*(2), 4–14. DOI: 10.3102/0013189X015002004

Smith, S. U., Hayes, S., & Shea, P. (2017). A critical review of the use of Wenger's Community of Practice (CoP) theoretical framework in online and blended learning research, 2000-2014. *Online Learning : the Official Journal of the Online Learning Consortium, 21*(1), 209–237. DOI: 10.24059/olj.v21i1.963

Strielkowski, W., Grebennikova, V., Lisovskiy, A., Rakhimova, G., & Vasileva, T. (2025). AI-driven adaptive learning for sustainable educational transformation. *Sustainable Development (Bradford), 33*(2), 1921–1947. DOI: 10.1002/sd.3221

Sultanow, E., Ulrich, M., Kamel, Z., Sebrak, S., Pomaskow, J., Gobinathan, B., . . . Grum, M. (2024). Capabilities of Gen AI. In *INFORMATIK 2024* (pp. 1553-1569). Gesellschaft für Informatik eV.

Sun, Y. (2021). A book review on teacher educator experiences and professional development: Perspectives from the Caribbean.

Sweeney, A. E., & George, L. (2024). STEM education in the Caribbean: Challenges, goals, and possibilities. *Caribbean Journal of Education and Development, 1*(1), 103–110. DOI: 10.46425/cjed1101019192

Sweeney, A. E., Williams, H. K., & George, L. (2024). STEM education research, policy and practice in the Caribbean: Imperatives for the next five years. *Caribbean Journal of Education and Development, 1*(1), 87–102. DOI: 10.46425/cjed1001018191

Tang, K. H. D. (2023). Student-centered approach in teaching and learning: What does it really mean? *Acta Pedagogia Asiana, 2*(2), 72–83. DOI: 10.53623/apga.v2i2.218

Taopan, L. S., Drajati, N. A., & Sumardi, S. (2020). TPACK framework: Challenges and opportunities in EFL classrooms. *Research and Innovation in Language Learning, 3*(1), 7–10. DOI: 10.33603/rill.v3i1.2763

Taylor, S. (2023). *Is UNESCO's guidance for generative AI (GenAI) in education & research "the solution" to the problem of GenAI adaptation in international schools? A critical analysis of policy recommendations through Carol Bacchi's What's The Problem Represented to Be? (WPR) Framework.* Wayfinder Learning Lab.

Thomas-Brown, K. (2021). The education system of Jamaica 28. *The Education Systems of the Americas*, 707.

Turner, D. A. (1974). Science in the 70's: Observations on science education in Jamaica. *Caribbean Quarterly*, *20*(2), 15–22. DOI: 10.1080/00086495.1974.11829221

UNESCO. (2020, August 19). Teacher development for online and blended learning to ensure quality education during COVID-19 in Jamaica. https://www.unesco.org/en/articles/teacher-development-online-and-blended-learning-ensure-quality-education-during-covid-19-jamaica

UNESCO. (2022). *Distance learning and teacher training strategies: Lessons from the Caribbean*. UNESCO Teacher Task Force. https://teachertaskforce.org/sites/default/files/2022-06/TTF_2022_Distance-learning-and-teacher-training-strategies-Lessons-from-the-Caribbean_EN.pdf

UNESCO. (n.d.). Education financing | #LeadingSDG4 | Education2030. https://www.unesco.org/sdg4education2030/en/education-financing

UNESCO Office in Kingston. (2024). *Caribbean artificial intelligence policy roadmap* (E. Simmons & A. M. Davis, Authors). https://doi.org/DOI: 10.58338/TELF3157https://unesdoc.unesco.org/ark:/48223/pf0000391996

United Nations. (n.d.). Sustainable Development Goal 4: Quality education. https://sdgs.un.org/goals/goal4

United Nations Development Programme. (2021). Goal 4: Quality education. https://www.ps.undp.org/content/papp/en/home/post-2015/sdg-overview/goal-4.html

U.S. Agency for International Development & Educational Quality Improvement Program I. (2011, December). *First principles: Designing effective education programs using information and communication technology (ICT) compendium*. https://www.edu-links.org/index.php/resources/first-principles-designing-effective-education-programs

Warner, S., Malik, M., & Mohammed, J. (2021). ICT professional development workshops and classroom implementation challenges: Perceptions of secondary school teachers in Trinidad and Tobago. [IJITL]. *International Journal of Innovation in Teaching and Learning*, *7*(1), 1–19. DOI: 10.35993/ijitl.v7i1.1507

Welsh, R. O. (2012). Overcoming smallness through education development: A comparative analysis of Jamaica and Singapore. *Current Issues in Comparative Education*, *15*(1), 114–131.

Wenger, E. (1998). *Communities of practice: Learning, meaning, and identity.* Cambridge University Press. DOI: 10.1017/CBO9780511803932

Weston, D. (2025, March 21). Education ministry aims to 'RAISE' students' performance in mathematics. *Jamaica Information Service.* https://jis.gov.jm/education-ministry-aims-to-raise-students-performance-in-mathematics/

Whittingham, N. (2022). *Key Motivating Factors of Worker Migration: The Migration of Experienced Jamaican Teachers* (Doctoral dissertation, Northcentral University).

Wilkinson, B. (2023, September 6). *Jamaican teachers head to North America, abandon local system.* Amsterdam News. https://amsterdamnews.com/news/2023/09/06/jamaican-teachers-head-to-north-america-abandon-local-system/

Williams, C. A. (2022). *The impact of professional development and administrative support on the motivation and engagement of Caribbean faculty and students in online programs.* ERIC. https://files.eric.ed.gov/fulltext/ED646223.pdf

Williams, E. V. (2020). *Investigating the impact of the integrated STEM program on student test scores in Jamaica.* Online Submission.

Williams-Buffonge, N. A. G. (2021). *Caribbean lecturers' self-efficacy and their perceived barriers to technology adoption* [Doctoral dissertation, Walden University].

Wilmot, A. M. (2025). Senior lecturers' feelings about their college leaders' treatment of their wellbeing: Implications for leadership readiness. *Power and Education, 17*(2), 17577438241312609. DOI: 10.1177/17577438241312609

Wooding, J. (2024, August 25). CXC embraces AI; Developing regional policy. *284 Media.* https://www.284media.com/education/2024/08/25/cxc-embraces-ai-developing-regional-policy/

World Bank. (2024, August 5). Empowering futures: Digital transformation in the Eastern Caribbean. https://www.worldbank.org/en/news/feature/2024/08/05/empowering-futures-digital-transformation-in-the-eastern-caribbean

Yadav, A. B. (2024). The development of AI with generative capabilities and its effect on education. [IJSR]. *International Journal of Scientific Research, 13*(5), 854–860.

# Compilation of References


Abdrakhmanov, R., Zhaxanova, A., Karatayeva, M., Niyazova, G. Z., Berkimbayev, K., & Tuimebayev, A. (2024). Development of a framework for predicting students' academic performance in STEM education using machine learning methods. *International Journal of Advanced Computer Science and Applications*, *15*(1). Advance online publication. DOI: 10.14569/IJACSA.2024.0150105

Adams, J. D. (2020). Designing frameworks for authentic equity in science teaching and learning: Informal learning environments and teacher education for STEM. *Asia-Pacific Science Education*, *6*(2), 456–479. DOI: 10.1163/23641177-BJA10016

Adarkwah, M. A., Badu, S. A., Osei, E. A., & Amponsah, A. (2025). ChatGPT in healthcare education: A double-edged sword of trends, challenges, and opportunities. *Discover Education*, *4*(1), 14. DOI: 10.1007/s44217-024-00393-3

Adeoye-Olatunde, O. A., & Olenik, N. L. (2021). Research and scholarly methods: Semi-structured interviews. *Journal of the American College of Clinical Pharmacy: JAACP*, *4*(10), 1358–1367. DOI: 10.1002/jac5.1441

Adri, M., Wahyuni, T. S., Zakir, S., & Jama, J. (2020). Using ADDIE instructional model to design blended project-based learning based on production approach. *International Journal of Advanced Science and Technology*, *29*(6), 1899–1909.

Ahmed, S. (2025). *Beyond human teachers: Post-humanist perspectives on AI, cultural inequities, and educational transformation. Journal of Posthumanism.* https://doi.org/DOI: 10.63332/joph.v4i3.1816

Ahmed, I., & Ishtiaq, S. (2021). Reliability and validity: Importance in medical research. *Methods (San Diego, Calif.)*, *12*(1), 2401–2406. DOI: 10.47391/JPMA.06-861 PMID: 34974579

Ainsworth, S. (2006). DeFT: A conceptual framework for considering learning with multiple representations. *Learning and Instruction*, *16*(3), 183–198. DOI: 10.1016/j.learninstruc.2006.03.001

Airey, J., & Linder, C. (2009). A disciplinary discourse perspective on university science learning: Achieving fluency in a critical constellation of modes. *Journal of Research in Science Teaching*, *46*(1), 27–49. DOI: 10.1002/tea.20265

al Hafidz, I. A., Sukaridhoto, S., al Rasyid, M. U. H., Budiarti, R. P. N., Mardhotillah, R. R., Amalia, R., Fajrianti, E. D., & Satrio, N. A. (2021). Design of Collaborative WebXR for Medical Learning Platform. *2021 International Electronics Symposium (IES)*, 499–504. DOI: 10.1109/IES53407.2021.9593951

Alalawi, K., Athauda, R., & Chiong, R. (2025). An extended learning analytics framework integrating machine learning and pedagogical approaches for student performance prediction and intervention. *International Journal of Artificial Intelligence in Education*, *35*(3), 1239–1287. DOI: 10.1007/s40593-024-00429-7

Al-Azawei, A., Serenelli, F., & Lundqvist, K. (2016). Universal Design for Learning (UDL): A content analysis of peer reviewed journals from 2012 to 2015. *The Journal of Scholarship of Teaching and Learning*, *16*(3), 39–56. DOI: 10.14434/josotl.v16i3.19295

Albano, S., & Longo, G. (2025). *Integrating generative AI in design education: A structured approach to client-centered interior design visualization*. AHFE International., DOI: 10.54941/ahfe1005930

Alenezi, M. (2023). *Blended Learning Motivation Support at the Saudi Electronic University: Utilizing Self-Determination Theory*. (PhD dissertation). Northern Illinois University.

Aligato, R. M., & Saligumba, R. P. (2025). The use of generative AI tools and their role in science learning among senior high school students. *International Journal for Multidisciplinary Research*, *7*(3), 44773. Advance online publication. DOI: 10.36948/ijfmr.2025.v07i03.44773

Al-Khalifa, S. N. (2022). The rapid evolution of educational technology: Implications for higher education. *Journal of Higher Education Theory and Practice*, *22*(16), 116–122.

Allemang, B., Sitter, K., & Dimitropoulos, G. (2022). Pragmatism as a paradigm for patient-oriented research. *Health Expectations*, *25*(1), 38–47. DOI: 10.1111/hex.13384 PMID: 34748689

Alnagrat, A., Ismail, R. C., Idrus, S. Z. S., & Alfaqi, R. M. A. (2022). A review of extended reality (XR) technologies in the future of human education: Current trend and future opportunity. *Journal of Human Centered Technology*, *1*(2), 81–96. DOI: 10.11113/humentech.v1n2.27

Álvarez-Siordia, F. M., Merino-Soto, C., Rosas-Meléndez, S. A., Pérez-Díaz, M., & Chans, G. M. (2025). Simulators as an innovative strategy in the teaching of physics in higher education. *Education Sciences*, *15*(2), 131. DOI: 10.3390/educsci15020131

Anderson, L. W. (Ed.). (2009). *A taxonomy for learning, teaching, and assessing: A revision of Bloom's taxonomy of educational objectives* (Abridged ed., [Nachdr.]). Longman.

Ansu-Kyeremeh, E. K., & Goosen, L. (2022). Exploring the Socioeconomic Facet of Online Inclusive Education in Ghana: The Effects of Technological Advancement in Academia. In Garcia, M. (Ed.), *Socioeconomic Inclusion During an Era of Online Education* (pp. 47–66). IGI Global., DOI: 10.4018/978-1-6684-4364-4.ch003

Antonio, D. (2020). *Continuing professional development (CPD) of teacher educators (TEs) within the ecological environment of the island territories of the Organisation of Eastern Caribbean States*. OECS. [Master's thesis, University of Liverpool]

Apprenticeship, C. Teaching the Crafts of Reading, Writing, and Mathematics. (2018). In A. Collins, J. S. Brown, & S. E. Newman, *Knowing, Learning, and Instruction* (1st ed., pp. 453–494). Routledge. DOI: 10.4324/9781315044408-14

Asare, S., Amoako, S. K., Biilah, D. K., & Apraku, T. B. (2023). The use of virtual labs in science education: A comparative study of traditional labs and virtual environments. *International Journal of Science Academic Research*, *4*(11), 6563–6569.

Association of Science Teachers of Jamaica. (n.d.). Home [Facebook page]. *Facebook*. Retrieved July 12, 2025, from https://www.facebook.com/ASTJamaica/

Ateeq, A., Alzoraiki, M., Milhem, M., & Ateeq, R. A. (2024). Artificial intelligence in education: Implications for academic integrity and the shift toward holistic assessment. *Frontiers in Education*, *9*, 1470979. DOI: 10.3389/feduc.2024.1470979

Ate, O., Parno, P., & Munfaridah, N. (2025). Multirepresentation in physics learning research: A content analysis review of trends, opportunities, and challenges. *Journal of Science Education Research*, *9*(1), 32–42. DOI: 10.21831/jser.v9i1.72954

Auditor General's Department Jamaica. (2021). *Auditor General's Department Annual Report FY2020/21*. https://auditorgeneral.gov.jm/wp-content/uploads/2022/01/2021_AuGD_Annual_Report.pdf

Awuah, F. K., & Ogbonnaya, U. I. (2020). Grade 12 Students' Proficiency in Solving Probability Problems Involving Contingency Tables and Tree Diagrams. *International Journal of Instruction*, *13*(2), 819–834. DOI: 10.29333/iji.2020.13255a

Bach, K. M., Hofer, S., & Bichler, S. (2024). *Adaptive Learning, Instruction, and Teaching in Schools: Unraveling Context, Sources, Implementation, and Goals in a Systematic Review. PsyArXiv*. DOI: 10.31234/osf.io/eyafq

Baesmat, K. H. (2024). Impedance analysis of adaptive distance relays using machine learning. *International Conference on Information Technology-New Generations*, 457–461. DOI: 10.1007/978-3-031-56599-1_57

Baesmat, K. H., Farrokhi, Z., Chmaj, G., & Regentova, E. E. (2025). Parallel multi-model energy demand forecasting with cloud redundancy: Leveraging trend correction, feature selection, and machine learning. *Forecasting*, *7*(2), 1–18.

Baesmat, K. H., & Latifi, S. (2023). A new hybrid method for electrical load forecasting based on deviation correction and mrmrms. *International Conference On Systems Engineering*, 293–303. DOI: 10.1007/978-3-031-40579-2_29

Baesmat, K. H., Masoudipour, I., & Samet, H. (2021). Improving the performance of short-term load forecast using a hybrid artificial neural network and artificial bee colony algorithm. *IEEE Canadian Journal of Electrical and Computer Engineering*, *44*(3), 275–282. DOI: 10.1109/ICJECE.2021.3056125

Baesmat, K. H., Shokoohi, F., & Farrokhi, Z. (2025). *Sp-rf-arima: A sparse random forest and arima hybrid model for electric load forecasting*. Global Energy Interconnection.

Baidoo-Anu, D., & Ansah, L. O. (2023). *Education in the Era of Generative Artificial Intelligence (AI): Understanding the Potential Benefits of ChatGPT in Promoting Teaching and Learning*.

Bailey, A., Powell-Wilson, D., Stone, S. M., Bartley-Ellis, J., Davies, R., & Edwards-Henry, A.-M. (2022). *STEM education in Jamaica: A case of practitioners*. ResearchGate.

Banda, H. J., & Nzabahimana, J. (2021). Effect of integrating physics education technology simulations on students' conceptual understanding in physics: A review of literature. *Physical Review. Physics Education Research*, *17*(2), 023108. DOI: 10.1103/PhysRevPhysEducRes.17.023108

Bandura, A. (1977). Self-efficacy: Toward a unifying theory of behavioral change. *Psychological Review*, *84*(2), 191–215. DOI: 10.1037/0033-295X.84.2.191

Bandura, A. (1986). *Social foundations of thought and action: A social cognitive theory*. Prentice Hall.

Bandura, A. (1998). Self-efficacy. In Friedman, H. (Ed.), *Encyclopedia of mental health* (Vol. 3, pp. 317–321). Academic Press.

Banh, L., & Strobel, G. (2023). Generative artificial intelligence. *Electronic Markets, 33*(1), 63. DOI: 10.1007/s12525-023-00680-1

Barianos, A. K., Logothetis, I., Kalogiannakis, M., & Vidakis, N. (2022). Teaching Ancient Greek Theatre Through In-Game Exploration: The Case of ThimelEdu. In *The Digital Folklore of Cyberculture and Digital Humanities* (pp. 186-205). IGI Global.

Barteit, S., Lanfermann, L., Bärnighausen, T., Neuhann, F., & Beiersmann, C. (2021). Augmented, Mixed, and Virtual Reality-Based Head-Mounted Devices for Medical Education: Systematic Review. *JMIR Serious Games, 9*(3), e29080. DOI: 10.2196/29080

Becerra-Labra, C., Gras-Martí, A., & Martínez-Torregrosa, J. (2012). Effects of a problem-based structure of physics contents on conceptual learning and the ability to solve problems. *International Journal of Science Education, 34*(8), 1235–1253. DOI: 10.1080/09500693.2011.619210

Bedada, T. B. (2021). *The use and effect of Geogebra software in Calculus at Wachemo University, Ethiopia: An investigation.* (Doctoral dissertation). University of South Africa (UNISA).

Belkina, M., Daniel, S., Nikolic, S., Haque, R., Lyden, S., Neal, P., Grundy, S., & Hassan, G. M. (2025). Implementing generative AI (GenAI) in higher education: A systematic review of case studies. *Computers and Education: Artificial Intelligence, 8*, 100407. DOI: 10.1016/j.caeai.2025.100407

Ben-Zion, Y., Einhorn Zarzecki, R., Glazer, J., & Finkelstein, N. D. (2024). Leveraging AI for rapid generation of physics simulations in education: Building your own virtual lab. *arXiv preprint* arXiv:2412.07482. http://doi.org//arXiv.2412.07482DOI: 10.48550

Berry, C., McCarthy-Curvin, A., Bramwell-Lalor, S., Moore, S., Newman, M., & Lambert, C. (2021). Massive open online courses: A source of effective professional development for in-service teachers. *Journal of Education and Development in the Caribbean, 19*(2), 112–144. DOI: 10.46425/j419028671

Bhat, B. A., & Neelam, N. (2023). An overview of the life and philosophy of John Dewey. *International Journal of Advanced Multidisciplinary Scientific Research, 6*(12). https://ijamsr.com/issues/6_Volume%206_Issue%2012/20240120_082027_6951.pdf

Bianchini, F. (2025). Generative Artificial Intelligence: A Concept in Progress. *Philosophy & Technology, 38*(2), 46. DOI: 10.1007/s13347-025-00875-8

Biggs, J. (1996). Enhancing teaching through constructive alignment. *Higher Education, 32*(3), 347–364. DOI: 10.1007/BF00138871

Bissessar, C. S. G. (2021a). Social learning and collaborative professional learning among caribbean teachers: implications for Praxis. *Teacher Learning and Professional Development, 6*.

Bissessar, C. (2021b). Comparing teacher professional development initiatives in three Caribbean countries. In *The handbook on Caribbean education* (pp. 23). University of the West Indies Press Bourne, P. A. (2022). An examination of mathematics performance in Jamaica: Insight into the basis for low enrolment in mathematics at the tertiary level. *International Journal of Transformation in Applied Mathematics & Statistics, 5*(1). https://science.eurekajournals.com/index.php/IJTAMS/article/view/286

Black, P., & Wiliam, D. (1998). Assessment and Classroom Learning. *Assessment in Education: Principles, Policy & Practice, 5*(1), 7–74. DOI: 10.1080/0969595980050102

Blonder, R., Feldman-Maggor, Y., & Rap, S. (2024). Are They Ready to Teach? Generative AI as a Means to Uncover Pre-Service Science Teachers' PCK and Enhance Their Preparation Program. *Journal of Science Education and Technology*. Advance online publication. DOI: 10.1007/s10956-024-10180-2

Bogna, F., Raineri, A., & Dell, G. (2020). Critical realism and constructivism: Merging research paradigms for a deeper qualitative study. *Qualitative Research in Organizations and Management, 15*(4), 461–484. DOI: 10.1108/QROM-06-2019-1778

Bozkurt, A., Karadeniz, A., Baneres, D., Guerrero-Roldán, A. E., & Rodríguez, M. E. (2021). Artificial Intelligence and Reflections from Educational Landscape: A Review of AI Studies in Half a Century. *Sustainability (Basel), 13*(2), 800. DOI: 10.3390/su13020800

Bradley, J. (2021). Achieving the aims of practical work with microchemistry. In *Research in chemistry education* (pp. 23–30). Springer International Publishing. DOI: 10.1007/978-3-030-59882-2_2

Brewe, E., Bartley, J. E., Riedel, M. C., Sawtelle, V., Salo, T., Boeving, E. R., Bravo, E. I., Odean, R., Nazareth, A., Bottenhorn, K. L., Laird, R. W., Sutherland, M. T., Pruden, S. M., & Laird, A. R. (2018). Toward a neurobiological basis for understanding learning in university modeling instruction physics courses. *Frontiers in ICT (Lausanne, Switzerland), 5*, 10. DOI: 10.3389/fict.2018.00010 PMID: 31106219

Brissett, N. O. (2022). Caribbean dreams: Education for more than just sustainable development. *The Journal of Environmental Education, 53*(1), 54–67. DOI: 10.1080/00958964.2021.2023448

Brooke, J. (1996). SUS-A quick and dirty usability scale. *Usability Evaluation in Industry, 189*(194), 4–7.

Brown, T. B., Mann, B., Ryder, N., Subbiah, M., Kaplan, J., Dhariwal, P., Neelakantan, A., Shyam, P., Sastry, G., Askell, A., Agarwal, S., Herbert-Voss, A., Krueger, G., Henighan, T., Child, R., Ramesh, A., Ziegler, D. M., Wu, J., Winter, C., Amodei, D. (2020). *Language Models are Few-Shot Learners* (Version 4). arXiv. DOI: 10.48550/ARXIV.2005.14165

Bruner, J. S. (1978). *Toward a theory of instruction* (8. pr). Harvard Univ. Press.

Brusilovsky, P., & Millán, E. (2007). User Models for Adaptive Hypermedia and Adaptive Educational Systems. In P. Brusilovsky, A. Kobsa, & W. Nejdl (Eds.), *The Adaptive Web* (Vol. 4321, pp. 3–53). Springer Berlin Heidelberg. DOI: 10.1007/978-3-540-72079-9_1

Bujang, M. A., Omar, E. D., Foo, D. H., & Hon, Y. K. (2024). Sample size determination for conducting a pilot study to assess reliability of a questionnaire. *Restorative Dentistry & Endodontics, 49*(1), e3. Advance online publication. DOI: 10.5395/rde.2024.49.e3 PMID: 38449496

Bulut, O., Shin, J., Yildirim-Erbasli, S. N., Gorgun, G., & Pardos, Z. A. (2023). An Introduction to Bayesian Knowledge Tracing with pyBKT. *Psych, 5*(3), 770–786. DOI: 10.3390/psych5030050

Bulut, O., & Wongvorachan, T. (2022). Feedback Generation through Artificial Intelligence. *The Open/Technology in Education. Society, and Scholarship Association Conference, 2*(1), 1–9. DOI: 10.18357/otessac.2022.2.1.125

Burns, M. (2023). *Distance education for teacher training: Modes, models, and methods* (2nd ed.). Education Development Center., https://inee.org/sites/default/files/Distance_Education_for_Teacher_Training_-_Modes%2C_Models%2C_and_Methods.pdf

Buys, T., Casteleijn, D., Heyns, T., & Untiedt, H. (2022). A reflexive lens on preparing and conducting semi-structured interviews with academic colleagues. *Qualitative Health Research, 32*(13), 2030–2039. DOI: 10.1177/10497323221130832 PMID: 36194785

Cabada, R. Z., Estrada, M. L. B., López, N. L., López, H. M. C., & Beltrán, V. M. B. (2023). APINET: A Methodology for Deploying Deep and Machine Learning Models as Services. *2023 Mexican International Conference on Computer Science (ENC)*, 1–7. DOI: 10.1109/ENC60556.2023.10508683

Cabada, R. Z., Estrada, M. L. B., Rivas, M. A. S., & Ibáñez, M. B. (2024). An Authoring Tool for XR Learning Environments. In *International Conference on Extended Reality* (pp. 192–208). DOI: 10.1007/978-3-031-71713-0_13

Caldarella, P., Larsen, R. A., Williams, L., Downs, K. R., Wills, H. P., & Wehby, J. H. (2020). Effects of teachers' praise-to-reprimand ratios on elementary students' on-task behaviour. *Educational Psychology*, *40*(10), 1306–1322. DOI: 10.1080/01443410.2020.1711872

Caribbean Community (CARICOM). (2005). *A harmonized policy framework for teacher education in the Caribbean* (OAS Hemispheric Project). https://caricom.org/documents/12940-aharmonizedpolicyframeworkforteachereducationinthecaribbean_(1).pdf

Caribbean Community (CARICOM). (2020). *CARICOM standards for teachers, educational leaders and teacher educators.* https://caricom.org/documents/caricom-standards-for-teachers-educational-leaders-and-teacher-educators/

Caribbean Community (CARICOM). (n.d.). *CARICOM standards for teachers, educational leaders and teacher educators.* https://caricom.org/documents/caricom-standards-for-teachers-educational-leaders-and-teacher-educators/

Caribbean Development Bank. (2024, October 3). CDB supporting regional education transformation with key initiatives. *CARICOM.* https://caricom.org/cdb-supporting-regional-education-transformation-with-key-initiatives/

Caribbean Examinations Council (CXC). (2019, July 1). New syllabuses to meet regional human resource development needs. https://www.cxc.org/new-syllabuses-meet-needs/

Caribbean Science Foundation (CSF). (n.d.). STEM teacher training workshops. https://caribbeanscience.org/stem-teacher-training-workshops/

Caribbean Telecommunications Union (CTU). (n.d.). Creative internet connectivity and classroom solutions to support Caribbean online learning. https://ctu.int/creative-internet-connectivity-and-classroom-solutions-to-support-caribbean-online-learning%EF%BF%BC/

Casteel, A., & Bridier, N. L. (2021). Describing populations and samples in doctoral student research. *International Journal of Doctoral Studies*, *16*(1), 339–362. DOI: 10.28945/4766

Castillo-Canales, D., Mancilla, A., Restrepo, R., & Martinez, F. (2022). *Teacher professional development supported by information and communication technologies: A case study of the "Teacher Training Program for Curricular Update 2016-2018 in Ecuador"*. Foundation for Information Technology Education and Development.

Cator, K., Schneider, C., & Vander Ark, T. (2014). *Preparing teachers for deeper learning*. Digital Promise. https://digitalpromise.org/2014/05/01/preparing-teachers-for-deeper-learning/

Cents-Boonstra, M., Lichtwarck-Aschoff, A., Denessen, E., Aelterman, N., & Haerens, L. (2021). Fostering student engagement with motivating teaching: An observation study of teacher and student behaviours. *Research Papers in Education*, *36*(6), 754–779. DOI: 10.1080/02671522.2020.1767184

Cervantes Juárez, E., & Sánchez Guzmán, D. (2024). Implementing the LSEESC methodology with AI-guided support for active learning in engineering physics courses. *2024 IEEE Frontiers in Education Conference (FIE)*. http://doi.org/DOI: 10.1109/FIE61694.2024.10893032

Chan, H. C., Hou, H.-T., Chien, C.-C., & Sung, Y.-T. (2024). Learning by playing with generative AI: Design and evaluation of a role-playing educational game with generative AI as scaffolding for instant feedback interaction. Journal of Research on Technology in Education, 56(1), 150–171. DOI: 10.1080/15391523.2024.2338085

Chapman, C., & Montecinos, C. (2025). Professional learning in Latin America and the Caribbean: Towards a networked learning system? *Professional Development in Education*, *51*(1), 1–6. DOI: 10.1080/19415257.2025.2446110

Chatterjee, A., & Hung, J. T. (2024). Socratic Mind: Scalable oral assessment powered by AI. In *Proceedings of the 11th ACM Conference on Learning @ Scale* (pp. 1–5). ACM. http://doi.org/DOI: 10.1145/3657604.3664661

Chatzopoulos, A., Kalogiannakis, M., Papadakis, S., Papoutsidakis, M., Elza, D., & Psycharis, S. (2021). DuBot: An open-source, low-cost robot for STEM and educational robotics. In *Handbook of Research on Using Educational Robotics to Facilitate Student Learning* (pp. 441-465). IGI Global Scientific Publishing.

Chen, S., Zhu, X., & Castillo, F. (2023). Integrating generative AI in knowledge building. *Computers & Education. Artificial Intelligence*, *5*, 100184. Advance online publication. DOI: 10.1016/j.caeai.2023.100184

Chen, T.. (2023). Artificial Intelligence in Adaptive Learning: A Review and Future Directions. *Educational Technology Research and Development, 71*(2), 353–370. DOI: 10.1007/s11423-022-10194-8

Chen, X., Xie, H., Zou, D., & Wang, F. L. (2023). A systematic review of AI in education: Implications for curriculum design and teacher development. *Computers & Education, 192*, 104633. DOI: 10.1016/j.compedu.2022.104633

Cheong, B. C. (2024). Transparency and accountability in AI systems: Safeguarding wellbeing in the age of algorithmic decision-making. *Frontiers in Human Dynamics, 6*, 1421273. Advance online publication. DOI: 10.3389/fhumd.2024.1421273

Cheung, G. W., Cooper-Thomas, H. D., Lau, R. S., & Wang, L. C. (2024). Reporting reliability, convergent and discriminant validity with structural equation modeling: A review and best-practice recommendations. *Asia Pacific Journal of Management, 41*(2), 745–783. DOI: 10.1007/s10490-023-09871-y

Chidziva, J. (2021). *Using ubuntu values to enhance disruptive pedagogies for effective and meaningful teaching of grade 12 Euclidean geometry.* (PhD thesis). UNISA.

Christie, S. T., Cook, C., & Rafferty, A. N. (2024). *Uncertainty-preserving deep knowledge tracing with state-space models* (Version 1). arXiv. DOI: 10.48550/ARXIV.2407.17427

Chukhlomin, V. (2024). Socratic prompts: Engineered dialogue as a tool for AI-enhanced educational inquiry. *Latin American Business and Sustainability Review, 1*(1), 1–14. DOI: 10.70469/labsreview.v1i1.10

Chung, J., Henderson, M., Pepperell, N., Slade, C., Liang, Y., & Yu, S. (2024). *Student use of generative AI.* ASCILITE Publications., DOI: 10.14742/apubs.2024.1153

Cipresso, P., Giglioli, I. A. C., Raya, M. A., & Riva, G. (2018). The Past, Present, and Future of Virtual and Augmented Reality Research: A Network and Cluster Analysis of the Literature. *Frontiers in Psychology, 9*, 2086. Advance online publication. DOI: 10.3389/fpsyg.2018.02086

Clandinin, D. J. (2008). Creating learning spaces for teachers and teacher educators. *Teachers and Teaching, 14*(5-6), 385–389. DOI: 10.1080/13540600802571304

Committee on the Development of an Addendum to the National Science Education Standards on Scientific Inquiry, Board on Science Education, Division of Behavioral and Social Sciences and Education, & National Research Council. (2000). *Inquiry and the National Science Education Standards: A Guide for Teaching and Learning* (S. Olson & S. Loucks-Horsley, Eds.). National Academies Press. DOI: 10.17226/9596

Conrad, M., & Nuebel, H. (2025). Learners' Acceptance of ChatGPT in School. *Education Sciences, 15*(7), 904. DOI: 10.3390/educsci15070904

Cooper, G. (2023). Examining Science Education in ChatGPT: An Exploratory Study of Generative Artificial Intelligence. *Journal of Science Education and Technology, 32*(3), 444–452. DOI: 10.1007/s10956-023-10039-y

Corbeil, J. R., & Corbeil, M. E. (2025). Teaching and learning in the age of generative AI.

Costa, A. L., & Garmston, R. J. (2016). *Cognitive coaching: A foundation for renaissance schools* (3rd ed.). Rowman & Littlefield.

Coy, A., James-Williamson, S., Bramwell-Lalor, S., Sadler-McKnight, N., McLean, N., Penugonda, V. R., & Rainford, M. (2019). A Review of a Tertiary Level Institution's Initiative for Enhancing Education in STEM at the Secondary School Level. *Journal of Education & Development in the Caribbean, 18*(1), 132–182. DOI: 10.46425/j061801u135

Creswell, J. (2012). *Educational research: planning, conducting and evaluating quantitative and qualitative research* (4th ed.). Pearson Education, Inc.

Creswell, J. W., & Creswell, J. D. (2018). *Research design: qualitative, quantitative, and mixed methods approaches* (5th ed.). SAGE.

Creswell, J. W., & Creswell, J. D. (2023). *Research design: Qualitative, quantitative and mixed methods approaches*. SAGE Publications.

Creswell, J. W., & Guetterman, T. C. (2024). *Educational research: Planning, conducting, and evaluating quantitative and qualitative research*. Pearson.

Creswell, J. W., & Plano Clark, V. L. (2017). *Designing and conducting mixed methods research* (3rd ed.). SAGE Publications.

Creswell, J. W., & Poth, C. N. (2007). *Qualitative inquiry and research design: choosing among five approaches*. SAGE.

Cross, J. I., Boag-Hodgson, C. C., & Mavin, T. J. (2023). Measuring Presence and Situational Awareness in a Virtual Reality Flight Simulator. *Aviation Psychology and Applied Human Factors, 13*(2), 83–94. DOI: 10.1027/2192-0923/a000250

Crupi, A., Costa, A., Thomas, A., & Khatri, P. (2024). *Unveiling the Future of Creativity and Innovation Management in the era of Generative Artificial Intelligence*. Retrieved from https://rnd2024.org/wp-content/uploads/2024/01/RND2024-Track-P3.pdf

Darling-Hammond, L., Oakes, J., Wojcikiewicz, S. K., Hyler, M. E., Guha, R., Podolsky, A., ... Harrell, A. (2019). *Preparing teachers for deeper learning* (Research brief).

Davidovitch, N., & Yavich, R. (2022). Teachers' attitudes to use of advanced technological tools as teaching and learning aids: From an inter-generational perspective. *The European Educational Researcher, 5*(1), 329-341. https://files.eric.ed.gov/fulltext/EJ1318682.pdf

Davies, C., & Fisher, M. (2018). Understanding research paradigms. *JARNA, 21*(3), 21–25.

Davishahl, J., & Haskell, K. (2024). Targeting representational competence and spatial skills development with hands-on models in calculus and statics. *ASEE PNW Section Conference Proceedings.* http://doi.org/DOI: 10.18260/1-2--31896

Davishahl, J., & Zhang, Z. (2024). Can hands-on statics improve student learning? *ASEE Annual Conference & Exposition Proceedings.* http://doi.org/DOI: 10.18260/1-2--48440

Dawadi, S., Shrestha, S., & Giri, R. A. (2021). Mixed-methods research: A discussion on its types, challenges, and criticisms. *Journal of Practical Studies in Education, 2*(2), 25–36. DOI: 10.46809/jpse.v2i2.20

De La Peña, S., & Maatubang, P. (2025). Inquiry-Based Science Using Five (5) E's Instructional Model: A Case Study. *European Journal of Contemporary Education and E-Learning*. https://doi.org/DOI: 10.59324/ejceel.2025.3(2).15

Devineni, S. K. (2024). AI-Enhanced Data Visualization: Transforming Complex Data into Actionable Insights. *Journal of Technology and Systems, 6*(3), 52–77. DOI: 10.47941/jts.1911

Devonish, D. (2016). *The cognitive coaching approach: A professional development model for science educators and for students' academic achievement* [Unpublished doctoral dissertation]. Northern Caribbean University.

Devonish, D. (2021, June). The role of professional organizations in education: The COVID-19 response in Jamaica by science teachers. *Revista Conexiones: Una experiencia más allá del aula, 13*(2), 42-55. https://www.mep.go.cr/sites/default/files/2revistaconexiones2021_a4.pdf

Devonish, D. (2025, March 26). *Harnessing AI-powered personalized learning for inclusive STEM education in Caribbean secondary schools* [Conference presentation]. Caribbean Association for the Advancement of Curriculum Studies, Fourth Virtual Conference.

Devonish, D. (2020). Assessment of the microscience kit intervention in secondary schools undertaken by the Ministry of Education Youth & Information, Jamaica under the UNESCO participation programme. *Ministry of Education, Youth & Information, Jamaica*. DOI: 10.13140/RG.2.2.32854.77127

Devonish, D., & Bennett, S. (2024). A toolkit intervention for school-aged Jamaican students: Strategy for collaborative involvement during the pandemic. *Caribbean Journal of Education and Development*, *1*(3), 77–95. DOI: 10.46425/cjed601036532

Devonish, D., Bennett, S., Hylton, K., King, J., & Barrett, D. (2025). Ensuring STEM teacher quality to meet the demands of the Caribbean labor market beyond the 21st century. In *Navigating leadership and policy management in education* (pp. 1–42). IGI Global.

Devonish, D., Lawrence, P., & Zamore, C. (2018). Voices of Pre-service Teachers on Science Pedagogy: A Case Study on the Challenges of Implementing Diverse Instructional Strategies into the Science lesson post University. *Journal of Arts Science & Technology*, *11*(1).

Dewey, J. (1938). *Experience and education*. Macmillan.

diGJamaica. (n.d.). Page 729 - Budget 2014-2015. http://digjamaica.com/app/webroot/edocs/Budget_2014-2015/files/assets/basic-html/page729.html

Distrik, I. W., Supardi, Z. A. I., & Jatmiko, B. (2021). The effects of multiple representations-based learning in improving concept understanding and problem-solving ability in electricity. *Journal of Physics: Conference Series*, *1796*(1), 012044. DOI: 10.1088/1742-6596/1796/1/012044

Dixon, R. A., & Hutton, D. M. (2016). STEM and TVET in the Caribbean: A framework for integration at the primary, secondary and tertiary levels. *Caribbean Curriculum*, *24*, 1–26.

Dolezal, N., & Motschnig, R. (2024). AI-supported personalization in science-based project learning: Case studies from European schools. *Education Sciences*, *14*(2), 211. DOI: 10.3390/educsci14020211

Dolezal, N., & Motschnig, R. (2024). The Impact of AI-Generated Instructional Videos on Problem-Based Learning. *Education Sciences*, *14*(1), 102. DOI: 10.3390/educsci14010102

Dolmans, D. H., Loyens, S. M., Marcq, H., & Gijbels, D. (2016). Deep and surface learning in problem-based learning: A review of the literature. *Advances in Health Sciences Education : Theory and Practice*, *21*(5), 1087–1112. DOI: 10.1007/s10459-015-9645-6 dos Anjos, J. B., Teixeira, M. R., & Ribeiro, A. S. (2024). Exploring ChatGPT in science education: Potential and limitations for conceptual learning. *Journal of Science Education and Technology*, *33*(2), 211–229.

Down, L. (2024). The future of Caribbean scholarly research: Towards greater community engagement. *Caribbean Journal of Education and Development*, *1*(1), 68–74. DOI: 10.46425/cjed801016484

Du Plooy, E., Casteleijn, D., & Franzsen, D. (2024). Personalized adaptive learning in higher education: A scoping review of key characteristics and impact on academic performance and engagement. *Heliyon*, *10*(21), e39630. DOI: 10.1016/j.heliyon.2024.e39630

Edelsbrunner, P., & Hofer, S. I. (2024). Examining and comparing the relation between representational competence and conceptual knowledge across four samples. *Frontiers in Education*, *9*, 1459603. Advance online publication. DOI: 10.3389/feduc.2024.1459603

Edelsbrunner, P., Malone, S., Hofer, S. I., Küchemann, S., Kuhn, J., Schmid, R., Altmeyer, K., Brünken, R., & Lichtenberger, A. (2023). The relation of representational competence and conceptual knowledge in female and male undergraduates. *International Journal of STEM Education*, *10*(1), 44. Advance online publication. DOI: 10.1186/s40594-023-00435-6 PMID: 37361927

Eguchi, A., Okada, H., & Muto, Y. (2021). Contextualizing AI education for K–12 students to enhance their learning of AI literacy through culturally responsive approaches. *Kunstliche Intelligenz*, *35*(2), 153–161. DOI: 10.1007/s13218-021-00737-3

El Fathi, T., Saad, A., Larhzil, H., Lamri, D., & Al Ibrahmi, E. M. (2025). Integrating generative AI into STEM education: Enhancing conceptual understanding, addressing misconceptions, and assessing student acceptance. *Disciplinary and Interdisciplinary Science Education Research*, *7*(1), 6. DOI: 10.1186/s43031-025-00125-z

Elder-Vass, D. (2022). Pragmatism, critical realism and the study of value. *Journal of Critical Realism*, *21*(3), 261–287. DOI: 10.1080/14767430.2022.2049088

Esnard, T., & Bristol, L. (2024). Grounding Caribbean educators and research(ers): Decolonial reflections with Professor Joel Warrican. *Caribbean Educational Research Journal*, *9*(1), Article 1. https://cavehill.uwi.edu/fhe/education/publications/past-issues/volume-9-number-1-october-2024/articles/01-full-text-esnard-and-bristol.aspx

Fakour, H., & Imani, M. (2025). Socratic wisdom in the age of AI: A comparative study of ChatGPT and human tutors in enhancing critical thinking skills. *Frontiers in Education*, *10*, 1528603. DOI: 10.3389/feduc.2025.1528603

Falmagne, J.-C., Cosyn, E., Doignon, J.-P., & Thiéry, N. (2006). The Assessment of Knowledge, in Theory and in Practice. In Missaoui, R., & Schmidt, J. (Eds.), *Formal Concept Analysis* (Vol. 3874, pp. 61–79). Springer Berlin Heidelberg., DOI: 10.1007/11671404_4

Farrokhi, Z., Kalhor, A., & Masouleh, M. T. (n.d.). Implementation and evaluation of object identification techniques on nao robot platform.

Farrokhi, Z., Baesmat, K. H., & Regentova, E. E. (2024). Enhancing urban intelligence energy management: Innovative load forecasting techniques for electrical networks. *Journal of Power and Energy Engineering*, *12*(11), 72–88. DOI: 10.4236/jpee.2024.1211005

Feng, S., Magana, A. J., & Kao, D. (2021, October). A systematic review of literature on the effectiveness of intelligent tutoring systems in STEM. In *2021 IEEE Frontiers in Education Conference (FIE)* (pp. 1-9). IEEE. DOI: 10.1109/FIE49875.2021.9637240

Figueira, A., & Vaz, B. (2022). Survey on synthetic data generation, evaluation methods and gans. *Mathematics*, *10*(15), 2733. DOI: 10.3390/math10152733

Filippi, S., & Motyl, B. (2024). Large Language Models (LLMs) in Engineering Education: A Systematic Review and Suggestions for Practical Adoption. *Information (Basel)*, *15*(6), 345. DOI: 10.3390/info15060345

Floridi, L., Cowls, J., Beltrametti, M., Chatila, R., Chazerand, P., Dignum, V., Luetge, C., Madelin, R., Pagallo, U., Rossi, F., Schafer, B., Valcke, P., & Vayena, E. (2018). AI4People—An Ethical Framework for a Good AI Society: Opportunities, Risks, Principles, and Recommendations. *Minds and Machines*, *28*(4), 689–707. DOI: 10.1007/s11023-018-9482-5

Foong, Y. P., Pidani, R., Sithira Vadivel, V., & Dongyue, Y. (2024). Singapore smart nation: Journey into a new digital landscape for higher education. In Kwok, A. O. J., & Teh, P.-L. (Eds.), *Emerging technologies in business: Innovation strategies for competitive advantage* (pp. 281–304). Springer Nature Singapore., DOI: 10.1007/978-981-97-2211-2_13

Freire, P. (2000). *Pedagogy of the oppressed* (30th anniversary ed.). Continuum.

Friel, S. N., Curcio, F. R., & Bright, G. W. (2001). Making Sense of Graphs: Critical Factors Influencing Comprehension and Instructional Implications. *Journal for Research in Mathematics Education*, *32*(2), 124. DOI: 10.2307/749671

Gadgil, S., Nokes-Malach, T. J., & Chi, M. (2012). Effectiveness of holistic mental model confrontation in driving conceptual change. *Learning and Instruction*, *22*(1), 47–61. DOI: 10.1016/j.learninstruc.2011.06.002

Gavira Durón, M., & Jiménez-Preciado, M. Á. (2025). *AI-enhanced Chemistry Learning: Evidence from Classroom-Based Simulations. Science Education International*, 36(2), 200–215. https://doi.org/DOI: 10.20362/sei2025.200215

Gentles, C. C. H. (2021). The work and professional identity of Caribbean teacher educators. In Smith, J., & Jones, A. (Eds.), *The handbook on Caribbean education* (pp. 43–65). Caribbean Press. DOI: 10.1108/978-1-64802-411-520251005

Gliem, J. A., & Gliem, R. R. (2003). *Calculating, interpreting, and reporting Cronbach's alpha reliability coefficient for Likert-type scales*. https://api.semanticscholar.org/CorpusID:146359317

Global Partnership for Education (GPE). (2025, February 5). Improving learning: What research says on the effectiveness and scalability of teacher professional development. https://www.globalpartnership.org/blog/improving-learning-what-research-effectiveness-scalability-teacher-professional-development

Goldschmidt, G., & Matthews, B. (2022). Formulating design research questions: A framework. *Design Studies*, *78*, 101062. Advance online publication. DOI: 10.1016/j.destud.2021.101062

Gomes, D. (2024). A Comprehensive Study of Advancements in Intelligent Tutoring Systems Through Artificial Intelligent Education Platforms. In Moreira, F. T., & Teles, R. O. (Eds.), (pp. 213–244). Advances in Educational Technologies and Instructional Design. IGI Global., DOI: 10.4018/979-8-3693-6170-2.ch008

Gonsalves, C. (2024). Generative AI's impact on critical thinking: Revisiting Bloom's taxonomy. *Journal of Marketing Education*, *46*(2), 02734753241305980. Advance online publication. DOI: 10.1177/02734753241305980

Goyal, A. (2025). AI as a cognitive partner: A systematic review of the influence of AI on metacognition and self-reflection in critical thinking. *International Journal of Innovative Science and Research Technology*, *10*(3), 1231–1238. DOI: 10.38124/ijisrt/25mar1427

Grandison, T. (2025, February 28). Jamaica and the Caribbean need a holistic AI roadmap. *The Gleaner*. https://jamaica-gleaner.com/article/commentary/20250228/tyrone-grandison-jamaica-and-caribbean-need-holistic-ai-roadmap

Grant, M. J., & Booth, A. (2009). A typology of reviews: An analysis of 14 review types and associated methodologies. *Health Information and Libraries Journal, 26*(2), 91–108. DOI: 10.1111/j.1471-1842.2009.00848.x

Greca, I. M., & Moreira, M. A. (2000). Mental models, conceptual models, and modelling. *International Journal of Science Education, 22*(1), 1–11. DOI: 10.1080/095006900289976

Griffith, S. A. (2019). Growth rate in CXC STEM subject entries: Implications for meeting the development needs of the Caribbean. *Journal of Research in STEM Education, 5*(2), 5. https://j-stem.net/index.php/jstem/article/view/82. DOI: 10.51355/jstem.2019.82

Guettala, M., Bourekkache, S., Kazar, O., & Harous, S. (2024). Generative Artificial Intelligence in Education: Advancing Adaptive and Personalized Learning. *Acta Informatica Pragensia, 13*(3), 460–489. DOI: 10.18267/j.aip.235

Gunkel, D. J. (Ed.). (2024). *Handbook on the ethics of artificial intelligence*. Edward Elgar Publishing., DOI: 10.4337/9781803926728

Gupta, P., Ding, B., Guan, C., & Ding, D. (2024). Generative AI: A systematic review using topic modelling techniques. *Data and Information Management, 8*(2), 100066. DOI: 10.1016/j.dim.2024.100066

Hamerski, P. C. (2024). Generative AI as a resource for creativity in computational physics. *Proceedings of the 55th ACM Technical Symposium on Computer Science Education* V. 2. http://doi.org/DOI: 10.1145/3626253.3635595

Hampson, T., & McKinley, J. (2023). Problems posing as solutions: Criticising pragmatism as a paradigm for mixed research. *Research in Education, 116*(1), 124–138. DOI: 10.1177/00345237231160085

Hasanova, N., Abduazizov, B., & Khujakulov, R. (2021). The main differences between teaching approaches, methods, procedures, techniques, styles and strategies. *JournalNX - A Multidisciplinary Peer Reviewed Journal, 7*(2), 371-375.

Hassanpouri Baesmat, K., & Shiri, A. (2019). A new combined method for future energy forecasting in electrical networks. *International Transactions on Electrical Energy Systems, 29*(3), e2749. DOI: 10.1002/etep.2749

Hattie, J., & Timperley, H. (2007). The power of feedback. *Review of Educational Research, 77*(1), 81–112. DOI: 10.3102/003465430298487

Her, P., & Hamerski, P. C. (2024). Investigating student perceptions of creativity and generative AI in computational physics. *2024 Physics Education Research Conference Proceedings*. http://doi.org/DOI: 10.1119/perc.2024.pr.Her

Hoekstra, R., Vugteveen, J., Warrens, M. J., & Kruyen, P. M. (2019). An empirical analysis of alleged misunderstandings of coefficient alpha. *International Journal of Social Research Methodology, 22*(4), 351–364. DOI: 10.1080/13645579.2018.1547523

Holmes, W., & Luckin, R. (2016). *Intelligence unleashed: An argument for AI in education*. Pearson : UCL Knowledge Lab.

Holmes, W., Bialik, M., & Fadel, C. (2019). *Artificial intelligence in education: Promises and implications for teaching and learning*. The Center for Curriculum Redesign.

Holmes, W., Bialik, M., & Fadel, C. (2022). *Artificial Intelligence in Education: Promises and Implications for Teaching and Learning*. Center for Curriculum Redesign.

Holstein, K., & Aleven, V. (2022). Designing for human–ai complementarity in k-12 education. *AI Magazine, 43*(2), 239–248. DOI: 10.1002/aaai.12058

Huang, L. (2023). Ethics of Artificial Intelligence in Education: Student Privacy and Data Protection. *Science Insights Education Frontiers, 16*(2), 2577–2587. DOI: 10.15354/sief.23.re202

Hunter, J. (2017, August 17). Maths coaches and specialists to attend training workshop. *Jamaica Information Service*. https://jis.gov.jm/maths-coaches-specialists-attend-training-workshop/

Hwang, H. S., Zhu, L. C., & Cui, Q. (2023). Development and Validation of a Digital Literacy Scale in the Artificial Intelligence Era for College Students. *KSII Transactions on Internet and Information Systems, 17*(8). Advance online publication. DOI: 10.3837/tiis.2023.08.016

Idrisov, B., & Schlippe, T. (2024). Program Code Generation with Generative AIs. *Algorithms, 17*(2), 62. DOI: 10.3390/a17020062

Inter-American Development Bank (IADB) & UNESCO. (2025). *AI and education: Building the future through digital transformation*. https://publications.iadb.org/publications/english/document/AI-and-Education-Building-the-Future-Through-Digital-Transformation.pdf

Întorsureanu, I., Oprea, S.-V., Bâra, A., & Vespan, D. (2025). Generative AI in education: Perspectives through an academic lens. *Electronics (Basel), 14*(5), 1053. DOI: 10.3390/electronics14051053

Introduction to Emerging Technologies for the Classroom. A Learning Sciences Perspective. (2013). In C. Mouza & N. C. Lavigne, *Emerging Technologies for the Classroom* (pp. 1–12). Springer New York. DOI: 10.1007/978-1-4614-4696-5_1

Isaacs, S., & Mishra, S. (2022). *Smart education strategies for teaching and learning: Critical analytical framework and case studies*. UNESCO Institute for Information Technologies in Education (UNESCO IITE).

Ismail, I. A., & Aloshi, J. M. (2024). Data Privacy in AI-Driven Education: An In-Depth Exploration Into the Data Privacy Concerns and Potential Solutions. In Keeley, K. L. (Ed.), (pp. 223–252). Advances in Educational Marketing, Administration, and Leadership. IGI Global., DOI: 10.4018/979-8-3693-5443-8.ch008

Jaggernauth, S. J. (2021). Modelling teacher efficacy change during a teacher professional development programme in Trinidad and Tobago. *Caribbean Curriculum, 28*.

Jamaica Gleaner. (2016, December 2). Digicel Foundation launches Phase Three of Mobile Science Lab initiative. *Jamaica Gleaner*. https://jamaica-gleaner.com/article/news/20161202/digicel-foundation-launches-phase-three-mobile-science-lab-initiative

Jamaica Information Service. (2025, April 23). EduHub develops revolutionary technology for student success in CSEC and CAPE exams. *Jamaica Information Service*. https://jis.gov.jm/eduhub-develops-revolutionary-technology-for-student-success-in-csec-and-cape-exams/

Jamaica Observer. (2023, June 29). STEM teacher training scholarship programme to be launched today. https://www.jamaicaobserver.com/2023/06/29/stem-teacher-training-scholarship-programme-to-be-launched-today/

Jamaica Observer. (2025, May 30). CXC failure rates: A crisis in Jamaican education. *Jamaica Observer*. https://www.jamaicaobserver.com/2025/05/30/cxc-failure-rates-crisis-jamaican-education/

Jamaica Teachers' Association. (2025, March 3). JTA proposes teacher rotation model to address migration crisis. https://www.jta.org.jm/content/jta-proposes-teacher-rotation-model-address-migration-crisis

Jamaica Teaching Council (JTC). (2022). *The Jamaica Teaching Council Act 2022*. https://japarliament.gov.jm/attachments/article/339/The-Jamaica-Teaching-Council-Act--2022.pdf

Jamaica Teaching Council. (n.d.). *Master teacher handbook.* https://jtc.gov.jm/masterteacherhm/

Jamali, H. (2025). Quantum-Accelerated Neural Imputation with Large Language Models (LLMs). *arXiv preprint arXiv:2507.08255.*

Jamali, H., Dascalu, S. M., & Harris, F. C. (2024). Ai-driven analysis and prediction of energy consumption in nyc's municipal buildings. *2024 IEEE/ACIS 22nd International Conference on Software Engineering Research, Management and Applications (SERA)*, pp. 277-283. IEEE, 2024. https://doi.org/DOI: 10.1109/SERA61261.2024.10685594

Jamali, H., Dascalu, S. M., Harris, J., & Wu, R. AI-Powered Adaptive Learning Interfaces: A User Experience Study in Education Platforms. *Frontiers in Computer Science, 7,* 1672081. https://doi.org/DOI: 10.3389/fcomp.2025.1672081

Jamali, H., Shill, P. C., Feil-Seifer, D., Harris, F. C., Jr., & Dascalu, S. M. (2023). A schedule of duties in the cloud space using a modified salp swarm algorithm. *IFIP International Internet of Things Conference*, 62–75.

Jamali, H., Watson, J., Dascalu, S. M., & Harris, F. C. (2025, April). Harmonized Data Drive: Standardizing and Unifying Smart Car Information Storage for Enhanced Forensics and Interoperability. In *2025 13th International Symposium on Digital Forensics and Security (ISDFS)* (pp. 1-6). IEEE.

Jamali, H., Dascalu, S. M., & Harris, F. C.Jr. (2025). A Systematic Review of Bio-Inspired Metaheuristic Optimization Algorithms: The Untapped Potential of Plant-Based Approaches. *Algorithms*, *18*(11), 686. DOI: 10.3390/a18110686

Jamali, H., Karimi, A., & Haghighizadeh, M. (2018). A new method of cloud-based computation model for mobile devices: Energy consumption optimization in mobile-to-mobile computation offloading. *Proceedings of the 6th International Conference on Communications and Broadband Networking*, pp. 32-37. 2018. https://doi.org/DOI: 10.1145/3193092.3193103

James, J. S. (2018, April). A model of professional development and best practice for primary science teachers. *Journal of Education and Development in the Caribbean*, *17*(1), 37–64.

Jaouadi, A., & Maaradji, A. (2024). ICT & Generative Artificial Intelligence Powered Hybrid Model for Future Education. *Cadmus*, *5*(3), 61–75.

Jauhiainen, J. S., & Guerra, A. G. (2023). Generative AI and ChatGPT in School Children's Education: Evidence from a School Lesson. *Sustainability (Basel)*, *15*(18), 14025. DOI: 10.3390/su151814025

Jayachandran, P., Kumar, S., & Anitha, S. (2024). Preparing future scientists: Integrating AI tools into secondary science curricula. *Science Education International, 35*(1), 45–56.

Jemetz, M., Dolezal, D., & Motschnig, R. (2025). *Secondary Teachers' Self-perceived AI Competences in Relation to Renowned European Digital Competence Frameworks* (pp. 3–17). DOI: 10.1007/978-3-031-73474-8_1

Jeyaseelan, S. M., Sobers, N. P., Grant, K., Vasquez, G. M., Blenman, S., & Hambleton, I. R. (2025). Implementing and evaluating a project to enable and encourage Caribbean data-sharing. *Revista Panamericana de Salud Pública = Pan American Journal of Public Health, 48*, e120.

Johri, A., Katz, A., Qadir, J., & Hingle, A. (2023). Generative artificial intelligence and engineering education. *Journal of Engineering Education, 112*(3), 572–577. Advance online publication. DOI: 10.1002/jee.20537

Joksimovic, S., Ifenthaler, D., Marrone, R., De Laat, M., & Siemens, G. (2023). Opportunities of artificial intelligence for supporting complex problem-solving: Findings from a scoping review. *Computers and Education: Artificial Intelligence.* DOI: 10.1016/j.caeai.2023.100138

Kaarlela, T., Padrao, P., Pitkäaho, T., Pieskä, S., & Bobadilla, L. (2022). Digital Twins Utilizing XR-Technology as Robotic Training Tools. *Machines (Basel), 11*(1), 13. DOI: 10.3390/machines11010013

Kaldaras, L., Wang, K. D., Nardo, J. E., Price, A., Perkins, K., Wieman, C., & Salehi, S. (2024). Employing technology-enhanced feedback and scaffolding to support the development of deep science understanding using computer simulations. *International Journal of STEM Education, 11*(1), 30. DOI: 10.1186/s40594-024-00490-7

Kalogiannakis, M., & Kanaki, K. (2022). Introducing computational thinking unplugged in early childhood education within the context of physical and natural science courses: A pilot study in Greece. In *Research Anthology on Computational Thinking, Programming, and Robotics in the Classroom* (pp. 197-222). IGI Global. DOI: 10.4018/978-1-6684-2411-7.ch010

Kalogiannakis, M., Papakonstantinou, N., & Sotiropoulos, D. (2025). From Support Tool to Learning Partner: A Systematic Review of GenAI Integration in University Science Labs. *Creative Education, 16*(9), 1364–1401. DOI: 10.4236/ce.2025.169083

Kamalodeen, V. (2024). Rapid response to professional development: How online teacher professional learning networks supported teachers in pandemic times. *Caribbean Journal of Education and Development, 1*(3), 149–156. DOI: 10.46425/cjed1001031940

Kamal, S. S. (2019). Research paradigm and the philosophical foundations of a qualitative study. *PEOPLE: International Journal of Social Sciences, 4*(3), 1386–1394. DOI: 10.20319/pijss.2019.43.13861394

Karpouzis, K. (2024). Plato's shadows in the digital cave: Controlling cultural bias in generative AI. *Electronics (Basel), 13*(8), 1457. DOI: 10.3390/electronics13081457

Kasneci, E., Seßler, K., Küchemann, S., Bannert, M., Dementieva, D., Fischer, F., Gasser, U., Groh, G., Günnemann, S., Hüllermeier, E., Krusche, S., Kutyniok, G., Michaeli, T., Nerdel, C., Pfeffer, J., Poquet, O., Sailer, M., Schmidt, A., Seidel, T., & Kasneci, G. (2023). ChatGPT for good? On opportunities and challenges of large language models for education. *Learning and Individual Differences, 103*, 102274. DOI: 10.1016/j.lindif.2023.102274

Kazemitabaar, M., Hou, X., Henley, A., Ericson, B. J., Weintrop, D., & Grossman, T. (2023). How novices use LLM-based code generators to solve CS1 coding tasks in a self-paced learning environment. *Proceedings of the 23rd Koli Calling International Conference on Computing Education Research*, 1–12. DOI: 10.1145/3631802.3631806

Keith, L. R., & Waldron, L. (2024). AI-driven educational paradigm for Sustainable Development Goal 4: A Caribbean perspective. In *The UWI Quality Education Forum* (No. 28, pp. 151-171).

Kelley, M., & Wenzel, T. (2025). Advancing Artificial Intelligence Literacy in Teacher Education Through Professional Partnership Inquiry. *Education Sciences, 15*(6), 659. DOI: 10.3390/educsci15060659

Khatri, K. K. (2020). Research paradigm: A philosophy of educational research. *International Journal of English Literature and Social Sciences, 5*(5), 1435–1440. DOI: 10.22161/ijels.55.15

Kirkpatrick, D. L. (1959). Techniques for evaluating training programs. *Journal of ASTD*, 1-13.

Kivunja, C., & Kuyini, A. B. (2017). Understanding and applying research paradigms in educational contexts. *International Journal of Higher Education, 6*(5), 26–41. DOI: 10.5430/ijhe.v6n5p26

Kix, G. (2024). *Teacher professional development: A research synthesis*. International Development Research Centre.

Knowles, M. S. (1984). Theory of andragogy: A critique. *International Journal of Lifelong Education*. Cambridge MA.

Knowles, M. (1977). Adult learning processes: Pedagogy and andragogy. *Religious Education (Chicago, Ill.)*, *72*(2), 202–211. DOI: 10.1080/0034408770720210

Knowles, M. S. (1975). *Self-directed learning: A guide for learners and teachers*. Follett Publishing Company.

Kodisang, S. M. (2022). *A framework towards improved instruction of probability to grade seven students: A case of South African schools in Mpumalanga province*. (PhD thesis). UNISA.

Koteluk, O., Wartecki, A., Mazurek, S., Kołodziejczak, I., & Mackiewicz, A. (2021). How do machines learn? Artificial intelligence as a new era in medicine. *Journal of Personalized Medicine*, *11*(1), 32. DOI: 10.3390/jpm11010032

Kozma, R., & Russell, J. (2005). Students becoming chemists: Developing representational competence. In Gilbert, J. (Ed.), *Visualization in science education* (pp. 121–145). Springer., DOI: 10.1007/1-4020-3613-2_8

Kuleto, V., Ilić, M., Dumangiu, M., Ranković, M., Martins, O. M. D., Păun, D., & Mihoreanu, L. (2021). Exploring Opportunities and Challenges of Artificial Intelligence and Machine Learning in Higher Education Institutions. *Sustainability (Basel)*, *13*(18), 10424. DOI: 10.3390/su131810424

Kumar, R., Eaton, S. E., Mindzak, M., & Morrison, R. (2023). Academic Integrity and Artificial Intelligence: An Overview. In Eaton, S. E. (Ed.), *Handbook of Academic Integrity* (pp. 1–14). Springer Nature Singapore., DOI: 10.1007/978-981-287-079-7_153-1

Kumar, S., Datta, S., Singh, V., Datta, D., Singh, S. K., & Sharma, R. (2024). Applications, challenges, and future directions of human-in-the-loop learning. *IEEE Access : Practical Innovations, Open Solutions*, *12*, 75735–75760. DOI: 10.1109/ACCESS.2024.3401547

Kuo, M.-M., Li, X., Qian, L., Obiomon, P., & Dong, X. (2024). *Deep Knowledge Tracing for Personalized Adaptive Learning at Historically Black Colleges and Universities* (Version 1). arXiv. DOI: 10.48550/ARXIV.2410.13876

Kwaah, C. Y. (2024). Social media use among basic school teachers in Ghana: Exploring opportunities and challenges. *Cogent Education, 11*(1), 2310978. Advance online publication. DOI: 10.1080/2331186X.2024.2310978

Lameras, P. (2022). A Vision of Teaching and Learning with AI. *2022 IEEE Global Engineering Education Conference (EDUCON)*, 1796–1803. DOI: 10.1109/EDUCON52537.2022.9766718

Laupichler, M. C., Aster, A., Schirch, J., & Raupach, T. (2022). Artificial intelligence literacy in higher and adult education: A scoping literature review. *Computers and Education: Artificial Intelligence, 3*, 100101. DOI: 10.1016/j.caeai.2022.100101

Lave, J., & Wenger, E. (1991). *Situated learning: Legitimate peripheral participation.* Cambridge University Press. DOI: 10.1017/CBO9780511815355

Law, L. (2024). Application of generative artificial intelligence (GenAI) in language teaching and learning: A scoping literature review. *Computers and Education Open, 6*, 100174. DOI: 10.1016/j.caeo.2024.100174

Lee, G.-G., & Zhai, X. (2024). Using ChatGPT for Science Learning: A Study on Pre-service Teachers' Lesson Planning. *IEEE Transactions on Learning Technologies, 17*, 1643–1660. DOI: 10.1109/TLT.2024.3401457

Lee, S. H., Park, J., & Kim, Y. (2023). Inquiry-Based Science Learning Supported by Generative AI: An Experimental Study in Secondary Education. *Asia-Pacific Science Education, 9*(1), 33–51.

Leidner, D. E., & Tona, O. (2021). The CARE Theory of Dignity Amid Personal Data Digitalization. *Management Information Systems Quarterly, 45*(1), 343–370. Advance online publication. DOI: 10.25300/MISQ/2021/15941

Lenette, C. (2022). What is participatory action research? Contemporary methodological considerations. In *Participatory action research: Ethics and decolonization* (pp. 1–18). Oxford University Press., DOI: 10.1093/oso/9780197512456.003.0001

Leon, M. (2024). Leveraging generative AI for on-demand tutoring as a new paradigm in education. *International Journal on Cybernetics & Informatics, 13*(5), 1–9. DOI: 10.5121/ijci.2024.130502

Létourneau, A., Deslandes Martineau, M., Charland, P., Karran, J. A., Boasen, J., & Léger, P. M. (2025). A systematic review of AI-driven intelligent tutoring systems (ITS) in K-12 education. *npj Science of Learning, 10*, 29. http://doi.org/DOI: 10.1038/s41539-025-00320-7

Lewis, J. (2020). Experimental design: ethics, integrity, and the scientific method. In *Handbook of research ethics and scientific integrity* (pp. 459–474). Springer International Publishing. DOI: 10.1007/978-3-030-16759-2_19

Liang, L. L., Fulmer, G. W., Majerich, D., Clevenstine, R. F., & Howanski, R. (2011). The effects of a model-based physics curriculum program with a Physics First approach: A causal-comparative study. *Journal of Science Education and Technology*, *21*(1), 114–124. DOI: 10.1007/s10956-011-9287-2

Lichtenberger, A., Kokkonen, T., & Schalk, L. (2024). Learning with multiple external representations in physics: Concreteness fading versus simultaneous presentation for Faraday's law. *Journal of Research in Science Teaching*, *61*(9), 2258–2290. DOI: 10.1002/tea.21947

Li, L. C., Grimshaw, J. M., Nielsen, C., Judd, M., Coyte, P. C., & Graham, I. D. (2009). Evolution of Wenger's concept of community of practice. *Implementation Science : IS*, *4*(11), 11. DOI: 10.1186/1748-5908-4-11

Lima, N. W. (2021). Michael Matthews and the development of History, Philosophy and Science Teaching: Thirty years after "the present rapprochement". *Review of Science, Mathematics and ICT Education, 15*(2), 101–121. http://doi.org/DOI: 10.26220/rev.3824

Lin, C.-H., Zhou, K., Li, L., & Sun, L. (2025). Integrating generative AI into digital multimodal composition. *Computers and Composition*, *75*, 102895. Advance online publication. DOI: 10.1016/j.compcom.2024.102895

Li, R., Wang, Y., Zheng, C., Jiang, Y.-H., & Jiang, B. (2024). Generating Contextualized Mathematics Multiple-Choice Questions Utilizing Large Language Models. In *International Conference on Artificial Intelligence in Education* (pp. 494–501). DOI: 10.1007/978-3-031-64315-6_48

Li, Z., Zhong, K., Wang, M., Zhao, X., & Zhang, Z. (2024). The transfer effect of computational thinking (CT)-STEM: A systematic literature review and meta-analysis. *International Journal of STEM Education*, *11*(1), 56. DOI: 10.1186/s40594-024-00498-z

Lochmiller, C. R. (2021). Conducting thematic analysis with qualitative data. *The Qualitative Report*, *26*(6), 2029–2044. DOI: 10.46743/2160-3715/2021.5008

Logothetis, I. B., Christinaki, E., Charalampakos, O., Katsaris, I., & Vidakis, N. (2022). Gamification techniques capitalizing on state-of-the-art technologies. In *The digital folklore of cyberculture and digital humanities* (pp. 206–229). IGI Global. DOI: 10.4018/978-1-6684-4461-0.ch012

Long, D., & Magerko, B. (2020). What is AI Literacy? Competencies and Design Considerations. *Proceedings of the 2020 CHI Conference on Human Factors in Computing Systems*, 1–16. DOI: 10.1145/3313831.3376727

Lourenço, O. (2012). Piaget and Vygotsky: Many resemblances, and a crucial difference. *New Ideas in Psychology*, *30*(3), 281–295. DOI: 10.1016/j.newideapsych.2011.12.006

Luckin, R., Holmes, W., Griffiths, M., & Forcier, L. B. (2022). *Intelligence Unleashed: An Argument for AI in Education*. OECD Education Working Papers. https://doi.org/DOI: 10.1787/5jlz8t8700j8-en

Luckin, R.. (2021). *Artificial Intelligence and the Future of Teaching and Learning*. U.S. Department of Education, Office of Educational Technology.

Lu, F., Li, Y., & Bao, Y. (2025). Deep Knowledge Tracing Integrating Temporal Causal Inference and PINN. *Applied Sciences (Basel, Switzerland)*, *15*(3), 1504. DOI: 10.3390/app15031504

Magana, A. J., Arigye, J., Udosen, A., Lyon, J. A., Joshi, P., & Pienaar, E. (2024). Scaffolded team-based computational modeling and simulation projects for promoting representational competence and regulatory skills. *International Journal of STEM Education*, *11*(1), 34. DOI: 10.1186/s40594-024-00494-3

Mahdavi, Z., Samavat, T., Javanmardi, A. S. J., Dashtaki, M. A., Zand, M., Nasab, M. A., Nasab, M. A., Padmanaban, S., & Khan, B. (2024). Providing a control system for charging electric vehicles using ANFIS. *International Transactions on Electrical Energy Systems*, *2024*(1), 9921062. DOI: 10.1155/2024/9921062

Mahoney, B. B., Oostdam, R., Nieuwelink, H., & Schuitema, J. (2023). Learning to think critically through Socratic dialogue: Evaluating a series of lessons designed for secondary vocational education. *Thinking Skills and Creativity*, *50*, 101422. DOI: 10.1016/j.tsc.2023.101422

Marshman, E., Maries, A., & Singh, C. (2024). Using multiple representations to improve student understanding of quantum states. *Physical Review. Physics Education Research*, *20*(2), 020152. DOI: 10.1103/PhysRevPhysEducRes.20.020152

Masrifah, M., Setiawan, A., Sinaga, P., & Setiawan, W. (2022). The effectiveness of using e-book based on multimodal representation and TPACK to improve ICT literacy of physics teachers. *AIP Conference Proceedings*, 020015. Advance online publication. DOI: 10.1063/5.0102620

Matthews, M. R. (2024). Thomas Kuhn and science education. *Science & Education*, *33*(3), 609–678. DOI: 10.1007/s11191-022-00408-1

McDonald, J., & Mercieca, B. M. (2021). What is a community of practice? In *Sustaining communities of practice with early career teachers* (pp. 1–19). Springer., DOI: 10.1007/978-981-33-6354-0_1

McTigue, E. M., & Flowers, A. C. (2011). Science Visual Literacy: Learners' Perceptions and Knowledge of Diagrams. *The Reading Teacher*, *64*(8), 578–589. DOI: 10.1598/RT.64.8.3

Méheut, M., & Psillos, D. (2004). Teaching–learning sequences: Aims and tools for science education research. *International Journal of Science Education*, *26*(5), 515–535. DOI: 10.1080/0950069032000161476 2

Mendezabal, M. J., & Tindowen, D. J. (2018). Improving students' attitude, conceptual understanding and procedural skills in differential calculus through Microsoft mathematics. *Journal of Technology and Science Education*, *8*(4), 385–397. DOI: 10.3926/jotse.356

Menzli, L. J., Smirani, L. K., Boulahia, J. A., & Hadjouni, M. (2022). Investigation of open educational resources adoption in higher education using Rogers' diffusion of innovation theory. *Heliyon*, *8*(7), e09885. Advance online publication. DOI: 10.1016/j.heliyon.2022.e09885

Meotti, M., & Magliozzi, D. (2025). Using artificial intelligence to navigate the new challenges of college and career. Harvard ALI Social Impact Review. Retrieved from https://www.sir.advancedleadership.harvard.edu/articles/using-artificial-intelligence-to-navigate-the-new-challenges-of-college-and-career

Merriam, S. B. (2018). Adult learning theory: Evolution and future directions. In *Contemporary theories of learning* (pp. 83–96). Routledge. DOI: 10.4324/9781315147277-6

Miller, E. L. (1999). Teacher development in the Caribbean. In Miller, E. L. (Ed.), *Education for All in the Caribbean in the 1990s: Retrospect and Prospect* (pp. 57–91). CARICOM.

Ministry of Education and Youth. Jamaica. (2022). *ICT in Education Policy 2022: Transforming lives, empowering citizens and enabling national development.* https://moey.gov.jm/wp-content/uploads/2022/07/ICT-in-Education-Policy-Jamaica-Ministry-of-Education-and-Youth-2022.pdf

Ministry of Education. (2015). *National Education Inspectorate Report*. https://drive.google.com/a/moey.gov.jm/folderview?id=0BzlAiS6fPqgZfldvQlFTaHcwc1FLSGxGLUNlaXY3RW9iUHRSNy00WlRVNGMzLXItRnl0eTg&usp=drive_web&pli=1&tid=0BzlAiS6fPqgZfkVzOGh1aWRPaXQ2WXFRcnpCT3JSZDc4ejRoeTB1MzJCMTZYYkpRQTlrc2s#list

Min, T., Lee, B., & Jho, H. (2025). Integrating generative artificial intelligence in the design of scientific inquiry for middle school students. *Education and Information Technologies*, *30*(11), 15329–15360. Advance online publication. DOI: 10.1007/s10639-025-13410-1

Miraz, M. H., Ali, M., & Excell, P. S. (2021). Adaptive user interfaces and universal usability through plasticity of user interface design. *Computer Science Review*, *40*, 100363. Advance online publication. DOI: 10.1016/j.cosrev.2021.100363

Mishra, P., & Koehler, M. J. (2006). Technological pedagogical content knowledge: A framework for teacher knowledge. *Teachers College Record*, *108*(6), 1017–1054. DOI: 10.1111/j.1467-9620.2006.00684.x

Mittal, U., Sai, S., Chamola, V., & Sangwan, D. (2024). A Comprehensive Review on Generative AI for Education. *IEEE Access : Practical Innovations, Open Solutions*, *12*, 142733–142759. DOI: 10.1109/ACCESS.2024.3468368

Molina, E., Cobo, C., Pineda, J., & Rovner, H. (2024). *AI Revolution in Education: What you need to know* (Brief N°1). World Bank. https://documents1.worldbank.org/curated/en/099734306182493324/pdf/IDU152823b13109c514ebd19c241a289470b6902.pdf

Molloy, K.. (2022). Barriers to conceptual understanding in high school science. *International Journal of Science Education*, *44*(1), 56–73. DOI: 10.1080/09500693.2021.1964825

Moore, S. L. (2007). David H. Rose, Anne Meyer, Teaching Every Student in the Digital Age: Universal Design for Learning: Association for Supervision and Curriculum Development, 1703 N. Beauregard St., Alexandria, VA 22311-1714, Product no. 101042, $22.95 ASCD members, $26.95 nonmembers, ISBN-0-87120-599-8. *Educational Technology Research and Development*, *55*(5), 521–525. DOI: 10.1007/s11423-007-9056-3

Mora, S., . . .. (2025, April 11). How AI can support teachers in Latin America. *Brookings Institution*. https://www.brookings.edu/articles/how-ai-can-support-teachers-in-latin-america/

Moura, D., Oliveira, M., & Silva, T. (2025). GenAI for learning science: A framework for multimodal understanding in physics and biology. *Educational Technology Research and Development, 73*(1), 55–70.

Moura, L., Barcaui, A., & Payer, R. (2025). AI and Financial Fraud Prevention: Mapping the Trends and Challenges Through a Bibliometric Lens. *Journal of Risk and Financial Management, 18*(6), 323. DOI: 10.3390/jrfm18060323

Mufit, F., Festiyed, F., Fauzan, A., & Lufri, L. (2018). Impact of learning model based on cognitive conflict toward students' conceptual understanding. *IOP Conference Series. Materials Science and Engineering, 335*(1), 012072. DOI: 10.1088/1757-899X/335/1/012072

Mukherjee, S., Le, C., & Chow, Y.-W. (2025). Generative AI-enhanced intelligent tutoring system for graduate cybersecurity programs. *Future Internet, 17*(4), 154. DOI: 10.3390/fi17040154

Musaev, A., Kadyrov, B., & Ospanova, N. (2025). Rethinking science education in the AI era: Challenges and innovations. *International Journal of STEM Education, 12*, 10.

Mweshi, G. K., & Sakyi, K. (2020). Application of sampling methods for the research design. *Archives of Business Research, 8*(11), 180–193. DOI: 10.14738/abr.811.9042

Ngugi, J., & Goosen, L. (2017). The Effects of Course Design Characteristics, Self-Regulated Learning and Knowledge Sharing in Facilitating the Development of Innovative Behaviour among Technology Students at Universities. *Proceedings of the Institute of Science and Technology Education (ISTE) Conference on Mathematics, Science and Technology Education* (pp. 80-86). Mopani Camp, Kruger National Park: UNISA Press.

Ngugi, J., & Goosen, L. (2019, October 25). Towards Smart Innovation for Information Systems and Technology Students: Modelling Motivation, Metacognition and Affective Aspects of Learning. (Á. Rocha, & M. Serrhini, Eds.) *Smart Innovation, Systems and Technologies, 111*, 90-99. DOI: 10.1007/978-3-030-03577-8_11

Nguyen, T. D. (2025). The supply and quality of STEM teachers. *Humanities & Social Sciences Communications, 12*(1), 359. DOI: 10.1057/s41599-025-04648-8

Nilmanee, T., Sintanakul, K., & Sakulviriyakitkul, P. (2024). The Design of a Learning Experience Platform using xAPI with Design Thinking Learning to Promote Innovation. [iJET]. *International Journal of Emerging Technologies in Learning, 19*(01), 54–67. DOI: 10.3991/ijet.v19i01.44277

Nkambou, R., Bourdeau, J., & Mizoguchi, R. (Eds.). (2010). *Advances in Intelligent Tutoring Systems* (Vol. 308). Springer Berlin Heidelberg., DOI: 10.1007/978-3-642-14363-2

Nurjanah, S., Martaputri, N. A., & Suardi, I. K. (2024). Artificial intelligence in physics education research in two decades: A bibliometric study from Scopus database. *Jurnal Pendidikan Fisika, 12*(2), 53–86. Advance online publication. DOI: 10.26618/jpf.v12i2.14745

O'Donoghue, T. (2018). *Planning your qualitative research thesis and project: An introduction to interpretivist research in education and the social sciences.* Routledge. DOI: 10.4324/9781351165563

Odden, T. O. B., Lauvland, A., Bøe, M. V., & Henriksen, E. K. (2023). Implementing the learning assistant model in European higher education. *European Journal of Physics, 44*(3), 035701. Advance online publication. DOI: 10.1088/1361-6404/acb39e

Ofori-Kusi, D. (2017). *An investigation into the use of problem-solving heuristics to improve the teaching and learning of mathematics.* (PhD thesis). UNISA.

Ole, F. C. B., & Gallos, M. R. (2023). Impact of formative assessment based on feedback loop model on high school students' conceptual understanding and engagement with physics. *Journal of Turkish Science Education, 20*(2), 333–355. DOI: 10.36681/tused.2023.019

Olney, A. M.. (2024). Enhancing Science Learning with AI-generated Molecular Simulations. *Computers & Education: Artificial Intelligence, 6*, 100093. DOI: 10.1016/j.caeai.2024.100093

Olney, A. M., Chounta, I.-A., Liu, Z., Santos, O. C., & Bittencourt, I. I. (Eds.). (2024). *Artificial Intelligence in Education. Posters and Late Breaking Results, Workshops and Tutorials, Industry and Innovation Tracks, Practitioners, Doctoral Consortium and Blue Sky* (Vol. 2150). Springer Nature Switzerland., DOI: 10.1007/978-3-031-64312-5

Onwuegbuzie, A. J., & Frels, R. K. (2016). *Seven steps to a comprehensive literature review: A multimodal and integrative approach.* SAGE Publications.

Onwuegbuzie, A. J., Leech, N. L., & Collins, K. M. T. (2010). Innovative data collection strategies in qualitative research. *The Qualitative Report, 15*(3), 696–726. DOI: 10.46743/2160-3715/2010.1171

Opara, I. M., & Ogbanu, G. I. (2023). Effect of Item Order on the Reliability of Mathematics Test among Secondary School Students in Rivers State. *Journal of Advances in Education and Philosophy*, *7*(11), 460–466. DOI: 10.36348/jaep.2023.v07i11.003

Ormerod, R. J. (2021). Pragmatism in professional practice. *Systems Research and Behavioral Science*, *38*(6), 797–816. DOI: 10.1002/sres.2739

Ortiz, E. A., Bos, M. S., Peraza, J. C., Giambruno, C., Levin, V., Oubiña, V., ... Zoido, P. (2024). *Learning can't wait: Lessons for Latin America and the Caribbean from PISA 2022.*

Ortiz, M., & Aliazas, J. V. (2021). Multimodal representation strategies in teaching science towards enhancing scientific inquiry skills among Grade 4. *International Multidisciplinary Research Journal*. Advance online publication. DOI: 10.54476/iimrj241

Pajares, M. F. (1999). Teacher beliefs. *Review of Educational Research*, *62*(3), 307–322. DOI: 10.3102/00346543062003307

Papadakis, S., & Kalogiannakis, M. (2022). Learning computational thinking development in young children with Bee-Bot educational robotics. In *Research anthology on computational thinking, programming, and robotics in the classroom* (pp. 926–947). IGI Global. DOI: 10.4018/978-1-6684-2411-7.ch040

Papadakis, S., & Kalogiannakis, M. (Eds.). (2024). *New Approaches in Mobile Learning for Early Childhood Education*. IGI Global., Retrieved from https://www.igi-global.com/book/new-approaches-mobile-learning-early/332803 DOI: 10.4018/979-8-3693-2377-9

Papanikolaou, K. A., Grigoriadou, M., Kornilakis, H., & Magoulas, G. D. (2003). Personalizing the Interaction in a Web-based Educational Hypermedia System: The case of INSPIRE. *User Modeling and User-Adapted Interaction*, *13*(3), 213–267. DOI: 10.1023/A:1024746731130

Papert, S. (1980). *Mindstorms: Children, computers, and powerful ideas*. Basic Books.

Park, H., & Zhang, J. (2023). Teacher Reflective Noticing and Scaffolding for Student-Driven Knowledge-Building Inquiry. In *Proceedings of the 17th International Conference of the Learning Sciences-ICLS 2023, pp.* 1054-1057. International Society of the Learning Sciences. http://doi.org/DOI: 10.22318/icls2023.567396

Parks, C. (2017). Beyond Compliance: Students and FERPA in the Age of Big Data. *Journal of Intellectual Freedom & Privacy*, *2*(2), 23–33. DOI: 10.5860/jifp.v2i2.6253

Patterson, C. (2025, April 28). Senate passes Jamaica Teaching Council Act, 2025, with 38 amendments. *Jamaica Information Service*. https://jis.gov.jm/senate-passes-jamaica-teaching-council-act-2025-with-38-amendments/

Pedrera, O., Barrutia, O., & Díez, J. R. (2025). Unveiling students' mental models and learning demands. *Research in Science Education*, *55*(5), 1399–1426. Advance online publication. DOI: 10.1007/s11165-024-10225-x

Peikos, M., Giannakos, M., & Papamitsiou, Z. (2025). The integration of TPACK and AI literacy for future-ready science teachers. *Education Sciences*, *15*(3), 338. DOI: 10.3390/educsci15030338

Pellas, N. (2025). The impact of AI-generated instructional videos on problem-based learning in science teacher education. *Education Sciences*, *15*(1), 102. DOI: 10.3390/educsci15010102

Pesovski, I., Santos, R., Henriques, R., & Trajkovik, V. (2024). Generative AI for Customizable Learning Experiences. *Sustainability (Basel)*, *16*(7), 3034. DOI: 10.3390/su16073034

Phillip-Durham, G., & Deasey Weinstein, T. (2025). Harnessing artificial intelligence for educational reform and workforce development: The case of the Cayman Islands. *The Round Table*, *114*(4), 1–20. DOI: 10.1080/00358533.2025.2507802

Phillips, L. M., Norris, S. P., & Macnab, J. S. (2010). *Visualization in Mathematics, Reading and Science Education*. Springer Netherlands., DOI: 10.1007/978-90-481-8816-1

Piaget, J. (1972). *To understand is to invent: The future of education*. Viking Press., Retrieved from https://unesdoc.unesco.org/ark:/48223/pf0000006133

Pinho-Lopes, M., & Powrie, W. (2025). Applying the Learning Science and Engineering with Electronic Spreadsheets Cycle (LSEESC) in geotechnical engineering education. In *Proceedings of the 20th International Conference on Soil Mechanics and Geotechnical Engineering* (pp. 240–248). International Society for Soil Mechanics and Geotechnical Engineering. https://www.issmge.org/uploads/publications/3/134/PT24-61PinhoLopes-Powrie.pdf

Polius, A. P. (2022). *Impact of initial training program on teachers' levels of satisfaction and effectiveness at primary schools in Saint Lucia* [Master's thesis, UNICAF University]. UNICAF University Digital Repository. https://www.unicafuniversity.ac.mw/thesis-publications/impact-of-initial-training-program-on-teachers-levels-of-satisfaction-and-effectiveness-at-primary-schools-in-saint-lucia/

Potkonjak, V., Gardner, M., Callaghan, V., Mattila, P., Guetl, C., Petrović, V. M., & Jovanović, K. (2016). Virtual laboratories for education in science, technology, and engineering: A review. *Computers & Education*, *95*, 309–327. DOI: 10.1016/j.compedu.2016.02.002

Racine, E., Kusch, S., Cascio, M. A., & Bogossian, A. (2021). Making autonomy an instrument: A pragmatist account of contextualized autonomy. *Humanities & Social Sciences Communications*, *8*(139), 139. Advance online publication. DOI: 10.1057/s41599-021-00811-z

Rahi, S. (2017). Research design and methods: A systematic review of research paradigms, sampling issues and instruments development. *International Journal of Economics & Management Sciences*, *6*(2), 1–5. DOI: 10.4172/2162-6359.1000403

Raslan, G. (2024). The impact of the zone of proximal development concept (scaffolding) on the students' problem-solving skills and learning outcomes. In K. Al Marri, F. A. Mir, S. A. David, & M. Al-Emran (Eds.), *BUiD Doctoral Research Conference 2023: Multidisciplinary Studies* (Lecture Notes in Civil Engineering, Vol. 473, pp. 59–66). Springer. http://doi.org/DOI: 10.1007/978-3-031-56121-4_6

Reeves, L. E., Bolton, E., Bulpitt, M., Scott, A., Tomey, I., Gates, M., & Baldock, R. A. (2021). Use of augmented reality (AR) to aid bioscience education and enrich student experience. *Research in Learning Technology*, *29*. Advance online publication. DOI: 10.25304/rlt.v29.2572

Rianti, R., Gunawan, G., Verawati, N., & Taufik, M. (2024). The effect of problem-based learning model assisted by PhET simulation on understanding physics concepts. *Lensa: Jurnal Kependidikan Fisika*, *12*(1), 28. Advance online publication. DOI: 10.33394/j-lkf.v12i1.8783

Ritter, S., Anderson, J. R., Koedinger, K. R., & Corbett, A. (2007). Cognitive Tutor: Applied research in mathematics education. *Psychonomic Bulletin & Review*, *14*(2), 249–255. DOI: 10.3758/BF03194060

Robinson, E. S. (2017). *Science content knowledge: A component of teacher effectiveness in a primary school in Jamaica* [Doctoral dissertation, Walden University]. ScholarWorks. https://scholarworks.waldenu.edu/dissertations/4019/

Robledo-Rella, M., & Toh, Y. R. (2024). Artificial intelligence in physics courses to support active learning. In *Proceedings of the 2024 10th International Conference on e-Society, e-Learning and e-Technologies (ICSLT)*. http://doi.org/DOI: 10.1145/3678610.3678631

Rogers, E. M. (2003). *Diffusion of innovations* (5th ed.). Free Press.

Roofe, C. (2022). Currere and Teacher Professional Development. In *The Lived Curriculum Experiences of Jamaican Teachers: Currere and Decolonising Intentions* (pp. 53–68). Springer International Publishing. DOI: 10.1007/978-3-030-99450-1_4

Saldaña, J. J. (2021). *The coding manual for qualitative researchers* (4th ed.). SAGE Publications.

Samavat, T., Nazari, M., Fuhong, L., & Yang, L. (2025). Optimizing stand-alone PV systems: A metaheuristic-enhanced fuzzy approach for adaptive MPPT. *China Communications*, *22*(1), 61–74. DOI: 10.23919/JCC.fa.2024-0224.202501

Samuels, A. J. (2022). *Principals' perspectives on integrating digital tools in the Jamaican primary curriculum* [Doctoral dissertation, Walden University].

Sanjeevikumar, P., Zand, M., Nasab, M. A., Eskandari, M., Samavat, T., Jahangiri, A., & Moradi, M. H. (2023). Power Electronics in Smart Grid. In Smart and Power Grid Systems–Design Challenges and Paradigms (pp. 1-20). River Publishers. DOI: 10.1201/9781003339557-2

Sebele-Mpofu, F. Y. (2020). Saturation controversy in qualitative research: Complexities and underlying assumptions. A literature review. *Cogent Social Sciences*, *6*(1), 1838706. Advance online publication. DOI: 10.1080/23311886.2020.1838706

See, B. H., Munthe, E., Ross, S. A., Hitt, L., & El Soufi, N. (2022). Who becomes a teacher and why? *Review of Education*, *10*(3), e3377. DOI: 10.1002/rev3.3377

Seel, N. M. (2014). Model-based learning and performance. In *Encyclopedia of the Sciences of Learning* (pp. 465–484). Springer., DOI: 10.1007/978-1-4614-3185-5_37

Selwyn, N. (2019). *Should robots replace teachers? AI and the future of education*. Polity Press.

Selwyn, N. (2022). The future of AI and education: Some cautionary notes. *European Journal of Education*, *57*(4), 620–631. DOI: 10.1111/ejed.12532

Shulman, L. S. (1986). Those who understand: Knowledge growth in teaching. *Educational Researcher*, *15*(2), 4–14. DOI: 10.3102/0013189X015002004

Shute, V. J. (2008). Focus on formative feedback. *Review of Educational Research*, *78*(1), 153–189. DOI: 10.3102/0034654307313795

Siddiqua, A. (2023). Critique of Research Methodologies and Methods in Educational Leadership. *World Journal of Education*, *13*(4), 16–24. DOI: 10.5430/wje.v13n4p16

Siemens, G. (2005). Connectivism: A Learning Theory for the Digital Age. *International Journal of Instructional Technology and Distance Learning*. https://www.itdl.org/Journal/Jan_05/article01.htm?utm_source=chatgpt.com

Singh, A. (2021). Quasi experimental design in scientific psychology. SSRN *Electronic Journal*. DOI: 10.2139/ssrn.3793568

Singh, J., Steele, K., & Singh, L. (2021). Combining the Best of Online and Face-to-Face Learning: Hybrid and Blended Learning Approach for COVID-19, Post Vaccine, & Post-Pandemic World. *Journal of Educational Technology Systems, 50*(2), 140–171. DOI: 10.1177/00472395211047865

Smagorinsky, P. (2018). Deconflating the ZPD and instructional scaffolding: Retranslating and reconceiving the zone of proximal development as the zone of next development. *Learning, Culture and Social Interaction*, *16*, 70–75. DOI: 10.1016/j.lcsi.2017.10.009

Smith, S. U., Hayes, S., & Shea, P. (2017). A critical review of the use of Wenger's Community of Practice (CoP) theoretical framework in online and blended learning research, 2000-2014. *Online Learning : the Official Journal of the Online Learning Consortium*, *21*(1), 209–237. DOI: 10.24059/olj.v21i1.963

Sotelo-Rivas, M. A. (2024). *BabloXR: Una herramienta de autor para el desarrollo de ambientes de aprendizaje en realidad extendida.*

Sotiropoulos, D., & Kalogiannakis, M. (2025). Using GenAI Tools to Enhance Teaching and Learning in Science. In *Proceedings of the 14th Hybrid Edition of the International Conference New Perspectives in Science Education*, 293-301, Italy-Florence: Filodiritto-Pixel, 19-21 March 2025, http://doi.org/DOI: 10.26352/L319_2420-9732

Sotiropoulos, D. J., & Meletiou-Mavrotheris, M. (2025). Postgraduate student teachers' perspectives concerning AI and its integration into STEAM teaching and learning. In Papadakis, S. (Ed.), *AI roles and responsibilities in education* (pp. 3–21). Springer., DOI: 10.1007/978-3-031-96855-6_1

Stamatakis, A., Logothetis, I., Petridis, K., Kalogiannakis, M., & Vidakis, N. (2025). Micro-Credentials Establish New Realities in Digital Education. In *Education, Integrating Micro-Credentials With AI in Open* (pp. 19-38). IGI Global Scientific Publishing.

Steinert, S., Avila, K. E., Kuhn, J., & Küchemann, S. (2024). Using GPT-4 as a guide during inquiry-based learning. *The Physics Teacher*, *62*(7), 618–619. DOI: 10.1119/5.0235700

Stratton, S. J. (2021). Population research: Convenience sampling strategies. *Prehospital and Disaster Medicine*, *36*(4), 373–374. DOI: 10.1017/S1049023X21000649 PMID: 34284835

Strielkowski, W., Grebennikova, V., Lisovskiy, A., Rakhimova, G., & Vasileva, T. (2025). AI-driven adaptive learning for sustainable educational transformation. *Sustainable Development (Bradford)*, *33*(2), 1921–1947. DOI: 10.1002/sd.3221

Sultanow, E., Ulrich, M., Kamel, Z., Sebrak, S., Pomaskow, J., Gobinathan, B., . . . Grum, M. (2024). Capabilities of Gen AI. In *INFORMATIK 2024* (pp. 1553-1569). Gesellschaft für Informatik eV.

Sun, Y. (2021). A book review on teacher educator experiences and professional development: Perspectives from the Caribbean.

Sun, Z.. (2024). Narrative-Driven AI Simulations for Learning Chemical Processes. *Educational Technology Research and Development*, *72*(1), 102–120. DOI: 10.1007/s11423-023-10212-6

Sürücü, L., & Maslakci, A. (2020). Validity and reliability in quantitative research. *Business & management studies: an international journal, 8*(3), 2694-2726.

Sweeney, A. E., & George, L. (2024). STEM education in the Caribbean: Challenges, goals, and possibilities. *Caribbean Journal of Education and Development*, *1*(1), 103–110. DOI: 10.46425/cjed1101019192

Sweeney, A. E., Williams, H. K., & George, L. (2024). STEM education research, policy and practice in the Caribbean: Imperatives for the next five years. *Caribbean Journal of Education and Development*, *1*(1), 87–102. DOI: 10.46425/cjed1001018191

Swindell, A., Greeley, L., Farag, A., & Verdone, B. (2024). Against artificial education: Towards an ethical framework for generative artificial intelligence (AI) use in education. *Online Learning : the Official Journal of the Online Learning Consortium*, *28*(2). Advance online publication. DOI: 10.24059/olj.v28i2.4438

Tang, K. H. D. (2023). Student-centered approach in teaching and learning: What does it really mean? *Acta Pedagogia Asiana*, *2*(2), 72–83. DOI: 10.53623/apga.v2i2.218

Tang, K. S., Cooper, G., Rappa, N., Cooper, M., Sims, C., & Nonis, K. (2024). A dialogic approach to transform teaching, learning and assessment with generative AI in secondary education: A proof of concept. *Pedagogies*, *19*(3), 493–503. DOI: 10.1080/1554480X.2024.2379774

Tang, K.-S. (2023). The characteristics of diagrams in scientific explanations: Multimodal integration of written and visual modes of representation in junior high school textbooks. *Science Education*, *107*(3), 741–772. DOI: 10.1002/sce.21787

Tankelevitch, L., Kewenig, V., Simkute, A., Scott, A. E., Sarkar, A., Sellen, A., & Rintel, S. (2024). The metacognitive demands and opportunities of generative AI. *Proceedings of the CHI Conference on Human Factors in Computing Systems (CHI '24)*. http://doi.org/DOI: 10.1145/3613904.3642902

Taopan, L. S., Drajati, N. A., & Sumardi, S. (2020). TPACK framework: Challenges and opportunities in EFL classrooms. *Research and Innovation in Language Learning*, *3*(1), 7–10. DOI: 10.33603/rill.v3i1.2763

Taşdan, M., Kartal, M., Gözüm, A. İ., & Kalogiannakis, M. (2025). Digital Transformation in School Management: Insights From Administrators' Perspectives. In *Empowering STEM Educators With Digital Tools* (pp. 275-320). IGI Global Scientific Publishing.

Taylor, S. (2023). *Is UNESCO's guidance for generative AI (GenAI) in education & research "the solution" to the problem of GenAI adaptation in international schools? A critical analysis of policy recommendations through Carol Bacchi's What's The Problem Represented to Be? (WPR) Framework*. Wayfinder Learning Lab.

Teresi, J. A., Yu, X., Stewart, A. L., & Hays, R. D. (2022). Guidelines for designing and evaluating feasibility pilot studies. *Medical Care*, *60*(1), 95–103. DOI: 10.1097/MLR.0000000000001664 PMID: 34812790

*The potential impact of Artificial Intelligence on equity and inclusion in education* (OECD Artificial Intelligence Papers). (2024). Organisation for Economic Co-Operation and Development (OECD). DOI: 10.1787/dee339a8-en

Thomas-Brown, K. (2021). The education system of Jamaica 28. *The Education Systems of the Americas*, 707.

Tiruneh, D. T., Gu, X., De Cock, M., & Elen, J. (2018). Systematic design of domain-specific instruction on near and far transfer of critical thinking skills. *International Journal of Educational Research*, *87*, 1–11. DOI: 10.1016/j.ijer.2017.10.005

Tomak, B., & Virlan, A. Y. (2024). Ethical Considerations in the Educational Use of Generative AI Technologies. In Ara, A., & Ara, A. (Eds.), (pp. 49–62). Advances in Computational Intelligence and Robotics. IGI Global., DOI: 10.4018/979-8-3693-1565-1.ch004

Tran, A., Angelikas, K., Rama, E., Okechukwu, C., Smith, D. H., & MacNeil, S. (2023). Generating Multiple Choice Questions for Computing Courses Using Large Language Models. *2023 IEEE Frontiers in Education Conference (FIE)*, 1–8. DOI: 10.1109/FIE58773.2023.10342898

Turner, D. A. (1974). Science in the 70's: Observations on science education in Jamaica. *Caribbean Quarterly*, *20*(2), 15–22. DOI: 10.1080/00086495.1974.11829221

U.S. Agency for International Development & Educational Quality Improvement Program I. (2011, December). *First principles: Designing effective education programs using information and communication technology (ICT) compendium*. https://www.edu-links.org/index.php/resources/first-principles-designing-effective-education-programs

UNESCO Office in Kingston. (2024). *Caribbean artificial intelligence policy roadmap* (E. Simmons & A. M. Davis, Authors). https://doi.org/DOI: 10.58338/TELF3157https://unesdoc.unesco.org/ark:/48223/pf0000391996

UNESCO. (2020, August 19). Teacher development for online and blended learning to ensure quality education during COVID-19 in Jamaica. https://www.unesco.org/en/articles/teacher-development-online-and-blended-learning-ensure-quality-education-during-covid-19-jamaica

UNESCO. (2022). *Artificial Intelligence and Education: Guidance for policy-makers*. United Nations Educational, Scientific and Cultural Organization.

UNESCO. (2022). *Distance learning and teacher training strategies: Lessons from the Caribbean*. UNESCO Teacher Task Force. https://teachertaskforce.org/sites/default/files/2022-06/TTF_2022_Distance-learning-and-teacher-training-strategies-Lessons-from-the-Caribbean_EN.pdf

UNESCO. (2023). *Guidance for generative AI in education and research*. UNESCO. https://unesdoc.unesco.org/ark:/48223/pf0000386693

UNESCO. (2024). *Guidance for generative AI in education and research*. http://doi.org/DOI: 10.54675/unesco.genai.2024

UNESCO. (n.d.). Education financing | #LeadingSDG4 | Education2030. https://www.unesco.org/sdg4education2030/en/education-financing

United Nations Development Programme. (2021). Goal 4: Quality education. https://www.ps.undp.org/content/papp/en/home/post-2015/sdg-overview/goal-4.html

United Nations. (n.d.). Sustainable Development Goal 4: Quality education. https://sdgs.un.org/goals/goal4

Van der Walt, J. L. (2020). Interpretivism-constructivism as a research method in the humanities and social sciences–more to it than meets the eye. *International journal of philosophy and theology, 8*(1), 59-68. doi:DOI: 10.15640/ijpt.v8n1a5

Van Dijk, J. (2020). *The digital divide* (2nd ed.). John Wiley & Sons.

VanLEHN, K. U. R. T.VanLEHN. (2011). The Relative Effectiveness of Human Tutoring, Intelligent Tutoring Systems, and Other Tutoring Systems. *Educational Psychologist, 46*(4), 197–221. DOI: 10.1080/00461520.2011.611369

Vasarainen, M., Paavola, S., & Vetoshkina, L. (2021). A Systematic Literature Review on Extended Reality: Virtual, Augmented and Mixed Reality in Working Life. *The International Journal of Virtual Reality : a Multimedia Publication for Professionals, 21*(2), 1–28. DOI: 10.20870/IJVR.2021.21.2.4620

Vashista, N., Gugnani, P., & Bala, M. (n.d.). *The Educator's Lens: Understanding the Impact of AI on Management Education.*

Verawati, N. N., & Sarjan, M. (2023). The philosophy of critical thinking in problem-based science learning. *Prisma Sains: Jurnal Pengkajian Ilmu dan Pembelajaran Matematika dan IPA IKIP Mataram, 11*(4), 992-1001. DOI: 10.33394/j-ps.v11i4.9101

Villegas-Ch, W., Buenano-Fernandez, D., Navarro, A. M., & Mera-Navarrete, A. (2025). Adaptive intelligent tutoring systems for STEM education: Analysis of the learning impact and effectiveness of personalized feedback. *Smart Learning Environments, 12*(1), 41. DOI: 10.1186/s40561-025-00389-y

Vlasopoulou, M., Kalogiannakis, M., & Sifaki, E. (2021). Investigating teachers' attitudes and behavioral intentions for the impending integration of STEM education in primary schools. In *Handbook of research on using educational robotics to facilitate student learning* (pp. 235–256). IGI Global Scientific Publishing. DOI: 10.4018/978-1-7998-6717-3.ch009

Walkington, C. A. (2013). Using adaptive learning technologies to personalize instruction to student interests: The impact of relevant contexts on performance and learning outcomes. *Journal of Educational Psychology, 105*(4), 932–945. DOI: 10.1037/a0031882

Walliman, N. (2021). *Research methods: The basics.* Routledge., DOI: 10.4324/9781003141693

Wang, J., & Fan, W. (2025). The effect of ChatGPT on students' learning performance, learning perception, and higher-order thinking: Insights from a meta-analysis. *Humanities & Social Sciences Communications, 12*(1), 621. DOI: 10.1057/s41599-025-04787-y

Wang, T., Lund, B. D., Marengo, A., Pagano, A., Mannuru, N. R., Teel, Z. A., & Pange, J. (2023). Exploring the Potential Impact of Artificial Intelligence (AI) on International Students in Higher Education: Generative AI, Chatbots, Analytics, and International Student Success. *Applied Sciences (Basel, Switzerland)*, *13*(11), 6716. DOI: 10.3390/app13116716

Wan, Y., Zhang, L., & Chen, Y. (2025). Impact pathways of AI-supported instruction on learning behaviors, competence development, and academic achievement in engineering education. *Sustainability (Basel)*, *17*(17), 8059. DOI: 10.3390/su17178059

Warner, S., Malik, M., & Mohammed, J. (2021). ICT professional development workshops and classroom implementation challenges: Perceptions of secondary school teachers in Trinidad and Tobago. [IJITL]. *International Journal of Innovation in Teaching and Learning*, *7*(1), 1–19. DOI: 10.35993/ijitl.v7i1.1507

Wasielewski, A. (2024). DALL-E in Flatland. *Media Theory*, *8*(1), 185–204. Advance online publication. DOI: 10.70064/mt.v8i1.1073

Weidlich, J., Fink, A., Frey, A., Jivet, I., Gombert, S., Menzel, L., Giorgashvili, T., Yau, J., & Drachsler, H. (2025). Highly informative feedback using learning analytics: How feedback literacy moderates student perceptions of feedback. *International Journal of Educational Technology in Higher Education, 22*(1), 43. http://doi.org/ : https://doi.org/DOI: 10.1186/s41239-025-00539-9 — URL

Welsh, R. O. (2012). Overcoming smallness through education development: A comparative analysis of Jamaica and Singapore. *Current Issues in Comparative Education*, *15*(1), 114–131.

Wenger, E. (1998). *Communities of practice: Learning, meaning, and identity.* Cambridge University Press. DOI: 10.1017/CBO9780511803932

Weston, D. (2025, March 21). Education ministry aims to 'RAISE' students' performance in mathematics. *Jamaica Information Service.* https://jis.gov.jm/education-ministry-aims-to-raise-students-performance-in-mathematics/

Wetzel, D. A., & Kani, J. (2025). Enhancing information literacy through generative AI in the library classroom. *Pennsylvania Libraries: Research & Practice*, *12*(2). Advance online publication. DOI: 10.5195/palrap.2024.302

Whittingham, N. (2022). *Key Motivating Factors of Worker Migration: The Migration of Experienced Jamaican Teachers* (Doctoral dissertation, Northcentral University).

Wilkinson, B. (2023, September 6). *Jamaican teachers head to North America, abandon local system.* Amsterdam News. https://amsterdamnews.com/news/2023/09/06/jamaican-teachers-head-to-north-america-abandon-local-system/

William, F. K. (2024). Interpretivism or constructivism: Navigating research paradigms in social science research. *International Journal of Research Publications, 143*(1), 134–138. DOI: 10.47119/IJRP1001431220246122

Williams, C. A. (2022). *The impact of professional development and administrative support on the motivation and engagement of Caribbean faculty and students in online programs*. ERIC. https://files.eric.ed.gov/fulltext/ED646223.pdf

Williams-Buffonge, N. A. G. (2021). *Caribbean lecturers' self-efficacy and their perceived barriers to technology adoption* [Doctoral dissertation, Walden University].

Williams, E. V. (2020). *Investigating the impact of the integrated STEM program on student test scores in Jamaica*. Online Submission.

Willis, J., Gibson, A., Kelly, N., Spina, N., Azordegan, J. M., & Crosswell, L. (2021). Towards faster feedback in higher education through digitally mediated dialogic loops. *Australasian Journal of Educational Technology, 37*(3), 22–37. http://doi .org/: https://doi.org/DOI: 10.14742/ajet.5977 — URL

Wilmot, A. M. (2025). Senior lecturers' feelings about their college leaders' treatment of their wellbeing: Implications for leadership readiness. *Power and Education, 17*(2), 17577438241312609. DOI: 10.1177/17577438241312609

Wilson, K. L., Doswell, J. T., Fashola, O. S., Debeatham, W., Darko, N., Walker, T. M., Danner, O. K., Matthews, L. R., & Weaver, W. L. (2013). Using Augmented Reality as a Clinical Support Tool to Assist Combat Medics in the Treatment of Tension Pneumothoraces. *Military Medicine, 178*(9), 981–985. DOI: 10.7205/MILMED-D-13-00074

Windschitl, M., Thompson, J., & Braaten, M. (2020). *Ambitious science teaching*. Harvard Education Press.

Wittmann, M. C. (2006). Using resource graphs to represent conceptual change. *Physical Review Special Topics. Physics Education Research, 2*(2), 020105. DOI: 10.1103/PhysRevSTPER.2.020105

Wooding, J. (2024, August 25). CXC embraces AI; Developing regional policy. *284 Media*. https://www.284media.com/education/2024/08/25/cxc-embraces-ai-developing-regional-policy/

Woolf, B. P., Lane, H. C., Chaudhri, V. K., & Kolodner, J. L. (2013). AI Grand Challenges for Education. *AI Magazine, 34*(4), 66–84. DOI: 10.1609/aimag.v34i4.2490

World Bank. (2024, August 5). Empowering futures: Digital transformation in the Eastern Caribbean. https://www.worldbank.org/en/news/feature/2024/08/05/empowering-futures-digital-transformation-in-the-eastern-caribbean

Wu, Y., Jia, F., Zhang, S., Li, H., Zhu, E., Wang, Y., Lee, Y. T., Peng, R., Wu, Q., & Wang, C. (2023). Mathchat: Converse to tackle challenging math problems with llm agents. *ArXiv Preprint ArXiv:2306.01337.*

Xavier, M. C., & Oliveira, S. (2024). Construction of knowledge with strategies enabled by generative artificial intelligence. In *Teaching, Learning and Technology Integration* (pp. 142–153). Springer. http://doi.org/DOI: 10.1007/978-3-031-76365-6_9

Xenakis, A., Dimos, I., Feidakis, M., Sotiropoulos, D., Kalovrektis, K., & Nikolaou, G. (2024). An LLM-based smart repository platform to support educators with computational thinking, AI, and STEM activities. In *Empowering STEM educators with digital tools* (pp. 107–136). IGI Global., DOI: 10.4018/979-8-3693-9806-7.ch005

Xenakis, A., Dimos, I., Feidakis, M., Sotiropoulos, D., Kalovrektis, K., & Nikolaou, G. (2025). An LLM-Based Smart Repository Platform to Support Educators With Computational Thinking, AI, and STEM Activities. In *Empowering STEM Educators With Digital Tools* (pp. 107–136). IGI Global Scientific Publishing.

Xi, J., & Lantolf, J. P. (2020). Scaffolding and the zone of proximal development: A problematic relationship. *Journal for the Theory of Social Behaviour, 51*(1), 25–48. http://doi.org/: https://doi.org/DOI: 10.1111/jtsb.12260 — URL

Xiaoyu, W., Zainuddin, Z., & Hai Leng, C. (2025). Generative artificial intelligence in pedagogical practices: A systematic review of empirical studies (2022–2024). *Cogent Education*, *12*(1), 2485499.

Yadav, A. B. (2024). The development of AI with generative capabilities and its effect on education. [IJSR]. *International Journal of Scientific Research, 13*(5), 854–860.

Yan, F., Hu, Y., Jia, J., Ai, Z., Tang, K., Shi, Z., & Liu, X. (2020). Interactive WebVR visualization for online fire evacuation training. *Multimedia Tools and Applications*, *79*(41–42), 31541–31565. DOI: 10.1007/s11042-020-08863-0

Yan, L., Greiff, S., Teuber, Z., & Gašević, D. (2024a). Promises and challenges of generative artificial intelligence for human learning. *Nature Human Behaviour*, *8*(10), 1839–1850. DOI: 10.1038/s41562-024-02004-5

Yan, L., Sha, L., Zhao, L., Li, Y., Martinez-Maldonado, R., Chen, G., Li, X., Jin, Y., & Gašević, D. (2024b). Practical and ethical challenges of large language models in education: A systematic scoping review. *British Journal of Educational Technology*, *55*(1), 90–112. DOI: 10.1111/bjet.13370

Yeboah, A. N., & Goosen, L. (2024). The Impact of Learner Content and User Interface Design on E-Learning Quality: Teaching in Times of Crises. In Scott, B., & Fox, M. (Eds.), *Cases on Economics Education and Tools for Educators* (pp. 136–159). IGI Global., DOI: 10.4018/978-1-6684-7583-6.ch006

Yeboah, A. N., & Goosen, L. (2025). Integration Strategies of Learner Content and User Interface Design in Higher Education: Teaching and Learning Online in Times of Crises. In Arinushkina, A. (Ed.), *Integration Strategies of Generative AI in Higher Education* (pp. 51–70). IGI Global., DOI: 10.4018/979-8-3693-5518-3.ch003

Yildirim-Erbasli, S. N., & Bulut, O. (2023). Conversation-based assessment: A novel approach to boosting test-taking effort in digital formative assessment. *Computers and Education: Artificial Intelligence*, *4*, 100135. DOI: 10.1016/j.caeai.2023.100135

Yildiz Durak, H., & Onan, A. (2025). A systematic review of AI-based feedback in educational settings. *Journal of Computational Social Science*, *8*(4), 96. DOI: 10.1007/s42001-025-00428-1

Yimer, S. T., & Feza, N. N. (2019). Learners' conceptual knowledge development and attitudinal change towards calculus using jigsaw co-operative learning strategy integrated with GeoGebra. *International Electronic Journal of Mathematics Education*, *15*(1). Advance online publication. DOI: 10.29333/iejme/5936

Youn, C. H., Salam, A. R., & Rahman, A. A. (2024). AI-Driven Tools in Providing Feedback on Students' Writing. *International Journal of Research and Innovation in Social Science*, *9*(03), 58–67. DOI: 10.47772/IJRISS.2024.903SEDU0006

Yousefi Nooraie, R., Sale, J. E., Marin, A., & Ross, L. E. (2020). Social network analysis: An example of fusion between quantitative and qualitative methods. *Journal of Mixed Methods Research*, *14*(1), 110–124. DOI: 10.1177/1558689818804060

Yuan, B., & Hu, J. (2024). Generative AI as a tool for enhancing reflective learning in students. *arXiv preprint*. http://doi.org//arXiv.2412.02603DOI: 10.36227/techrxiv.173324189.99227671/v1

Zawacki-Richter, O., Bai, J. Y. H., Lee, K., Slagter van Tryon, P. J., & Prinsloo, P. (2024). New advances in artificial intelligence applications in higher education? *International Journal of Educational Technology in Higher Education*, *21*(1), 32. DOI: 10.1186/s41239-024-00464-3

Zawacki-Richter, O., Marín, V. I., Bond, M., & Gouverneur, F. (2023). Systematic review of research on artificial intelligence applications in higher education – where are the educators? *International Journal of Educational Technology in Higher Education, 20*(1), 1–48. DOI: 10.1186/s41239-023-00412-y

Zhai, C., Wibowo, S., & Li, L. D. (2024). The effects of over-reliance on AI dialogue systems on students' cognitive abilities: A systematic review. *Smart Learning Environments, 11*(1), 28. DOI: 10.1186/s40561-024-00316-7

Zhai, X. (2023). ChatGPT for Next Generation Science Learning. *XRDS: Crossroads. The ACM Magazine for Students, 29*(3), 42–46. DOI: 10.1145/3589649

Zhang, C., & Villanueva, L. E.Lizelle E. Villanueva. (2023). Generative artificial intelligence preparedness and technological competence: Towards a digital education Teacher Training Program. *International Journal of Education and Humanities, 11*(2), 164–170. DOI: 10.54097/ijeh.v11i2.13753

Zhang, Y., & Zhang, X. (2024). Opportunities and challenges of using generative AI to personalize education. *Frontiers in Artificial Intelligence, 7*, 1460651. DOI: 10.3389/frai.2024.1460651

Zheng, W., Lu, S., Cai, Z., Wang, R., Wang, L., & Yin, L. (2024). PAL-BERT: An Improved Question Answering Model. *Computer Modeling in Engineering & Sciences, 139*(3), 2729–2745. DOI: 10.32604/cmes.2023.046692

Zhou, B., Xu, J., & Zhao, J. (2024). Research on animated physics courseware technology for digital media. *Applied Mathematics and Nonlinear Sciences, 9*(1), 20242161. Advance online publication. DOI: 10.2478/amns-2024-2161

Zhou, X., Zhang, Z., Xie, X., & Zhang, J. (2025). Deep learning based knowledge tracing in intelligent tutoring systems. *Scientific Reports, 15*(1), 21395. DOI: 10.1038/s41598-025-07422-7

Zhou, Y.. (2024). Algorithmic Fairness in AI-Driven Learning Environments: A Critical Review. *AI and Ethics, 5*(1), 88–103. DOI: 10.1007/s43681-023-00279-w

Zuccarini, G., & Malgieri, M. (2024). Modeling and representing conceptual change in the learning of successive theories: The case of the classical-quantum transition. *Science & Education, 33*(3), 717–761. DOI: 10.1007/s11191-022-00397-1

Zwickl, B., Hu, D., Finkelstein, N., & Lewandowski, H. (2014). Model-based reasoning in the physics laboratory: Framework and initial results. *Physical Review Special Topics. Physics Education Research, 11*(2), 020113. DOI: 10.1103/PhysRevSTPER.11.020113

# About the Contributors

**Michail Kalogiannakis** is a Professor at the Department of Special Education of the University of Thessaly in Greece and an Associate Tutor at the School of Humanities at the Hellenic Open University. He graduated from the Physics Department of the University of Crete and continued his post-graduate studies at the University Paris 7-Denis Diderot (D.E.A. in Didactic of Physics), University Paris 5-René Descartes-Sorbonne (D.E.A. in Science Education) and received his PhD degree at the University Paris 5-René Descartes-Sorbonne (PhD in Science Education). His research interests include: science education, STEM Education, mobile learning for science education, GenAI in science education, distant learning and science education, and computational thinking in science education. He has published over 180 articles in international conferences and journals and has served on the program committees of numerous international conferences. Professor Michail Kalogianakis is recognised as being in the top 2% of scientists worldwide within his field, according to the Stanford-Elsevier global rankings of scientists.

**Dimitrios Sotiropoulos** is a member of the teaching laboratory staff of the Department of Special Education of the University of Thessaly. His qualifications include a PhD on the use of digital technology in science education (University of Athens), a Master's Degree (M.Sc.) in Science Education (University of Athens) and a Bachelor's Degree (B.A.) in Physics (AUTh). He has extensive experience in teaching at all levels of education and in training teachers in the use of new technologies in educational practice. He has taught computing and science at primary, secondary and post-secondary levels. At the tertiary level, for several years he has taught numerous courses on the pedagogical use of digital technology. He has also supervised students in the preparation of their postgraduate theses. He has also participated in a variety of European education programmes, including Erasmus+, Horizon 2020 and previous initiatives. His postdoctoral thesis concerned the design and implementation of a functional, user-friendly and useful web platform for teachers and students. His research interests focus on the scientific disciplines and the use of new technologies in education. In particular, his recent academic research focuses on the pedagogical integration of emerging technologies, especially Generative Artificial Intelligence (GenAI), in STEM and STEAM education. He has presented his research at numerous academic conferences, journals and forums in Greece and abroad.

***

**María Lucía Barrón-Estrada** received her PhD in Computer Science from the Florida Institute of Technology in 2004. She works as Professor at the TecNM-Instituto Tecnológico de Culiacán (México). Her research topics mainly include Artificial Intelligence on Education, Affective Computing, and Extended Reality on Education.

**Víctor Manuel Bátiz Beltrán** received the BSc degree in computer science from the Instituto Tecnológico de Culiacán (México) in 1997 and the MSc degree in business administration from the Universidad Tecmilenio (México) in 2007. He also received the MSc degree in computer science from Tecnológico Nacional de México Campus Culiacán (México) in 2021. He also holds a PhD in Engineering Science from the Tecnológico Nacional de México Campus Culiacán (Mexico). His research interests include the areas of artificial intelligence, generative AI, affective computing, intelligent learning environments, natural language processing, and automatic personality recognition. He also teaches computer systems engineering at the Instituto Tecnológico de Culiacán.

**Saikat Baul** is a dedicated professional with a profound passion for science and technology, driving his commitment to a career in computer science. Currently, he holds the position of Lecturer in the Department of Computer Science at American International University-Bangladesh. Before this role, he served as an Instructor in the same department, showcasing his expertise and commitment to academic excellence. In 2022, Saikat Baul successfully earned his Bachelor's degree in Computer Science and Engineering (CSE) from American International University-Bangladesh (AIUB), laying the foundation for his journey in the field. His academic journey continued as he pursued and completed his Master's in Computer Science Specialization in Software Engineering (SE) from American International University-Bangladesh (AIUB) in 2023. His research interests are diverse, focusing on Software Engineering and Computer Vision.

**Debbie Devonish** is an Associate Professor, and leading voice on the intersection of educational policy, pedagogical readiness, and emerging technologies within the Caribbean. She is the Vice Dean of the Faculty of Science & Sport at Utech, Jamaica. An experienced educator, Devonish is a trained teacher who holds an MPhil. in Entomology and a Ph.D. in Educational Leadership with emphasis on professional Development for Science Educators. Devonish focuses on teacher agency and infrastructural preparedness in STEM fields. Her current research, including this critical IGI Global chapter, addresses a significant literature gap by proposing a contextually adapted professional development framework for GenAI integration among Science educators. Devonish's primary research interests include: culturally authentic professional development, research methods, digital transformation, and policy development in resource-constrained educational environments. Her contributions offer practical guidelines for organizational structure and policy commitment, underscoring the imperative for deliberate action to drive national progress.

**Leila Goosen** is a full professor in the Department of Science and Technology Education of the University of South Africa. She holds a C2 rating via the South African National Research Foundation. Prof. Goosen was an Associate Professor in the School of Computing, and the module leader and head designer of the fully online signature module for the College for Science, Engineering and Technology, rolled out to over 92,000 registered students since the first semester of 2013. She usually supervises around ten Masters and Doctoral students, and has successfully completed supervision of 43 students at postgraduate level. Previously, she was a Deputy Director at the South African national Department of Education. In this capacity, she was required to develop ICT strategies for implementation. Before that, she had been a lecturer of Information Technology (IT) in the Department for Science, Mathematics and Technology Education in the Faculty of Education of the University of Pretoria. Her research interests have included cooperative work in IT, effective teaching and learning of programming and teacher professional development.

**Hossein Jamali** is a Research Assistant in the Department of Computer Science and Engineering at the University of Nevada, Reno. His research focuses on human-centered AI applications in education, learning analytics, and intelligent tutoring systems. His work explores the intersection of artificial intelligence, educational technology, and learning sciences, with particular emphasis on developing adaptive systems that enhance personalized learning experiences. He has published several papers on AI-driven mechanisms, educational data, and interactive visualization techniques.

**Dip Nandi** is working as the associate dean in the faculty of science and technology in american international university-bangladesh (aiub). Prior to this, he served as the director, faculty of science and technology and head, undergraduate program in the department of computer science in aiub. Prof. Nandi has completed his phd from rmit university australia, msc from the university of melbourne and bsc from american international university-bangladesh. His research interest includes e-learning, software engineering, data mining and information systems.

**Aldo Uriarte Portillo** earned his master's degree in computer science and his doctorate in engineering sciences from the Culiacán Institute of Technology. He is a member of the Mexican National System of Researchers. His main research interests are Augmented Reality and AI applied to education.

**Apostolos Xenakis** is currently an Assistant Professor at the Department of Digital Systems, University of Thessaly (UTH). He holds a PhD from the Electrical and Computer Engineering department of UTH since 2014. He has worked in several companies as a network analyst and engineer and participates in National and EU funded projects, as a researcher and scientific coordinator. His research interests include networking technologies, wireless sensor networks and IoT, communications, optimization algorithms, quantum technologies and educational robotics. Finally, he is a member of IEEE and ACM and contributes as a co - editor in several engineering journals.

**Christos Xenakis** studied Physics at the University of Thessaloniki with a scholarship from the State Scholarships Foundation (I.K.Y.), followed by postgraduate studies in Science Education and a PhD in Physics. He has specialized in France (Paris-VI and Académie de Lyon) and in the UK (University of Southampton). He has taught Physics in Secondary Education, served as Principal of the 1st High School of Volos, School Advisor for Natural Sciences, and as a Member of the former Pedagogical Institute. He also worked as a Physics Teacher and Coordinator of the Natural Sciences Department at the European School of Brussels-III in Belgium. He has collaborated for many years with the National Hellenic Research Foundation as an External Researcher, taught at the University of Thessaly (Department of Mechanical Engineering), and at the School of Pedagogical and Technological Education (ASPETE). He has published numerous research papers in Greek and international journals, as well as books for students, university learners, and the general public. He is Vice President of the Board of the Hellenic Astronomical and Space Society and an active member of other scientific organizations such as A.E.D.E. (Association Européenne des Enseignants). He has been honored with the Silver ECU Medal by the Council of Europe for his contribution to education.

**Ramón Zatarain-Cabada** received his PhD in Computer Science from the Florida Institute of Technology in 2003. He works as Professor at the Instituto Tecnológico de Culiacán (México). His research topics mainly include Artificial Intelligence on Education, Affective Computing, and Extended Reality on Education.

**Nofamataro Zebua** is a writer and researcher. He earned his bachelor's degree from the Biology Education Program at FKIP-Universitas Nias Raya. Subsequently, the author received a scholarship from LPDP RI to continue his studies at Universitas Negeri Malang, where he pursued a Master's degree in Biology Education and graduated in 2025. The author also enjoys writing articles for media outlets such as goonewsfromindonesia.com and kompasiana.com. His research interests include biology, biology education, ethnobiology, critical thinking skills, literacy, and the professional development of biology teachers.

**Yan Piter Basman Ziraluo** started higher education in 2005 and continued his studies in Biology Education at IKIP Gunung Sitoli, which he completed in 2010. During college, he actively worked as an honorary teacher in several private schools on Nias. After graduating, she served as Principal of Senora Private Junior High School and Regional Auxiliary Teacher at SMA Negeri 1 Fanayama, which strengthened her dedication to education. In 2011, she continued her Master of Education Management studies at HKBP Nommensen University with the support of the foundation where she teaches. Despite experiencing health problems, in 2013 he was accepted as a lecturer at STKIP Nias Selatan (now Nias Raya University), where he has served until now. She completed her master's degree in 2015 at Padang State University through a scholarship from the South Nias Education Foundation. At Universitas Nias Raya, she is active as a lecturer, student supervisor, and involved in various academic quality development activities, both at the study program level and internal quality assurance institutions. In 2022, he successfully passed the doctoral program selection at the State University of Malang through the LPDP scholarship, marking his long-term commitment to improving the quality of higher education in Indonesia.

# Index

www.ingramcontent.com/pod-product-compliance
Lightning Source LLC
LaVergne TN
LVHW080902300926
849162LV00003B/523